CONTEMPORARY REALISM

The Seavest Collection

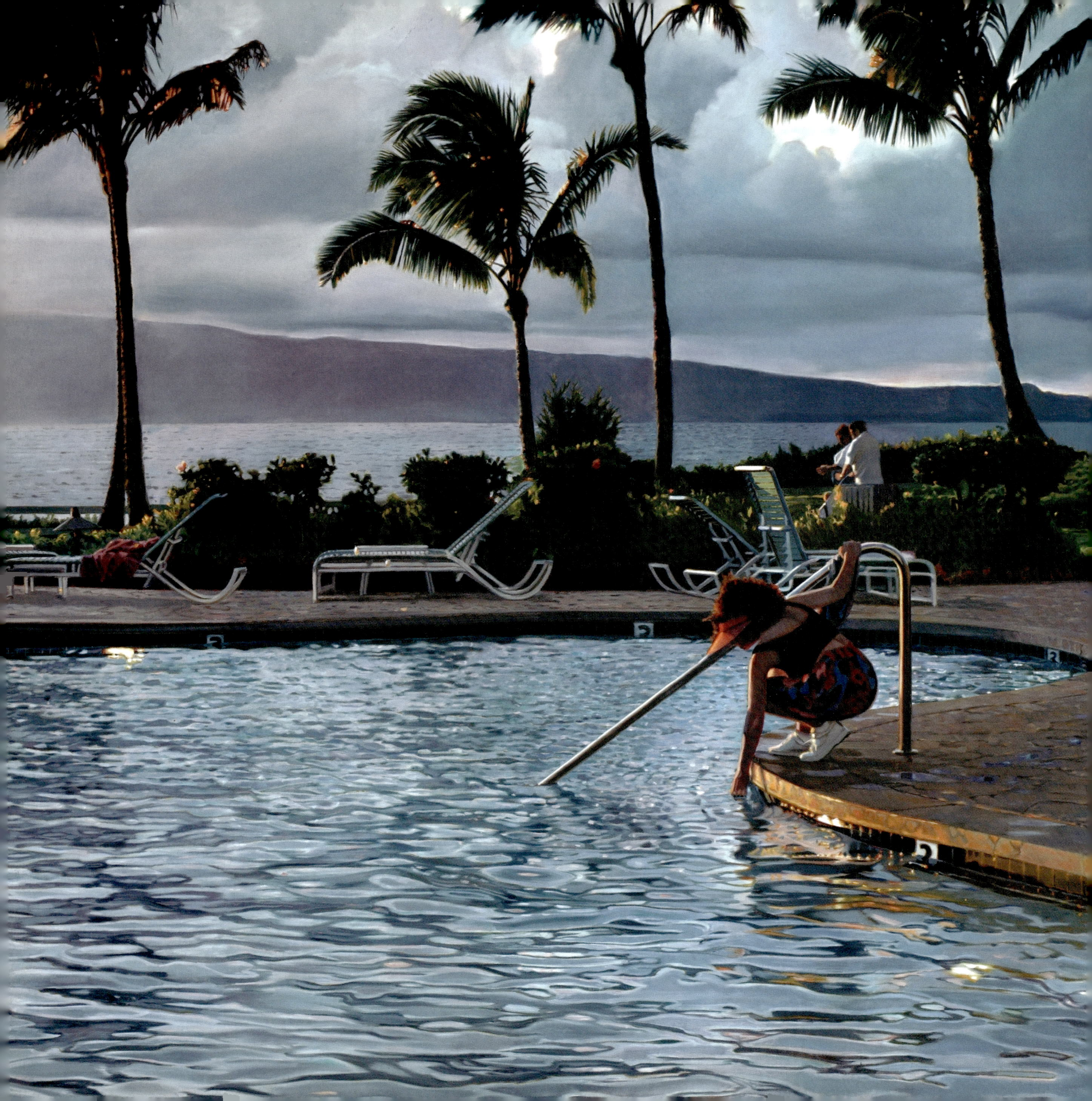

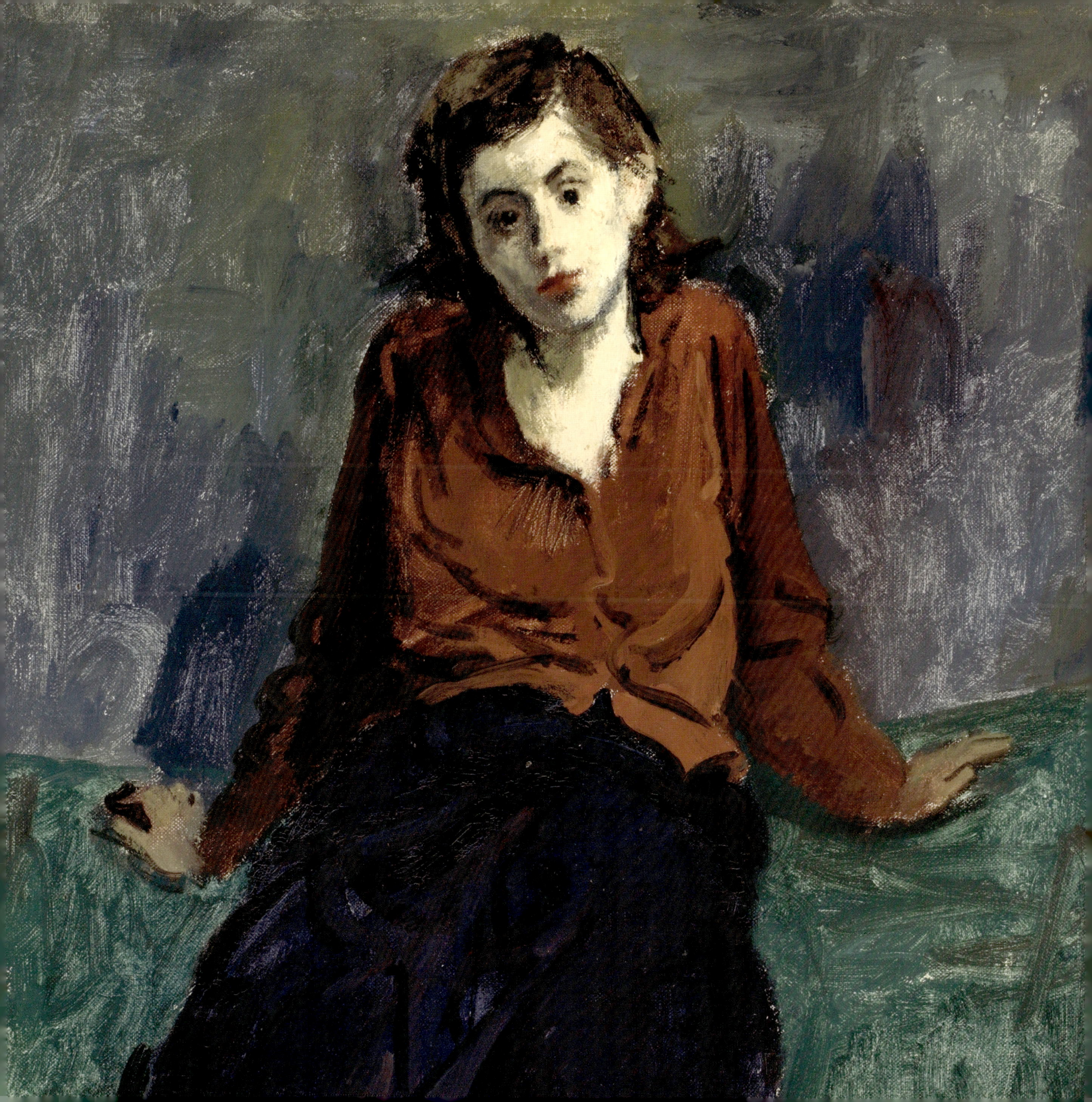

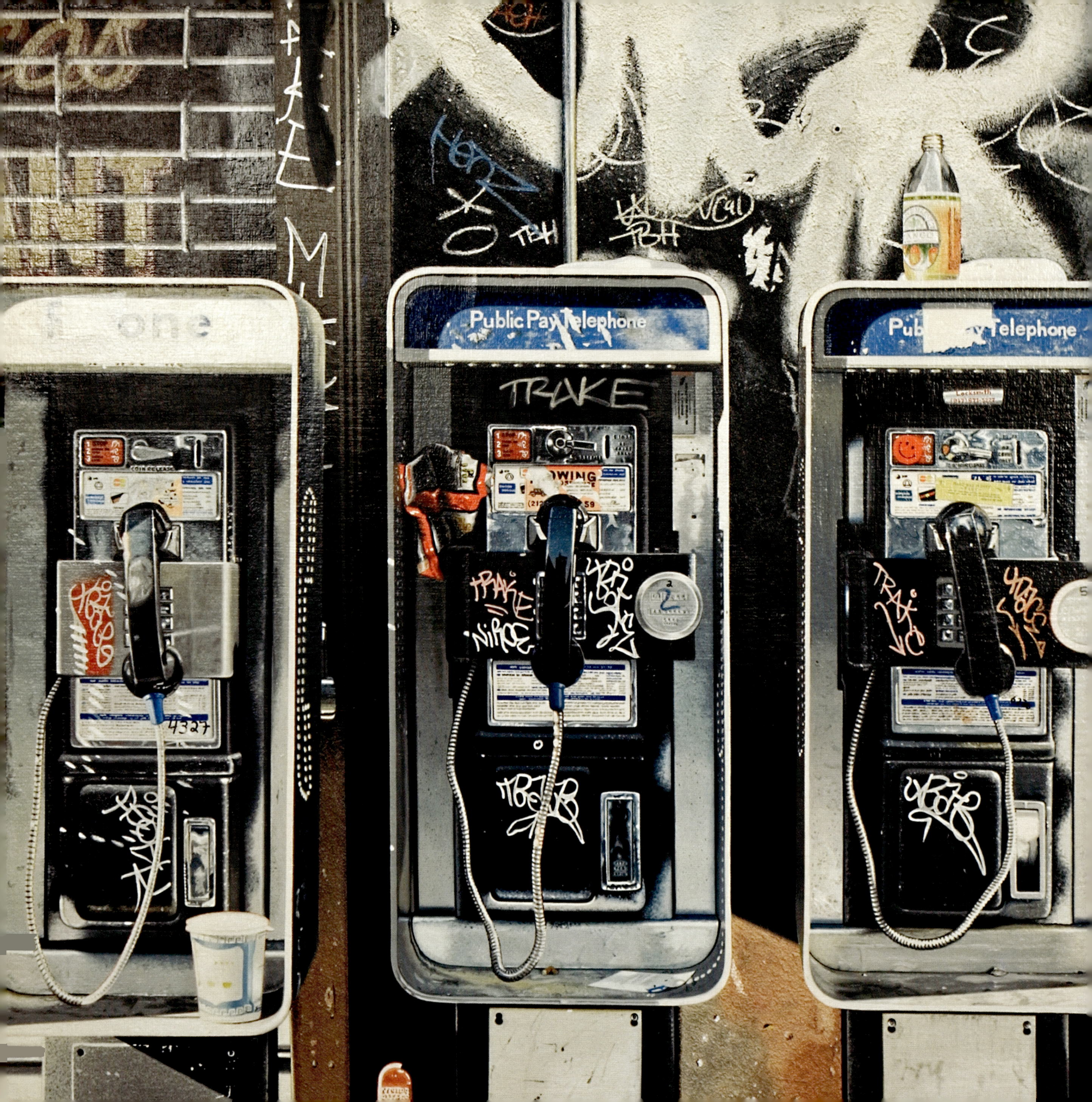
Public Pay Telephone
TRAKE

CONTEMPORARY REALISM

The Seavest Collection

Richard D. Segal and Monica M. Segal

Essays by Jared Pruzan

Introduction by Dede Young

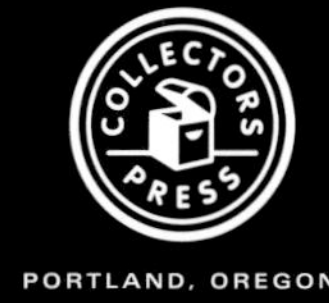

PORTLAND, OREGON

Cover Design: Kevin A. Welsch, Sara Blum
Design: Jerry Soga
Editors: Lindsay S. Brown, Jade Chan, Elizabeth Fuller
Index: Corine Milano

Library of Congress Cataloging-in-Publication Data

Segal, Richard D.
Contemporary realism : the Seavest collection / by Richard D. Segal and Monica M. Segal ; essays by Jared Pruzan ; introduction by Dede Young.
p. cm.
Includes bibliographical references and index.
ISBN 978-1-933112-37-4 (hardcover : alk. paper)
1. Realism in art. 2. Art, American--20th century--Catalogs. 3. Art, American--21st century--Catalogs. 4. Segal, Richard D., 1954---Art collections--Catalogs. 5. Segal, Monica M., 1956---Art collections--Catalogs. 6. Art--Private collections--United States--Catalogs. I. Segal, Monica M., 1956- II. Pruzan, Jared. III. Title.

N6512.5.R4S44 2007
709.73'074--dc22

2007000604

Distributed by Publishers Group West

ISBN 10: 1-933112-37-9
ISBN 13: 978-1-933112-37-4

First American Edition

Printed in China
9 8 7 6 5 4 3 2 1

Collectors Press books are available at special discounts for bulk purchases, premiums, and promotions. Special editions, including personalized inserts or covers, and corporate logos, can be printed in quantity for special purposes. For further information contact: Special Sales, Collectors Press, Inc., P.O. Box 230986, Portland, OR 97281. Toll free: 1-800-423-1848.

To see a full catalog of Collectors Press books visit www.collectorspress.com.

Table of Contents

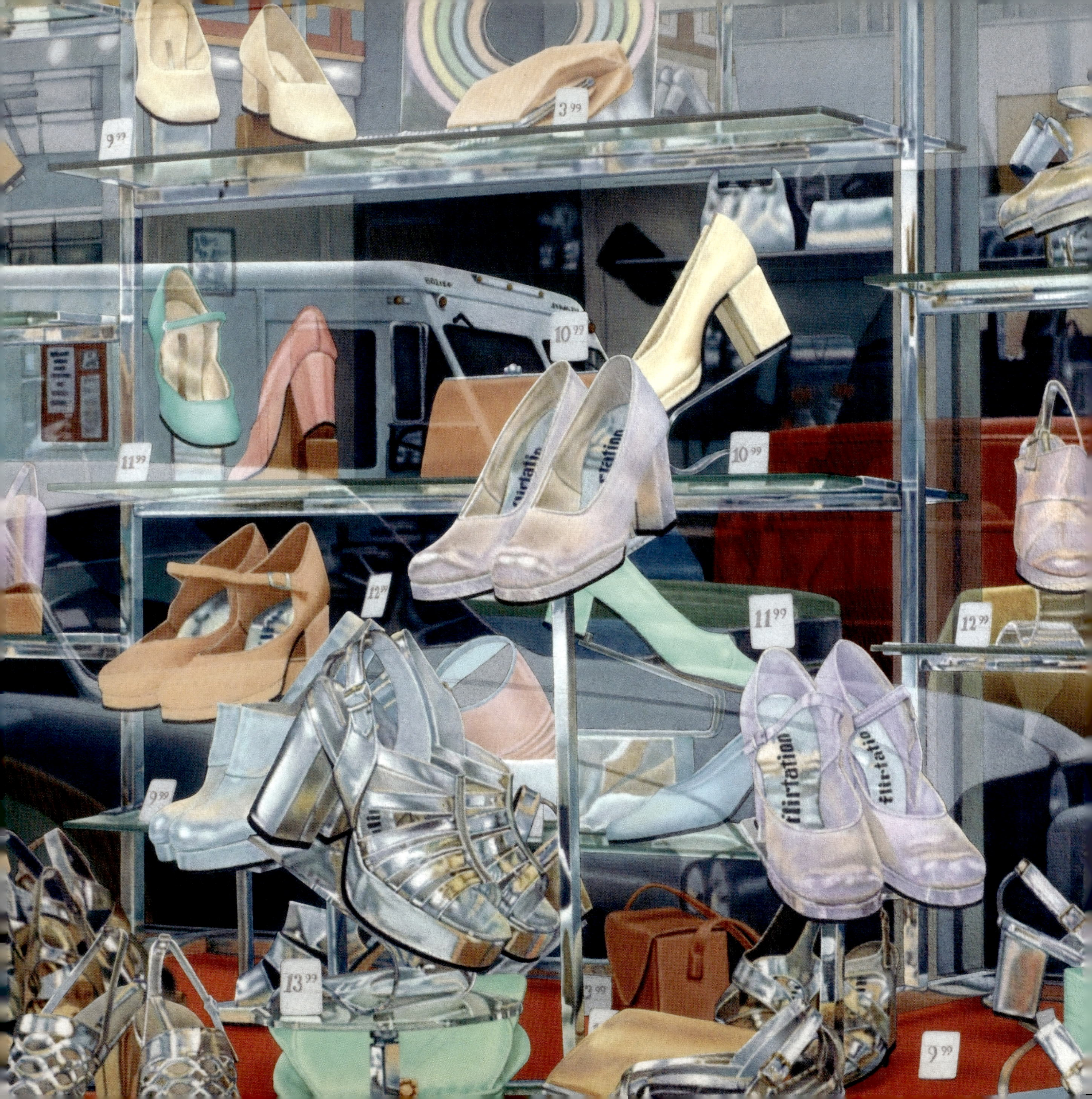
9 99
3 99
10 99
11 99
10 99
flirtation
12 99
11 99
12 99
9 99
flirtation
flirtation
13 99
9 99

Preface

Monica and I began this collection in 1980 when we discovered the art of Romare Bearden and subsequently purchased two of his collages. We had no idea at the time that these were to be the first of hundreds of acquisitions to follow, nor did we appreciate the lifelong journey upon which we had embarked. The collection has evolved as the years have passed. At the outset, we seem to have been drawn to urban landscapes and tightly rendered Photorealist paintings; later the works have tended to be more figurative and a little more painterly, but we have always focused on representational art, works with identifiable subjects and the evident presence of the artist's hand. We have purchased what has appealed to us rather than what was popular, but like everyone, our tastes have been molded by the fashions of the times and influenced by the subtle but insistent evolution of art and artists. We have selected for this book a sampling of our collection, and, limited by space, have tried to distill the presentation to suggest both the breadth and depth of our interests. We have included works by household names and also works by artists for whom this book represents a first-time publication. What we have left out and what we have chosen should by no means be taken as evidence of preference of one artist over another. We hold all the art we collect in the highest esteem and wish that we could fit much more in this book. It is our hope that with this presentation we will stimulate broader support for all the artists whose work we collect, all the galleries we frequent, all the museums we patronize, and all the passions we pursue.

Most of the works in our collection are hanging on the walls of our residences and offices. We therefore have an intimate and tangible relationship with these works that no individuals outside our immediate family will ever have. That said, we still do not believe that our collection is exclusively ours. Art is the legacy of its creators to the world in which they live and the generations that follow. So while custody may vest with us, ownership is truly universal. Visitors to our home, whether they be friends, family, or strangers, show little restraint in offering their opinions on the art on our walls. While people never tell us they don't like our furniture, rugs, or wallpaper, they often feel free to say they don't like this piece or that painting, or they don't get what the artist was up to, or they don't understand why that is even considered art. I hope our readers are moved to react with similar candor. Art is meant to establish a connection between the artist and his or her audience, whoever and wherever it might be. Artists don't create their work merely to reach the individuals who purchase it. We offer this publication as a way to further that audience and give greater voice to the art we collect and admire.

One of the most frequent comments from our visitors is that there is a lot of nudity in the collection. About one-third of the works in the book portray nudity; in the collection as a whole, fewer than ten percent are nudes. Still, it is a common observation and hints at a general underlying discomfort with the subject. There is a good reason that artists paint nudes, and it's not just because they can. The human mind is wired to respond to nudity. It's probably the most innate and most intense natural reaction we have. If their audience is programmed to react to specific stimuli, it seems logical that artists seeking to engage viewers would gravitate to that subject matter. This means the artists are doing their job. They are making connections and reaching out, and the audience is taking notice. Still, I'd like for once for someone to ask me, "Why so many trees?"

We are also often asked why we collect realism and other representational art. I often reply, "Because I have no imagination." The real answer is that it is what we respond to. I can certainly appreciate abstract art. I think anyone who has seen the works of the great abstract expressionists, the minimalists, and the color field artists understands that artificial constructs can convey aesthetic pleasures and messages as powerfully as images that are natural and recognizable. Being an English major in college and a lifelong reader of fiction, I can certainly appreciate that nonvisual conceits can be powerful and tangible, therefore validating the impact and importance of conceptual art. I do believe, however, that art in whatever form is an artifact, the physical manifestation of the talents and abilities of the most extraordinary of the men and women who walk among us. The best comment on art that I could hope to hear, but probably never will, is, "My six-year-old can't do that." I have four children, all uniquely talented in my biased eyes, but they "can't do that." My wife and I "can't do that" and most readers of this book "can't do that." But the artists whose work we present in these pages can do that; the human race can do that, and we celebrate in this book and in our collection the limitless possibilities that are inherent in our species and will be left forever to mark our presence, our achievements, and our triumphs.

Richard Segal

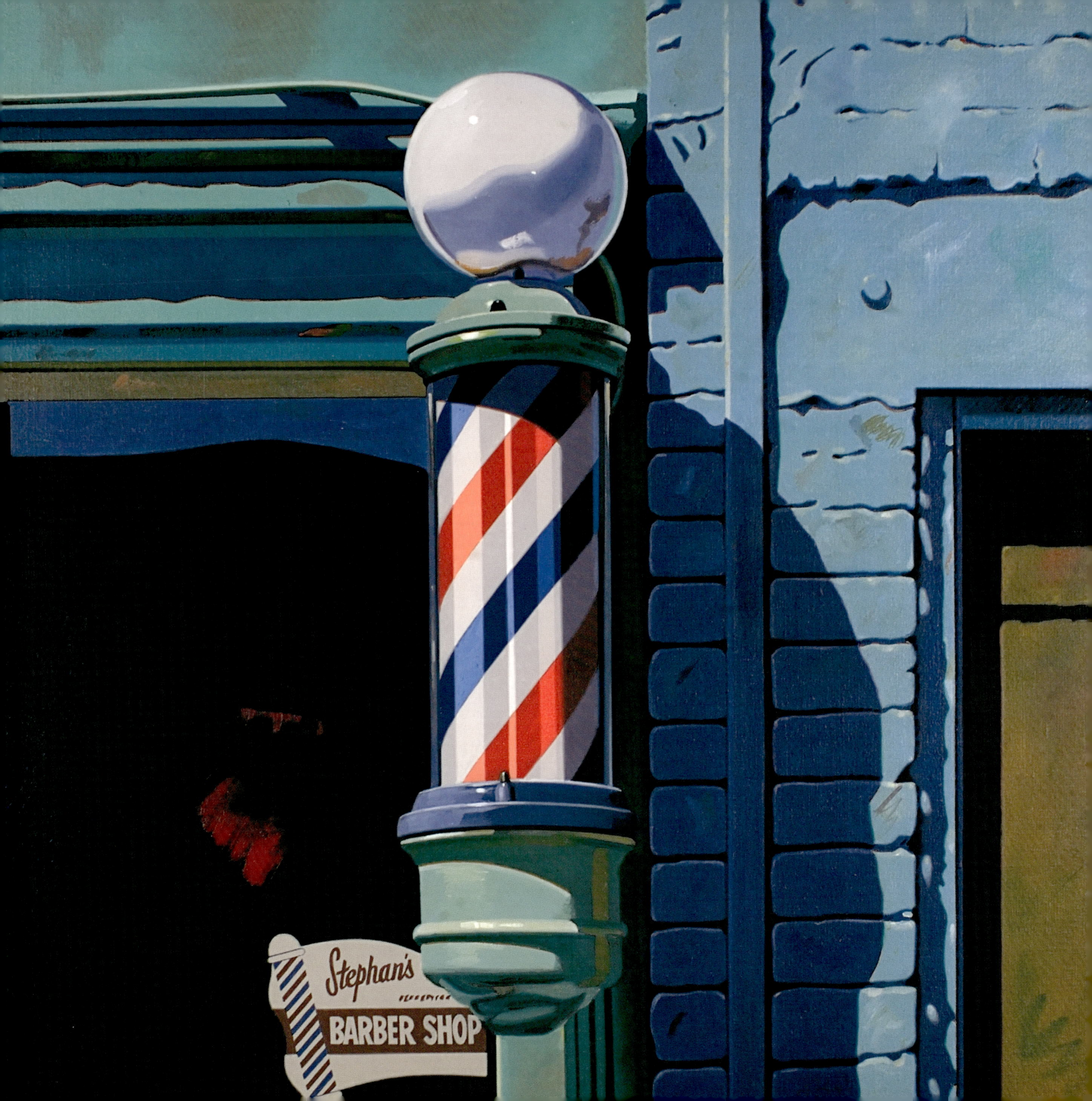
Stephan's
BARBER SHOP

Introduction

The reflection of *the real* in images of the world around us has held a special fascination and has been one of art's most potent subjects. In the United States between the two world wars, realism dominated the scene, and only the rise of Abstract Expressionism caused an interruption before realism once again became a prevailing style in American art, finding a fresh voice in the 1960s and gaining momentum in the 1970s. It was in the aftermath of the realist revival in the 1970s that the Seavest Collection of Contemporary Realism began, and it extends to the present to include examples by a younger generation of artists whose worldview challenges past canons and who are creating art far beyond strict categorization.

Since 1980, Rick and Monica Segal have built the Seavest Collection through a process of avid searching and collecting that Rick has described as "an addiction that filled my soul with the peace that comes from understanding." This addiction—or passion or affliction, as many collectors confess—"has been informed by the belief that there exists an object out there in the wilds of the world that, when discovered, obtained, and displayed, will further the quest to build for oneself a nest that with its very presence and appearance provides us with the sense of security and belonging that comes from the knowledge that we are at home." The fact that art can bring a more grounded or expanded meaning to the experience of daily life is not inherently revelatory, but the commitment to continually update an otherwise historic collection, to question and reconsider the meaning and value of these objects in the context of culture and one's life today, and to never hit a saturation point is indeed remarkable.

Considered in terms of its particular focus, this collection becomes an extraordinary story that runs parallel to life. It reveals not only the historic arc of realism as a genre, but the activity of collecting in the marketplace and a growing and changing taste for objects that reflect both the outside world and the complex inner world of the collector. The Segals' discovery of and appreciation for the profusion of subjects and styles over the past twenty-six years of collecting have come together to form a personal document that is generously shared in this public forum.

Collecting art creates a kind of connective tissue to the world. It is a means to face the reality of global life and deepen one's relationship to it. As the Seavest Collection developed, it naturally gained depth and diversity, but its starting point was the acquisition of works defined clearly within the canon. Today, we consider these earlier works masterful, beautiful, or important historic records of the moment, but they also gain new meaning when judged in light of recent sociopolitical developments. The collection expresses an authentic respect for the richness and range of realism without being academic or a textbook case survey.

When assessed carefully, this volume gives us more than a representation of the world we live in. It also conveys the collectors' active response to the cultural shift in the United States that saw more inclusion of women and minority artists. Recent additions to the collection include female nudes portrayed by female artists, which had previously been defined and portrayed by men. The recent acquisition of work by Asian-American artists further attests to the contemporizing of a previously narrowly defined "American" art and an expansion of the notion of "belonging" that stimulated the forming of the collection. Younger generations of artists whose work significantly broadens the tight focus of the first generation of realists include Don Brown, Will Cotton, Amie Dicke, Hilary Harkness, Marcus Harvey, Sean Henry, Damien Loeb, Grayson Perry, Richard Phillips, Marc Quinn, Alexis Rockman, Xavier Veihan, Kara Walker, Cynthia Westwood, and Lisa Yuskavage. Just as surely as the history of realism is being rewritten, the collectors are on the move, participating in the expanded discussion by supporting new art, which gives the collection its particular liveliness and a fluidity of range to what we might think of as prototypical realism.

Two reasonable approaches to examining the collection are to think in terms of historic groupings, such as Pop Art and Photorealism, and to categorically break down these ninety-some reproductions into groupings according to subject matter. Portraits are in the lead, followed by American scene/landscape, the female nude, still life, and self-portraits. No one subject can be singled out as most important, and each general category includes iconic works by American masters as well as works by younger, international artists who push the canon with thought-provoking work.

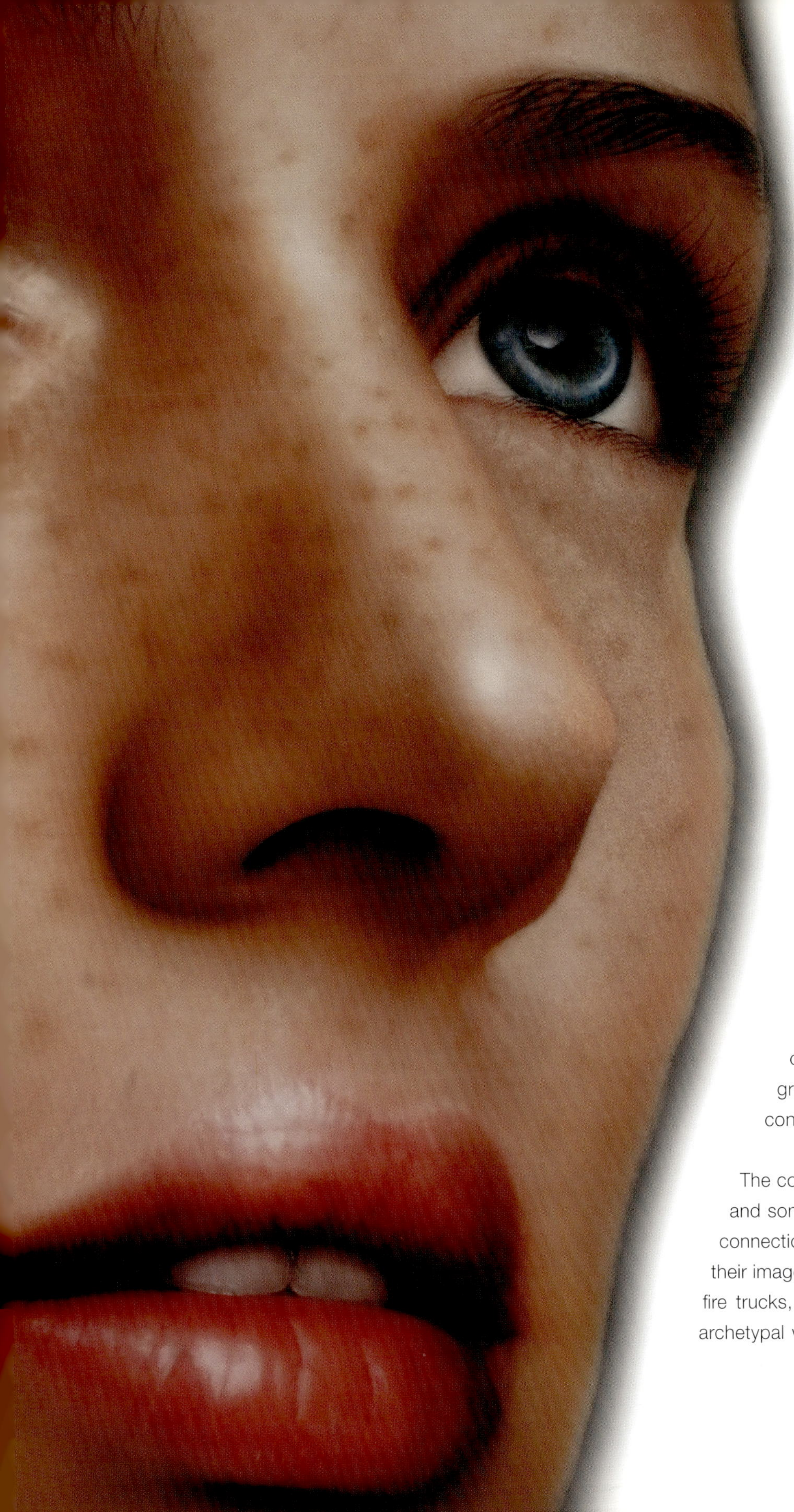

Central to the early development of the collection is the inclusion of numerous artists connected to Pop Art, which in the 1960s was the hottest movement in art, readily accepted by broad audiences due to its basis on imagery drawn from the everyday realities of the commercial world dominant in American culture. Artists were quickly assimilated into the market system and packaged in a way that reflected corporate models. Included in the collection are groundbreaking artists such as Jim Dine, Marisol, Robert Rauschenberg, Larry Rivers, James Rosenquist, and George Segal, all of whom considered the contemporary world as "a painting in itself," infinitely quotable in fractions or whole parts. They all were on the scene early in their careers with a more radical and experimental art that brought the viewer's perception of reality into question by incorporating actual consumer products and detritus into their work, which at times bordered on kitsch. They produced large enough bodies of work, however, for the critics to seriously debate. These artists further expanded the physical plane and created a greater sense of theater in art, both of which were important developments in art.

Pop artists are credited with the return of the nude in art. The examples in the collections by Robert Overby, Mel Ramos, John Wesley, and Tom Wesselmann are sexually charged fantasy images that play out in divergent styles. Younger artists who continue to consider the female image in the world of advertising include Hilo Chen, Amie Dicke, and Richard Phillips. In fact, there is no more contemporary an example of a return to Pop Art than Phillips's *Sissel* (2002), a larger-than-life red, white, blue, and blonde deadpan portrait of a woman showing us a diamond ring in a velvet box. The chilled expression on her flawless face is painted on the scale of a commercial billboard and is a manifestation and mirror of the strangely real, grand obsession with youth culture and luxury objects that is the lifeblood of contemporary America.

The cool, detached style of the Photorealists is mediated by the use of photography and sometimes airbrush to obtain veracity in an image. The viewer makes an instant connection with the person, place, or object in the painting, but artists also ingrained in their images cultural truths for us to ponder. Diners, shop windows, city streets, bridges, fire trucks, and parades are classic subjects for the Photorealist. In the collection are archetypal works by John Baeder, Tom Blackwell, Davis Cone, Robert Cottingham, Don

Eddy, Ralph Goings, Ron Kleemann, and Idelle Weber. As seen in Weber's *Cooper Union Trash* (1974), we are confronted squarely with a dirty reality. It focuses on a familiar scene that, though unpeopled, is a telling portrait of American consumer values.

The tightness of Photorealism gave way to a more expressionistic approach as the 1970s progressed. Among the artists in the collection who have worked in a less tightly wrought style are Jennifer Bartlett, Romare Bearden, Richard Diebenkorn, Eric Fischl, Neil Jenney, Fairfield Porter, Richard Prince, and Lisa Yuskavage. Exemplifying extremes of style are Philip Pearlstein and Eric Fischl. Pearlstein's *Two Nudes with Horse Weathervanes & Punch* (1988) is a highly controlled painting of a studio interior, a classic, almost academic, setup. This painting is hard-edged and harsh, from the lighting and claustrophobic space to the gravity that seems to pull the figures down to an almost lifeless state. The polar opposite of Pearlstein's work is Fischl's sun-drenched *Lapping Sounds Along the Shore* (1996–97), a painterly image encoded with complex psychological readings that defy the lift caused by an initial glance. This work transmits the clear but elusive experience of that moment in life when all the good stuff is happening, the rare but real stuff we later relish in memory with yearning and anxiety, because we always knew it could not last.

Many realists have dedicated themselves almost exclusively to portraits and self-portraits, a favorite subject for artists throughout history. In recent decades, the symbolic aspect of portraiture has expanded to include the heroic, ideal images of man associated with ancient Greek sculpture. Nicolas Africano, Stephan Balkenhol, William Beckman, Don Brown, Will Cotton, John De Andrea, Till Freiwald, Tim Gardner, Gregory Gillespie, Robert Graham, Sean Henry, Alex Katz, Karen Kilimnik, Robert Longo, Alice Neel, Evan Penny, Richard Phillips, Marc Quinn, Kiki Smith, Xavier Veilhan, and Lisa Yuskavage all play with encoded notions of beauty, and in so doing, their work becomes a compelling commentary on human frailty, insecurity, narcissism, and spiritual and moral decay.

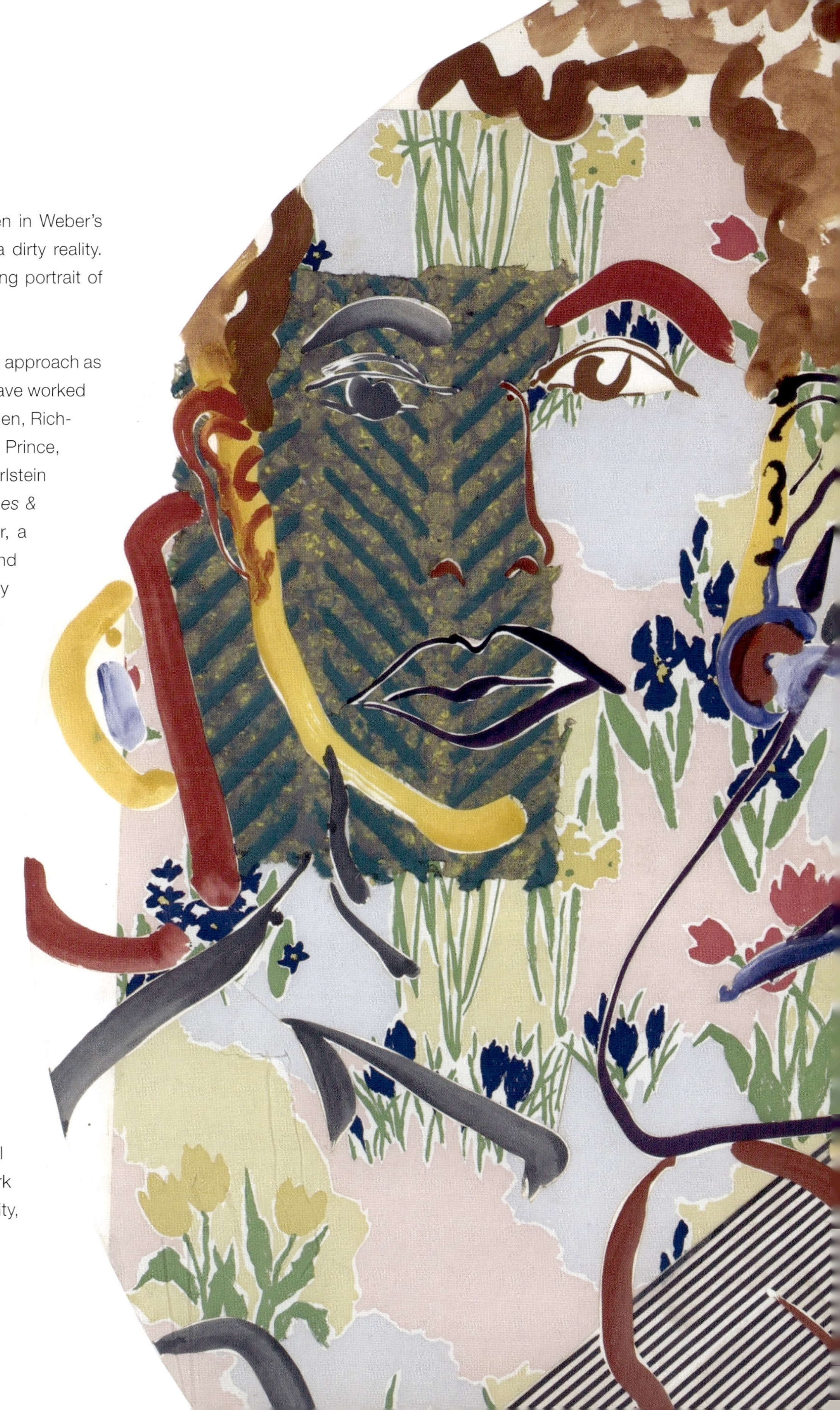

One of the most startling portraits in the collection is Marc Quinn's white marble sculpture, *Selma Mustajbasic* (2000), which is modeled after a young woman who is an amputee. This work obliterates the Platonic ideal, yet imitates its material, proportion, and smooth finish. By choosing to sculpt human forms that are physically imperfect, Quinn resolutely denies the body as important to the realities of existence, yet strangely relates the amputation to fragmentation of antiquities. Moreover, he infers that our interior life completes us, a reference to spirituality that is relatively out of favor today.

In images of the landscape, artists choose to signify the action and residue of our existence, abbreviating the details of the story to intensify the reality. Herein lies the most pressing political commentary in the realist genre, a fascinating subject too extensive to discuss fully, but which is encapsulated in the work of two artists whose artistic choice could not be more contrary. Kara Walker's *Shiny Penny* (1995) is a jet-black cutout silhouette that depicts an absolutely perverse and threatening story that is both easy and difficult for the viewer to complete in detail. This simple work speaks volumes as an historic narrative of the American South and of depravity in general. Conversely, Alexis Rockman's *Disneyworld II* (2005) is painted in the high traditional style of the Hudson School, filled with detail that forecasts the future as a grim reality resulting from casual and careless human actions. Here we see the fast-forward chronicle of society's legacy foretold by Idelle Weber's trash bin.

Walker and Rockman's political and moral messages affect new analysis of the collection. James Rosenquist's cellophane-wrapped doll, Alex Katz's *Amanda*, and Jennifer Bartlett's boat at the sandy shore, all lose their offhand innocence and accrue a strangely ominous nuance. In fact, if we look at this new generation of artists in the Seavest Collection, we see indicators of the realities of the post-9/11 world, which challenges our previous perspectives of a bridge, a skyscraper, a shop window, a fire truck, or an airplane.

Art is often viewed strictly in the marketplace in cold terms as a commodity to be bought and sold. The Seavest Collection of Contemporary Realism is evidence that it is indeed more than that. These works attest to the enduring and expressive power of realism. The collection, shared in this forum, conveys the capacity of artists to describe our cities and the people in them with an unflinching eye, as well as their ability to embed in their work the economics and politics of our time, and informs us of the high value placed on art as part of our everyday existence.

Dede Young
Curator of Modern and Contemporary Art
Neuberger Museum of Art
SUNY Purchase, New York

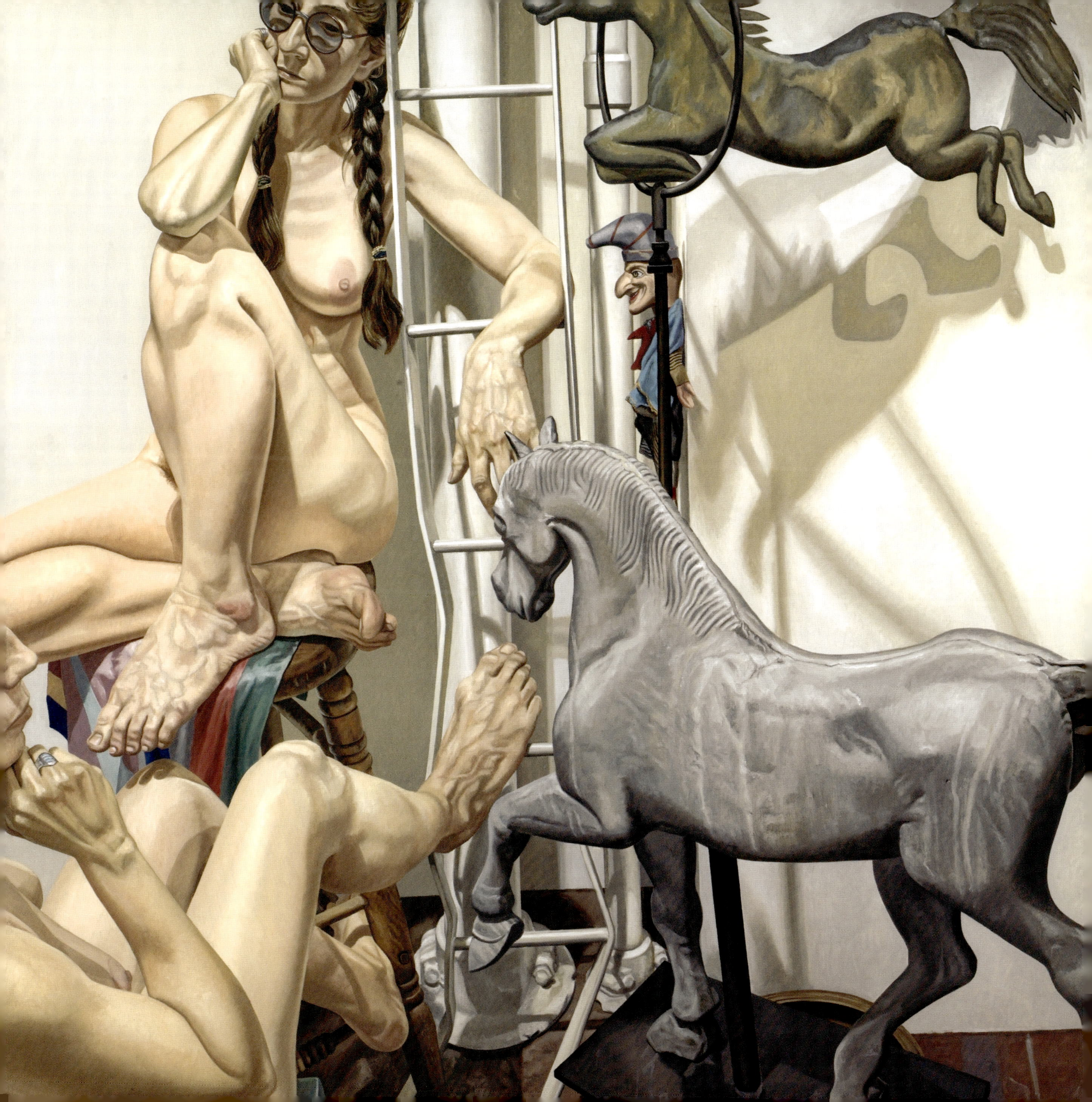

Real

Art

Till Freiwald 1963-

From a distance, it would be easy to mistake Till Freiwald's oversized, unemotional portraits of male and female faces with those made famous by Chuck Close. Unlike Close, however, whose works reveal an endlessly complicated betrayal of the overall image after more detailed inspection, Freiwald prefers to leave his huge watercolor paintings flat, with broad expanses of uninflected color that belie what Ken Johnson calls the realistic topography of the face.[1] This imparts the massive figure with an eerie absence that quickly becomes oppressive given the unbroken gaze. As Johnson wrote, "They loom and glow mysteriously like giant ghosts."[2]

Nevertheless, the mechanics that gave life to these giant hyperrealist ghosts are even more unique than their resulting creation. Unlike most artists painting under the rubric of Photorealism, most of whom typically rely on photographic images projected onto enormous screens, Freiwald claims to paint entirely from memory. Before starting a large-scale work, he creates smaller studies of men and women, ironically in more detail than their larger successors. In the transcription from study to memory to large-scale image, Freiwald tones down the effects of light on the canvas and brings his diverse models toward a predictable mean, which is always somewhat simplified if not intentionally abstract. This process tends to create an idea of a person who feels strangely numb, scarcely alive, and certainly not individualized.[3]

Given Freiwald's artistic process, his use of watercolors—seldom thought of as an edgy medium—actually raises a compelling attack on the perceived nature of hyperrealism: while it appears perfectly realistic, Freiwald only captures his memory of reality, and promises no accuracy beyond that which is sufficient to convince his audience of such a person's existence. With the simple step of the photographic conduit removed, Freiwald posits a lingering doubt over the veracity and honesty of photorealism, reminding us that every such work must always pass through the mind and hand of the artist.

[1] Johnson, "Till Freiwald," E36.
[2] Ibid.
[3] "Till Freiwald," press release.

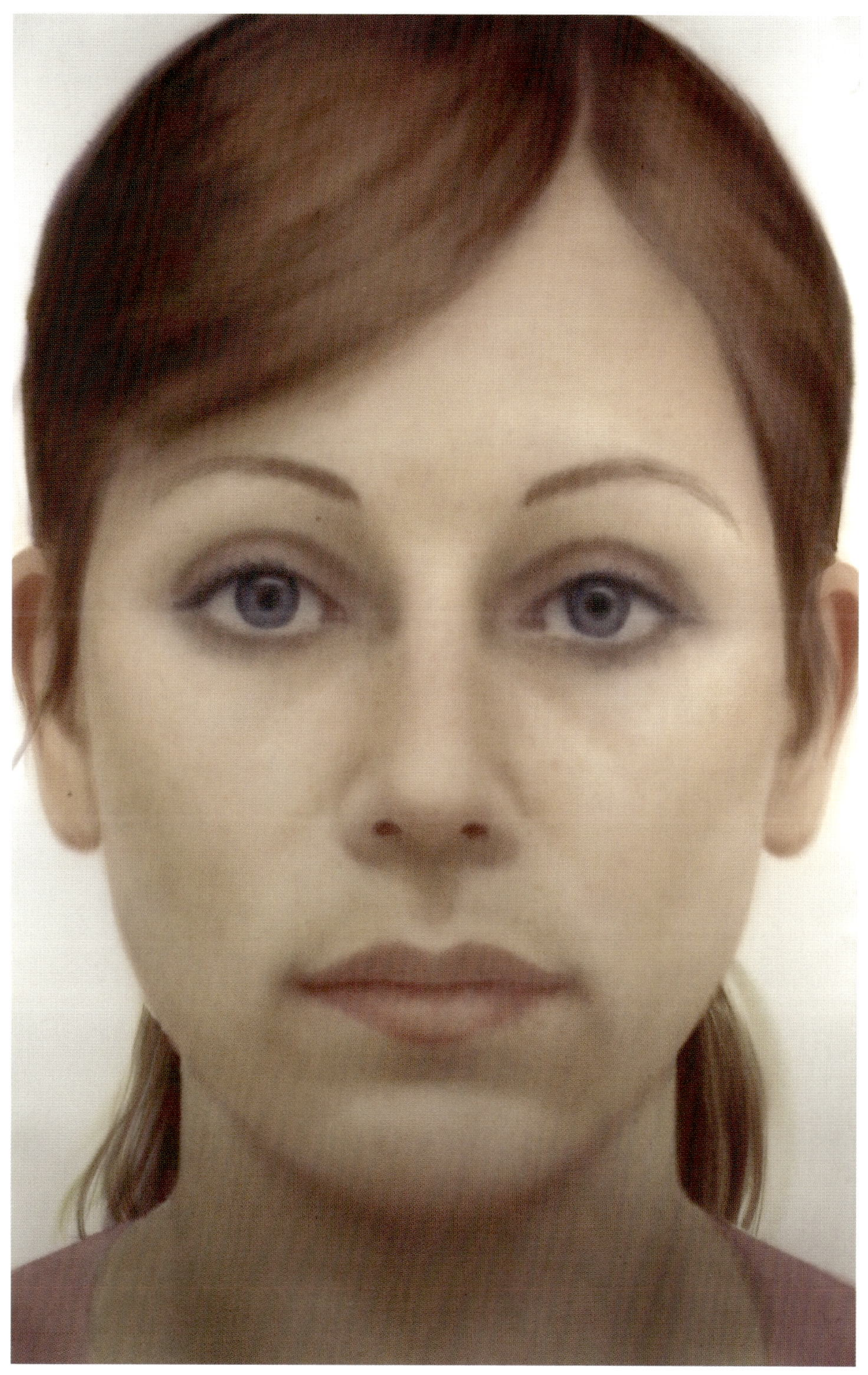

Untitled 2004
Watercolor on paper, 90″ x 60″

Nicolas Africano 1948-

Through its evocation of classical sculpture in both material and pose, Nicolas Africano's musing figure seems to consider her place in the complicated history of the female nude in Western art. Her connection to this broader question, inextricably woven into her morbid countenance and remote expression, serves to permanently distinguish Africano's small-scale figure from the realm of decorative, collectible figurines to which she might otherwise belong.[1]

Africano's *Untitled (Reclining Nude)* dialogues with an argument as old as the style he sought to imitate, vacillating between depictions of the female nude as boldly aggressive and demurely modest. Of course, Africano straddled this binary not out of any personal indecision, but for the very purpose of identifying and reinforcing the timelessness of the irresolvable debate. Similarly, Africano refused to allow his sculpture to evoke any single desire to the exclusion of another, prompting his viewer to protect and possess equally.[2] In this way, his nude becomes both bewitching and off-putting—and somewhat problematic for its insistent duality.

But Africano redeemed his work by grounding it in reality; he openly used his wife, Rebecca, as the subject of his work to suggest that the aura surrounding such a longstanding debate need not impede the exploration of its personal relevance, especially for the modern artist. As Arden Reed observed in *Art in America*, Africano's "obsessive, adoring study of one body—his wife's—as if he were trying poignantly, again and again, to get it right" is reflective of the intensely personal but historically indeterminable nature of the female nude for an artist like Africano.[3] Whether personally or historically motivated, however, Africano seemed to employ the female nude as a vehicle for a Foucaultian inquiry into gender performance in the arts and, more importantly, into the ever-evolving relationship between artist, audience, and the visually objectified. Though some have attempted to describe Africano's work as an outright celebration of the beauty of classical forms and an expression of their ongoing poignancy in the modern world, even such praise tends to reveal the ingenious duality inherent in his sculptures. For example, one critic praised Africano's glass figures as "unapproachably beautiful," deviating from their Greek and Roman predecessors only through an increased softness, which imbues his nudes "with a kind of romanticism that allows us to see them as human rather than as divine."[4] Of course, this merely leads the viewer back to the central concern of Africano's work so that in the end, *Untitled (Reclining Nude)* seems as much an expression of the Platonic ideal of the female form as it is an indictment of the legitimacy of such a limiting and simplistic concept.

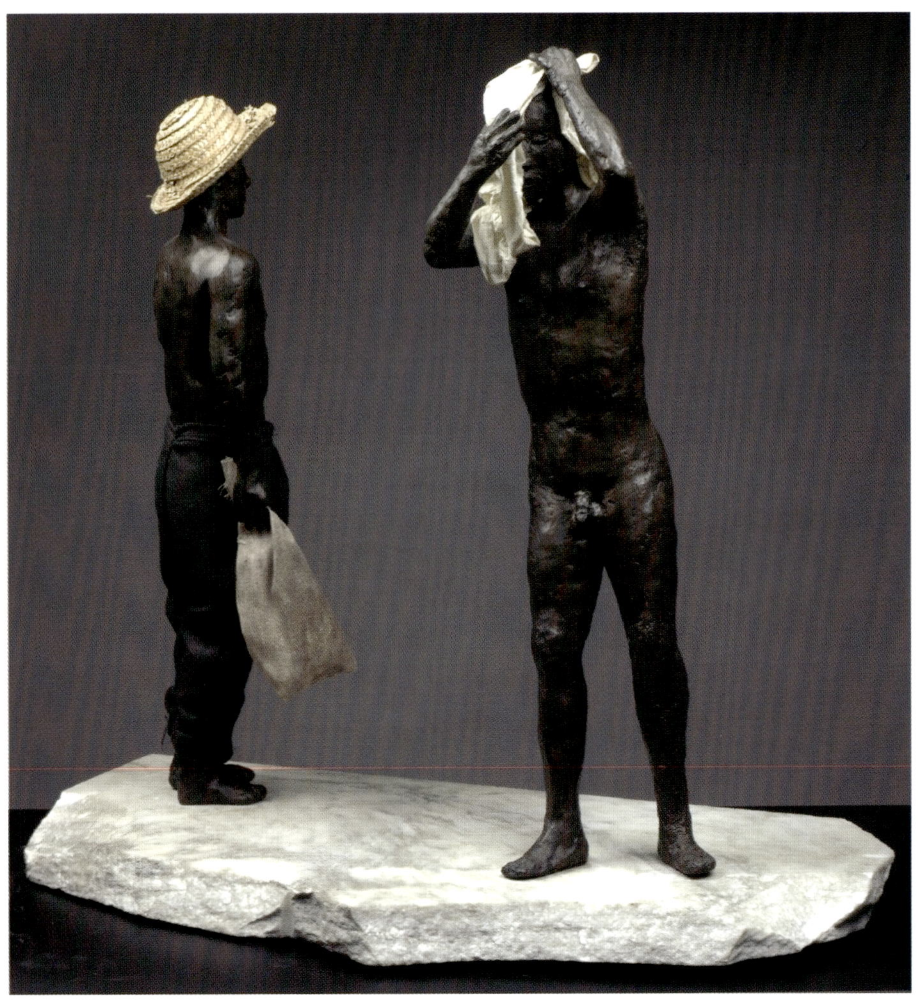

The Bathers 1986-87
Bronze, straw, and cloth, 20″ x 23″ x 11 1/2″

[1] Richard, "Nicolas Africano," 19.
[2] Ibid.
[3] Reed, "Nicholas Africano at Allene Lapides," 118.
[4] Hawkins, "Modern Spins on Classical Beauty," 56.

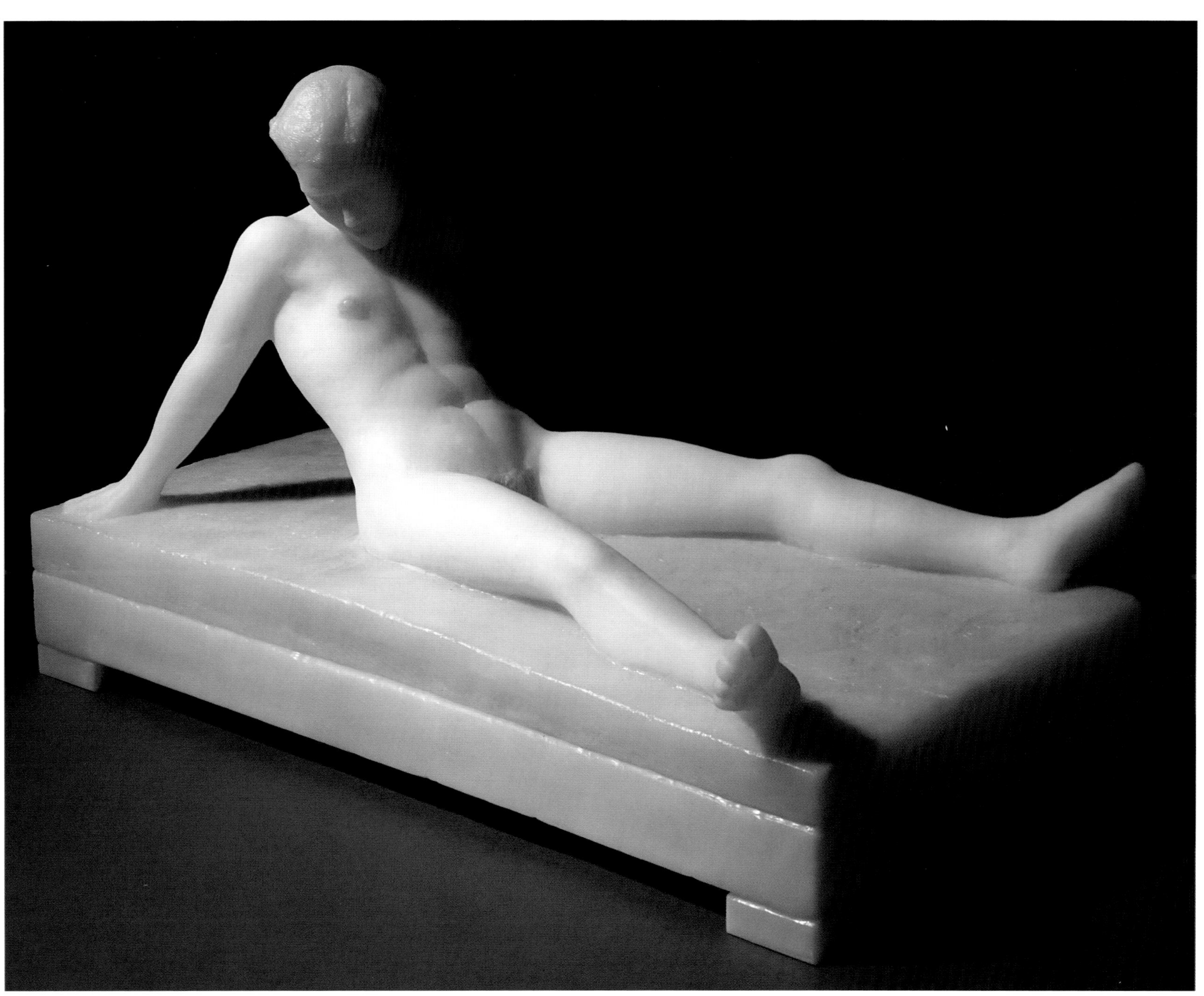

Untitled (Reclining Nude) 1998
Cast glass, enamel paint 13″ x 10 1/4″ x 21 3/4″

Hilo Chen 1942-

As a first-generation Photorealist, Hilo Chen separates himself from the hard-lined engine parts, chrome diners, and crisp commercial objects depicted by his contemporaries in the movement by focusing instead on the human figure. Accordingly, Louis Meisel categorizes Chen as "the primary painter of the nude in the movement,"[1] a title earned by his obsessive portrayal of hundreds of female nudes at the beach, painted sporadically over the course of three decades.

At first glance, Chen's nudes relate to their surroundings just as his oeuvre stands in regard to Photorealism writ large, pitting the sensuously beautiful female form against ubiquitous, contemporary artifacts: radios, soda cans, and coolers—necessitated by a day at the shore—flank his airbrushed goddesses with a hauntingly iconic presence.[2] Yet Chen seemed willing to cauterize any further exploration into their relationship for the sake of emphasizing the minute variations in skin tone, light, and shadow that saturate his foregrounded beauties with desire and envy—it is a treatment that can leave one wondering "whether his painting is an indictment, or a tacit approval, of soft pornography."[3]

Though his beach series appears to produce yet another in the line of soft-core pinups, according to Christine Lindey, "These paintings do not seem to deal with the subjects as much as the trite manner in which they are portrayed in non-art imagery."[4] Lindey suggests that Chen's work actually approaches the dangerous ground of satire: it exposes popular culture's pictorial conventions of sexuality by adopting them while relying on scale and context to transform his images into a form that transcends the very conventions utilized.[5]

Formally, Chen's paintings owe more to photography than satire. In *Beach #115*, the steep viewing angle places the audience in the position of the cameraman, complete with its "limited viewing space and depth of field."[6] The result is an instant, extemporaneous image of a woman whose flirtatious adjustment to her hair seems reminiscent of last-minute preparations for a photo shoot. She even presents the image of a cover model, concealing her true identity behind the cool façade of orange sunglasses.

Despite this exteriority, the immediate universe Chen presents seems to imitate an overly idealized lifestyle, one in which there is a perfectly harmonious transition from the woman's light-draped skin to the sun-bleached sand. It is all too incredible to be reality. In this way, Chen's beach paintings can be read as a parody of our enduring inner fantasies, and the sheer proliferation and breadth of his series should be seen as a testimony to the fantasy's relentless occupation of our minds, which seemingly cannot be assuaged. One even learns to read the bronzed nude as a fantasy equally exotic and exaggerated as that represented by the towel in *Beach #115*. Despite their different stylizations—one airbrushed, the other a cartoon—in Chen's view, they can both be equally comical.

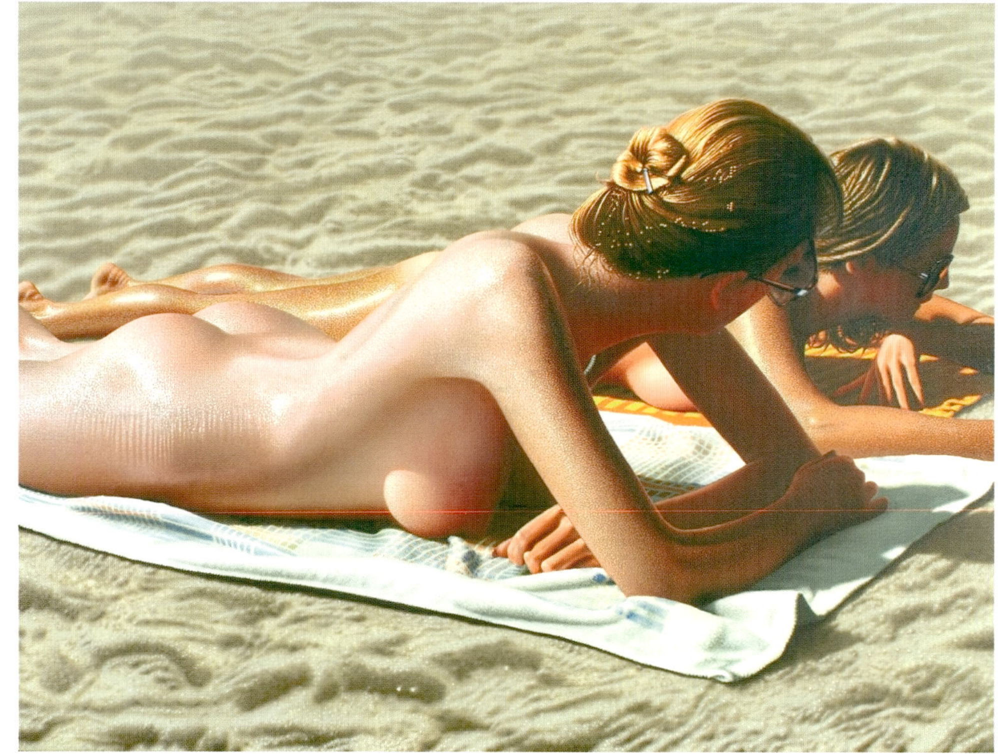

Beach #154 2006
Oil on canvas, 36″ x 48″

[1] Meisel, *Photo-Realism*, 434.
[2] Yoskowitz, "Hilo Chen," 57.
[3] Lindey, *Superrealist Painting & Sculpture*, 85.
[4] Ibid.
[5] Ibid.
[6] Yoskowitz, "Hilo Chen," 14.

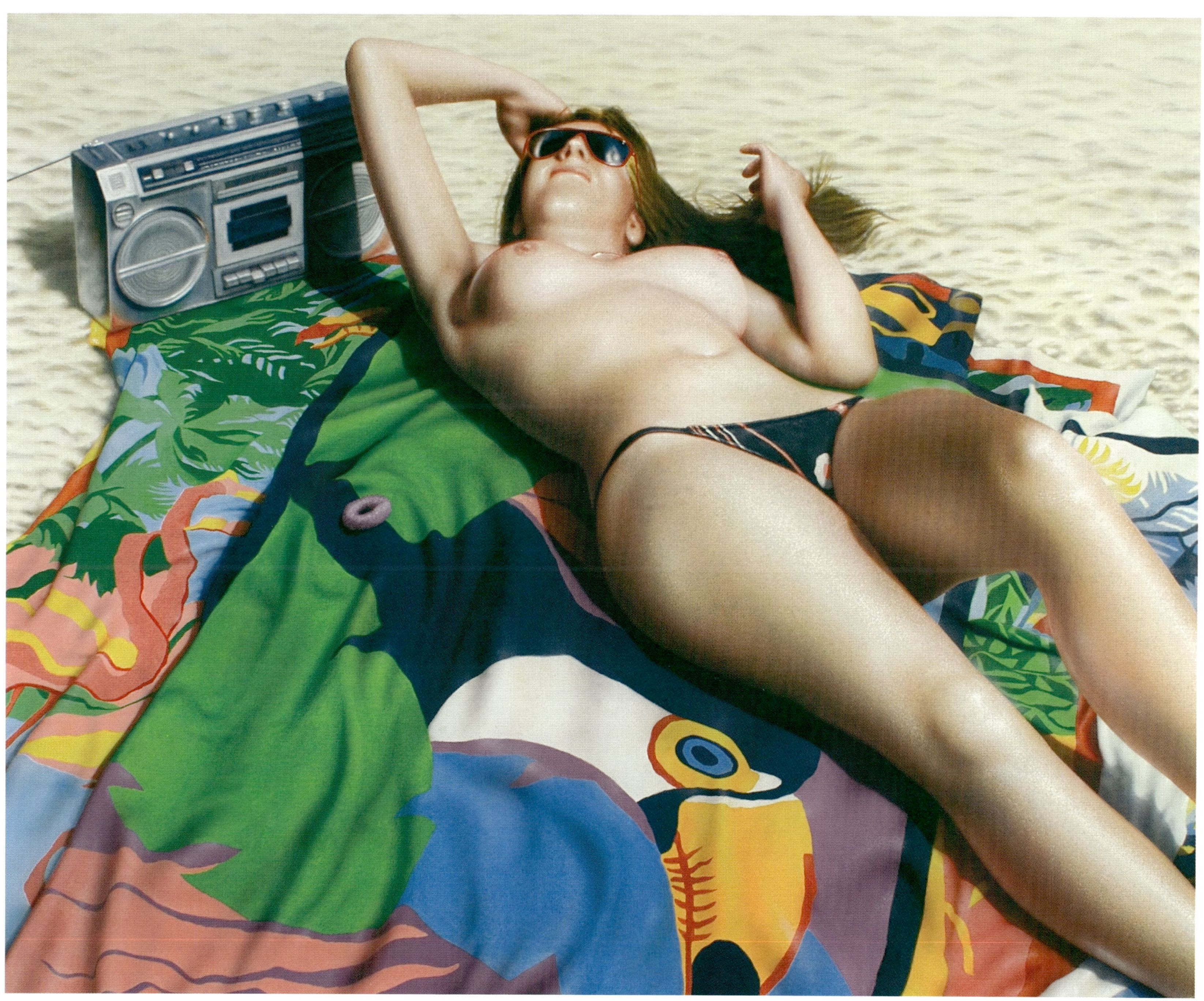

Beach #115 1989
Oil on canvas, 40″ x 50″

Tim Gardner 1973-

Playing on two of the most prevalent leisure distractions of the middle-class bourgeoisie—snapshot photography and watercolor—Tim Gardner explores what significant depth he can invest in those mediums often reserved for sweet portraits, panoramic landscapes, and other polite pleasantries.[1] While much of his work seems to attack this low-brow culture through its subject matter, centering on inebriated young adults on spring break and overtly macho displays of athleticism, others like *Untitled (Jim and Bhoadie on Mt. Temple*) come dangerously close to the typical snapshot. It is only Gardner's ability to inject scenes of hypermasculinity, such as the achievement of conquering a famous Canadian Rocky Mountain, with moments of unusual fragility that clearly pushes his oeuvre away from clichéd imagery.

Gardner achieves this degree of strange intimacy and vulnerability as much through watercolor's natural delicacy as through the diminutive scale of his work.[2] In his slightly hazed deviation from Photorealism, Gardner is able to present a scene of male bonding that is at once truthful and sensitive: his figures scarcely touch, yet they seem content in each other's company.

Perhaps some of the intimacy is achieved through Gardner's relation to his subjects: Jim, his father, and Bhoadie, his brother, are only two of the many family members whose photographs he transforms into highly aestheticized formal scenes. But it is in the distance Gardner also builds into his work that a self-reflective perspective on the meaning of art begins to emerge. By choosing source material in which minute subjects are set among grand, sublime landscapes, Gardner allows his work to dialogue with that of artists like Casper David Friedrich and Thomas Cole. As a result, the snapshot aesthetic seems as much culturally derived as it is historically informed.[3] It is no longer simply a captured moment of the tourist's gaze or a claim of ownership on a piece of Americana, but a greater challenge to the notions of which types of art are banal and which are deserving of the greater privilege of aura.[4]

[1] Molon, "Tim Gardner," 120.
[2] Ibid.
[3] Ibid.
[4] Ibid.

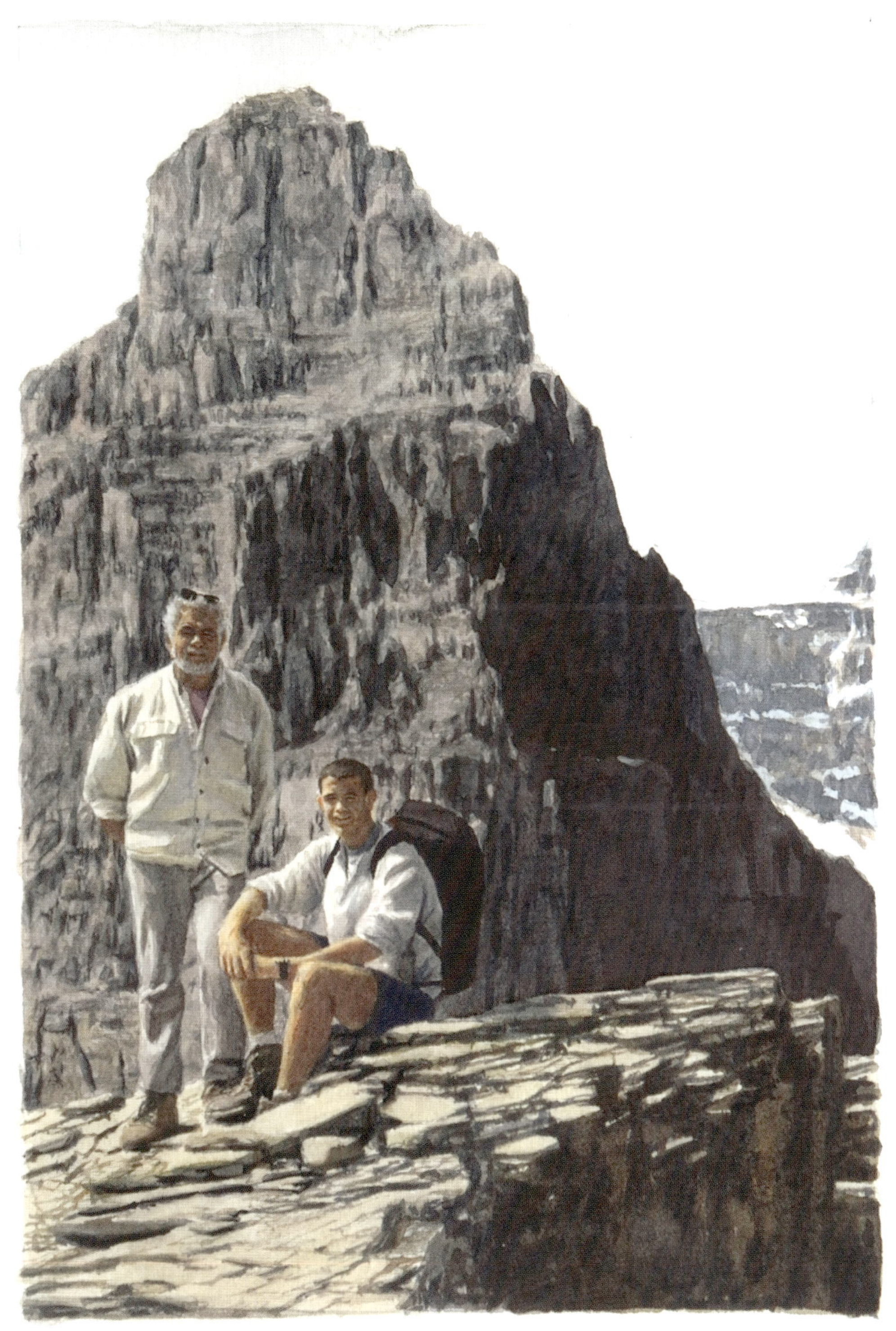

Untitled (Jim and Bhoadie on Mt. Temple) 2002
Watercolor on paper, 8 3/4″ x 6″

William Bailey 1930-

It is no longer enough for a modern still-life painting to succeed by the rules of its genre; even when an artist's skills equal those of his predecessors, his work must also contend with the zeitgeist of his age. As such, the work is called upon to stake some revisionary statement, to redefine what still life means for a modern world. It must succeed not only as a work of art but also as a representative—or even as a spokesperson.

William Bailey's modern transumption of the still-life genre is in many ways also a return to its traditional ideals. It is a process that seeks the order and formal beauty characteristic of such history while acknowledging the dense shadow it casts in order to progress beyond it. His allusive titles evoke a nostalgia for Old Europe and for the small Italian towns like Tuscan Arezzo that produced artists as influential as Piero della Francesca, renowned for the graceful curves of his figures and the simplicity of his still lifes.

For Bailey, the shadow cast by his work's historicity is not only a figurative motif; it is also a literal manifestation. Shadow defines the objects in his work, driving their often complicated relationships toward moments of upstaging, supporting, pointing, and ignoring.[1] But this, it seems, is precisely Bailey's contribution to the revision of still life: for the artist, still life is a form of "figure" painting not simply because it entails the creation of recognizable representations, but because it is also "figurative," or non-literal.[2] In this way, his surface of interconnected, uninterrupted objects is evocative of his work's continuum with history. His egg is not simply a technical challenge, but also a symbol of his works as topologically simple and self-contained pieces. His particular use of light and tonality is not merely mimetic of the conditions of his studio, but meant to induce a sense of silence and meditative gaze not unlike the artist's own gaze on history.

Just as *Arezzo Still Life* centers on the relationships between objects on the canvas, so too is it concerned with its larger relationships beyond the canvas. The struggle for claims of prominence and authority extend beyond the ceramic structures, centuries into the past.[3] Bailey's work is meant to show and to tell and, most of all, to exercise the facility of still life to function as a communicative art, even if only self-referentially so.[4]

[1] Briganti and Hollander, *William Bailey*, 21.
[2] Ibid., 16-17.
[3] Ibid., 21.
[4] Ibid., 24.

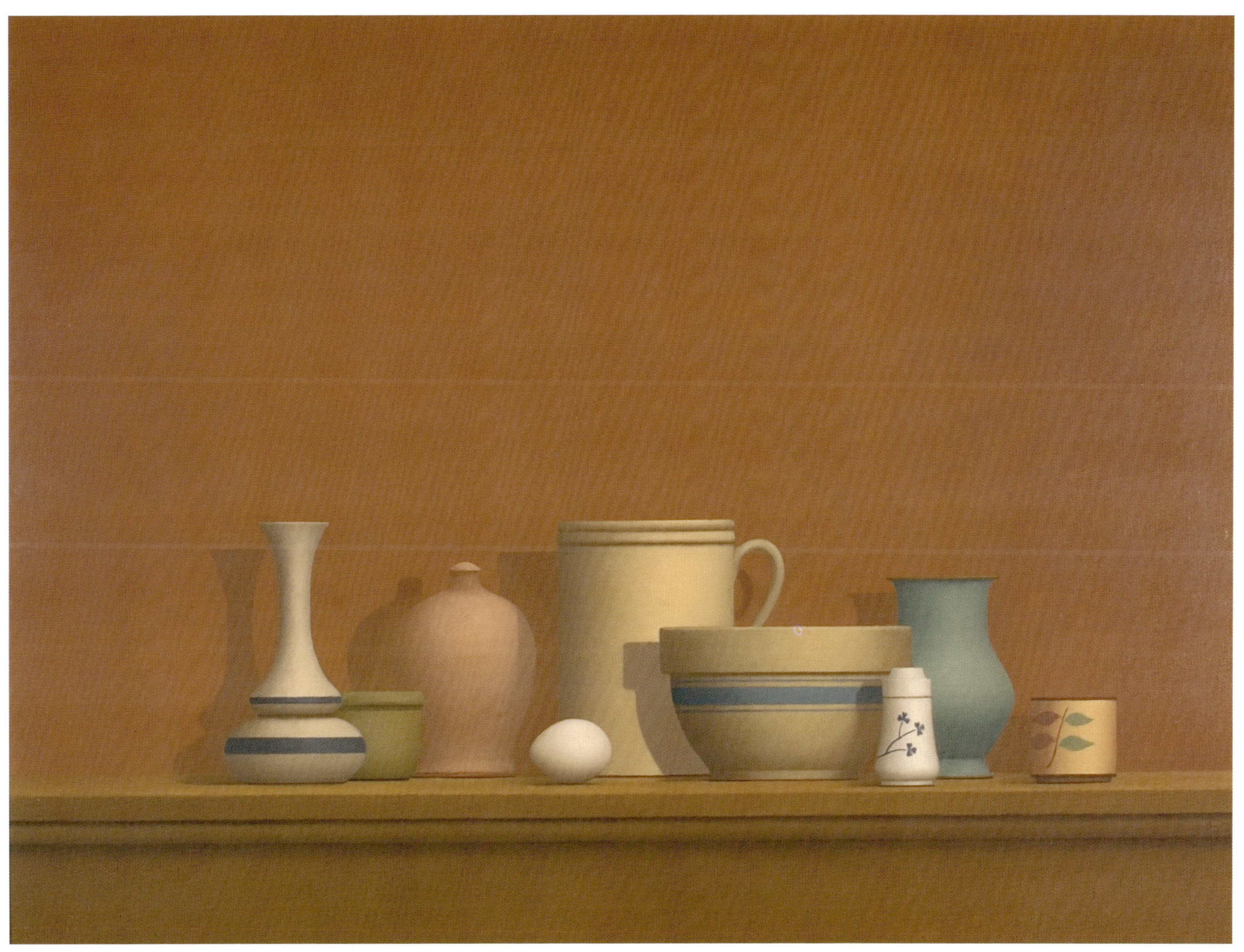

Arezzo Still Life 1979
Oil on canvas, 30″ x 40″

Colette Calascione 1971-

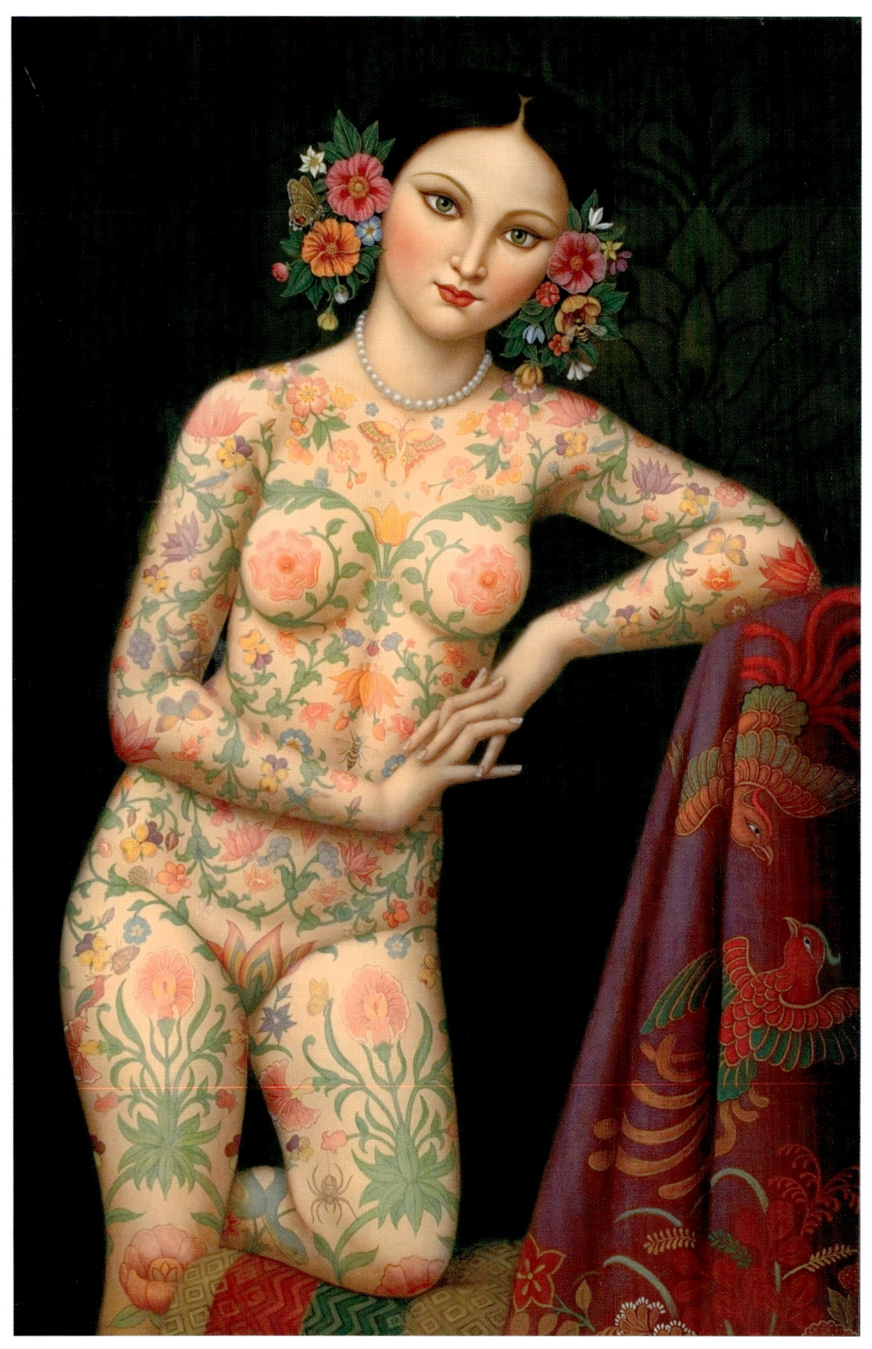

Illumination 2004
Oil on panel, 30″ x 20″

Jennifer Bartlett 1941-

Although Jennifer Bartlett's choice of gardens, lakes, and boats for subject matter would typically conjure thoughts of recreation, as curator Marge Goldwater wrote, "her approach to art is anything but leisurely."[1] Bartlett's career as a painter has been marked by relentless attempts to understand all possible permutations of a situation, and to survey nature and culture from a dizzying array of vantage points, changes in medium, and even shifts in dimensionality. Accordingly, she works almost exclusively in series.

At Sands Point #21 is part of an investigatory series that spans fifty-two attempts to capture the area on the North Shore of Long Island where Bartlett spent the summer following an exhibition in New York. The vignette occupies a middle ground in the series, both in its chronological position and in its size—works range between 12 x 12" to 84 x 84"—but more importantly, in its style and content. While some appear overly idyllic, without any inhibition to the paradise displayed before our eyes, others portray a storm-torn landscape complete with black sky and swirling waters. *At Sands Point #21* partially blocks the viewer's access through the presence of a picket fence in the foreground, yet leaves the picturesque scene perfectly unmarred, tranquil, and above all, free from any evidence of human habitation. As such, the canvas is also caught in the middle of tension, unsure if it is granting a piece of nature or preserving it. In all likelihood, Bartlett also felt the effects of the extended catch twenty-two: her appreciation of the unblemished setting and a corresponding desire to enjoy it is set alongside the knowledge that such use can only lead to its destruction.

Bartlett's work is also an investigation into what defines a place. For her, the boat serves as a symbol of liberty, adventure, and Ulyssian homecomings, while the fence is emblematic of order, reason, and demarcation. Together, these symbols define Sands Point as a place of retreat, as a place of suspended reality, and as a place where moments of introspection inevitably broach the lofty material encoded in its semiotic imagery.[2]

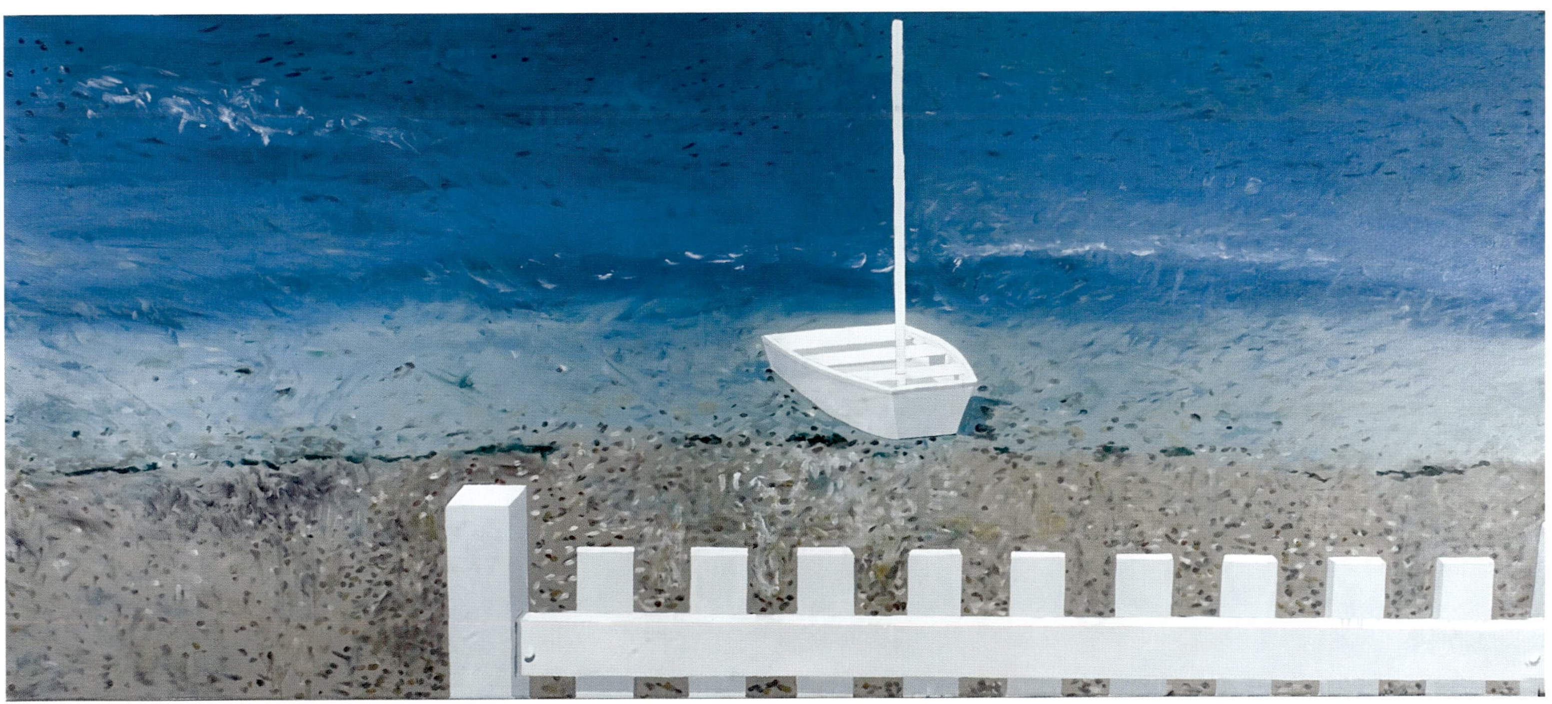

At Sands Point #21 1986
Oil on canvas, 36" x 84"

[1] Marge Goldwater, "Jennifer Bartlett: On Land and Sea," *Jennifer Bartlett* (New York: Abbeville Publishers, 1989) 39.
[2] Smith, "Flooding the Mind's Eye," 136.

William Beckman 1946-

William Beckman is one of many artists in the Collection who quickly grew uncomfortable painting under the umbrella label of Photorealism. Though his early work masterfully fulfilled the genre's technical demands, his methodology of razor stripping showed him to be rather conflicted, seeking both the faithful rendering of reality and its simultaneous deconstruction—so much so that he often shaved the canvas down to a bare, representation-free weave. As Carl Belz, Director Emeritus of the Rose Art Museum, wrote of Beckman's inclusion as a Photorealist, "If the realist label survives [his painting], I only hope it will in the end have come to connote the work's deep embodiment of lived human experience."[1]

In particular, critics have understood Beckman's work to go beyond aesthetic reflection, to capture the underlying structural network of daily experience as witnessed in its countless interpersonal relationships. Unlike many Photorealists who rely on source material and photographic projection, Beckman works entirely from human models posing for hundreds of hours in his studio. As a result, Beckman's work often seems to center on his relationship with the subject and, more generally, on the connections humans form between themselves.[2] Recognizing both the difficulty of developing meaningful relationships and their intensity once formed, Beckman seeks to craft portraits that both represent and force such a connection to be established.

Study for a Classical Woman functions as this kind of vehicle, candidly and aggressively daring the viewer to engage with its subject, who presents herself naked and without embellishment "for no apparent reason other than to discomfort anyone who dares to observe her."[3] In other words, Beckman attempted to construct an honest and concentrated relationship, free from pretense, or as the Frye Art Museum termed it in reference to the artist's method, "stripped of sentiment."[4] In many ways, the viewer has no choice but to be drawn into the woman. There is no superfluous background detail nor foreground space, only a cropped, encroaching body and an unrelenting stare that demands and holds one's attention.

Unlike many of his earlier works, however, which featured then-wife Diana as a similarly disarming, nude siren, Beckman's *Study for a Classical Woman* appears to withhold something of herself from the relationship, obstructing the viewer from complete access with her hand and avoiding overt connection through shaded eyes. By situating her on a detached portion of a sectional sofa, Beckman unexpectedly calls attention to her solitude and further confuses the proposition of forming a relationship with the subject by suggesting that she has already formed a physical connection with the chair, which appears to mimic her concealed body. Is she consumed by this relationship, or is she simply that much more open to involving herself with a variety of objects and viewers?

If one can look to the Photorealist conclusion of *Classical Woman* (1988-1991), many of these issues appear to resolve, ultimately aligning more closely with Beckman's typical themes of directness and connection. Yet viewed on its own, *Study for Classical Woman* presents perhaps a more compelling stance on the multidimensional reality of relationships: the back-and-forth struggle for control that can take place in establishing any formal involvement with another, and the extent to which one is willing to open before seeking reciprocity.

[1] Belz, introduction to *William Beckman*, 8.
[2] Ibid., 19.
[3] Valdez, "William Beckman at Forum," 126-127.
[4] Resource Library Magazine, "Painting on the Edge."

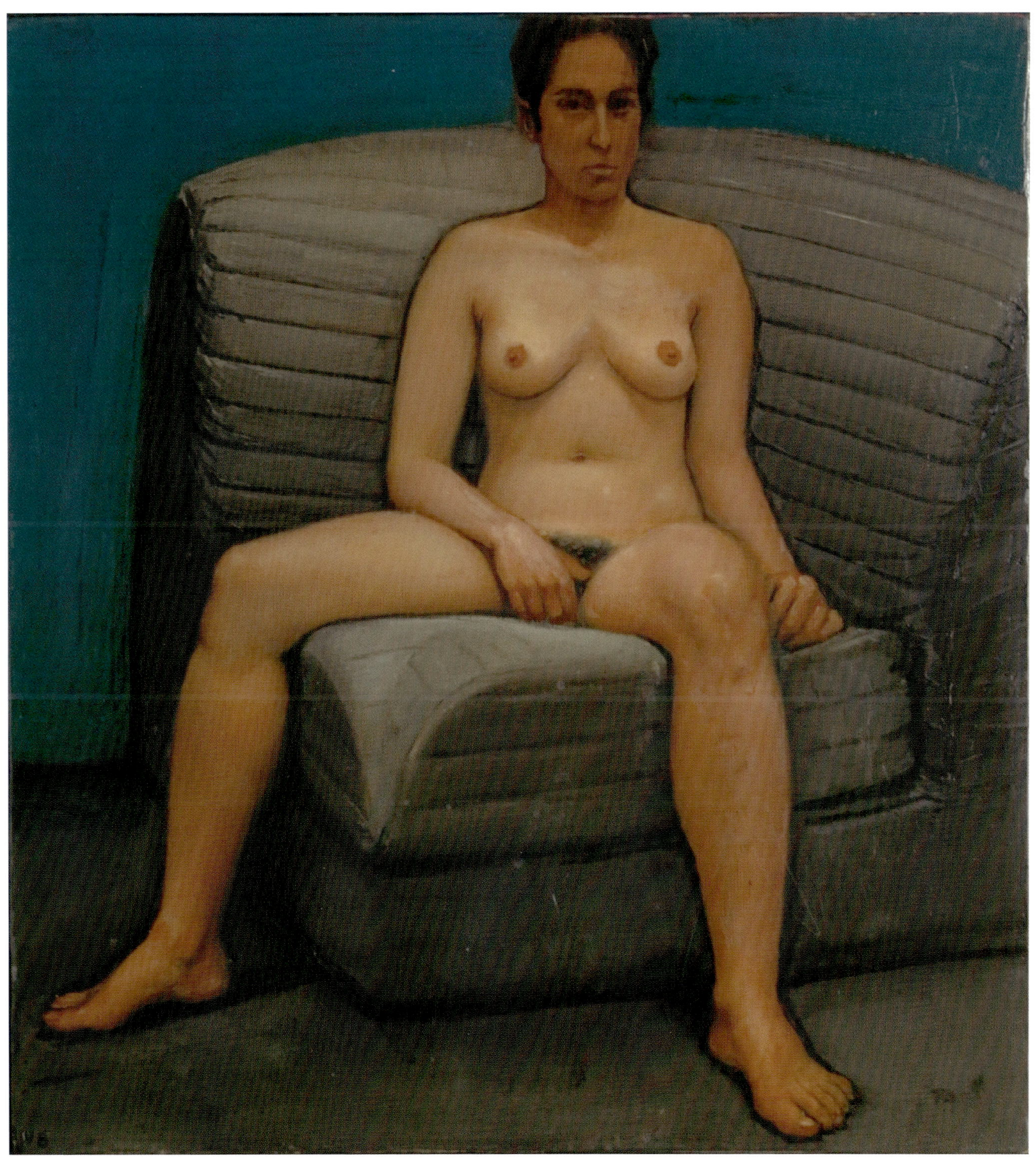

Study for a Classical Woman 1991
Oil on panel, 15 1/2″ x 14 1/4″

Fairfield Porter 1907-1975

Painted in the last year of his life, at the age of sixty-eight, Fairfield Porter's *Still Life* is a testament to the artist's ability to create successful works without repetition, formula, or a dependence on signature motifs. As he said in an interview, "Composition isn't good because something is repeated but because it is not...If there's something that never occurs again in a painting, that's what gives it its unique quality."[1]

Porter's *Still Life* is a watercolor *Intimisme*, a veritable homage to the influence exerted on his career by French Postimpressionists Pierre Bonnard and Édouard Vuillard. Seeking to reinvigorate their use of unmodulated color and unique description of light for an American audience, Porter chose a distinctly national domestic setting: a country kitchen with views of the outdoors through the screened-in porch. The scene is completed with wholesome details such as country-store butter and farm-fresh milk. Porter also sought to adopt their use of simple domestic interiors as stages for the battle between figure and ground, horizontals and verticals, and even between crowded details and their propensity to meld into large-scale, luxurious patterns.[2]

On the whole, the work's quiet energy invites its viewer into the scene, pushing one's eye past the table, past the mediating porch, and ultimately into the misty blue of the outdoors.[3] Porter's use of pattern and color nearly replace perspective in the definition of space, resulting in a conflation of the country kitchen with its inspirational—or literal, in the case of the milk, flowers, and fruit—outdoor source.[4] Moreover, the white of the paper comes through as the grid of the windows—its verticals reflecting on the table—extending directly off the paper and providing a visual link between Porter's fictional world and the viewer's own reality. For Porter, such a simple, life-affirming scene was intended to be reproduced by American families everywhere.

As Hilton Kramer wrote in a review for the *New York Times*, Porter's painting was "the art of conservation...standing in relation to the more radical modes of artistic expression very much as our parks and gardens and surviving areas of unmolested countryside stand in relation to our overpopulated urban centers...We seek in them the renewal of spirit that stands aloof from the very concept of dynamism—a spirit which nourishes itself on nuances of feeling which are, if anything, the very obverse of dynamic change and disruption."[5] For a work such as *Still Life*, Kramer's metaphor and description of the artist are particularly appropriate: Porter's work endures as a simplified version of life, a source of renewed spirit achieved only through its nuances of light, pattern, and definition of space, producing a world as appealing as that of the masters of *Intimisme*.

[1] Quoted in Spike, *Fairfield Porter*, 9.
[2] Bonito, *Get Real*, 100.
[3] Ibid., 102.
[4] Ibid.
[5] Kramer, "Art of Conservation," D33.

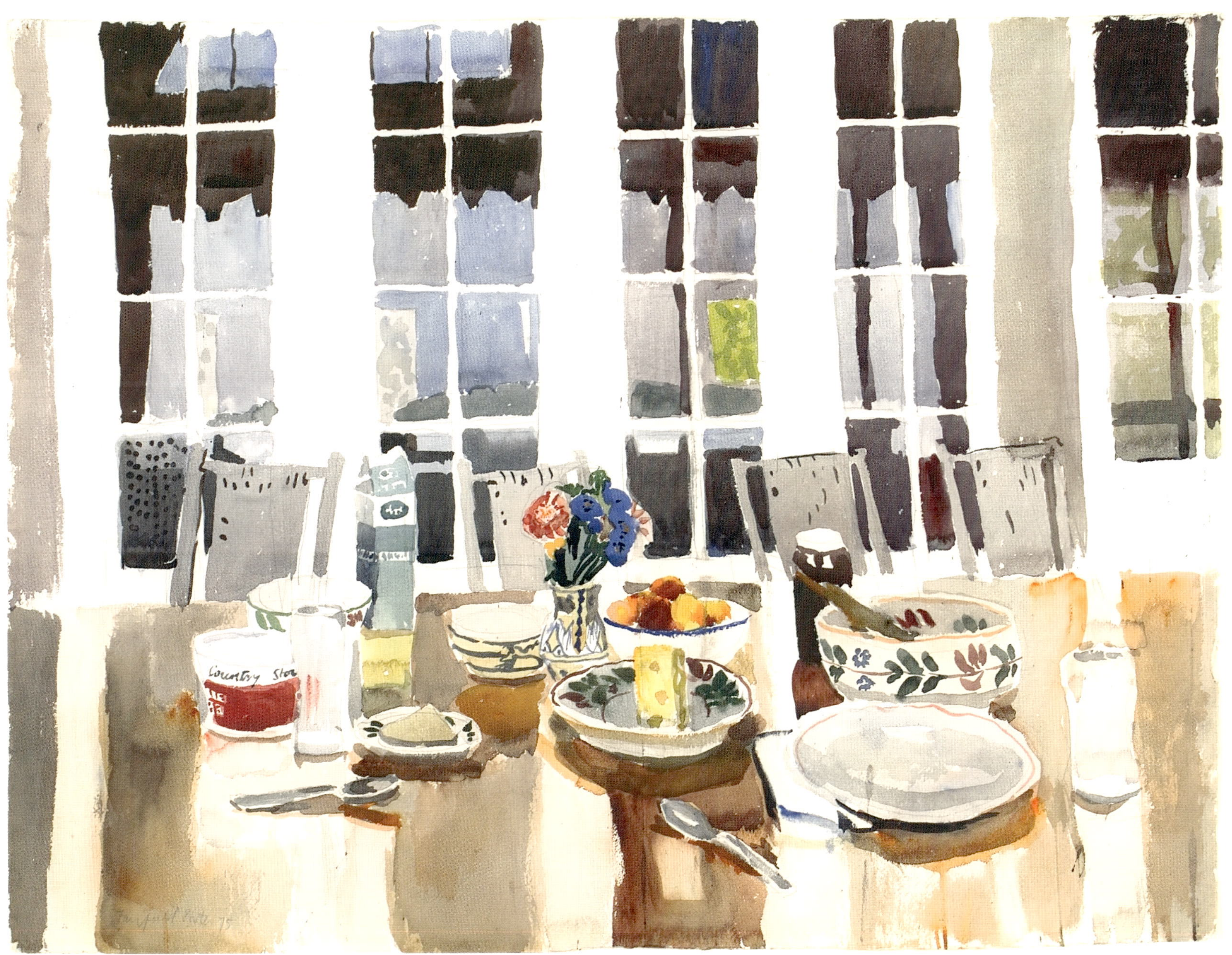

Still Life 1975
Watercolor on Paper, 22 1/2″ x 30 1/2″

Romare Bearden 1914-1988

Romare Bearden's collages have always sought to embrace themes from diverse times and places by imbuing each disparate end with the same unique sense of character and physical presence.[1] He aimed for a unified work that lent insight on all that we share across racial lines and a depiction of difference with the noble balance of equality. Even late in life, however, the coherent integration of so much was never a smooth process and his work reflected it. Serrated and truncated edges of paper, bleeding and abrasive blocks of color, terse and elliptical narratives, and distortions of scale and perspective each stand as an indispensable badge of the unresolved tension Bearden sought to identify and ultimately erase.[2]

On the heels of *Profile/Part I, The Twenties*, which served as Bearden's first autobiographical installment, the artist produced another series of nineteen collages chronicling the institutions, people, places, and events that significantly impacted his life during the 1930s. As the decade that continued the Harlem Renaissance, the thirties were embodied in meccas of African American culture like Leroy's Jazz club and its legendary Sunday nights, which Bearden captured in *Uptown Sunday Night Session*, The Apollo Theater, and the Lafeyette Theater, which Bearden captured in *Johnny Hudgins Comes On*.[3]

When the painting was exhibited in New York in 1981, *Johnny Hudgins Comes On* was displayed with the accompanying text: "He was my favorite of all the comedians. What Johnny Hudgins could do through mime on an empty stage helped show me how worlds were created on an empty canvas."[4] For Bearden, sometimes it was just that simple. Like many of Bearden's other pieces, *Johnny Hudgins Comes On* also captures a subject matter that serves as an allegory for racial tension and unity. As a minstrel tap dancer, Johnny Hudgins was known as much for his seemingly unattached limbs as for his use of blackface, calling special attention to this facet of his performance through use of the name Johnny Hudgins and The Blackbirds. As such, Hudgins presented Bearden with the unique situation of a man who drew upon a stereotyped notion of the same race and culture to which he owed his success. Ironically, Hudgins seemed to link white and black culture, regardless of this circumstance, and in Bearden's system of logic, Hudgins showed that whites and blacks could unite—perversely or otherwise—or at least share the same "stage," be it the Lafayette Theater or Bearden's own canvas.

As one of only a few well-known black American artists, Bearden's work is constantly called upon to represent and define African American culture. Though Bearden was more interested in attaining universals, he does seem to approach such an aim through the lens of the African American experience, paying special attention not to marginalize or essentialize that experience.[5] In Johnny Hudgins, Bearden found yet another shared cultural memory that freed him from the closed circle of Black culture, offering an outlet for further interrogation of the past and a vehicle for pushing the divided canon of modern art back into a convergent path.

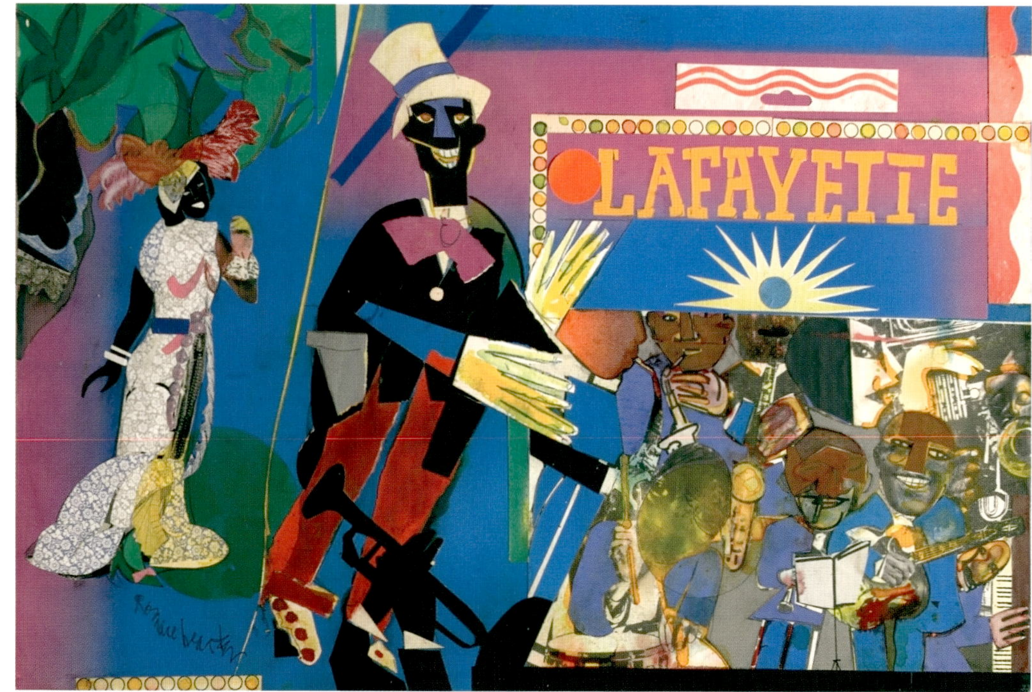

Johnny Hudgins Comes On: Profile/Part II, The Thirties Series 1981
Collage and mixed media, 16″ x 24″

[1] Fine, Romare Bearden, 4.
[2] Kennel, "Bearden's Musée Imaginaire," 153.
[3] Fine, "Romare Bearden," 107-110.
[4] Bearden, *Collages: Profile/Part II: The Thirties*, 39.
[5] Kennel, "Bearden's Musée Imaginaire," 153.

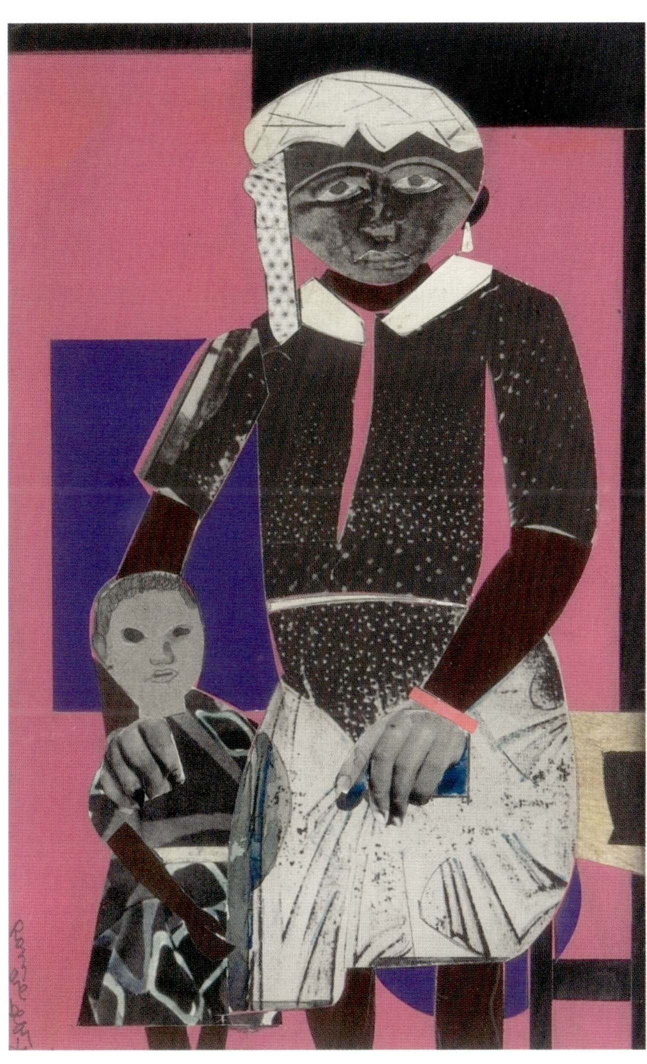

Mother and Child 1978
Collage and mixed media, 12″ x 7″

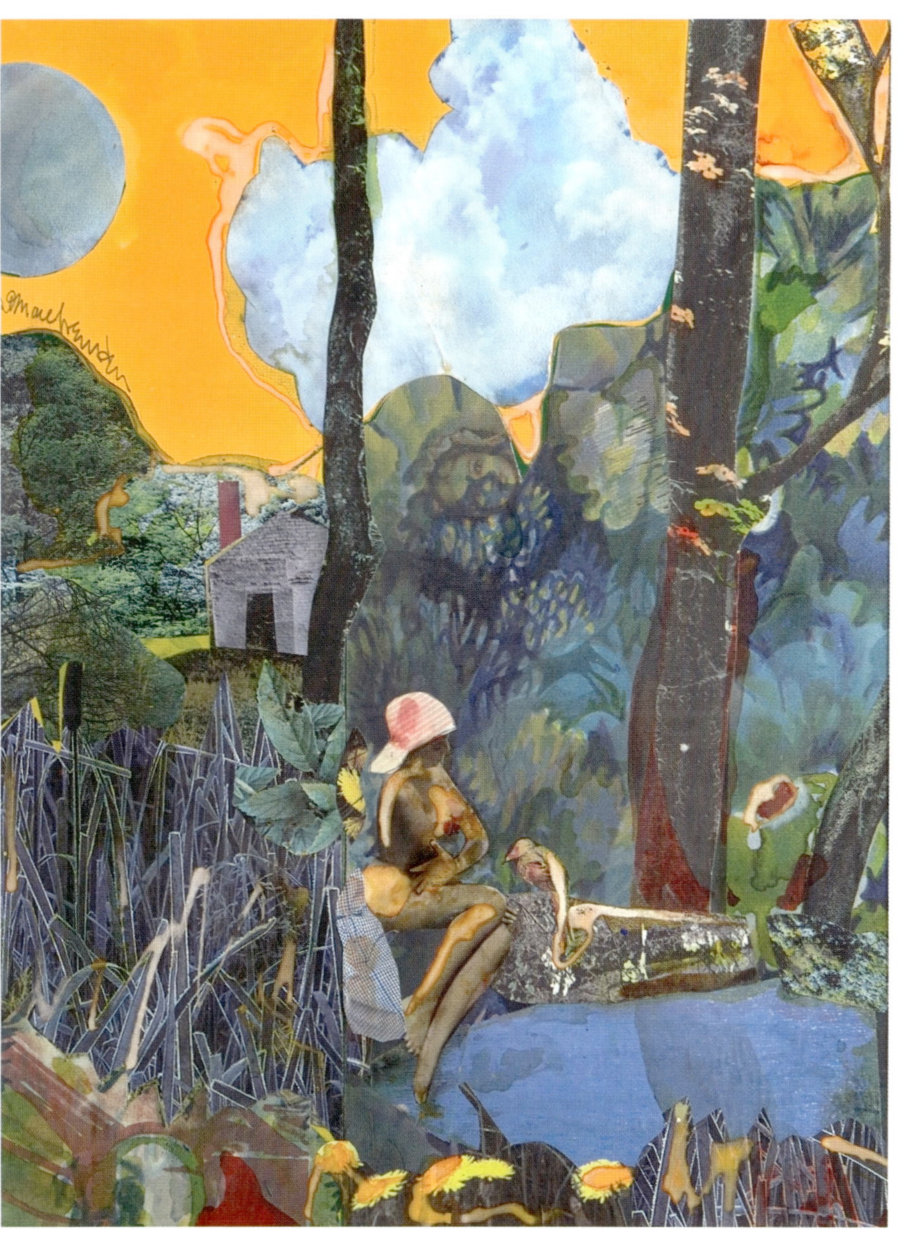

Mecklenburg Autumn 1981
Collage and mixed media on Masonite, 18″ x 14″

Karen Kilimnik 1955-

Drawing upon television, theater, and cinema for inspiration as often as she looks to Raeburn, Stubbs, or Desportes, Karen Kilimnik provides her own point of entrée to enchanting fictional worlds through the simple act of painting whatever she enjoys.[1] As she explained in the afterword to her retrospective, "To me painting is like magic—it's fun being able to paint a big house, or lots of animals...[It's] as if they are mine now."[2] Through such "scatter" painting, Kilimnik gains access to both the substantive and tangentially fictional elements of daily life that are otherwise unavailable to her, especially those that enter through the special effects and fairy-tale storylines of the entertainment industry.

Chloe is part of a portraiture series of characters from the cult 1971 British horror film *The Blood on Satan's Claw*, directed by Piers Haggard and based on three short stories by Robert Wynne-Simmons. As Kilimnik wrote, the *Blood on Satan's Claw* series was done "partly as a way to be part of that seemingly fun environment."[3] Like the film, which employs the hallucinatory air of a dream set in seventeenth-century England, Kilimnik developed her work as a means to gain access to another era, to momentarily achieve a sense of otherness and escape. Seeking to emulate the suspenseful and eerie camera angles of the horror genre, Chloe is set against the backdrop of a dark forest, partly obscured by a branch as she either recedes into the darkness or emerges from it. By paralleling the spiritual possession of characters in the film, Kilimnik seeks to be possessed thematically by her work, employing the temporary, pleasurable loss of control as her central motif.

Kilimnik's work is not a painterly reproduction of a still screen shot, but rather a fictitious moment in the artist's imagination. Because Chloe is a minor character, Kilimnik is able to cast her into a new storyline, reinventing and observing her as the painting unfolds along a yet-untaken journey. Although Chloe carries a specific set of allusions, it is her interaction with the viewer's current reality that is more striking, such as slightly parted lips that seem hauntingly ready to speak yet which remain mute. By importing the figure of Chloe into a new fictional world, Kilimnik sought to amplify the pleasure derived from the representational reality of filmic drama, disseminating the redoubled effect for an audience that Kilimnik hopes will share in her preferred script.[4]

[1] Schwabsky, "Karen Kilimnik," 174.
[2] Karen Kilimnik, *Karen Kilimnik Paintings*, 311.
[3] Ibid., 312.
[4] Ibid., 312-314.

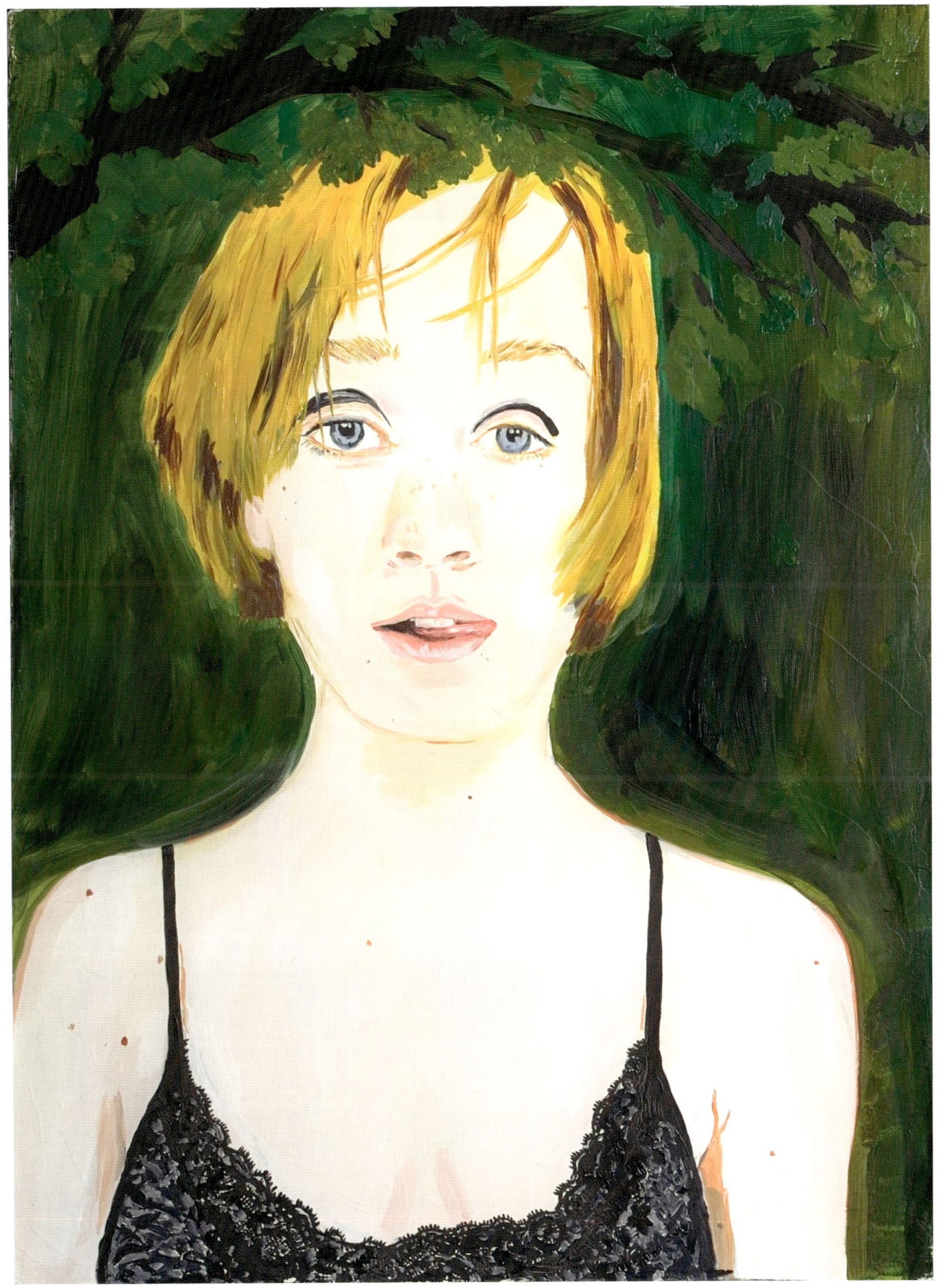

Chloe (from Blood on Satan's Claw) 1996
Oil on canvas, 24″ x 18″

Tom Blackwell 1938-

Though he is considered one of the original Photorealists, Tom Blackwell has remained at the forefront of the movement throughout its duration and has arguably elevated his prominence from one of its central artists to having his *Odalisque Express* featured on the cover of Louis K. Meisel's *Photorealism at the Millennium*, the third installment of the genre's unofficial directory.

His increased importance can, in part, be attributed to the change in Blackwell's subject matter as it evolved from simple chromatic motorcycles to the multi-layered worlds contained and reflected in plate-glass store windows, which brought with them an increased complexity seldom before seen in Blackwell's paintings. In 1985, Blackwell supported his interest in this new subject matter, writing, "For several years I have been interested in dealing with the formal issues involved in juxtaposing and overlapping images, but I also wanted to bring a more emotional, personal, and deliberately evocative element into the work. Painting store windows with their double and triple reflective images, which I did for several years, started me thinking about the idea of pentimento...I wanted to use this effect in a deliberate way, having one image literally coming through another."[1]

Blackwell's *Odalisque Express* employs his playful infatuation with the by-products of pentimento to an absurd degree, overlapping levels of reality and non-reality as though amusing himself by copying Jean-Augustine-Dominique Ingres' famous *La Grande Odalisque*, only to transparently superimpose one of his signature storefront windows directly on top. As a palimpsest, Blackwell's work fulfills the evocative qualities he sought in 1985, relying upon his viewer to both recognize the figure as a visual pun of another storefront mannequin and to recall the gamut of emotions that the perfectly concealed concubine has historically invoked.

Of course, in this process Blackwell reveals his true use of the figure as well; his painting serves to visually elaborate on the subtle ways Ingres covered the sensitive parts of his nude, preserving Ingres' original positioning and clothing while expanding upon the complex visual obstruction from the reflection of street traffic on one side of the window to objects for sale on the other. In turn, this connection of the woman to objects of desire—and even objects for sale, since the odalisque was originally a female slave for the Turkish sultan—is solidified by Blackwell's centering of Alexander's department store, a once-famous merchandiser on Lexington Avenue in Manhattan. Though Blackwell had thus updated the idealized, desirable object, he duly noted its permanence, and by interlacing these many visual levels around a common theme of objectification and commodification, Blackwell was able to take found images—both the pre-existing artwork and the photograph of city life from which he worked—and transform them into a poetic and perfectly realistic chaos.

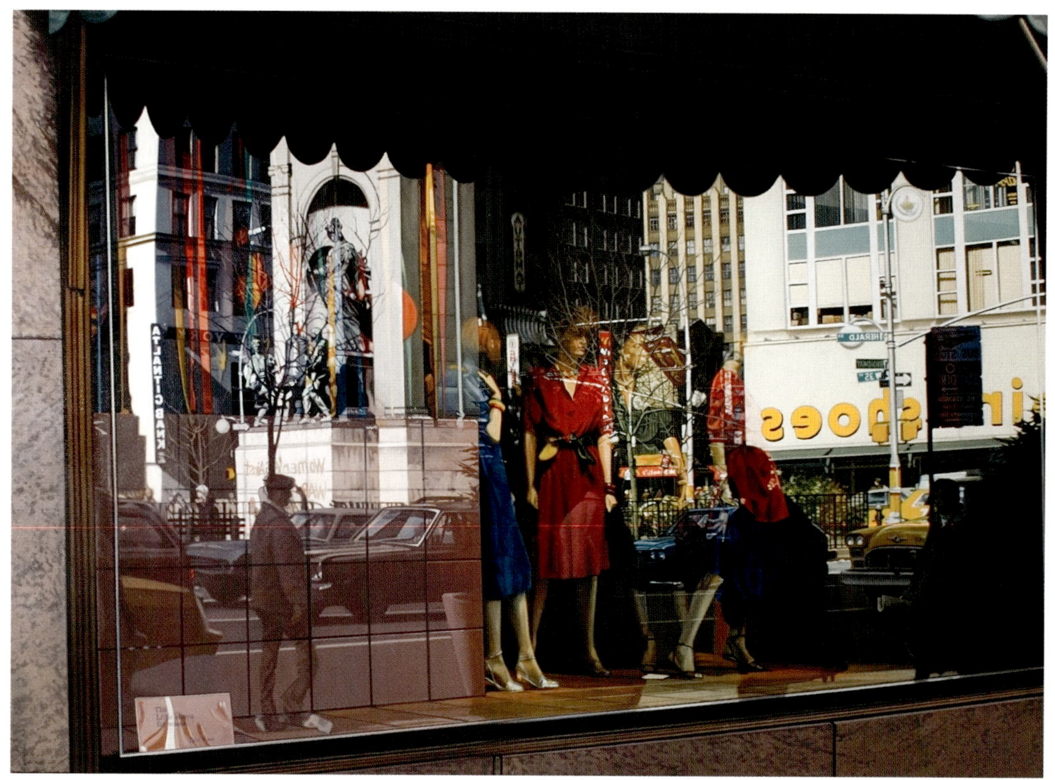

Herald Square 1983
Oil on linen, 60″ x 84″

[1] Blackwell, *Tom Blackwell: New Paintings.*

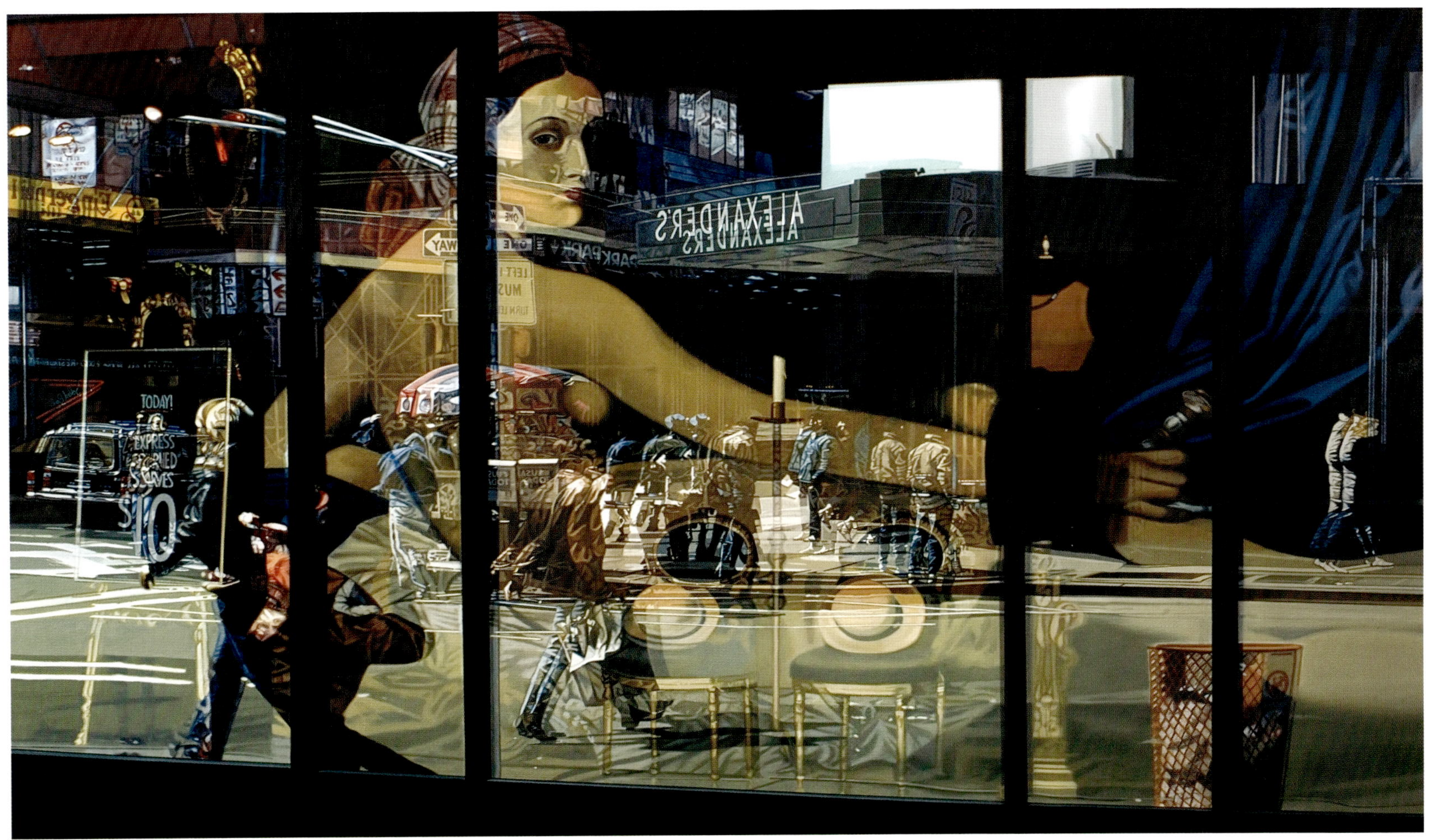

Odalisque Express 1992-93
Oil on linen, 61″ x 93 1/2″

Audrey Flack 1931-

Credited with the first Photorealistic painting, *Kennedy Motorcade* (1964), Audrey Flack turned her efforts to sculpture in the early 1980s in order to find "solidity on many levels" in an art world that was "out of control, structureless, oversized, and temporary."[1] As she explained in her manifesto on the process of creation, *Art and Soul: Notes on Creating*, "I need[ed] the substance of sculpture, the compactness of scale reduction in the form of a recognizable human figure—something solid, real, tangible. Something to hold and to hold on to."[2]

Flack found just this in a series of six large Medusa heads, each differing slightly in medium but with a similarly commanding weight and presence that invaded its space of display. Taking the mythical figure of Medusa as her subject, Flack entered into dialogue not only with the historical use of the goddess in art but with the central use of the figure in modern feminist literature as well. Flack is particularly attentive to her beauty, rebuffing the past male presupposition that Medusa's punishment was her ugliness.[3] Flack was also aware that, in an art world dominated by men, her work would automatically be judged on its political implications, so she chose an exclusively female pantheon for her sculpture, reworking ancient mythological legends for her modern criterion.[4]

For Flack the myth of Medusa was still unresolved and, more importantly, able to be reclaimed on account of its many twists and turns. Espied and raped by Poseidon in the temple of Athena, Medusa was ironically punished by the jealous and fickle goddess for the transgression that occurred at her altar. Yet, despite changing Medusa's hair into snakes, Athena was unable to destroy her beauty, and Medusa continued to pose a great threat to any man who stared at her long enough to be turned to stone. Still, the curse of Medusa's beauty survived and ultimately led to her demise when Perseus raped the goddess before beheading her. In a final act of repentance, however, Athena saved Medusa's blood and gave it to Poseidon, who congealed it into coral and endowed it with Asclepian powers of healing.

Aspects of the Medusa sculpture—the ongoing tension between materiality and spirituality, the real and the mythical, and, of course, the use of multivalent symbols as vehicles for political, emotive, and personal threads—are anticipated by Flack's career as a painter.[5] Like her canvases, *Flack's Colossal Head of Medusa* is densely packed, replete with endless symbolic iconography from the complicated myth: Her head is adorned in shells—emblems of Medusa's ultimate role as a healer—and flanked by strands of rope that symbolically pull her in opposite directions, for use as both a masculinized virago and as a feminist heroine.[6] Deer horns evoke Medusa's gentility and vulnerability, which led to her repeated victimization.

Ultimately, Flack portrayed Medusa as a sacrificial creature whose value is only now being realized. The snakes that frame her chin serve as a beard-like, androgynous force typical of feminist criticism, and Pegasus emerges from the back of her head as a message of hope for the future. Flack also chose to embellish the snakes, rejecting their Christian connotation as the seducers of Eve and privileging their role as symbols of wisdom in Egyptian and Indian beliefs. Lastly, the decapitated, spherical head seems to serve as a metaphor for the parallel rape of the earth for profit—innocent yet unfairly ravished, vulnerable yet potentially vengeful, as symbolized by the real bullet imbedded in the foreground.[7]

Flack's *Colossal Head of Medusa* stands as a paragon of strength, both feminine and androgynous. It is a stanchion of reinvention and a modern reworking of the semiotic coding of the female body.[8]

[1] Casteras, "Breaking the Mold," 103.
[2] Flack, *Art and Soul*, 26.
[3] Casteras, "Breaking the Mold," 122.
[4] Ibid., 103.
[5] Ibid.
[6] Ibid., 122.
[7] Ibid., 122-125.
[8] Ibid., 126, 129.

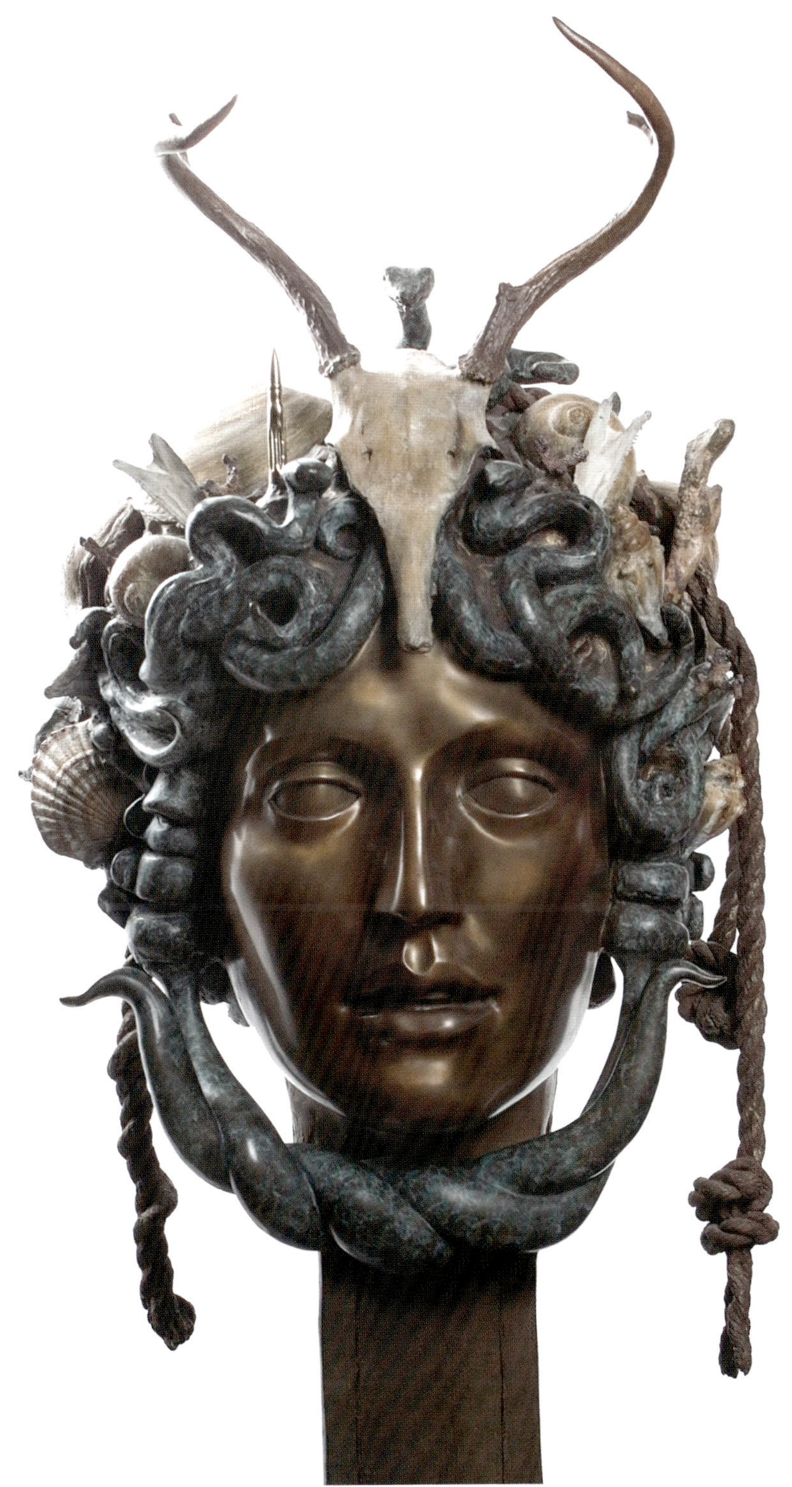

Colossal Head of Medusa 1991
Patinated and gilded bronze, 36″ x 36″ x 18″

Anthony Brunelli 1968-

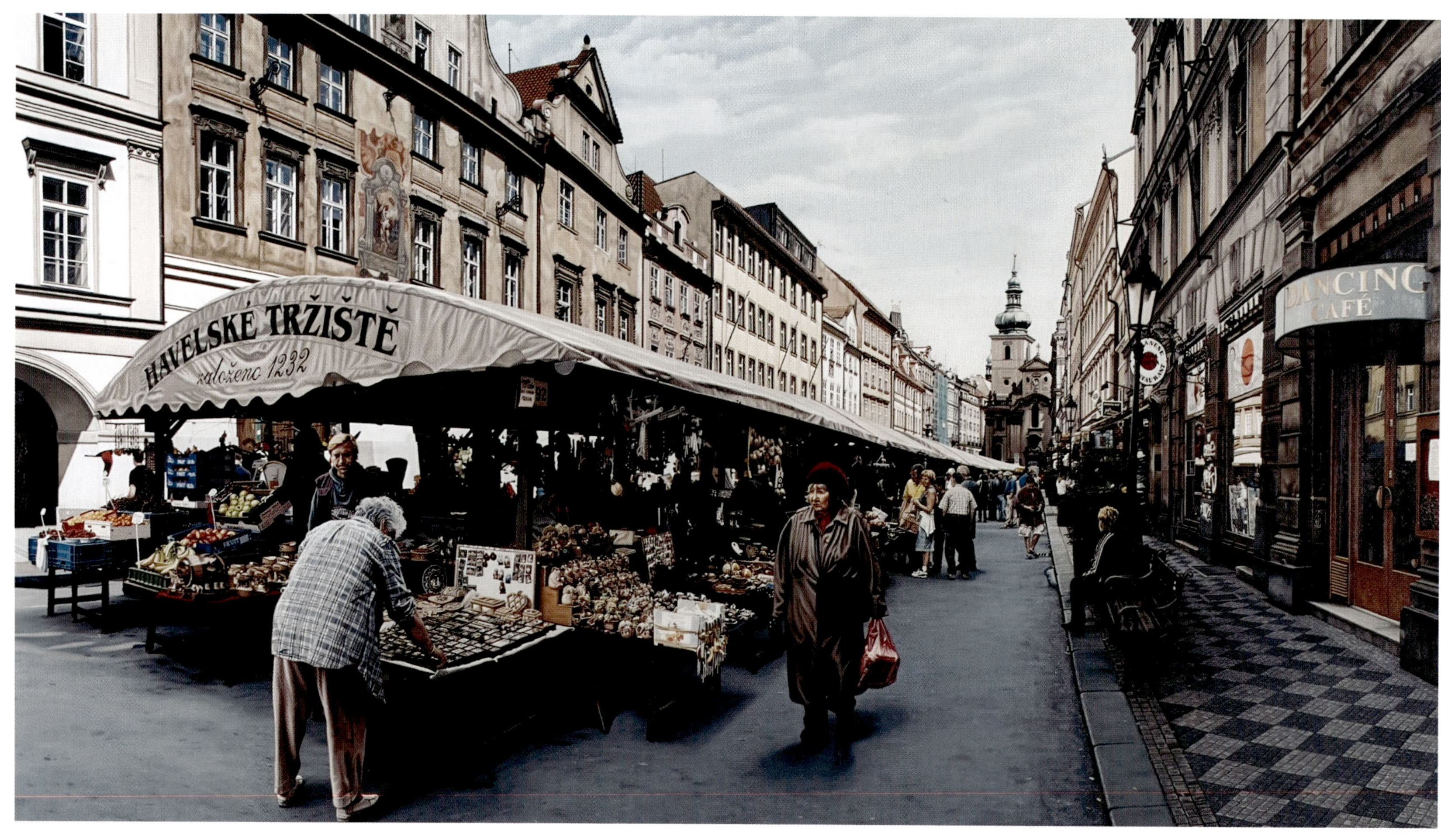

Prague Market 2006
Oil on linen, 36 1/4″ x 65″

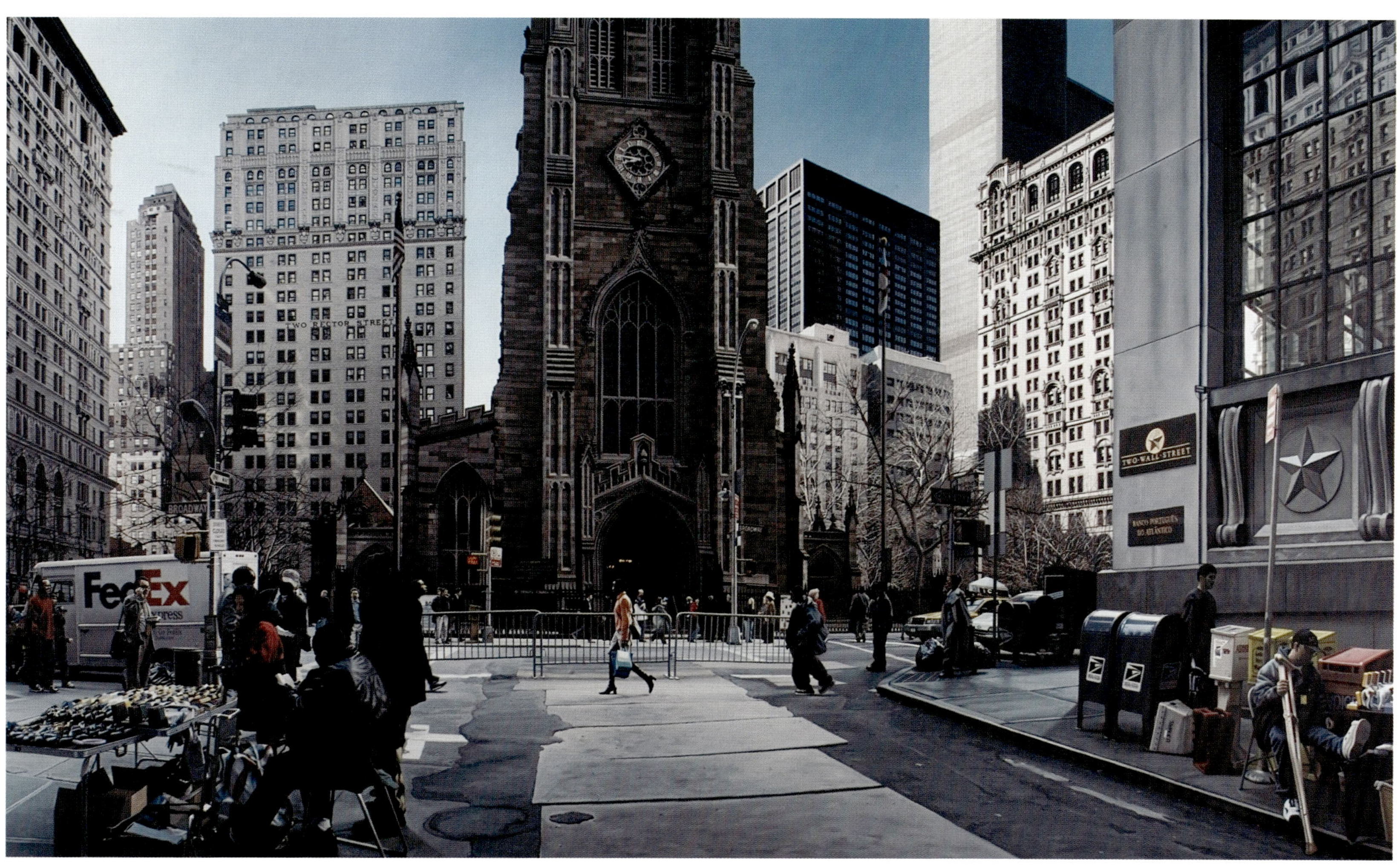

Trinity 2003
Oil on canvas, 50″ x 87″

Marisol (Escobar) 1930-

After witnessing her figurative sculptures alternately praised as witty, sardonic Pop Art and condemned as naïve, folkloric decoration over the course of three decades, Marisol began to produce portraits of other artists as a means of reflecting on the tribulations and demands of her chosen vocation.[1] Taking admired subjects as varied as Georgia O'Keeffe, Louise Nevelson, Pablo Picasso, and Marcel Duchamp, Marisol faced the challenge of taming the eccentric personalities of these illustrious artists into bulky, standardized slabs of wood. For such a task, Marisol developed a stylistic approach in which, as Dominick Lombardi wrote, "Representational punctuates Minimal...in an odd sort of purity" that enabled Marisol to enhance defining characteristics of her predecessors in a unified series without sacrificing their unique identities.[2]

Marisol's most ambitious portraits in this vein are found in her series on the surrealist René Magritte, with whom she identifies closely as a fellow master of absurdist displacement and social critic of the middle class.[3] Crafting Magritte's knowing, stoic countenance, Marisol employs several variations on a single theme: she carves relief into one sculpture, sketches outlines onto a concave surface in another, and combines both techniques to create three-dimensional illusions of the artist's features in other works.[4] In every representation, however, Marisol leaves Magritte's body in the wood's original shape to draw attention to the presentation of his face. In *Magritte VI*, for example, which portrays the artist in a later stage of life, Marisol scarcely separates Magritte from the original block of wood, endowing him with a regal bearing derived from his authoritative, kindly demeanor.[5] Since only his face is given an intricate carving, the viewer is forced to acknowledge the decades of creative struggle that have left the artist's expression permanently careworn—the price he has paid to earn his sagacious air.[6]

Unlike Marisol's portraits of other artists, whom she depicts seated to provide such venerated colleagues with a place of rest, Marisol always depicts Magritte as a perfectly rigid soldier, as if permanently standing on guard to serve his artistic cause despite the physical effects of its struggle. Armed only with one of his iconic props—an umbrella, left open to symbolize the ease with which he incorporated everyday objects into the surrealistic vocabulary—Magritte awaits society's inevitable need for him to once again take flight into the artistic realm of imagination, or at least to inspire his fellow artists to take up the journey in his stead.[c]

[1] Quoted in Raynor, "Marisol Sculpture from Leonardo Painting."
[2] Lombardi, "Master of Contemporary Art," 9, c. 1.
[3] Heartney, "Sculptor of Modern Life," 22.
[4] Lombardi, "Master of Contemporary Art," 9, c. 1.
[5] Heartney, "Sculpture of Modern Life," 18.
[6] Ibid., 15.
[7] Ibid., 22.

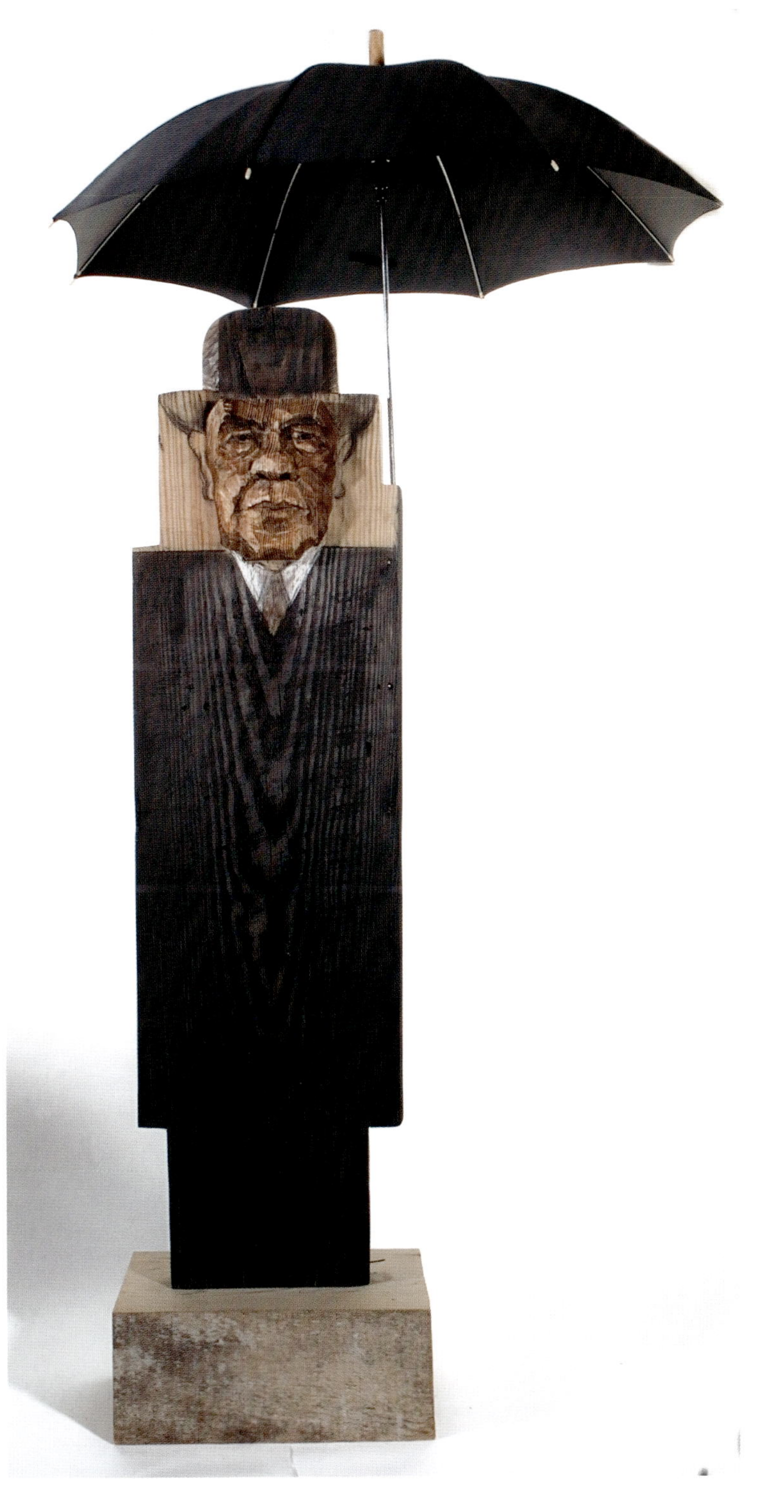

Magritte VI (Pushed Out Face) 1998
Wood and oil, 69″ x 33″ x 33″

Davis Cone 1950-

Rivaled only by John Baeder's obsession with the American diner, Davis Cone's unwavering commitment to vintage and classic movie theaters on Main Street have granted the artist a distinguished place among Photorealists, enabling the exploration of a single subject matter through various angles, different atmospheric conditions, and unique light situations, such as those presented by neon and fluorescent displays.[1] Perhaps because no other aspect of American architecture elicits such a strong feeling of nostalgia, Davis's paintings are evocative of simple hometown pleasures, even as they are overwhelmed from within by the fantasy and glamour of Hollywood.[2] As Cone himself described the aim of works such as *Thompson*, "I hope my paintings reflect [the] love I have for the theaters and that they can reawaken, for an instant, personal memories for the viewer as well. It's only one of the levels I hope the viewer will meet my paintings on, but it is an important one for me—that nonartistic gut reaction."[3]

Artistically, Cone elicits powerful results as well, painting in a manner that is extremely technical yet somehow devoid of any grandiloquence. His style allows the subject matter to speak for itself through a dispassionate rendering that connects with the viewer through its verisimilitude. Cone also chronicles the influence of 1930s deco style, specifically its quirky combination of Hollywood glitter and small-town ambience that juxtaposed marvelously gaudy landmarks with the dowdy streets they so often inhabited.[4] *Thompson* presents just such an example, from its sleek lines and gleaming curves of the decorative band atop the marquee to the rectilinear and geometric details on its crown, all of which were impossibly chic and perfectly art deco.[5] The theater's vertical name sign is also a descendant of the skyscraper boom of the deco period, reinforced by the uppermost antenna spire and the step-back motif, both elements shared by structures such as the Empire State and Chrysler buildings.[6]

Yet set alongside ghostly evidence of another declining small town in Cone's native Georgia—embodied by details such as the dented fender, and the "For Sale" sign in the adjacent vacant storefront—such deco details seem blaringly ironic; even the theater itself is aging, as gaps in the marquee and cracks in the paint begin to show. As a result, the entirety of the scene begins to reveal the naïve desire of theaters to embrace each and every popular design during the height of the movie house boom, even when such a pursuit wasn't necessarily in stride with the rest of the town. Ironically, however, this seems to be the very same naïveté that afforded such towns their quirky, innocent charm and nostalgic appeal in the first place, a paradox that Cone is so adept at capturing in his subtle and startlingly realistic manner.

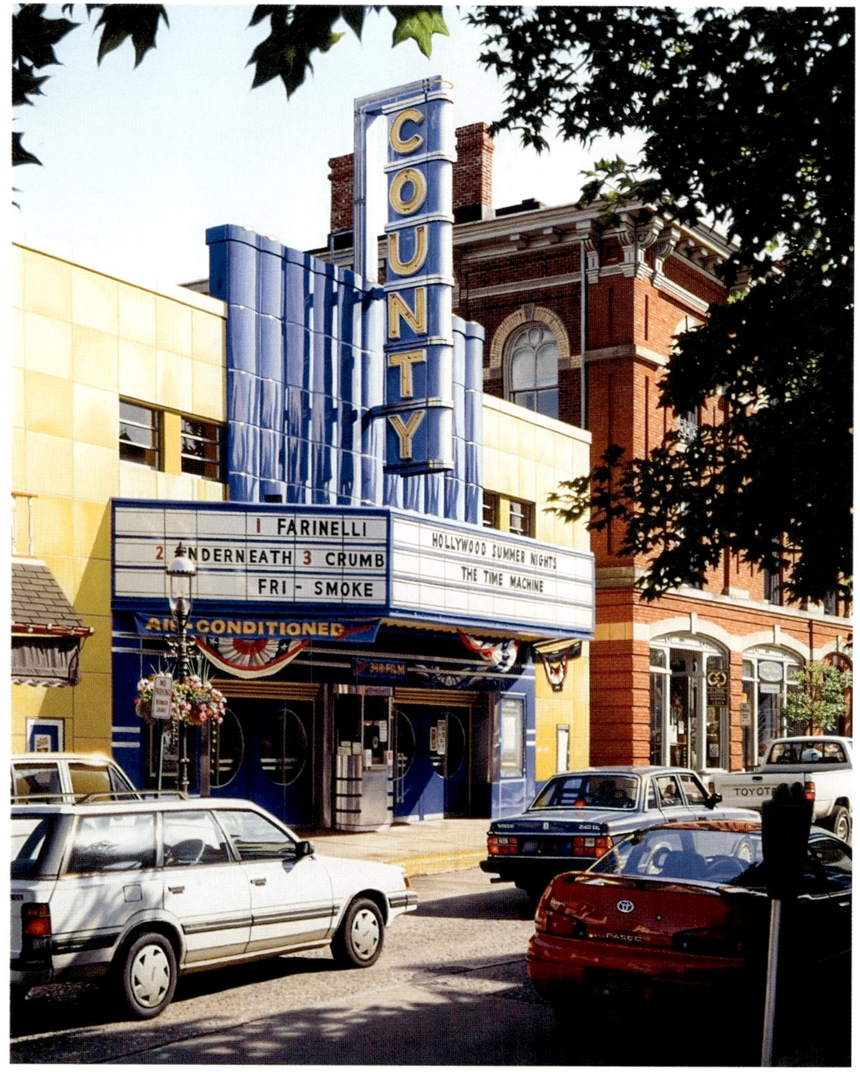

County 1999
Acrylic on canvas, 18 3/4" x 15 1/8"

[1] Meisel, *Photorealism Since 1980*, 123.
[2] Chase, *Hollywood on Main Street*, 11.
[3] Ibid., 17.
[4] Ibid., 12.
[5] Ibid., 53.
[6] Ibid.

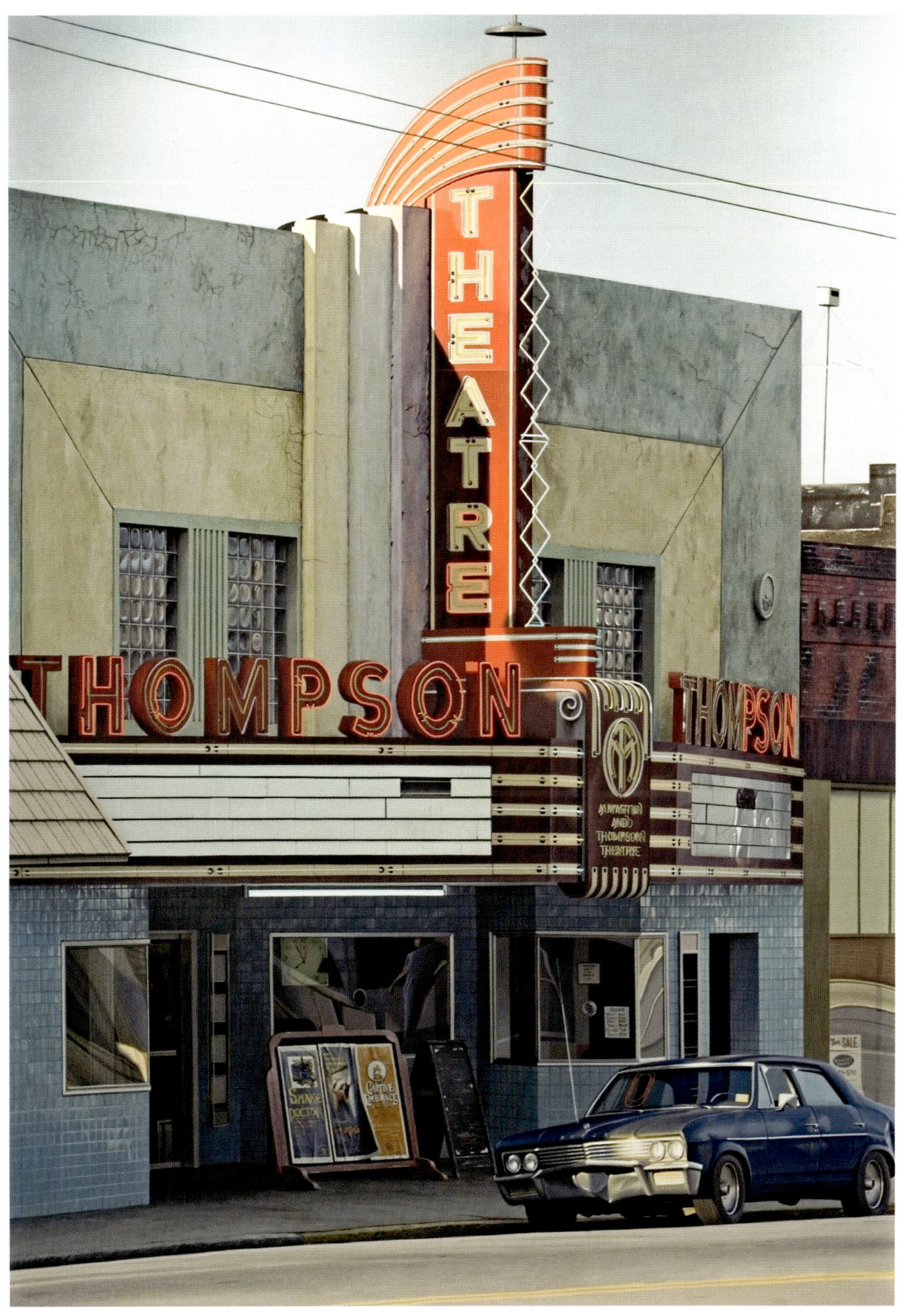

Thompson 1980
Acrylic on canvas, 55″ x 39″

John Baeder 1938-

For more than two decades, John Baeder has been a connoisseur of the American roadside, traveling the country to photograph and document diners and the culture that encompasses them and compiling source material for his hyperrealistic compositions. Baeder's unswerving, compulsive attraction to the diner as an icon of Americana has resulted in nearly three hundred works on the subject, all of which catalog the architectural structures, the evolving moods they embody, and the varied environments they inhabit.

Though most of Baeder's diners are situated in suburban locales, some, like *Empire Diner*, occupy an urban environment and therefore seem to represent a fast-disappearing element of vernacular simplicity within the metropolitan fabric.[1] Baeder himself described the Empire Diner as "out of place" on the lower west side of Manhattan—that is, until it "changes garb [at night], and turns into a nocturnal melody for Gotham's chic."[2] As he explained further, the Empire Diner is "just what you'd expect when a bright group of restaurateurs gets hold of a diner and capitalizes on the past."[3] It is a token of the neodiner concept in which an early 1940s Fodero diner that catered to truckers is revamped for an upscale crowd—its clientele drawn in by overdramatic elements such as the projected Eat sign and the miniature sculpture of its namesake made digestible and souvenir-sized.[4] Seizing on the recent fad of retro styling, the Empire Diner stands as an emblem of the successful translation of image into profit.

However cynical Baeder's description may seem, he fully intended for his work to celebrate the Empire Diner for the creativity involved in reworking past images and styles for a modern audience. In many ways, Baeder saw this process as parallel to his own and even included a concise homage to the influence of John Sloan and other Ashcan school artists in the "dusky shapes beside the Empire Diner."[5] In this way, just as each diner derived its persona as much from its environment as from the personality of those who ran and owned it, so too was Baeder's work a fusion of the quirky structures themselves and his own ability to rework historical techniques and styles in order to pursue an entirely new genre.

[1] Bonito, *Get Real*, 12.
[2] Baeder, *Diners, Revised and Updated*, 94.
[3] Ibid., 94.
[4] Ibid.
[5] Scully, Preface to Baeder, *Diners, Revised and Updated*, 6.

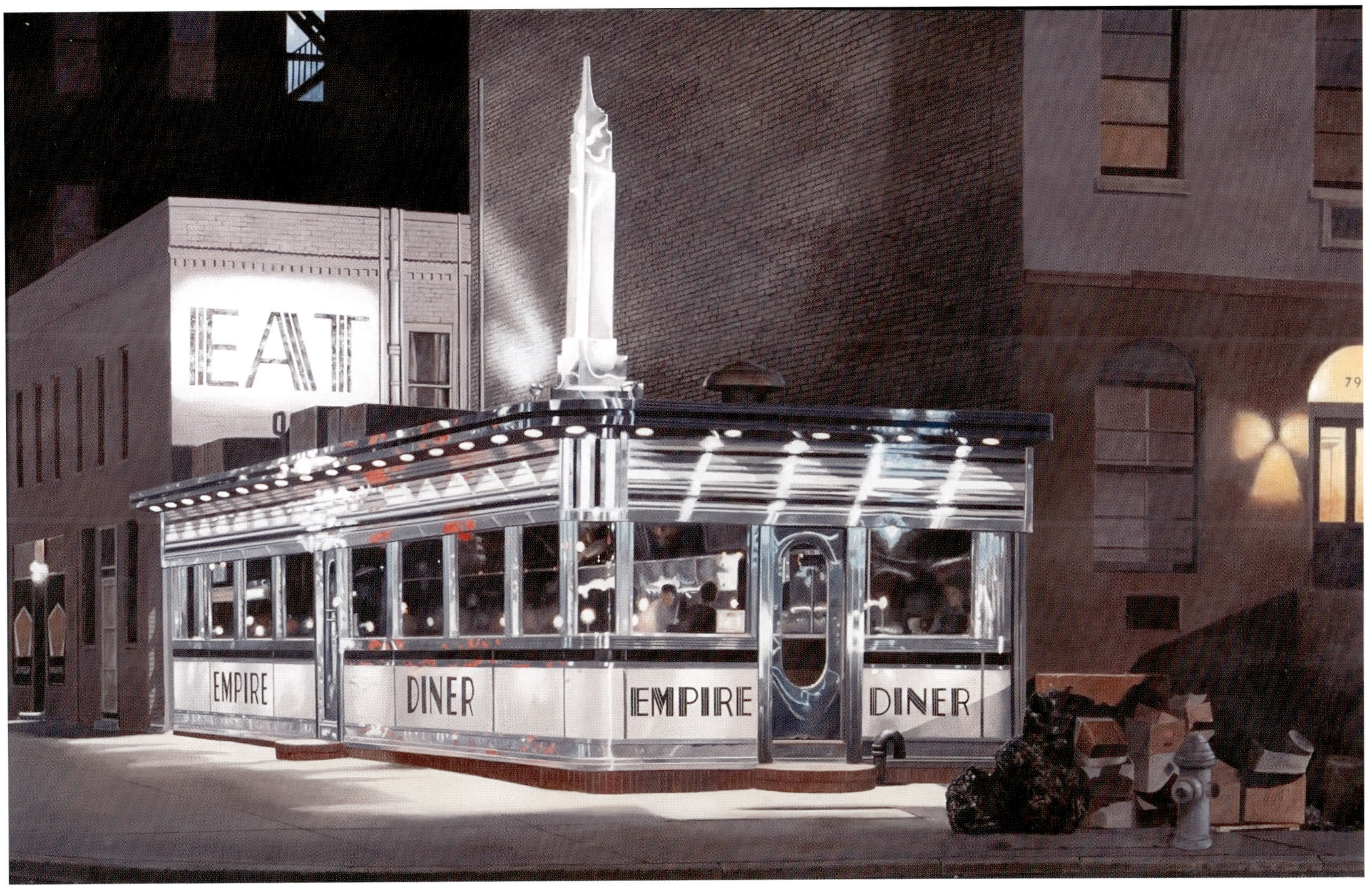

Empire Diner 1999
Oil on canvas, 30 3/4″ x 48″

Amy Cutler 1935-

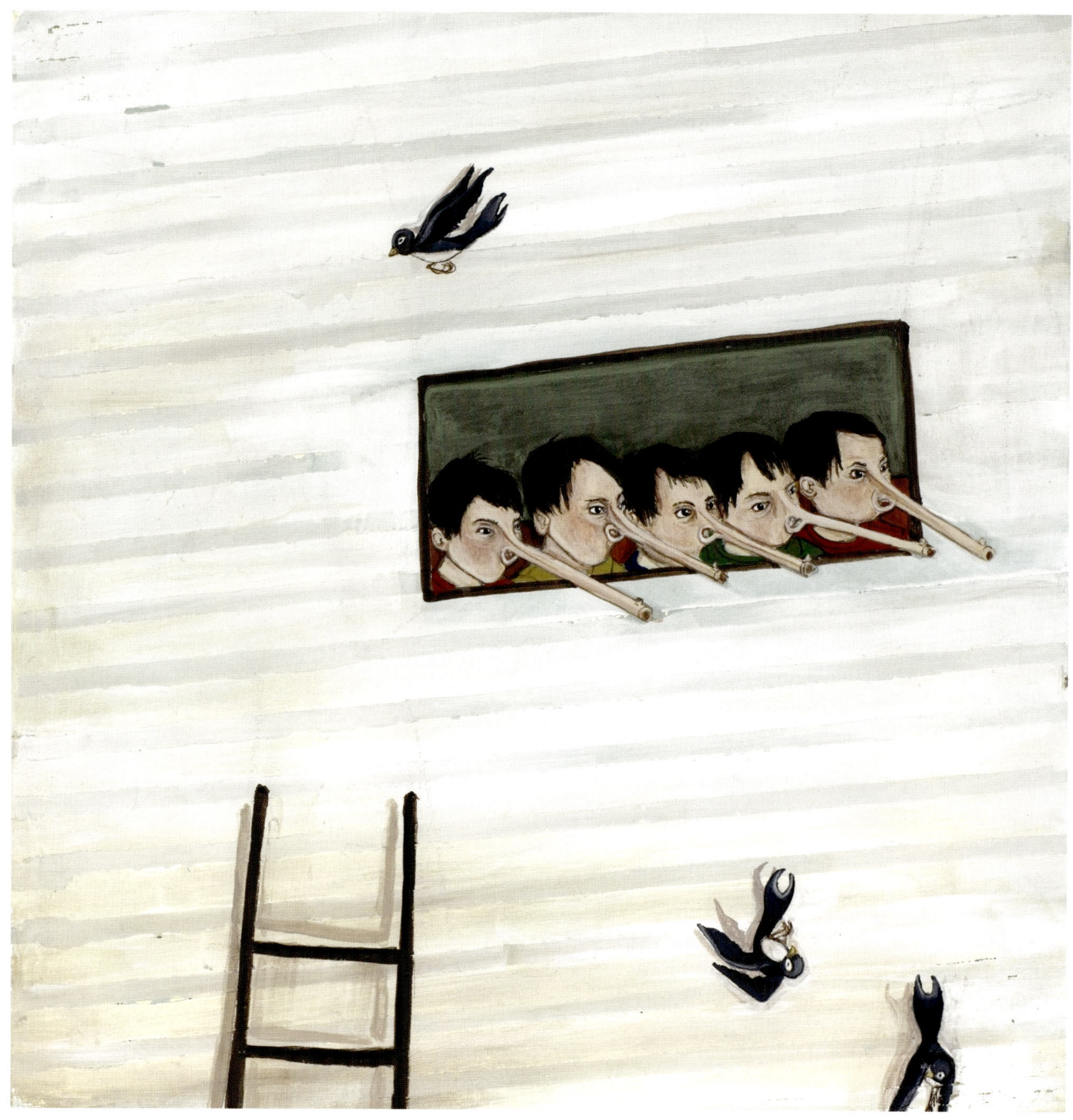

Bird Watchers 2002
Casein, Flashe on Wood, 7 1/2″ x 7 1/2″

Sara Lucas 1962

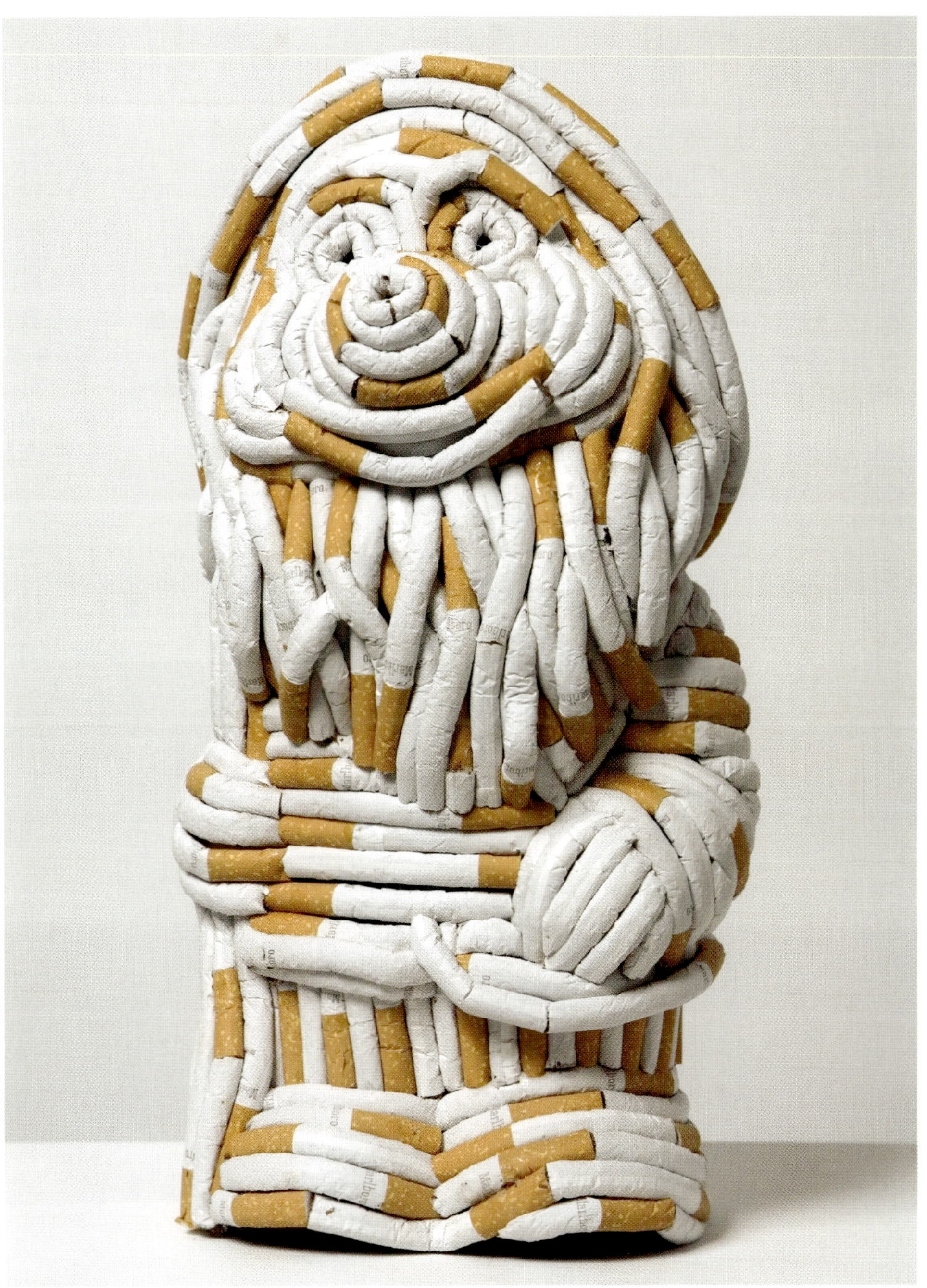

Gnorman 2006
Plastic cast gnome and cigarettes, 11 3/8″ x 7 7/8″ x 7 1/2″

Will Cotton 1965-

Deeply rooted in the visual vocabulary of advertising, Will Cotton's paintings develop an exaggerated form of consumer desire. In *Ice Cream Cavern*, Cotton exploited the power of this desire, offering both his nude model and a cavern of sweets for the same purpose: to tantalize.[1] Even the Mary Boone Gallery's description of the work as a "landscape of drippy vanilla ice cream and sticky syrup" reads more like a menu caption intended to whet the appetite than a typical press release.[2]

Using a satirically realistic style, Cotton's setting remains pure fantasy—a scene of empty calories and endless pleasure.[3] As Edward Leffingwell of *Art in America* wrote, Cotton's paintings are developed within the "consumerist romance; their themes are immediate gratification, availability, abundance."[4] Yet as much as Cotton prepared his audience to envelop themselves in their desire, he was also careful not to give away his nude too easily, cloaking her precisely in the gluey ice cream and perpetrating the game of longing by turning her away from our voyeuristic gaze.

The painting's "sticky materialism" relentlessly parodies the convergence of gluttony and heterosexual male fantasy as a distinctly tangible yet impossible reality—one that is inescapably attractive nonetheless. His use of explicitly lush palettes, heavenly and intense light, and airy texturing permits the work to appear as though on the verge of disappearing, casting Cotton's entire universe as an essentially fleeting and perfect fantasy.[5] In the chocolate mountains of *Devil's Fudge Falls* and the strawberry pools of *Old Faithful*, Cotton did little to extract his viewer from the reverie his paintings induce.

At the same time, such an overt, embellished fantasy also holds within it the capacity to force the viewer to confront rather than delight in his desire, as it threatens to melt at any moment. In this way, Cotton's *Ice Cream Cavern* questions our tendency to designate the female body as an item for consumption and suggests that our need to repeatedly indulge in such fantasies might also expose their illusion. As Roberta Smith of the *New York Times* lightheartedly noted, "Like simple carbohydrates, they don't supply much nutrition."[6] Eventually, Cotton's overindulgence suggests, we will have to turn to more substantial sources.

[1] Hindry, "Will Cotton's Giant Confections," 12.
[2] Mary Boone Gallery, *Ice Cream Cavern.*
[3] McQuid, "Adding a Stroke," C18.
[4] Leffingwell, "Will Cotton at Mary Boone," 158.
[5] Valdez, *Curve: The Female Nude*, 59.
[6] Leffingwell, "Will Cotton at Mary Boone," 158.

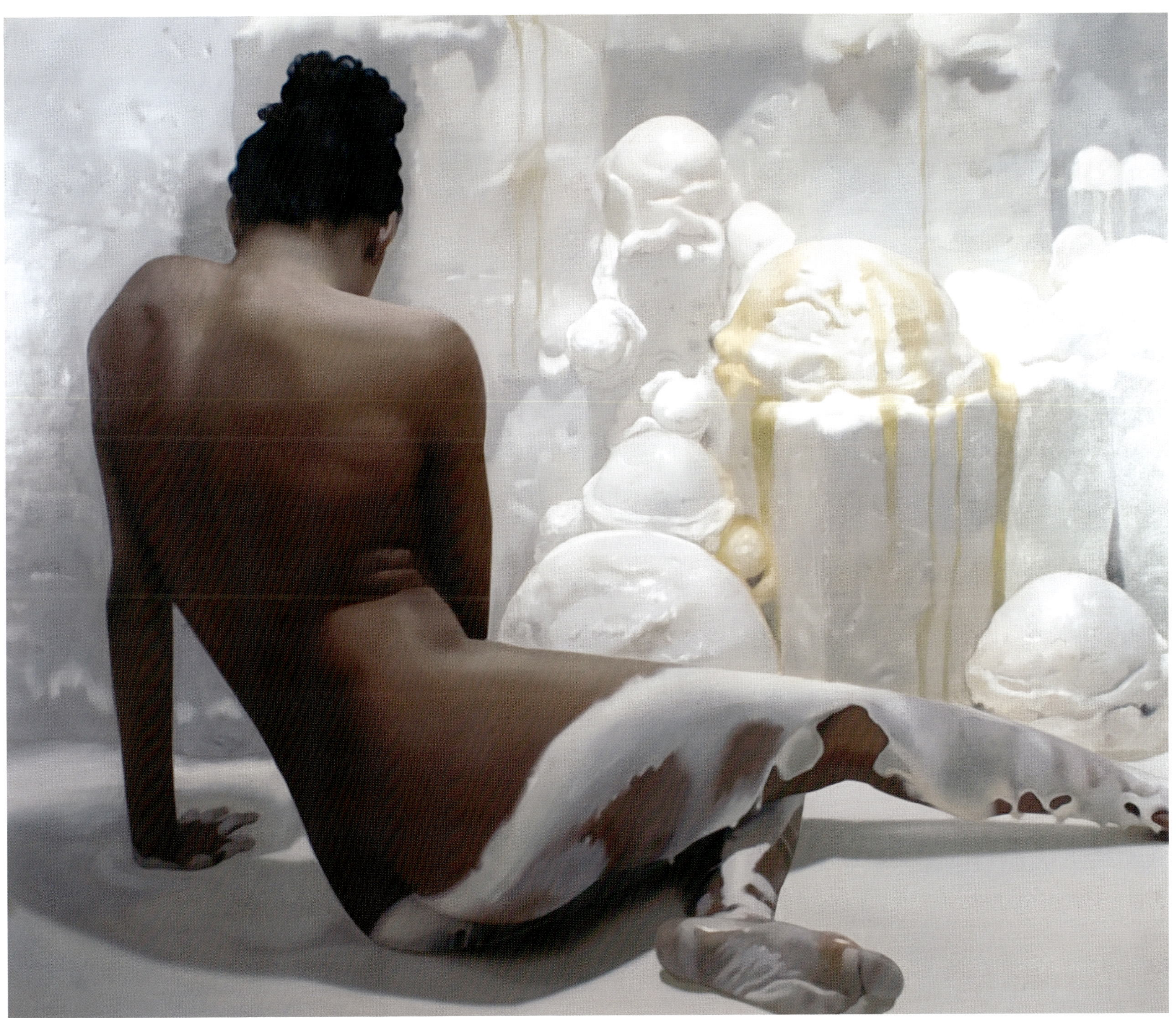

Ice Cream Cavern 2003
Oil on linen, 70″ x 80″

Alex Katz 1927-

For Alex Katz, a painting's success is not achieved through "what it means but how it appears."[1] Consequently, he seeks the minimal level of detail that will permit his work to function as a realistic illusion without supplying a single superfluous stroke toward the establishment of narrative themes. Logically devoid of sentimentality and free from the burden to operate on philosophical, psychological, or social grounds, his oeuvre stands as an iconoclastic disputation of the notion that traditionally styled work must address humanistic expectations simply because it avoids the telos of Abstract Expressionism.[2]

The nucleus of Katz's legacy, therefore, will not be formed by his programmatic themes but by his multifaceted use of color to supply everything from the optical perception of light to the suggestion of varying depths and the definition of a picture plane.[3] As Katz explained, "I can't think of anything more exciting than the surface of things. Just appearance."[4] As such, a work like *Amanda* applies a frontal pressure that exerts itself on the plain surface, foregrounding the girl's face through its massive, dominating scale and sharply defined separation from the red background. In order for the color to be felt fully, all elements alien to its presence were removed: impasto brushwork, realistic shadowing, and the gradation of hues affected by the light source. As a result, the commissioned work, which was later sold when the subject fell on hard times, is immediate and aggressive, uncontaminated by any painterly facture and functioning entirely within its high color key.[5]

By the late 1960s, Katz began to work more from drawings and sketches than from photographs. The transition actually pushed Katz toward Perceptual Realism as he abandoned the nostalgia and personal narrative he associated with photography. Amanda was finalized after a number of such sketched studies (see figure 1), all of which seem to strive toward an openness of surface and already appear free from any trace of the literary that Katz so feared.

Throughout his career, Katz was conscious of the contradiction inherent to portraiture, especially as a modernist, figurative work. Aware that his paintings existed as both a representation of a real three-dimensional person and as an actual two-dimensional plane, Katz chose to confront the issue head-on, challenging the limits of the genre by rendering his figure as flatly as possible. In fact, "the more closely Katz depicted reality, the more conscious of the picture plane he became," resulting in a style that was as conceptual as it was perceptual, greatly influenced by the original tenets of abstraction.[6]

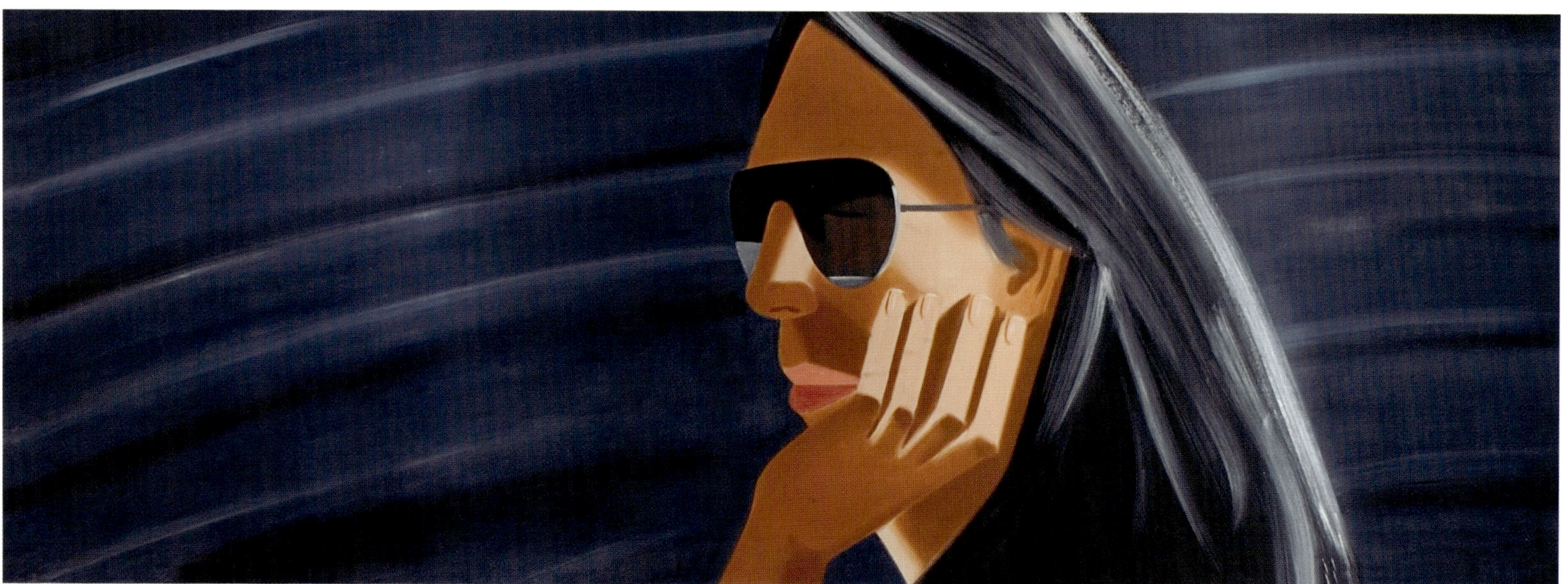

Dark Glasses 1989
Oil on canvas, 40" x 112"

[1] Vincent Katz, "Plunk 'Em Down", 59; quoted in Sandler, *Alex Katz: A Retrospective*, 17.
[2] Sandler, *Alex Katz: A Retrospective*, 21-24.
[3] Ibid., 20.
[4] Katz, "On Art and Artists," 9.
[5] Sandler, *Alex Katz: A Retrospective*, 19,12.
[6] Ibid., 11.

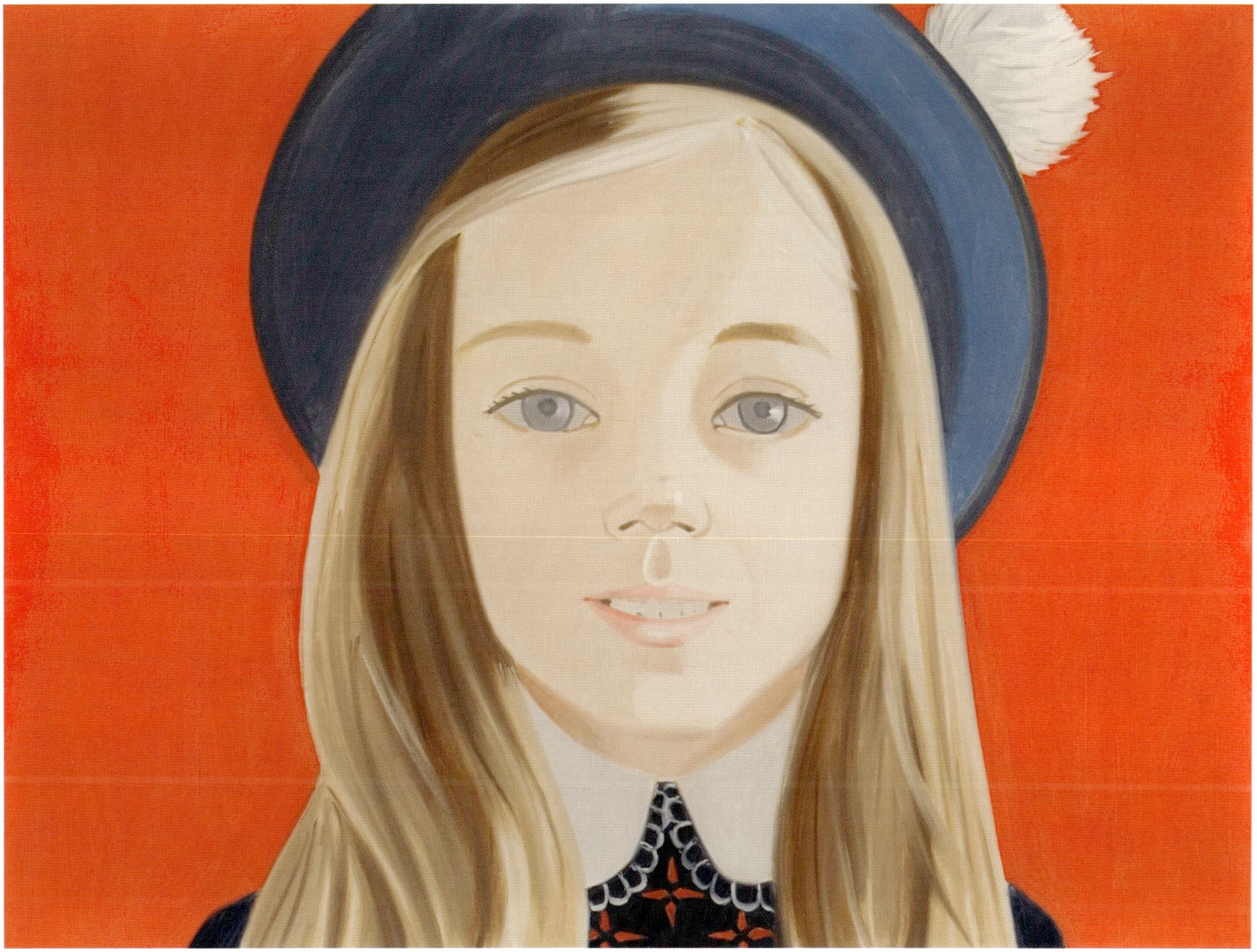

Amanda 1973
Oil on canvas, 34″ x 48″

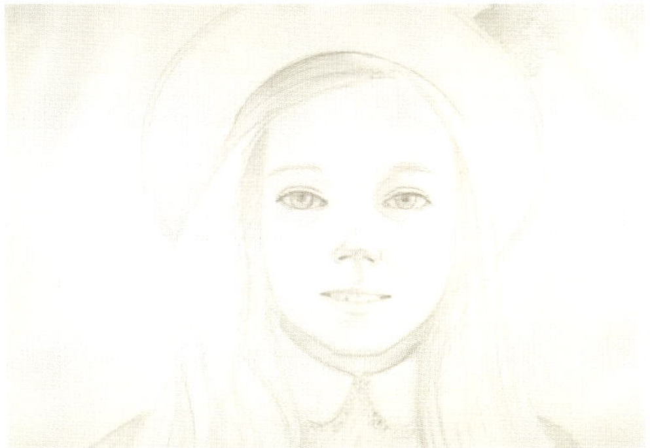

Figure 1

Alexis Rockman 1962-

As a child, Alexis Rockman was raised around dinosaur skeletons, taxidermy armadillos, and anthropological dioramas from across the globe. His mother, archaeologist Diana Wall, assisted Margaret Mead at the American Museum of Natural History in Manhattan and exposed Rockman to a veritable playground of science, technology, and history at an early age.[1] Imbued with the imagination of childhood, the museum helped foster Rockman's unique fusion of science-fiction and science-fact, a hybrid intellectual–pop culture style that lent itself just as readily to Discovery Channel projects as to illustrated storybooks for the Bronx Zoo.[2]

But as Rockman came of age into a world of mass pollution, biological warfare, and global warming, he began to stray from the optimistic, Frederic Church-inspired landscapes of the museum toward a darker, "H. G. Wellsian sensibility that the world of living things, despite its superficial charms, has become a dangerous place."[3] Rockman has since made a career codifying this ideology in such lurid caveats as the Brooklyn Museum of Art's large-scale mural, *Manifest Destiny*, which projects iconic Brooklyn three thousand years in the future, flooded beneath eighty-five feet of water and overrun with mutant ocean life and toxic waste due to its citizens' brazen misuse of natural resources. But his concern for mankind's destruction of its habitat is not limited to urban epicenters: natural settings in Guyana, Tanzania, and the Amazon, which the artist visited for research, are all equally positioned to perish. "As a result of environmental hazards, animal extinction and genetic engineering," Elizabeth Hayt wrote, "nature is no longer seen as a paradise that forever regenerates itself. The current perception of nature is anti-Arcadian: all that appears to be alluring conceals something appalling."[4]

In *Disneyworld II*, Rockman set about destroying yet another American icon, metonymically attacking the commercialism and unsustainable tourism that he sees eroding the planet. There is also an element of violence, symbolized by the ruined, atomic warhead-shaped ride from 20,000 Leagues under the Sea, which now rests in the residual sludge. "Rockman's art has long wallowed in [this] exquisite primal ooze," Roberta Smith wrote. "His grim grotesqueries of mutant animals, dank swamps and pearlescent sunsets depict a world that is both pre-human and post-apocalyptic in a style that might be called Technicolor Bosch."[5]

Yet for all of Rockman's prophetic negativism, Holland Cotter argued, "His approach is basically that of 19th-century American artists like Thomas Cole, moralizing history painters who presented reality not as it was, but as it might be. Cole's *Course of Empire*, a depiction of a civilization destroyed through a failure of self-vigilance, was a political warning aimed at the America of his day. The same could be said of Mr. Rockman's painting."[6] Rockman himself seems to agree: "I've been very deliberate about using the Hudson River school language...The Industrial Revolution and the Hudson River school were really tied in to the idea of using natural resources. Global warming, unimaginable in the 19th century, is obviously its dark side."[7] In works like *Manifest Destiny* and *Disneyworld II*, Rockman utilizes the language of the Hudson River school to its maximum effect, giving his viewers realistically rendered hypotheses for the globe's next set of "unimaginable" outcomes.

[1] Yablonsky, "New York's Watery Grave," 28.
[2] Hammond, "Rockman at Gorney + Lee," 134.
[3] Hayt, "Nature Painting," 37.
[4] Ibid.
[5] Smith, "Realism with a Vengeance," 18.
[6] Cotter, "Brooklyn-ness, 36.
[7] Quoted in Yablonsky, "New York's Watery Grave," 28.

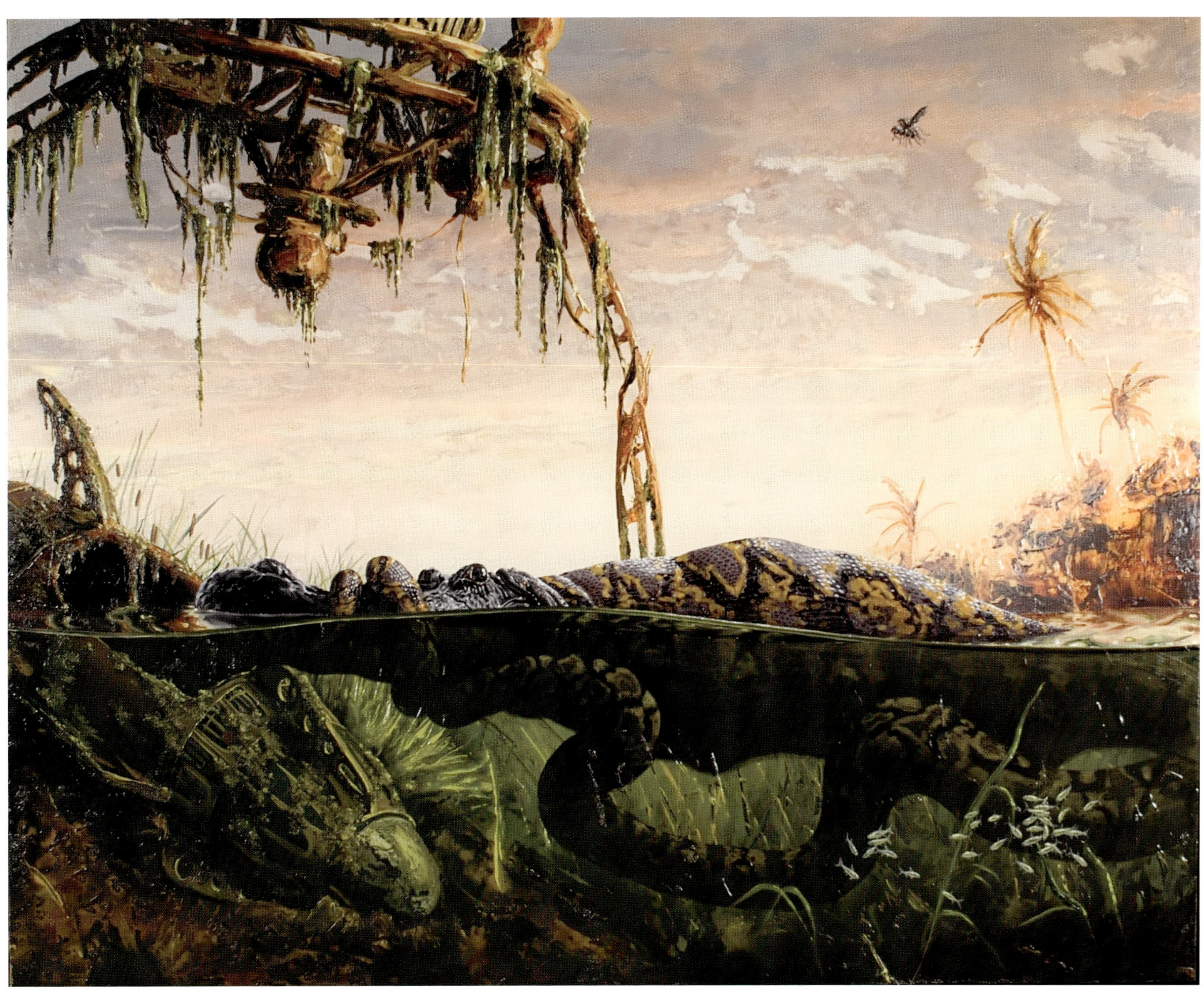

Disneyworld II 2005
Oil on wood, 44″ x 56″

Amie Dicke 1978-

In 2000, Amie Dicke participated in her first major public exhibition, an Amsterdam group show entitled "It is strange to be so many women."[1] In retrospect, the project's billing seems to accurately foreshadow the next five years of Dicke's career, which the artist would devote almost exclusively to new means of relating to the multifarious images of beautiful women in the world of fashion and entertainment.

With only scalpel and black pen, Dicke began crafting full-page beauty magazine advertisements into delicate spider webs of ink and poster, positive and negative space, meaning and deliberate absence. The filiform remains—which, given their ornamental feminine grace, have elicited praise as the modernization of Botticelli—are often excessively thin and fragile, and the effect is an impermanence that bespeaks both the universality of delicate beauty and the transience of fashionable beauty trends.[2]

Moreover, Dicke's work seems to serve as an intervention against the icons of beauty- magazine culture, be it Yves Saint Laurent or Polo Ralph Lauren. While some of her art achieves this through its titles, such as the provocatively named *Gisele Wants Out*, Dicke more commonly suggests the emptiness of her subject through the dark, sad cavities of her work, which the German critic Wieteke van Zeil called "lace prison[s] full of voids."[3] In a world in which the faces most familiar to us are often those of celebrities and not of friends and family, Dicke attempts to counteract this alarming tendency by reducing the aura of models and actresses to "dark phantom traces of their photo shoot selves."[4]

Once much of the fashion filler has been removed, Dicke then inks over accessories and design details, erasing the compositional elements to buttress the underlying suggestion of fragility and, to a greater extent, to ask why we place such value in something so temporary.[5] Dicke's models regularly appear to be crying over their decaying, vacant states, which, given the structural continuity of their tears and bodies, also threatens the very fabric of their existences. It is a violent process, reflected in the blood-red lips, severed mouths, and intricate veins that constitute her women, as well as in the artistic plastic surgery involved in cutting, slicing, and incising her women. But in a way, through this same process, Dicke has actually endowed her models with a certain depth and permanence they lacked while serving in the glossy pages of weekly fashion magazines.[6]

[1] *It is strange to be so many women*, Ellen de Brujne projects & Diana Stigter Inc., Amsterdam, 2000.
[2] van Zeil, "The Promise of Beauty," 68-69.
[3] Ibid., 67.
[4] Sholis, "Traces of Beauty," 197.
[5] Ibid., 198.
[6] Ibid.

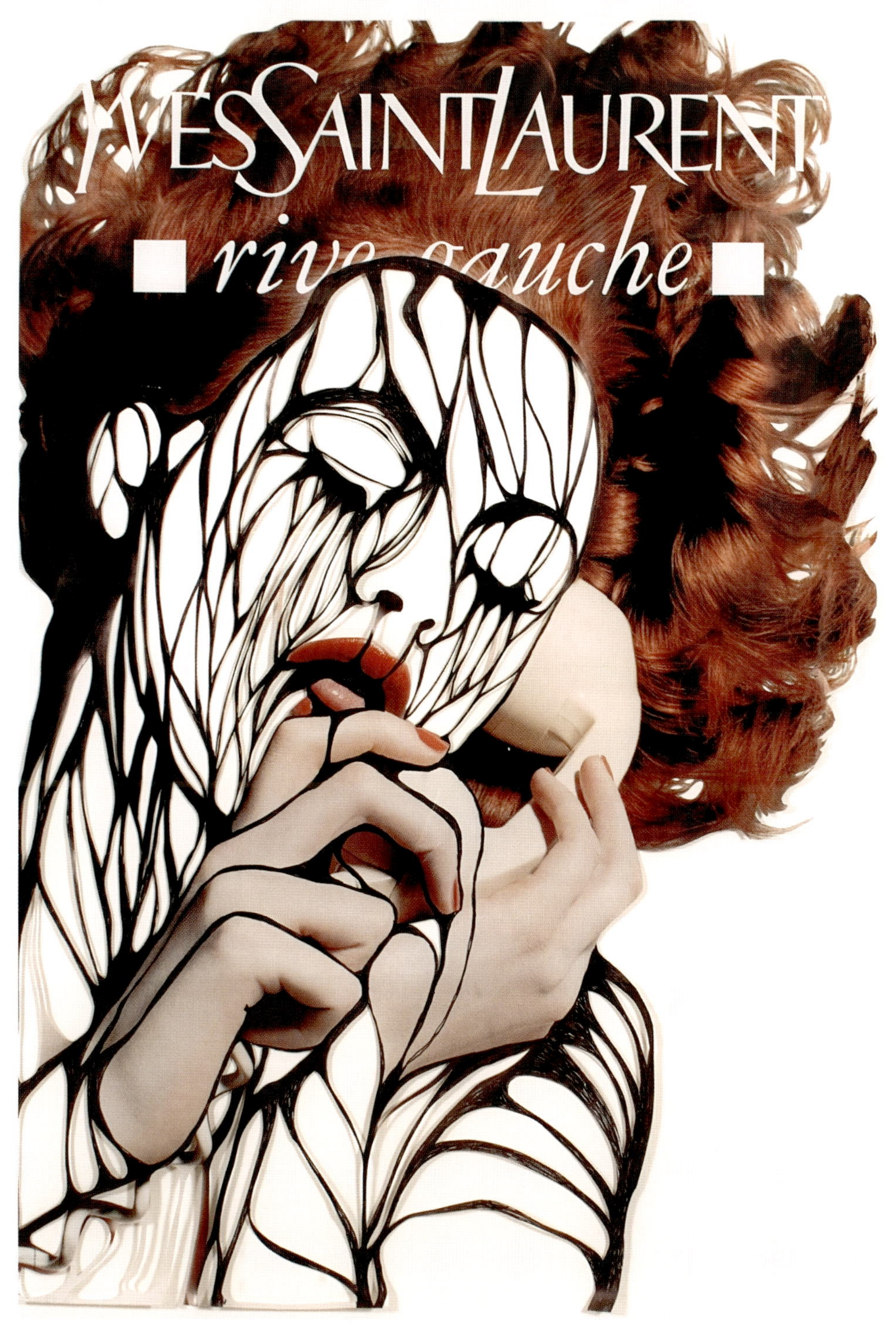

I Suck My Tongue in Remembrance of You 2004
Cutout, ink on poster paper, 69″ x 47″

Don Eddy 1944-

In many ways, Don Eddy's work seems to epitomize the principles of Photorealism: his airbrushed paintings faithfully reproduce even the most technically complicated and multi-layered scenes, as if completed to prove that he was able to capture anything with a brush just as well as he could with a camera. Nevertheless, it is an artistic genre Eddy detests being pinned to, seeing the themes of such art as both limiting and inferior to his own.

Accordingly, *Silver Shoes* does its part to distance Eddy thematically from other Photorealists, even while its style excels by the rules of the genre. Employing a preoccupation particular to the artist, *Silver Shoes* is dominated by the use of a storefront window, which serves as a vehicle for studying the visual effects of transparency and reflection. The technique created many formal and compositional challenges, which Eddy resolved by simultaneously capturing all three planes—the store window, its contents, and the world it reflects—rather than blurring any one level as a camera would. The result, however, also allowed Eddy to manipulate the relationships of objects on different pictorial planes in order to derive more moralistic elements. For example, Eddy's shoes tempt and mingle with pedestrians and traffic; patches of cityscape are reduced to temporary, translucent decals on a silver shoe; and appearance-altering high heels seem ready to assume their role in the outside world with which they already visually intermixed.[1]

It is in this jumbled matrix that Eddy planted his thematic message, introducing the complicated relationship many Americans have with their material culture. By overwhelming the eye and failing to provide any single focus point, Eddy thrusts his viewer into a state of visual chaos equivalent to the spiritual meaninglessness associated with an overemphasis on commercial goods.[2] The glittery, dazzling spectacle mocks its depicted commodities by showing them in all their opulence, only to turn around and segment them behind connotations of imprisonment and fragile transparency. In the end, Eddy hopes that his literal reflection might breed inner reflection on the part of his audience, but he is eternally cautious in his approach, knowing all too well that the airbrush he employs himself is used far more commonly for causes rather antithetical to his own.

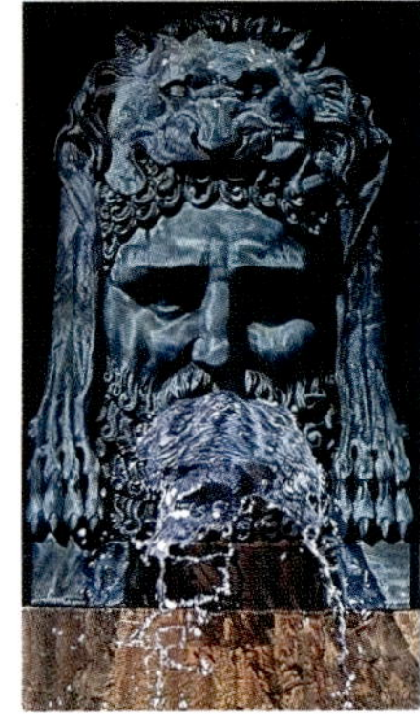

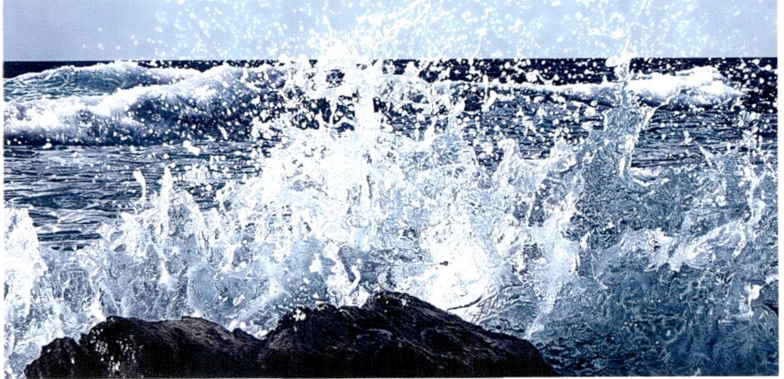

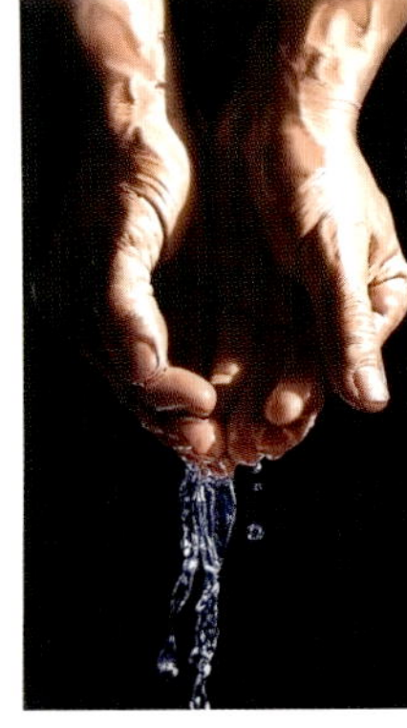

Aqueous Lumina 1993
Acrylic on canvas (in three panels), 74" x 50"

[1]Bonito, *Get Real*, 34.
[2]Kuspit, "Spiritual Realism," 25.

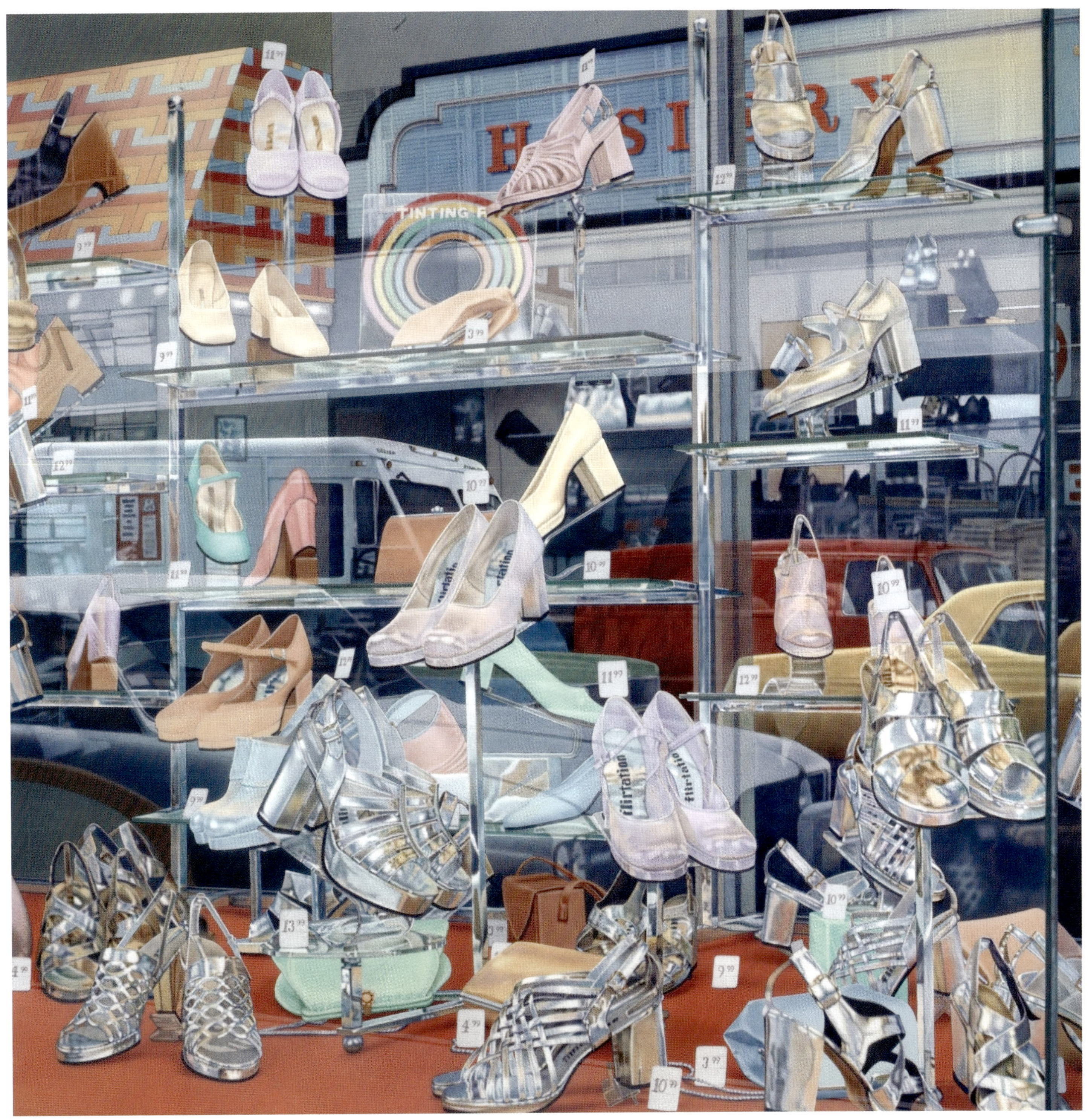

Silver Shoes 1972
Acrylic on canvas, 40 3/8″ x 40 1/2″

John DeAndrea 1941-

To label John DeAndrea a verist sculptor is often more a dismissal of his work than a productive categorization, as critics have continuously reacted unsympathetically to the overt hyperrealism of his life-sized sculptures. Made directly from casts of models and painted as naturalistically as possible, DeAndrea, like his contemporary Duane Hanson, has even been known to accessorize his figures with real hair, shoes, jewelry, and clothing, leaving critics to doubt the creative input of his work.

Ironically, his figures seem designed specifically to remain blasé in the face of such criticism. Often aloof in self-absorbed reflection, his figures distance themselves from their surroundings as well as their onlookers, rendering anything that might be uttered in their direction wholly moot, be it laudatory or admonishing.

As Dennis Adrian noted early in DeAndrea's career, however, this emotional removal of his figures serves another purpose as well, since it "allows us to satisfy our voyeuristic nosiness without feeling that we are being rude or giving affront to the 'subject,' much as one comfortably rubber necks at different types on the bus or as long as the object of scrutiny is unaware of being gazed at."[1] By positioning his figures as lost in reverie or dark reflection, DeAndrea simultaneously invites his viewers to speculate at the cause of their concerns and promises that any such speculation will not be noticed.

Tara certainly exudes both sides of this characteristic, though she also serves as a departure from many of DeAndrea's other pervasive themes. Unlike his typical sculptures, she is neither a nude nor fully life-sized. As a petite, youthful, and attractive figure, *Tara* would easily have qualified for his customary handling, but her raison d'être seems more akin to the logic of Degas' famous *Little Fourteen-Year-Old Dancer*[2] than some of his more risqué dancers. While *Tara* carries the same erotic potential as most of DeAndrea's other figures, her downsized proportions and her allusion to Degas make her more easily identifiable with high art than with a wax figure or an artist-made mannequin. Similarly, her role as a dancer breaks the stiff sense of inactivity that dominates most of his work.

Nevertheless, it is this same potential for activity—especially toward an activity so closely linked with aesthetic beauty and human grace—that locates *Tara* as a Galatean threat to break from her bronze mold, once and for all joining her modern Pygmalion as a man-made creation that easily rivals its natural counterpart.[3]

[1] Adrian, *Real and Ideal*, 1-16.
[2] Degas, *Petite Danseuse de Quatorze Ans, Statuette en Cire* (The Little Fourteen-Year-Old Dancer) c. 1881.
[3] Harrison, "Rodin and His Descendants," 32.

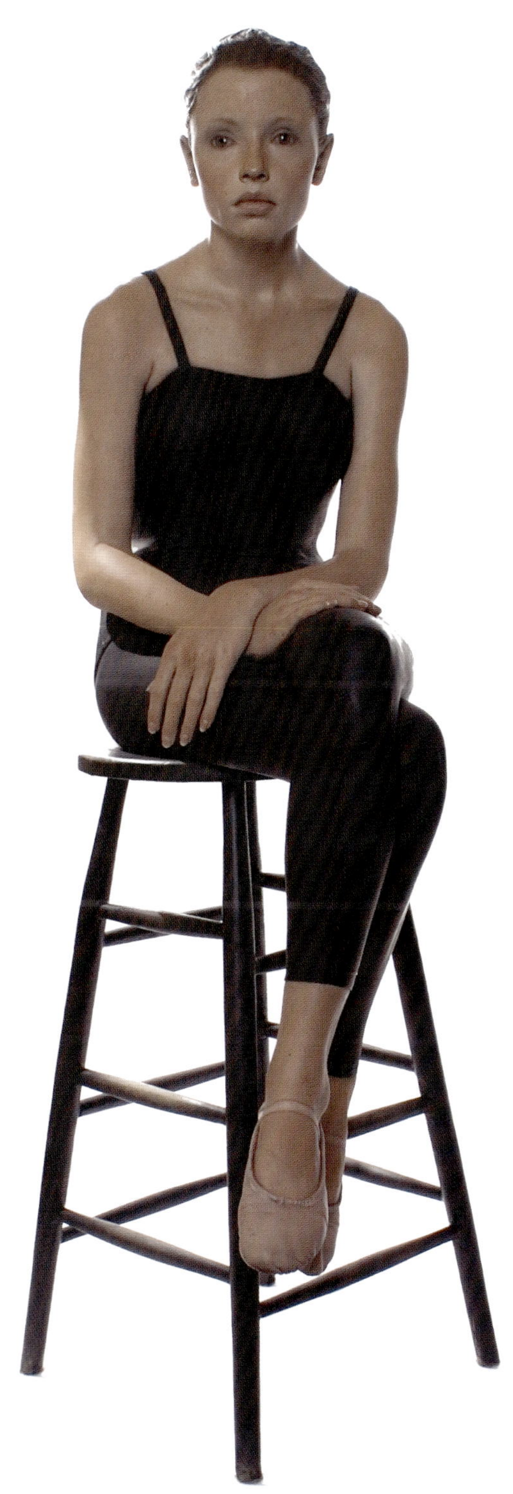

Tara 2002
Polychromed bronze, 54 1/2″ x 13 1/2″ x 28″

Stephan Balkenhol 1957-

If bronze or stone elevates its subject, then surely wood domesticates it.[1] Stephan Balkenhol's figure sculptures foster this association in every way, thriving as serial Mr. Everyman that neither possess any sense of personal identity nor wither from its void. They were created simply to exist, totems of normality that solidify as sculpture long before they become real people. As Balkenhol once said, "I want everything at once: sensuality, expression but not too much, vivacity but no superficial verbiage, instantaneity but no anecdote, wit but no bad jokes, self-irony but no cynicism. And above all, a beautiful silent figure, moved, meaningful and meaningless."[2] As such, Balkenhol provides himself a tightrope of success that offers very little room for deviation toward either the concrete or the abstract, and so his figures must float between their two natural tendencies.

Works such as *Three Men on a Sculpted Pedestal* counteract their lack of narrative quilting through an exaggerated structural stability: its figures are arranged triangularly and firmly grounded to their pedestal, weighed down by the original bulk of the wood and never fully released.[3] They also seem to ground themselves by referring back to their creator and to the furious, rough artistic process of which they still bear marks.

Clearly, Balkenhol did not seek to hide his method or his materials; instead, he allowed the wood to become a symbolic gesture of the naturalism inherent in his work. He left the original wood as the color of his figures' skin and even permitted the wood's irregularities and knots to serve as normal blemishes and imperfections.[4] As such, his work echoes the eternal struggle between nature and human intervention, a fight that seems at once violent and perfectly reconciled in the silent, stable figures.

Like many of his other works, Balkenhol's *Three Men on a Sculpted Pedestal* flirts with the "pitfalls and potentials" of narrative, hinting at the reiteration of type inherent to society and the paradoxical isolation that invariably accompanies it.[5] He inhibited any relationship from developing immediately between his figures but allowed for such a possibility in another space and another future. He employed a scale that is both distancing in its distortion of reality and familiar in its evocation of comic-book kitsch. In the end, what results is something that stands almost unabashed, neither as hero nor villain, particular nor overly general, motionless nor entirely without life, but simply the concatenation of so many paradigmatic states that it eventually launches a dialogue out of the desire to explain. Only then can the work be completed, momentarily supplying the narrative that Balkenhol intentionally omitted.[6]

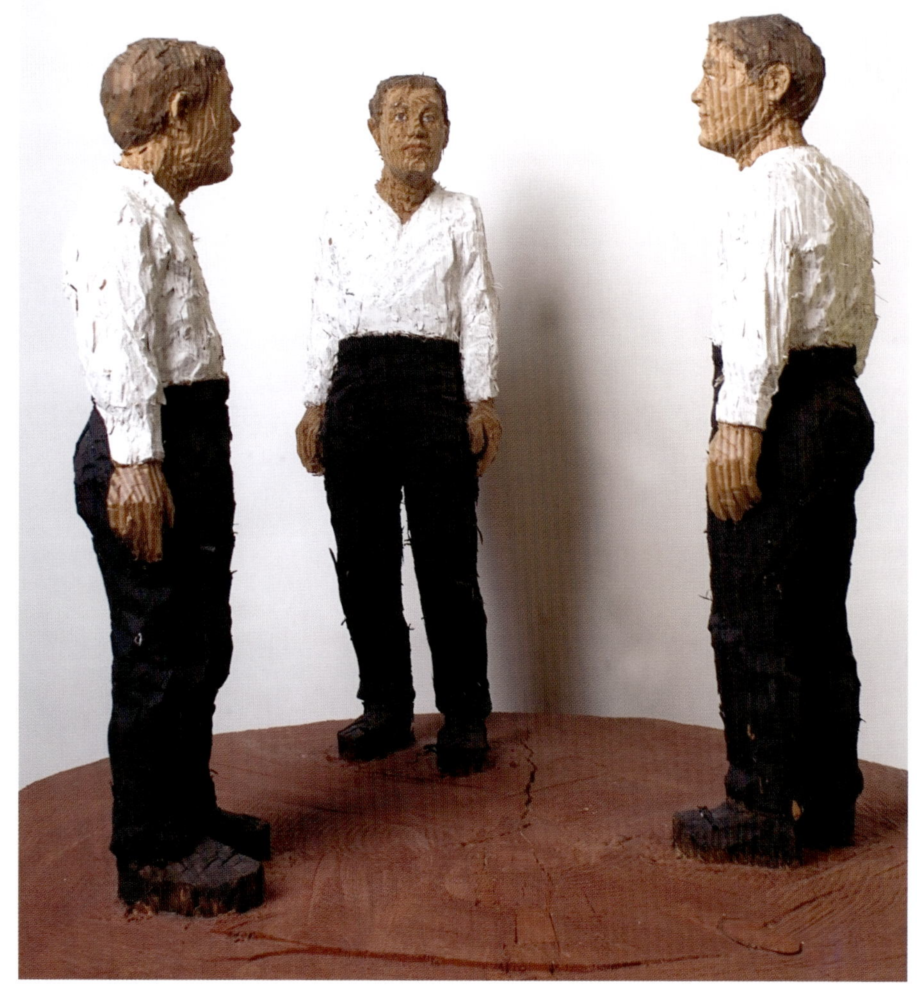

[1] Kent, "The Company of Strangers," 3.
[2] Quoted in Fernandez-Cid, "A Matter of Weight," 143.
[3] Desmarais, *Stephan Balkenhol.*
[4] Kent, "The Company of Strangers," 2.
[5] Ibid., 4.
[6] Koepplin, "Stephan Balkenhol," 149.

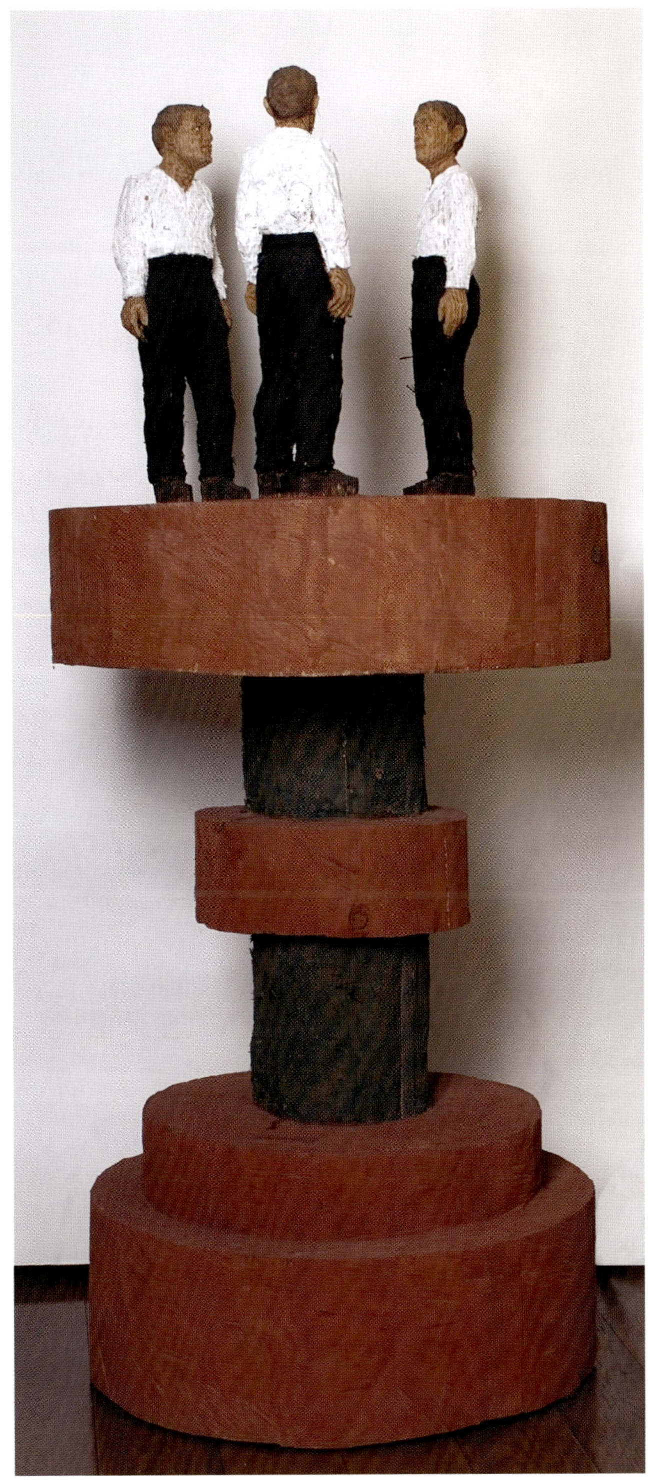

Three Men on a Sculpted Pedestal 2000
Painted douglas fir, 68″ x 31 1/2″ (diameter)

Janet Fish 1938-

Janet Fish once said in an interview, "It seemed to me that composition is about grabbing the viewer's eye and keeping it there in the painting and trying to keep that eye moving around the painting and not let it escape."[1] Through the interlacing of landscape and still life, Fish accomplished this aim in *Dog Days*, a representational scene of a reverie gone adrift on a bright summer day.

The title, then, is both whimsical and informative, granting the viewer a sense of place that is otherwise absent in the ambiguous background. But before ever reaching the dogs of the title, one's eye must enter at the work's focal point: the translucent angular vase from which the painting spreads along its diagonals. The resulting path confronts its viewer with additional still-life figures before leaving the comfortably defined tabletop objects for a background landscape painted in the indistinct language of abstraction.

At this point, distortions of scale begin to challenge the viewer. Most noticeably, the front dog does not appear far away enough to warrant his dwarfed status, nor does the background appear defined enough to presume his particular locale. The viewer is suddenly unsure of the work's realism, which Fish furthers by playing with color to change an object's apparent size and light to unite and divide space at unusual places, such as in the temporary table runner derived from the flow of light through a vase.[2]

In this way, Fish slowly built to her point: although a work may appear realistic, it does not follow that it must also be easily digested and understood. In fact, she aimed to contradict the expected, leading her viewer "from areas of stability to areas of indeterminate spatial relation" for the very purpose of defamiliarization.[3] In its cyclical motion from one plane to the next, Fish's composition wanders along with her imagination, forcing its viewer to seek respite from her play—to become like a dog in shade—in order to finally cease analyzing and simply follow the visual marvel as it unfolds before the eyes.[4]

[1] Quoted in Katz, *Janet Fish Paintings*, 28.
[2] Bonito, *Get Real*, 50; Katz, *Janet Fish Paintings*, 34.
[3] Katz, *Janet Fish Paintings*, 28.
[4] Ibid., 37.

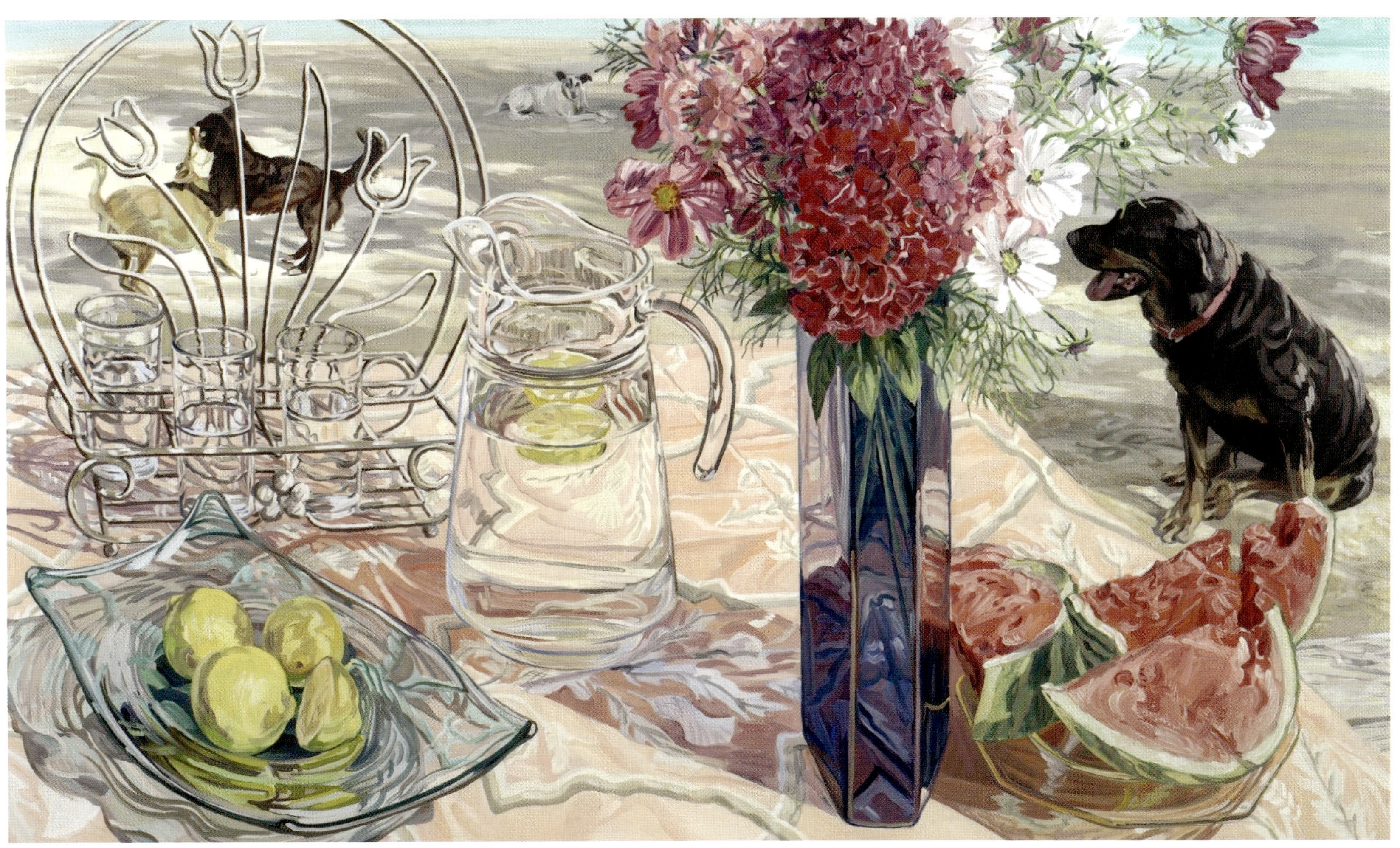

Dog Days 1993
Oil on canvas, 46″ x 80″

Emily Eveleth 1960-

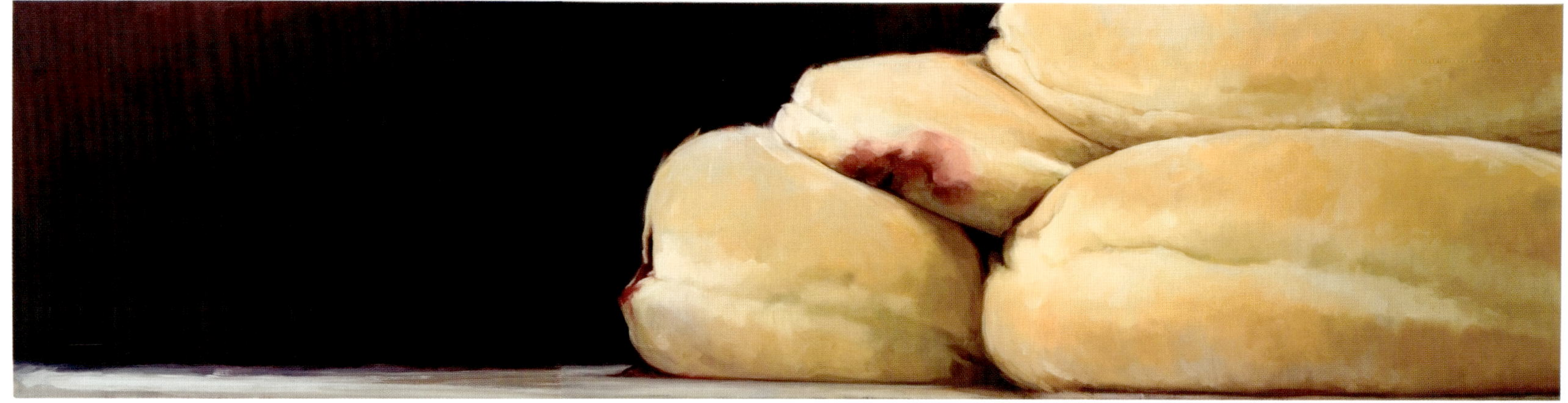

Truce 2005
Oil on canvas, 44″ x 177″

Scott Prior 1949-

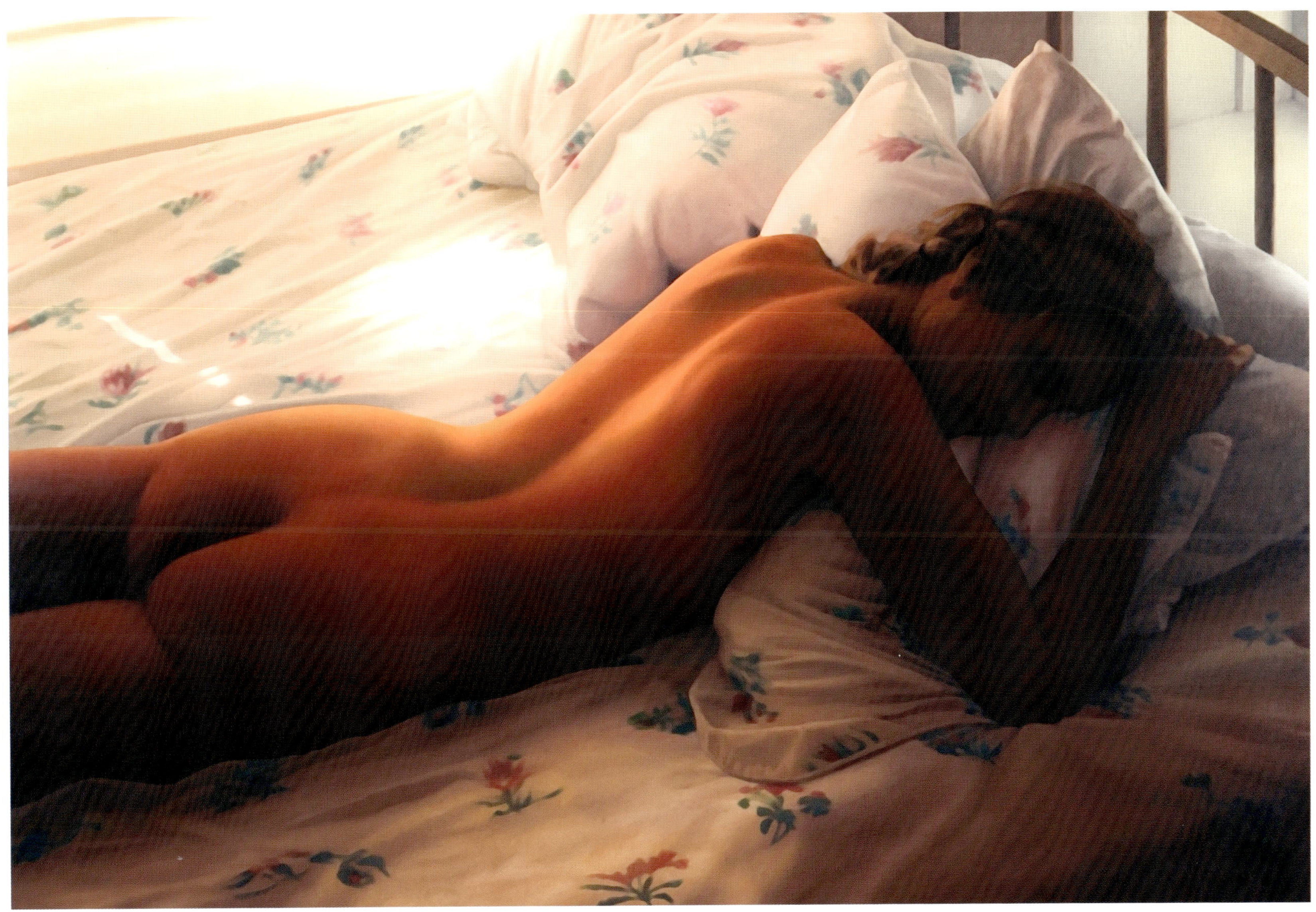

Nanny Sleeping 2002
Oil on linen, 28″ x 41 1/2″

Eric Fischl 1948-

Eric Fischl once wrote bluntly, "For me the water represents the place we've come from, whether by way of biology or immigration. I've always been fascinated by our obsession with hanging out at the beach. In a metaphorical way it's like hanging out really close to where we came from, which is analogous to sex. It's like wanting to play with and meditate on the mysteries of this thing that we've come from and can never go back to. You can go ten feet into the water but you can't live in it, so you have to return to the shore."[1]

In many ways, *Lapping Sounds Along the Shore* seems to illustrate Fischl's words, endowing them with an added narrative significance. Not only is the erotic figure engaged in a waterside, Freudian reclamation of sexuality—conveyed by the phallic stick pointed toward her in the coy game of fetch—but she is also reputed to be the mistress of a well-known collector of contemporary American art. Knowing that the same buyer would be at the Gagosian Gallery to see this work, Fischl seems to dangle her presence as a symbolic caveat: like the sojourn in the water, time in her companionship must also be temporary, and one ultimately has to "return to the shore."

As such, while Fischl's painting casts all the necessary facets of a high-stakes potboiler in the elite, postwar art world, it does not do so to the detriment of his artistic beliefs.[2] Rather, it adheres to the prescriptive cosmology Fischl outlined when he wrote, "I would say that narrative is a large part of the sexual domain insofar as it has as components an object, an audience, and a motive and that the search for satisfaction, the completion of desire, requires tactics––strategies for dominance, strategies for submission, for attraction, and for fulfillment...We are the culture of the individual. Life is expressed meaningfully by representation of the intimate and the personal. The upside is the brassiness of our irreverence. The downside is our loneliness."[3] Accordingly, Lapping Sounds Along the Shore can easily be viewed as a narrative of the sexual domain, replete with the necessary components of the objectified mistress, the scandalized audience/buyer, Fischl's uncurbed motivation to comment, and, of course, the strategy needed to carry on an affair. Furthermore, his isolated, downcast figure seems the quintessential representation of the intimate and the personal; in essence, the work is a fleeting, unmasked glimpse of a brassy, flirtatious woman at the moment of her greatest loneliness.

To pursue Fischl's words further is to see that, like his earlier work capturing the psychological landscape of suburban America, *Lapping Sounds Along the Shore* is successful precisely because it maintains the conflict between "emotional needs and [the] pursuit of perfection...which gives my work its vulnerability. It is for me always an uneasy truce that is arrived at in the painting."[4] As much as the narrativized actors in *Lapping Sounds Along the Shore* adhere to this directive in their presumed actions beyond the canvas, so too does the work itself fundamentally attempt to balance the emotional input of the depicted scene with its aesthetic concretion in perfect color, line, and form.

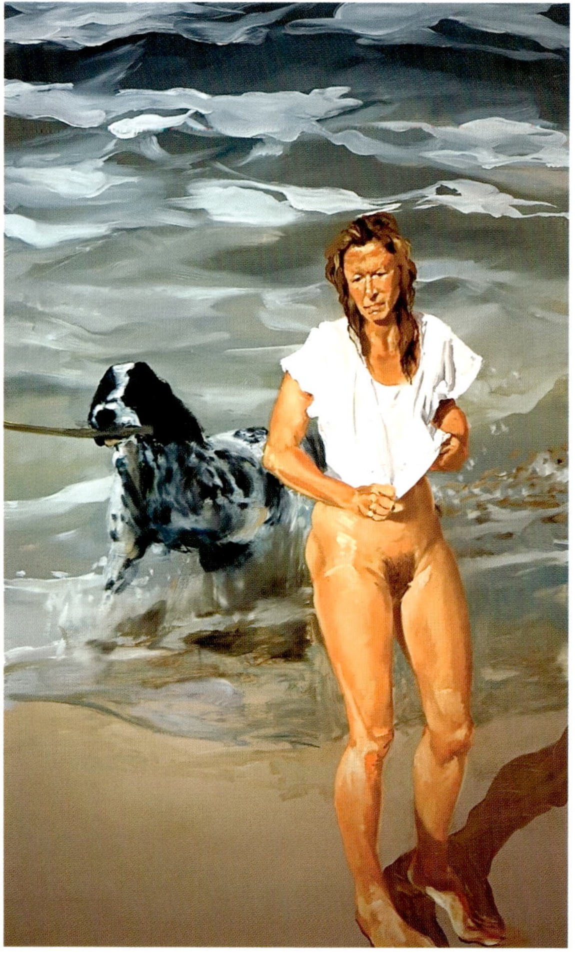

Lapping Sounds Along the Shore 1996-97
Oil on linen, 74″ x 47″

[1] Fischl, "Fischl on Fischl," 152.
[2] Johnson, "Mary Boone: Eric Fischl."
[3] Fischl, "Dialogue with Eric Fischl," 98.
[4] Ibid., 99.

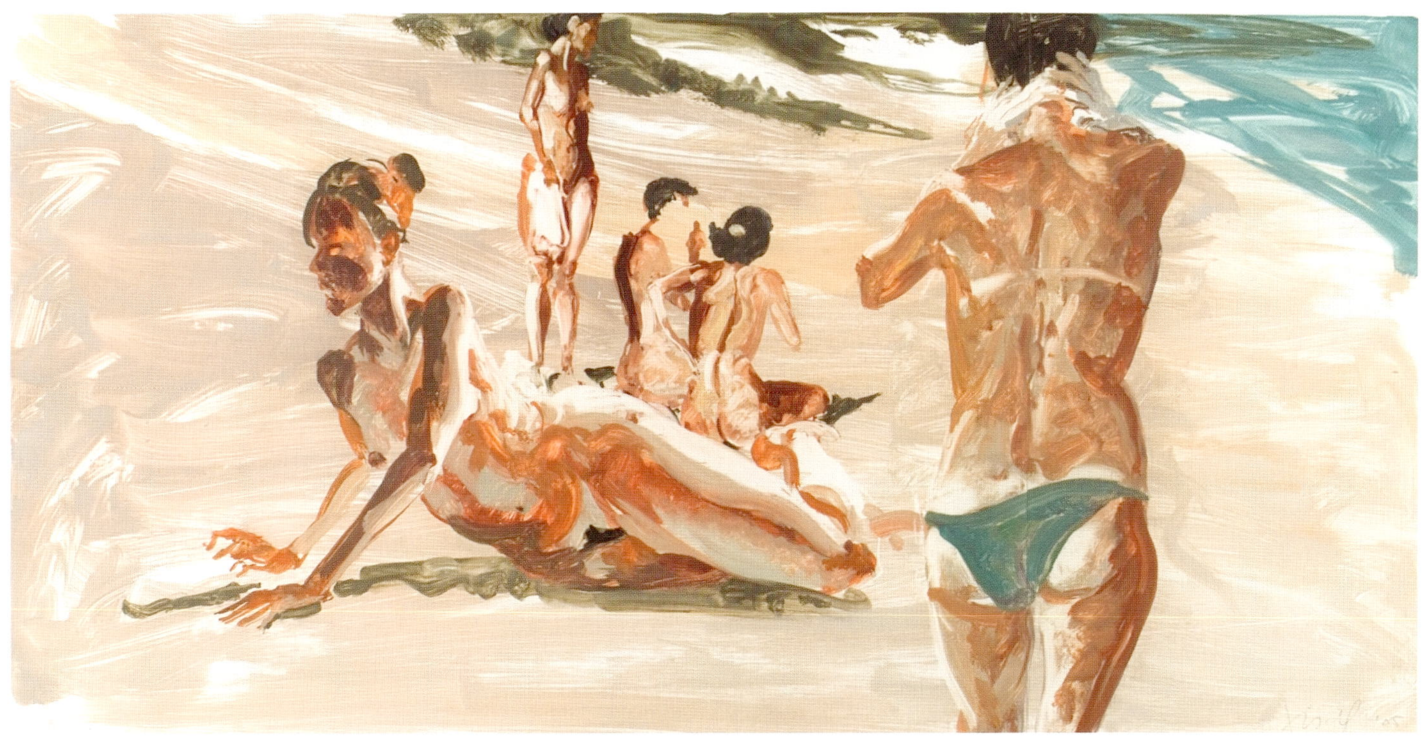

Untitled 2005
Oil on paper, 28″ x 55″

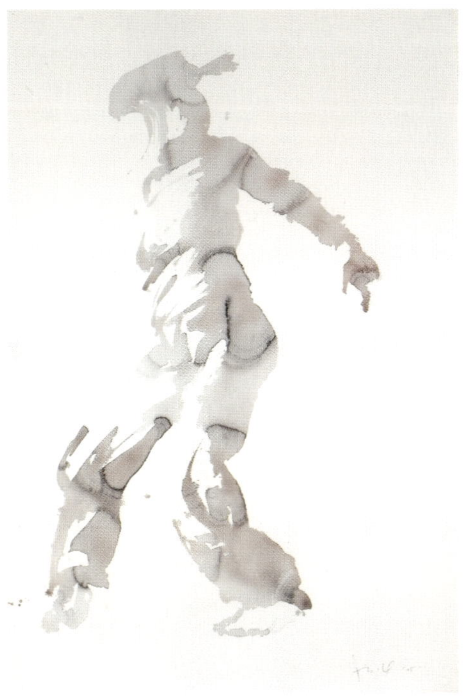

Untitled 2006
Watercolor, 60″ x 40″

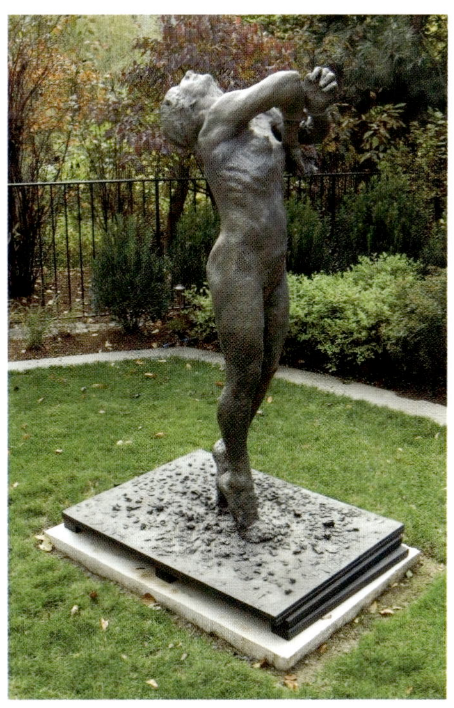

Untitled (Arching Woman) 2005
Bronze, 75″ x 48″ x 36″

Jim Dine 1935-

In the early 1960s, between his pioneering experimentation with the Happenings movement and his reluctant acceptance of an important role in the development of Pop Art, Jim Dine became preoccupied with finding a suitable autobiographic avenue. After exploring printmaking, photography, Environmental Theater, dozens of painting formats, and even poetry, Dine serendipitously struck upon his ideal symbol for the self.

"I'd been trying to find a way to make a self-portrait besides just looking in the mirror," Dine admitted in an interview for a retrospective of his work from 1959 to 1969. "One Sunday, in the *New York Times Magazine*, I saw this ad for bathrobes, and it was a bathrobe with nobody in it. It looked like me. It looked like my physique. So I thought, if I use this, I really can make a miraculous self-portrait."[1]

Returning quickly to his multidirectional explorations, Dine then set out to amend, annotate, adapt, and contort his newly designed symbol for the self. In the Seavest Collection's *Self Portrait*, for example, Dine added an element of assemblage art to his watercolor rendering of the now-famous bathrobe. Through the three-dimensional element of an affixed rock, *Self Portrait* served Dine not only as another cryptic autobiographical artifact, but as the type of bridge that he typically constructed when moving from a format like painting to sculpture.

Though the garment is modified in this way, *Self Portrait* also complies with many of the tenets of Dine's bathrobe series, most noticeably incorporating the habitual beheading of his symbolic self into the painting. While some critics have argued that this construct allows Dine to project a certain endless multiplicity of the self, others have claimed that it simply points viewers to the underlying human geometry of the figure rather than misleading elements of personality or behavior.[2]

As Dine himself saw it, his bathrobe series permitted him "a way to make structure for [him]self."[3] As the empty fabric magically conforms to Dine's shape, it stabilizes and separates the temporary and the permanent; removing fleeting emotion or spurious philosophy until only the physical space he occupies remains. Though it is possible to see the attached rock, which serves no role beyond the mere occupation of space, as a symbolic extension of such a viewpoint, it is far more likely just another found object, similar to the bathrobe, that struck Dine as appropriate for this particular work—as he perpetually crafted footholds to propel himself from one realm of the art world to the next.

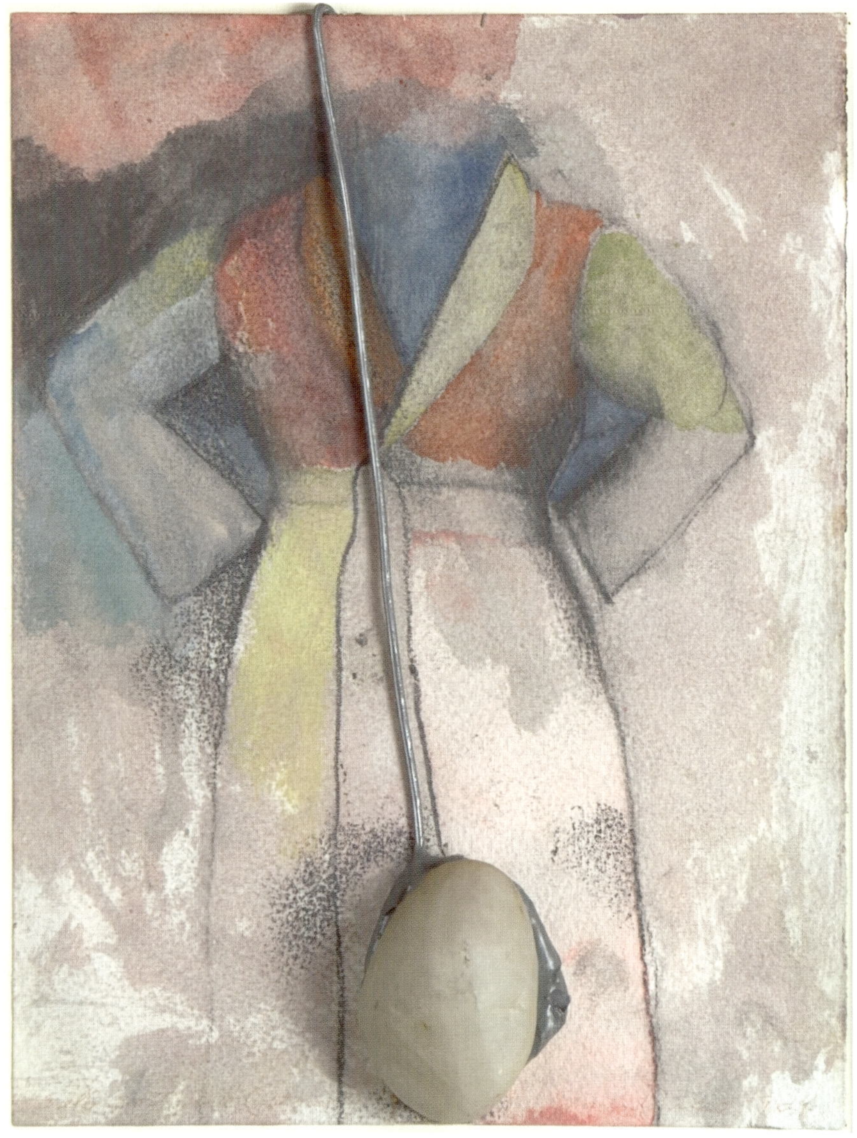

Self Portrait 1964
Watercolor (with stone and string), 9″ x 7″

[1] Quoted in Bell, Celant, and Dine, "Walking Memory: A Conversation," 192.
[2] Johnson, "From Modernism Backward"; Katz, "Symbols for the Self," 12.
[3] Quoted in Bell, Celant, and Dine, "Walking Memory: A Conversation," 192.

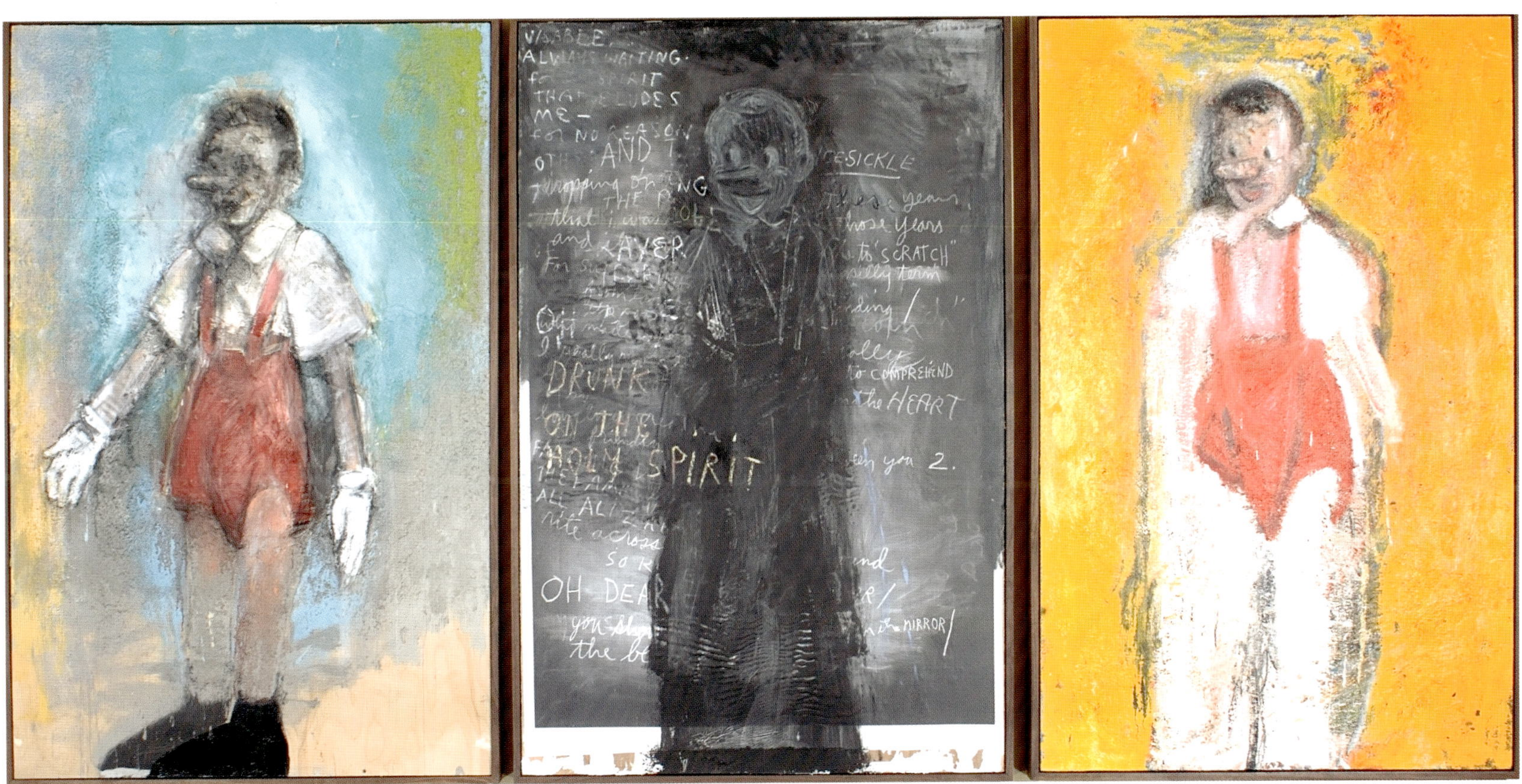

Prayer on the Mirror 2004
Oil on wood with charcoal, pastel, acrylic, 72″ x 147 3/4″

Viola Frey 1933–2004

Though best known for her miniature bric-a-brac figurines of men in power-suits and women in 1950s patterned dresses, Viola Frey devoted the last decade of her life to assembling a legion of massive ceramic figures, the diaspora of which has since found addresses across the country at high-profile collections such as the Bellagio Hotel's in Las Vegas.[1]

In many ways, the larger-than-life figures are a fitting summation of Frey's relentless quest to unite the drama of painting with the physical presence of ceramics. Early in her career, Frey distinguished herself among ceramicists through the pursuit of an emotive use for color, which she first learned under the tutelage of Mark Rothko while pursuing an MFA at Tulane University.[2] At the time, Frey realized, "Painting had a great influence on my ceramics. The ceramic objects were made immeasurably more effective by color used to emphasize the internal stresses of the work and that color itself added to the external visual exchanges between the stability of the clay and the very active environment in which they existed. Color intensifies an object's participation in its surrounding space and light."[3]

By the 1970s, Frey became even more aware of her objects' participation in their natural environment as she began to work outdoors in the backyard of her Oakland home, where changes in shadow and light prompted her to explore what colors best complemented the blues and greens of her workspace.[4] Today, the massive figures reflect her quest: displayed outdoors, the abstract badges of color not only narrate their ongoing paroxysmal processes of self-signification, but also serve to assimilate them within their surroundings. To add drama to the composition, Frey employed patchwork blocks of yellow and red, both balancing the figure against the pure blues and greens of the water and grass and driving the breakup of color and light as one's eye travels across its surface and setting.[5] As Frey often termed it, she was exploring the dissolution of surface.

In *Man and Vase*, Frey not only captured the broader color themes typical of her later work, but she also explored her place in the history of ceramics. Through the inclusion of the prototypical ceramic creation—the vase—Frey introduced the notion of ceramics as a *craft*, as opposed to a high art. In frustration, it seems, the figure seeks to kick over the vase, once and for all liberating himself from his condescendingly popular rank. But as Frey depicted it, he is incapable of pushing the vase over completely, for doing so would mean destroying his own image, which is reproduced in so many permutations on the vessel. In the end, the vase is as much a consequence of "the potter's sense of volumetric form" as the figure itself, and accordingly, Frey was as incapable of denying her source material as she was of perpetuating the ceramic tradition without the modifications of color and scale that became so central to her oeuvre.[6]

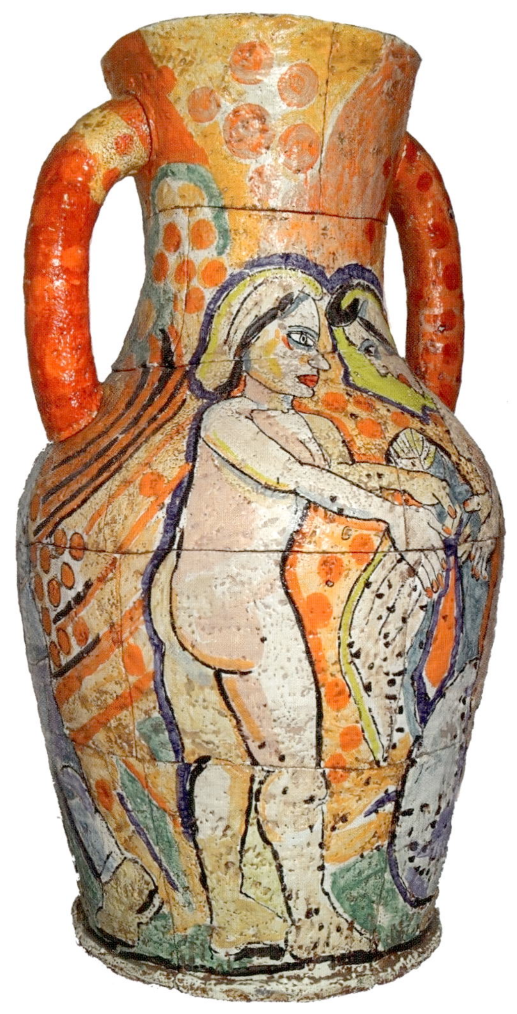

Conversation Urn: Viola's Theory 2000
Ceramic, 80" x 40" (diameter)

[1] Clark, "Viola Frey [Obituary]," 75.
[2] Jana, "Viola Frey: Survey of Work," 83.
[3] Frey, *Unpublished Statement*, 1.
[4] Jana, "Viola Frey: Survey of Work," 83-87.
[5] Clark, "Cracks in the Sidewalk," 13.
[6] Ibid., 16.

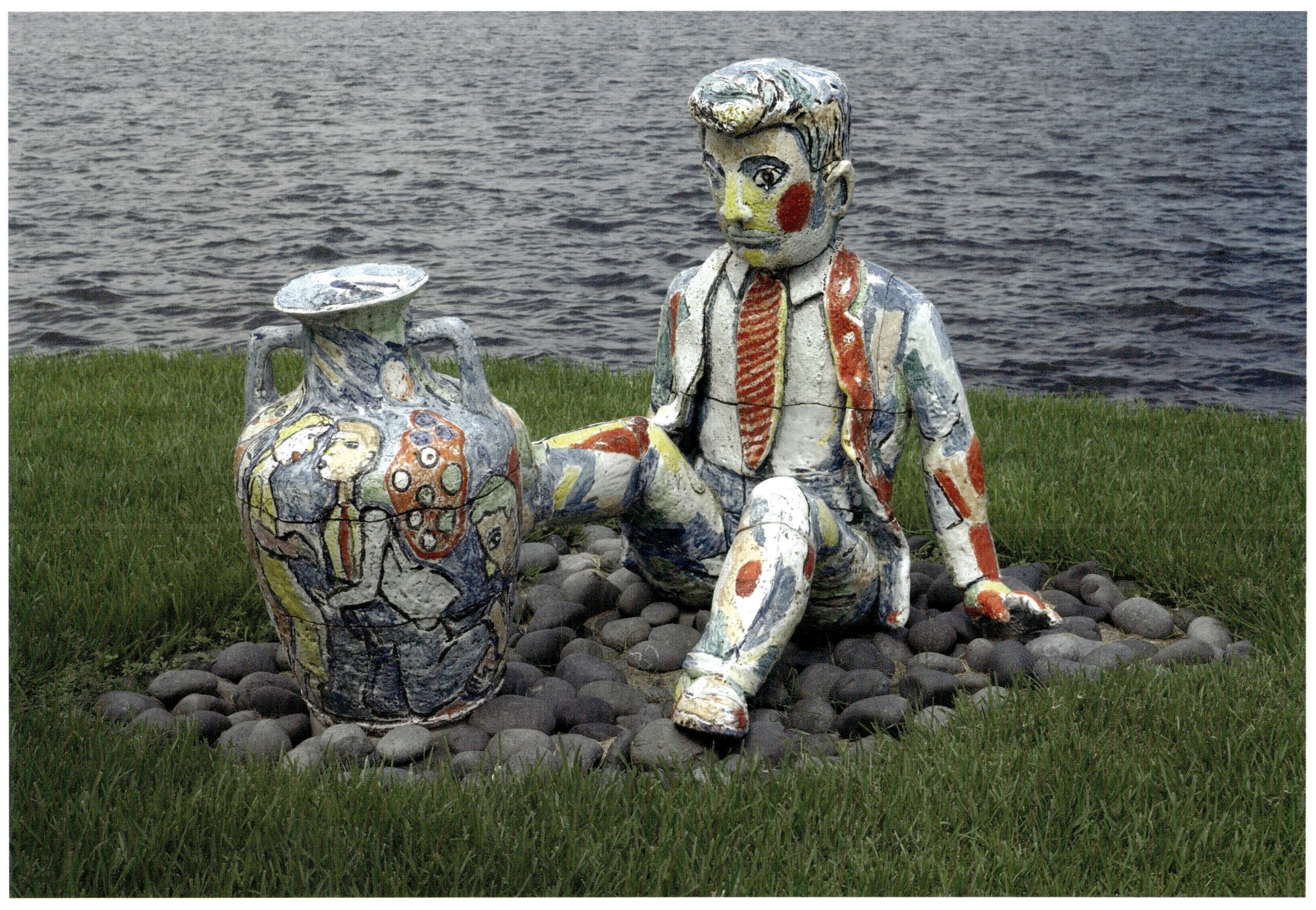

Man and Vase 1996
Ceramic, 66″ x 88″ x 66″

Don Jacot 1949-

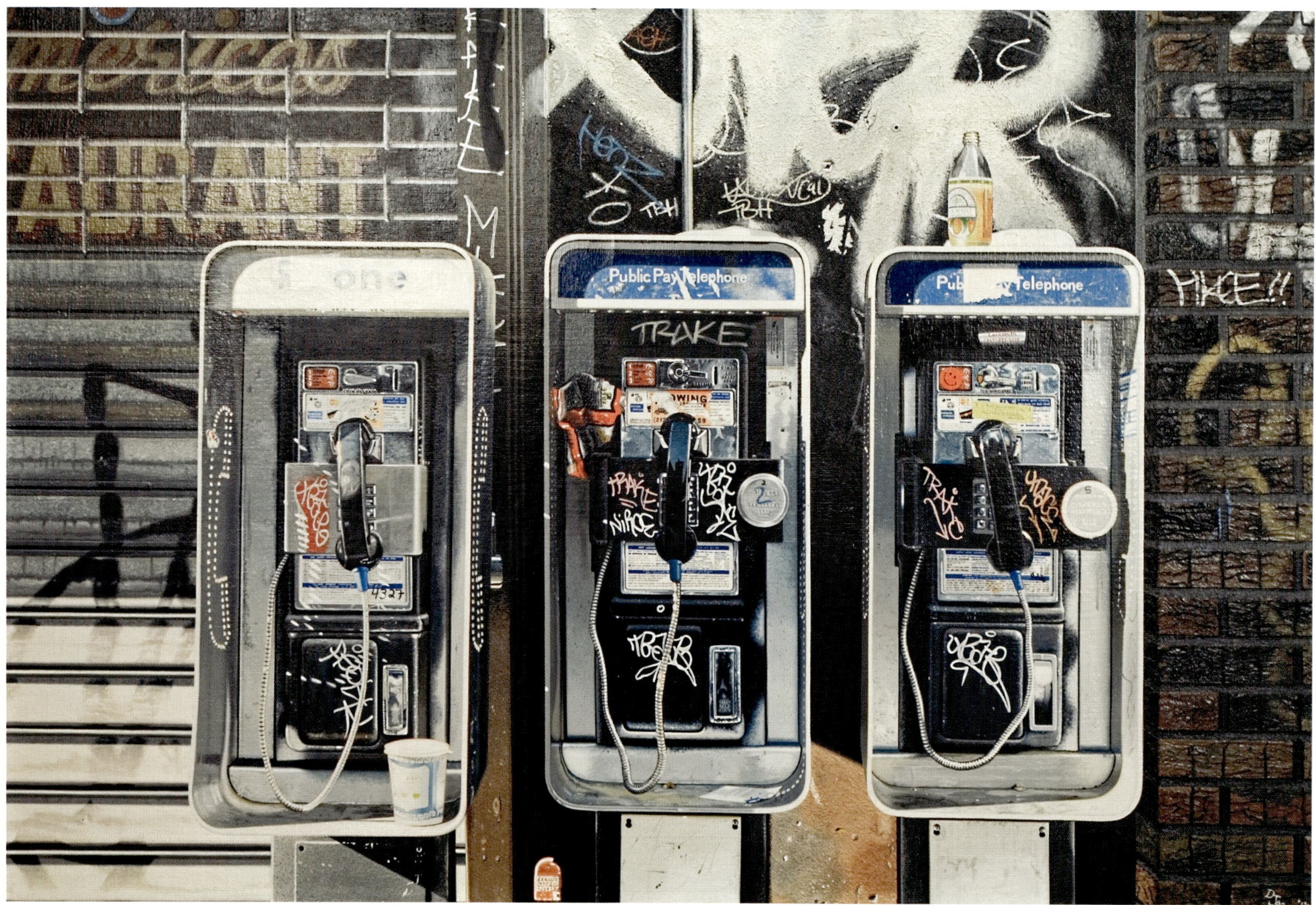

Pay Phones 1995
Oil on linen, 24″ x 36″

Chie Shimizu 1971-

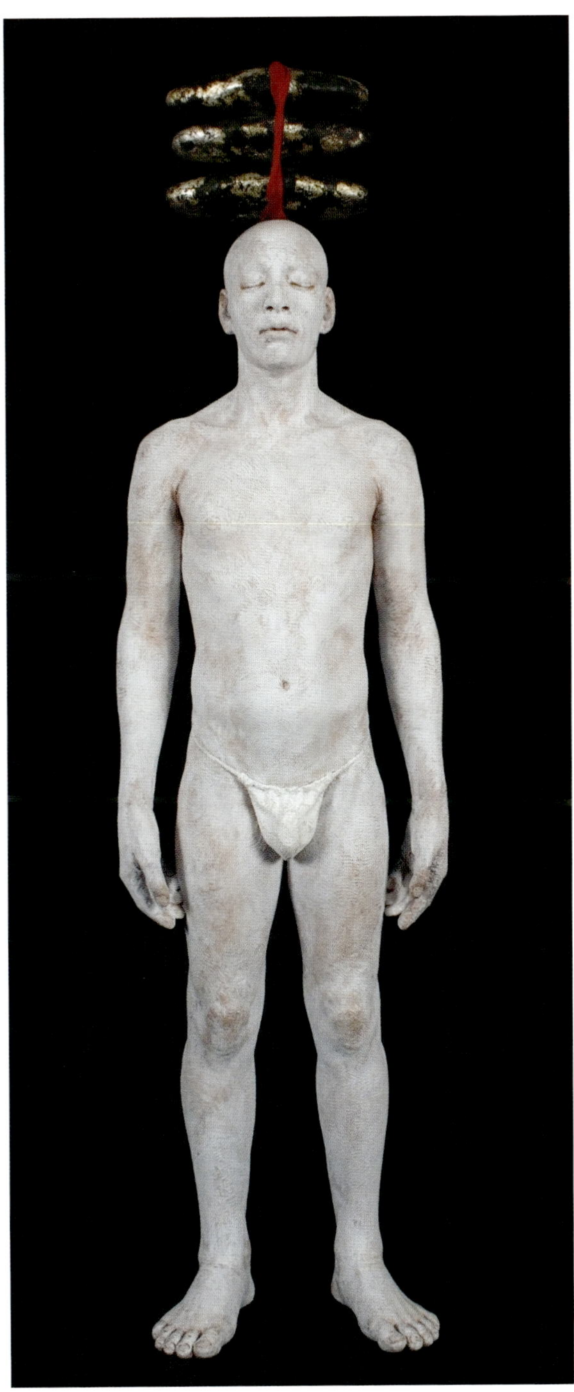

Untitled 2005
Ultracal, plaster, pigment, gofun (seashell powder) and silver leaf, 42 1/2″ x 12″ x 4″

Gregory Gillespie 1936–2000

Gregory Gillespie was quick to defend the many large, twenty-year-old canvases scattered in various stages of completion about his studio, saying, "Even something that is not so successful can be recycled, repainted, brought to life again."[1]

Such was the case with *Rick and the Large Mandala*, commissioned by Richard Segal after a chance connection to Gillespie's alma mater, Cooper Union, led him to purchase a small portrait during a charity auction. When Segal traveled to Gillespie's studio to take source photographs for the portrait, he stood in front of a particularly large painting for one of the pictures—what was then an early version of *Large Mandala*. After Gillespie developed the photographs, he found himself drawn to the image of Segal positioned in front of the existing painting and immediately conceived of synthesizing his shrine series with the commissioned portrait; what was supposed to be a 10" x 20" painting developed into a life-sized portrayal.

Regardless of the success of *Large Mandala* beforehand, for Gillespie his new subject seemed to have "brought it to life again." Perhaps this was a proper testament to Segal's underlying passion for art and his collection, which he once described as a "quest to build for one's self a nest that with its very presence and appearance provides us with the sense of security and belonging that comes from the knowledge that we are at home." For the first time, not only was Segal at home *with* his art, but in the eyes of Gillespie, he was at home in it as well.

Adapting the work by removing some of its darker imagery and personal ghosts, such as the oversized brush stroke of an Abstract Expressionist and various sexually explicit sketches, Gillespie superimposed his portrait of Segal onto the center of the canvas. By reworking the painting's symbols, Gillespie was better able to "explore the tension inherent in portraiture between the depiction of the body as a still-life object and as a representation of the human soul" as he saw it in Segal.[2]

As is the case in all of Gillespie's art, the "weird, unpredictable nature" of his images "makes them appear to have sprung from a perpetually opened Pandora's box," resulting in a work that is "literary, intellectual, and content-ridden, while at the same time, fraught with angst."[3] However, as a mandala—a design symbolic of the universe—the work places its subject at the center of a world only to surround him with images of its fragility, transience, and chance, represented by a roll of tape, a shoe, and even a lucky rabbit, respectively. Gillespie balanced these images with emblems of another kind: tools of progress, a bag for the fruits of one's labor, and even a phallic gourd to represent the roots of a patriarch.

Despite such a varied tableaux, the painting seems, first and foremost, to caution against reading into any one of these symbols too deeply. After all, as evidenced by its drastic shift in subject matter, "its construct...has changed over the years, different images coming and going...changed as our individual worlds change,"[4] constantly brought to life again by the people we encounter, the things we learn, and the artistry we seek in all of its forms.

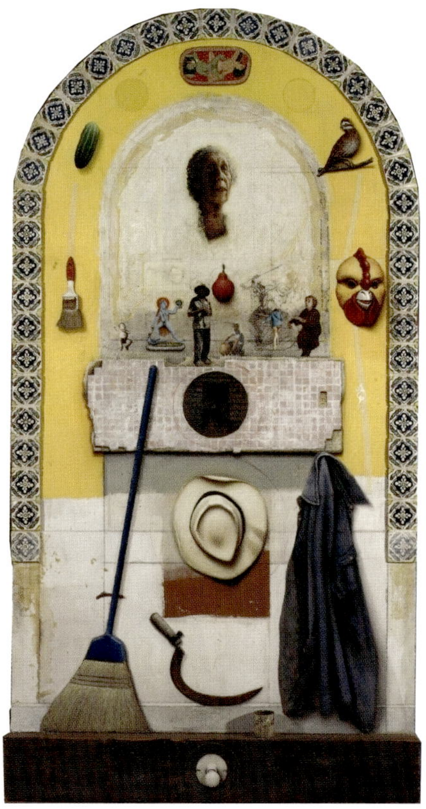

Godmother Shrine 1990
Oil and alkyd on board, 107″ x 56″

[1] Gillespie, "Interview with Gregory Gillespie," 56.
[2] Duncan, "The Self," 157.
[3] Ibid., 154.
[4] Quoted in Belz, "Gregory's Vision," 45.

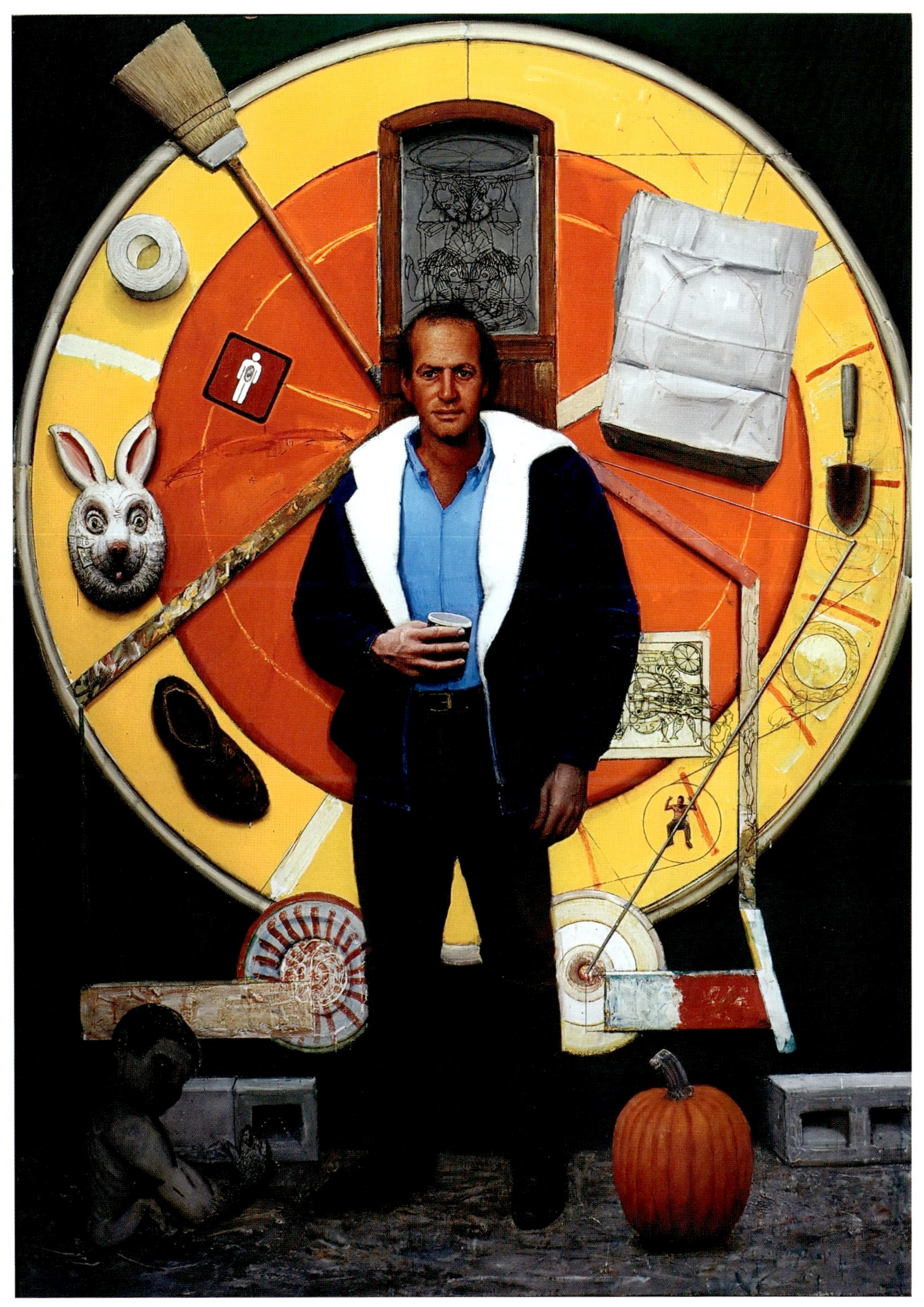

Rick and Large Mandala 1995-97
Oil and alkyd on board, 108″ x 90″

Jonathan Seliger 1955 –

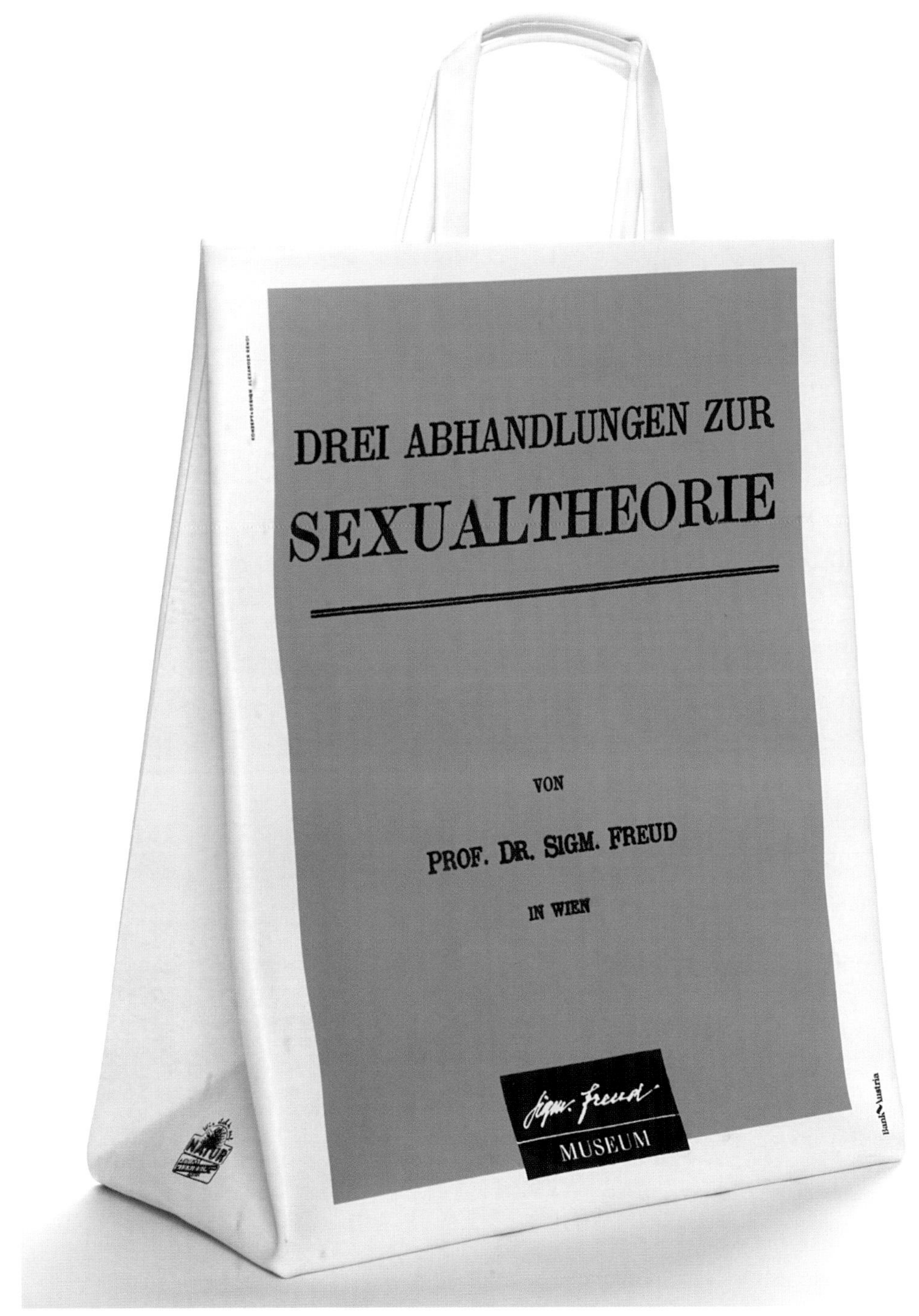

The Dr. Will See You Now 2001
Oil, alkyd, acrylic, and modeling paste on canvas, 13″ x 12″ x 6 1/2″

Robert Gniewek 1951–

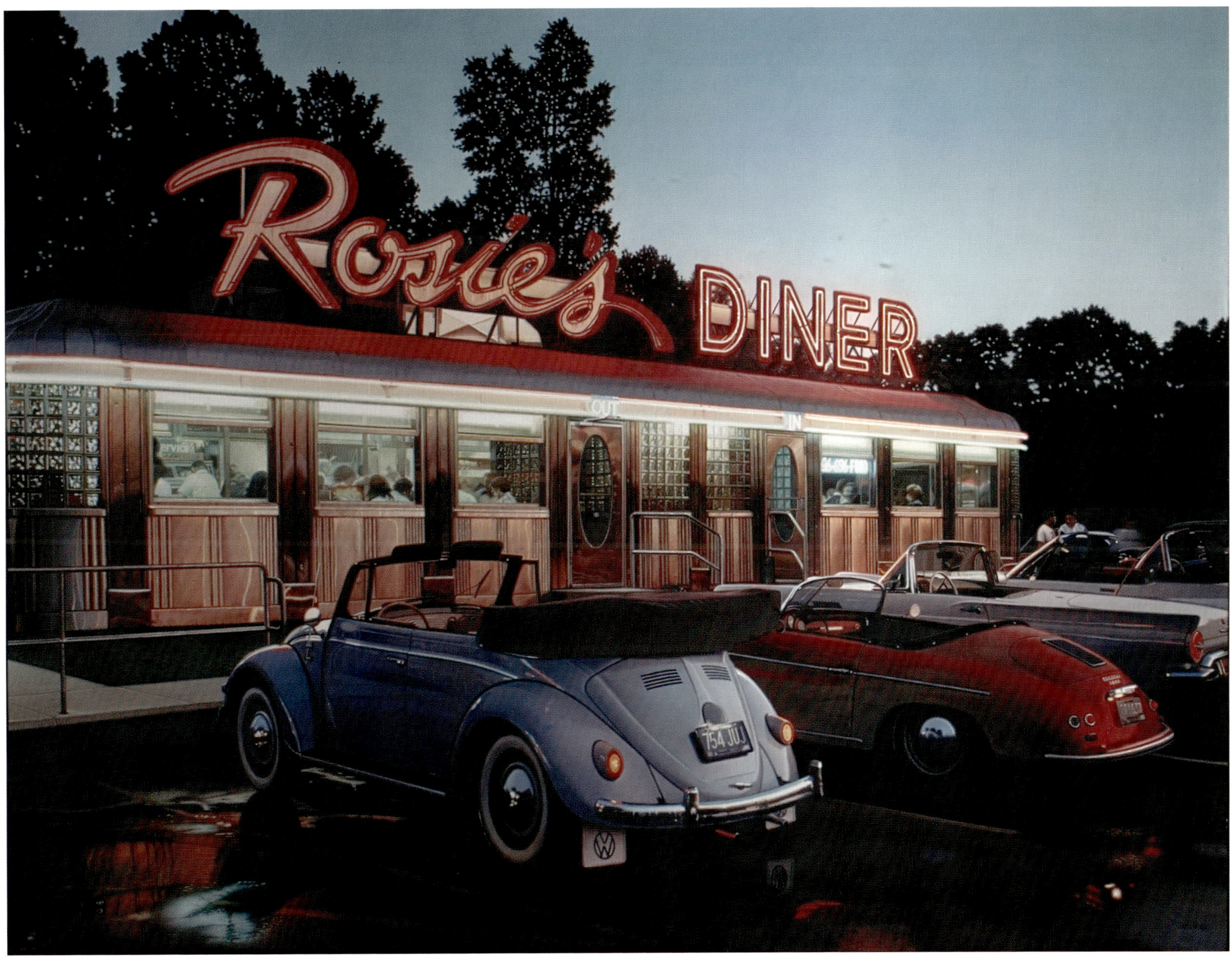

Rosie's Diner #7 2004
Oil on linen, 30″ x 40″

Ralph Goings 1928-

When Pop Art began to validate his burgeoning interest in the materiality of American culture, Ralph Goings's experimentation with realism seemed to take on new spirit, not only recording the quotidian fabric of life but magnifying it as well. In the 1970s, Goings began this transition, zooming in on his normal subject matter of diners and small-town eateries, and exploding the scale of tabletop commodities, which perpetually evolved alongside the world of marketing and brand-name packaging.[1]

As Goings seems to indicate in *Sugar*, through his commodity lens, it is evident that daily life has become patently overcomplicated when even simple condiments are no longer clear-cut and the supply of options begins to outnumber any demands of necessity. In the Collection's piece, despite its prominent role in the title, the sugar appears scarcely able to outperform its synthetic equivalents and is, in fact, the dwindling minority in the scene—a development made all the more ironic by the technique of simplification that Goings imposed upon the tabletop landscape to highlight the slipping values of his nostalgic vignettes.

In *Sugar*, Goings again takes disposable, mundane items from the periphery of our vision and repositions them as emblems of Americana, dismantling the hierarchy of subject matter in order to reflect upon those aspects of modern culture curiously absent from representation in high art.[2] Visually, Goings had little trouble defending his classification of everyday items as definitively modern: glass containers appear as crystalline architectural elements, while polished silver surfaces and hyperreal textures are rich in pictorial and sensory illusion. Each element serves as a miniature study of the way light is shaped by those objects that disrupt its trajectory, and as a result, the totality of the still life emerges with an unapologetic interest in the gleaming surfaces and repeated geometries offered by the sleek modern world.[3]

Through its subject matter, *Sugar* evokes an equally contemporary sense of the freewheeling mobility and fast-paced, caffeinated lifestyle to which most Americans subject themselves.[4] Though the condiments are devoid of their end-user participants, the captured scene is undoubtedly democratic and middle class, displaying emblems of the brief social pleasantries scheduled during bouts of refueling for yet another busy day.[5]

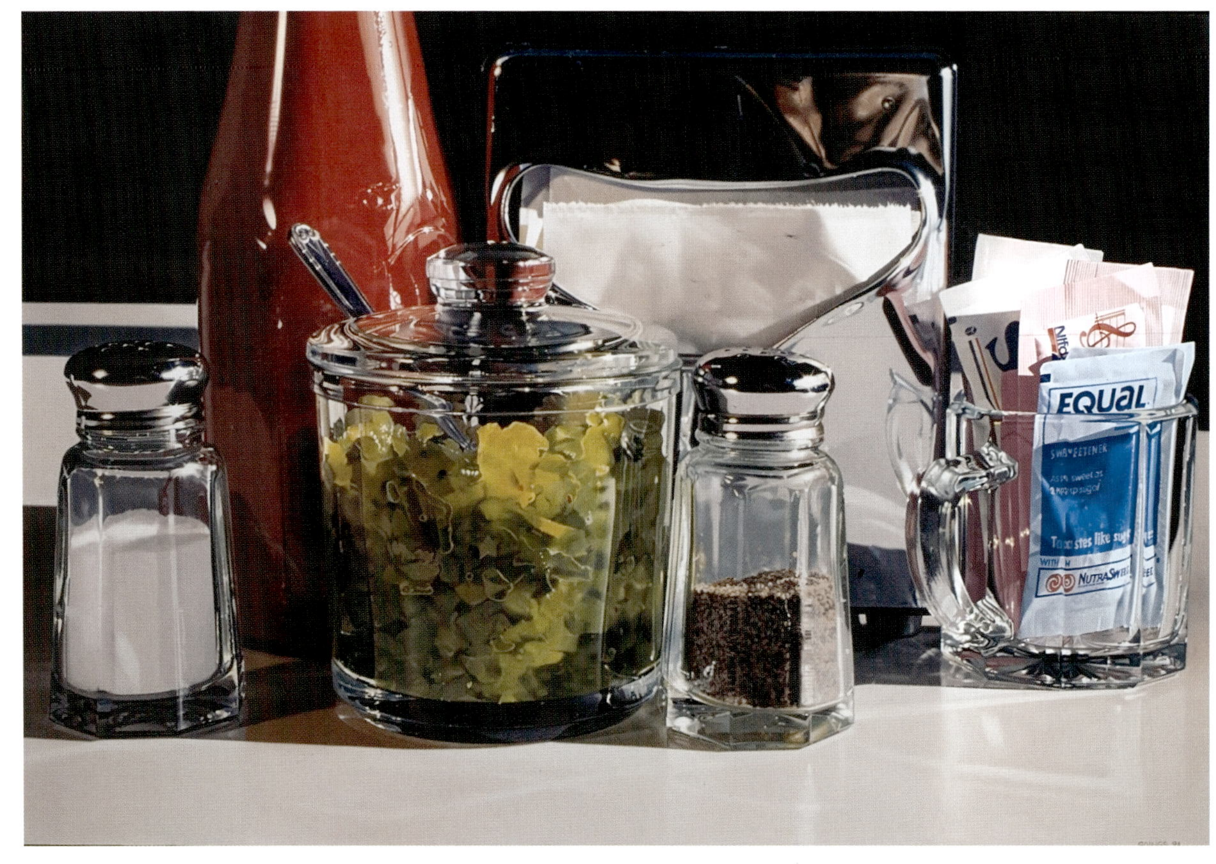

Relish 1994
Oil on linen, 44″ x 64 1/2″

[1] Bonito, *Get Real*, 64-66.
[2] Meisel, *Photorealism at the Millennium*, 131.
[3] Lucie-Smith, "Ralph Goings: America's Vermeer," 3. Meisel, *Photorealism at the Millennium*, 131.
[4] Lucie-Smith, 3.
[5] Bonito, *Get Real*, 64.

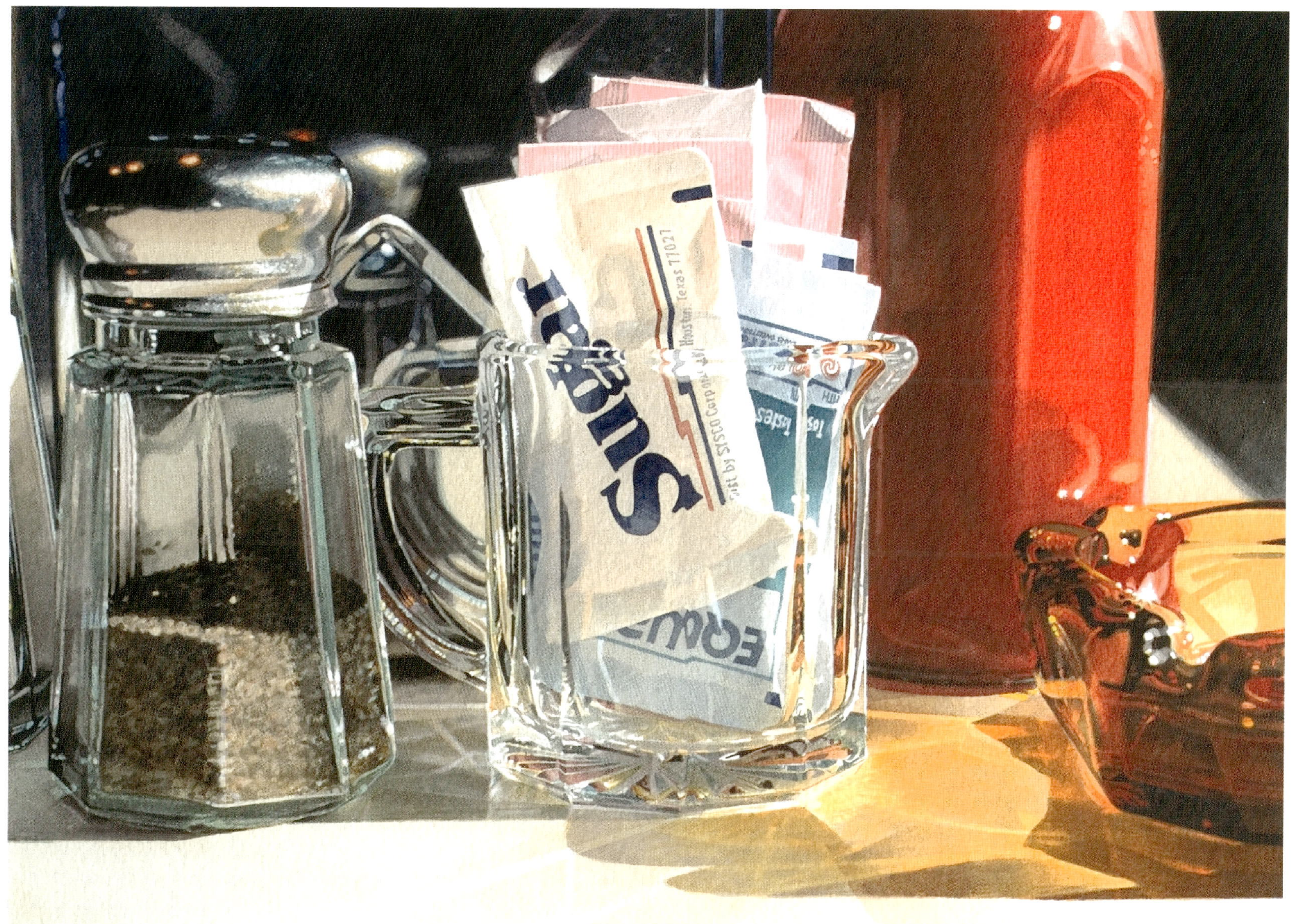

Sugar 1993
Watercolor on paper, 11 1/2″ x 16 1/4″

Sean Henry 1965-

Caught between action and inaction, Sean Henry's figures seem to hesitate before proceeding, locked in consideration over the next path to take at one of life's crossroads.[1] His *T.P.O.L.R. (The Path of Least Resistance)* makes this motif explicit, presenting a small-scale sculpture that gazes at a course rather countercurrent to the one down which his momentum carries him, so much so that his mind seemingly has no control over the progress and direction of his feet. Paradoxically, Henry leads his viewer to believe that the anonymous man has a great deal of mental agility despite his static pose and personal inertia.[2] At the same time, however, one also gets the sense that he is engaged in distinctly unfocused thought, which provides for a tabula rasa that the viewer is compelled to fill with personally informed, prosaic narration.

The ambiguity of the title does little to hinder such external interjection and serves as a possible allusion to a popular self-help book for managers. Even as an unintentional allusion, Robert Fritz's *The Path of Least Resistance: For Managers*, an abbreviated guide to success in the corporate world, seems an appropriately mixed metaphor, bridging the gap between the figure's quotidian existence and the path that might lead to an improved life. Of course, Henry acknowledged that he does not expect his figure to attempt the more difficult course, nor do the visual cues of his clothing suggest he is intent on such a choice. Instead, he simply adopts the logo of a major corporation, framing it as the vapid centerpiece of his identity.

Invariably intertwined with identity, the heavy, tactile clothes are also key symbols of status, and the bold block letters easily label the figure with an unassuming honesty that continues through his wrinkled blue jeans and blue-collar jacket. As the writer and curator Barbara Krulik once remarked, Henry's figures are men who have "rolled up their sleeves and put in a hard day's work."[3] But as such, they also appear vacant, demoralized by their situation and the difficulty of escape, exasperated by the ever-present possibility of another path.

[1] Moncrieff, (*Here and Now*), 25-26.
[2] Krulik, Sean Henry, 6.
[3] Ibid., 3.

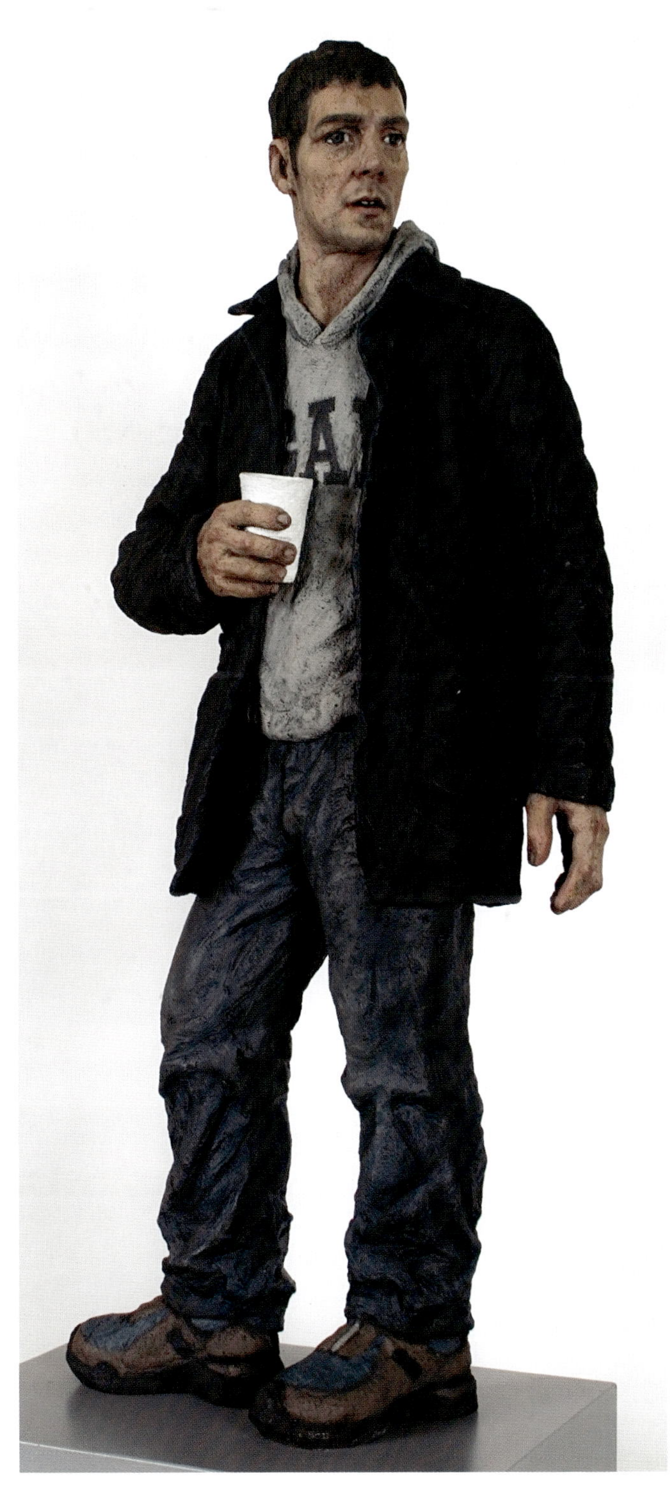

T.P.O.L.R. (The Path of Least Resistance) 2002
Bronze, oil paint, 20 1/2″ x 8 1/2″ x 6″

Juan Gonzalez 1942-1993

Juan González employs a marriage of dualities in *Rembrandt's Hands, Vermeer's Frame and the Passing of the Moth*, his painting-within-a-painting that prominently includes a miniature reproduction of an earlier work, *Vermeer's Frame* (1990). The conflation of so many opposites—and of multiple paintings—within a single trompe l'oeil frame quixotically broadens the painting's artistic and historical reach beyond the simple confines of his own work while also re-centering it on a distinctly personal level, for it is as much a chronicle of influence as an inlet to the significance stirred within.

The multi-layered structure of *Rembrandt's Hands, Vermeer's Frame and the Passing of the Moth* is purposefully difficult to digest, since González did not let go of his secrets transparently. On this account, the lower edge of the painting, which is dominated by an austere darkness that seems to spill over to the artist's emotional reworking of Vermeer's *A Lady Standing at the Virginal*, threatens to obscure his allusion, which is itself transformed through graying palette and authorial insertion of the artist.[1] The overall effect of looming obfuscation is increased by its juxtaposition with dense, tightly wound golden flowers, which form a potentially explosive backdrop for the central visual subject of the work, the conjoined *Rembrandt's Hands*.

In this pivotal allusion, González drew on Rembrandt's *Isaac and Rebecca (The Jewish Bride)*, ca. 1666, to highlight the fruitful union of opposites and the unexpected parallels that exists for an artist like González, who incessantly synthesized his own contemporary art with clashing Renaissance and classical styles. Any such union, González suggested, is equally and inevitably productive. In the artist-provided example of Isaac and Rebecca, it is González himself, who painted both male and female hands using his own as models, who appears as the faceless androgyne born from the synthesis of certain nominal dualities: man and woman, light and dark, birth and death.[2] As Irene McManus wrote in a retrospective of the artist's work, "*Rembrandt's Hands* immerses itself in everything that Gonzalez ever found beautiful. It is an authentic vision, rare in a contemporary artist, of a golden paradise of roses, of love and death, entered through the dark door of *Vermeer's Frame* and predicting the artist's ascent to Dante's 'Celestial Rose,' the vast theater of paradise."[3] As McManus suggested, González deployed such charged symbols to construct a visual coding of the fruitful life and work cycles—replete with his own dualities and antitheses—that led to his gradual ascension from darkness to lightness and, ultimately, even to his own acceptance of death by its reduction to a purely artistic illumination.[4]

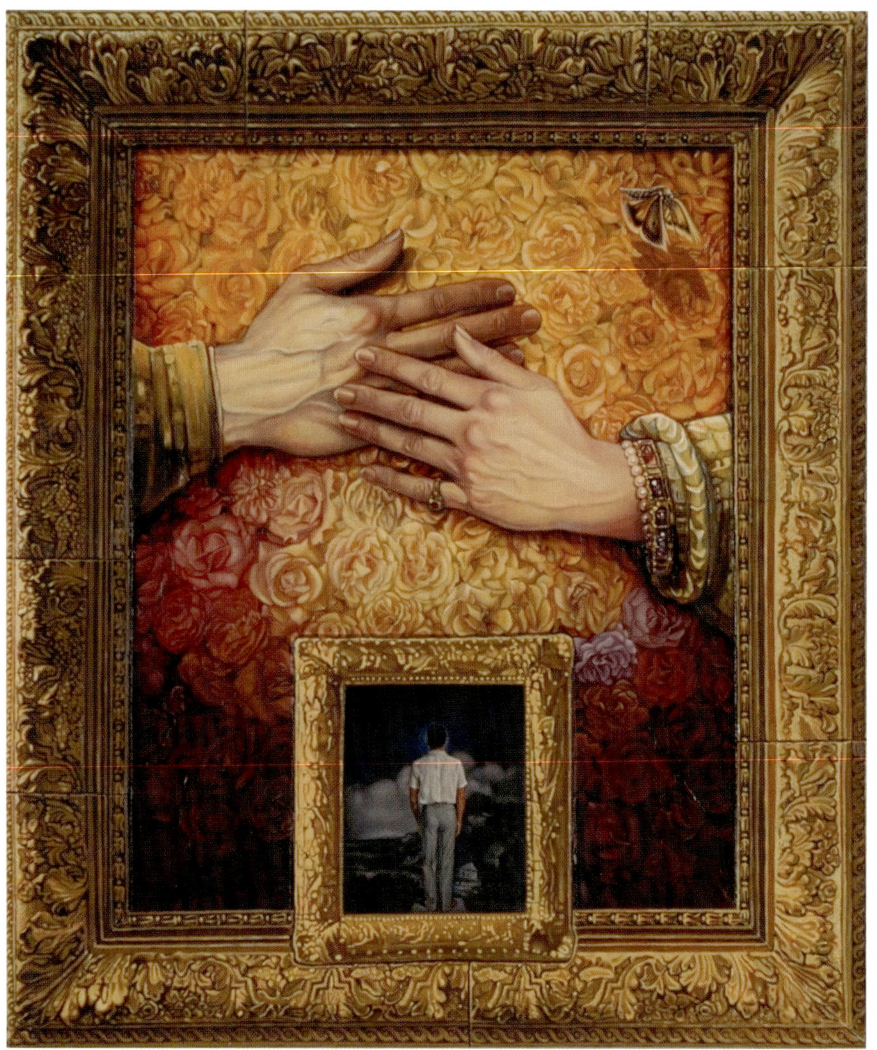

Rembrandt's Hands, Vermeer's Frame and the Passing of the Moth 1990
Mixed mdia, 33″ x 29″

[1] McManus, Dreamscapes, 158.
[2] Ibid.
[3] Ibid.
[4] Ibid.

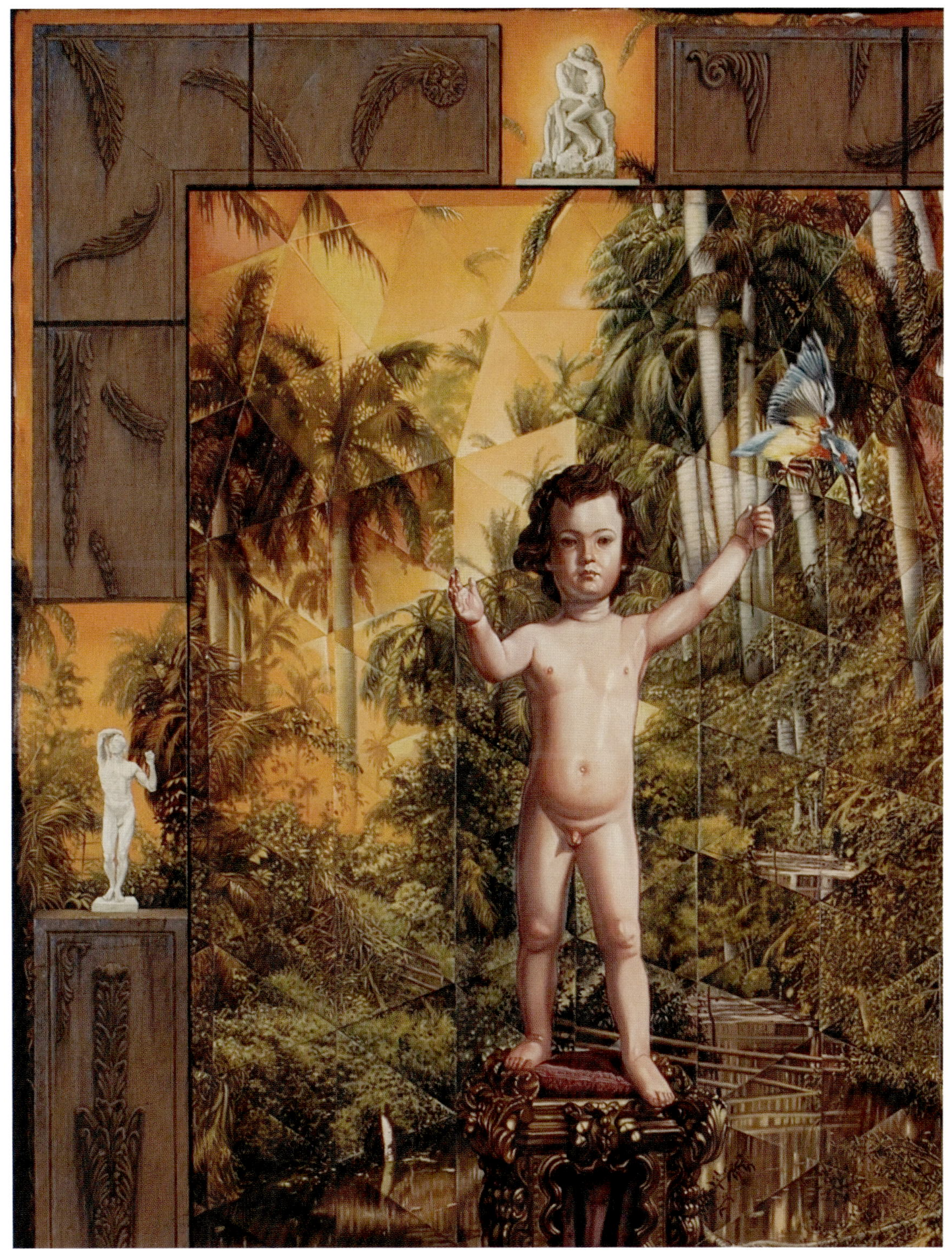

Memory Piece 1990
Oil on wood and silk mounted on honeycomb panel, 43″ x 34″

John Wesley 1928-

In a press release for John Wesley's solo exhibition at the Harvard University Art Museum in 2001, curators described the "conspicuous characteristics of his work since the early seventies" as a symbiosis of six fundamental traits: "insistent flatness, powdered pastel palette, cartoon/cinematographic narratives, embrace of the sexually charged encounter, sophisticated anthropomorphism, and mannered drawing."[1] Certainly, *December 5* is a product of such Wesley ingredients, from its dominant baby blues and cotton-candy pinks to its overtly sexual subject matter. But as much as *December 5* follows the hallmarks of Wesley's oeuvre, it also seems to launch a new course of introspection that borders on self-doubt, thereby marking a drastic departure from the impersonal social wit and blank-faced irony typical of the artist's best-known work.

It is widely agreed in critical circles that Wesley quelled the sexual appetite apparent in his work by adhering to a cartoon, comedic style that is too far removed from reality to alarm or disturb his viewers. As Carolyn Christov-Bakargiev wrote, "He has dealt with this issue [of sexuality] by avoiding any direct portrayal of women: since the beginning of his practice, there has been no 'cinema of the real,' nor photorealism, nor any direct appropriation of images of bodies. He paints, rather, a fictional world of animated figures, a dream landscape of the mind."[2] Although the style of *December 5* maintains this dream landscape, it seems as though the very subject of the painting has finally startled awake from the dream, rising from her pillow as if to escape the canvas itself. No longer do the stylized line and dreamy palette suffice to justify the prescribed role of sexual objectification. In this way, the strikingly naked figure may fulfill her role as the means of sexual satisfaction through her protruding chest and suggestive hand posture but she also demands to break beyond the boundaries of this role, literally raising herself above it all. In the narrative structure of the painting, however, she is ironically trapped in the voyeur's dream even as she is able to wake from her own slumber, and it is only by raising herself beyond the limits of the canvas that the woman is afforded any hope of escape, for the onlooker is forced to imagine the continuation of her body in his own space and the fantasy is thoroughly punctured.

As Christov-Bakargiev continued, "Wesley grew up desiring women, as some men do. With his delicate sensibility and profound humanity, he has found a way to portray this desire in such a way that he could question his own (male, authoritarian) gaze."[3] Ultimately, this is the role of *December 5*: to celebrate and capture his fantasy nude while simultaneously providing her with an escape from his gaze and, just as importantly, acknowledging the unending sexual power to control him. This cyclical power dynamic has necessitated Wesley to paint his pastel fantasies endlessly throughout his career.

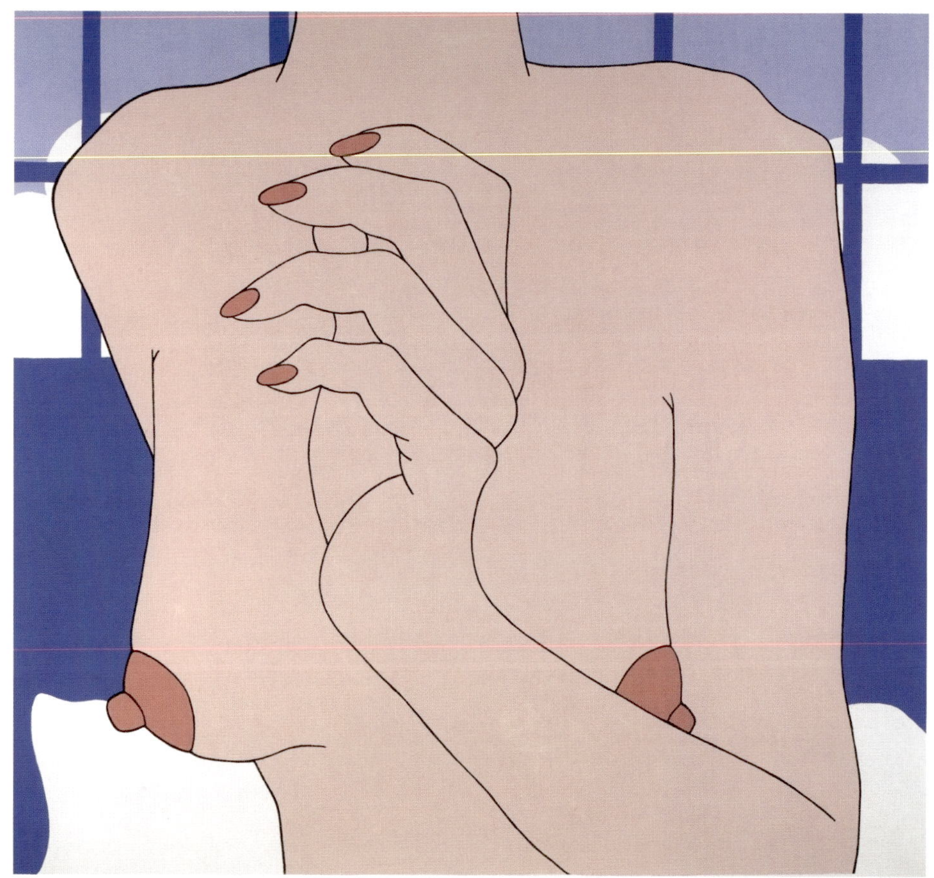

December 5 1998
Acrylic on canvas, 46″ x 50″

[1] Harvard University Art Museum, "Pictoral Strategies."
[2] Christov-Bakargiev, "John Wesley's *Capricci*," 30.
[3] Ibid., 30.

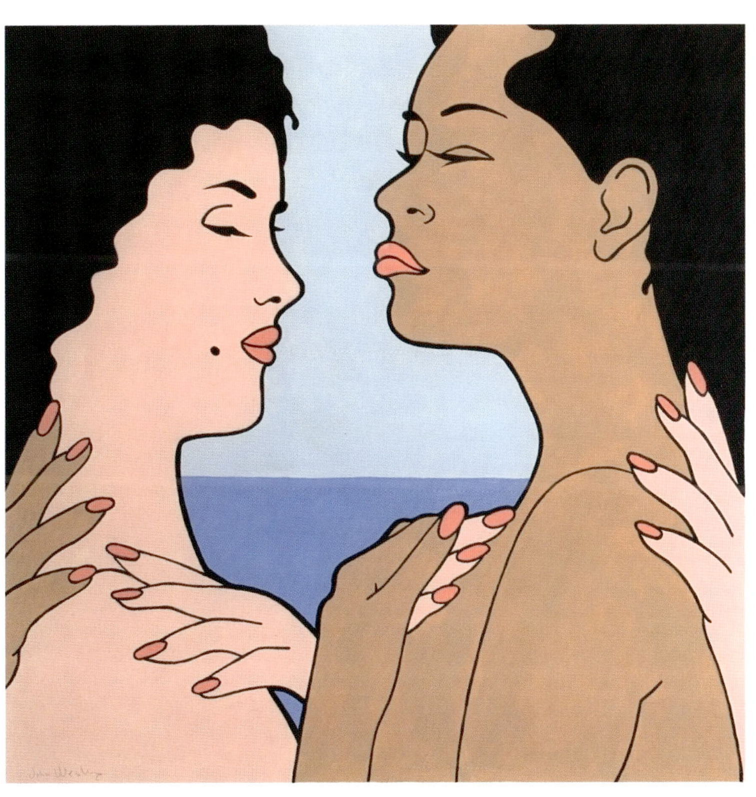

Untitled (Two Girls with Hands) 2004
Acrylic on paper, 22 1/2″ x 22 1/2″

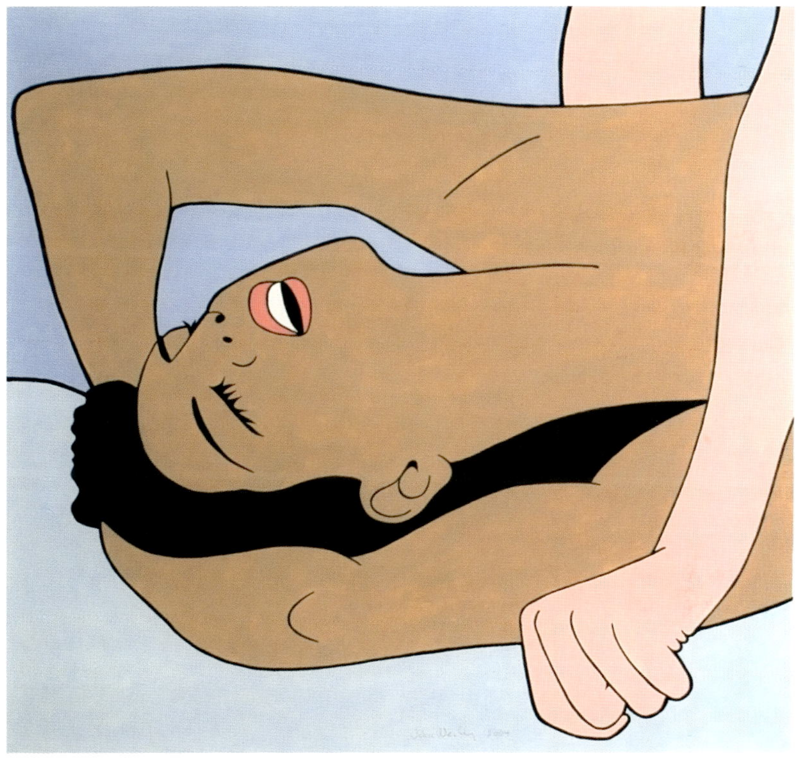

Untitled (Brown Woman with Mouth Open) 2004
Acrylic on paper, 22 1/2″ x 24″

Robert Graham 1938-

Be it the *Olympic Gateway* at the 1984 Los Angeles games, the Duke Ellington Memorial in Harlem, or the Franklin Delano Roosevelt Memorial in Washington D.C., sculptor Robert Graham is best known for his controversial works of art let loose in the public sphere. After experimenting with encased miniature worlds of wax erotica in the 1960s, Graham increased the scale of his art and opened it to larger audiences in the 1970s. In the transition, as Joseph Giovannini wrote for the *New York Times*, "He switched mediums, and sensibilities, creating with a clinician's eye anatomically perfect, genitally detailed female bronze figures...[with] proud, independent body postures."[1] Although the nonverbal power of his expressionless figures was praised by many critics, the public deemed such defiant and brazen nudity inappropriate for Graham's chosen subject matter, such as honoring artistic and political leaders or greeting international spectators.[2]

Removed from the context of their overpowering environments, however, Graham's figures tend to reveal a more personal, subdued "ascetic distance" that belies the public outcry he has received.[3] In a series of sculptural portraits depicting the model Stephanie, for example, Graham presented a stoic, poised individual, unaffected by her nudity or representational condition. The result, as Agustín Arteaga wrote in an exhibition catalog, "is a relic which maintains the essence of the model's personality, from which the artist has sequestered that reflexive, contained attitude, with a particular sense of greatness and calmness."[4] Graham himself commented on the intensely individualistic nature of his three-dimensional portraiture in 1982 saying, "The only way I can make them is as effigies of a particular person."[5]

Yet over time, his art has grown to be considerably more fragmentary and less holistic, prompting critics to proclaim that Graham "wants us to remember that these are sculptures, not people."[6] In the Collection's *Stephanie Fragment*, for example, industrial bronze-work replaces the lower half of the model's torso, mimicking her spine and intestine with stiff, austere metal. She is completed, but not naturally. In other works, the fragmentation of the body is brought to the hyperbolic extreme without mechanical replacement of parts, as in the Joe Lewis Memorial, where an enormous severed fist is made to represent the entire man. The rationale Graham created in this process was that a sculpture need not look like Rodin's—or even John De Andrea's or Duane Hansen's—to realistically capture the potential dignity and strength of the human experience. Instead, it need only suggest the potency of a body or the proud character of a countenance in order to stand for the vitality and dignity of mankind. In the wake of this effort, Graham often became "an archeologist of his own production," digging through the fragments of his creations for appropriate representations of his lofty ideals.[7]

[1] Giovannini, "Acts of Devotion," 39, c. 1.
[2] Sánchez, "Robert Graham, the Nude," 37.
[3] Arteaga, "Robert Graham, Sculptor," 23.
[4] Ibid., 26.
[5] Quoted in Gluek, "Art People; A French Invasion," C.
[6] Taplin, "Robert Graham at Gagosian," 111.
[7] Arteaga, "Robert Graham, Sculptor," 27.

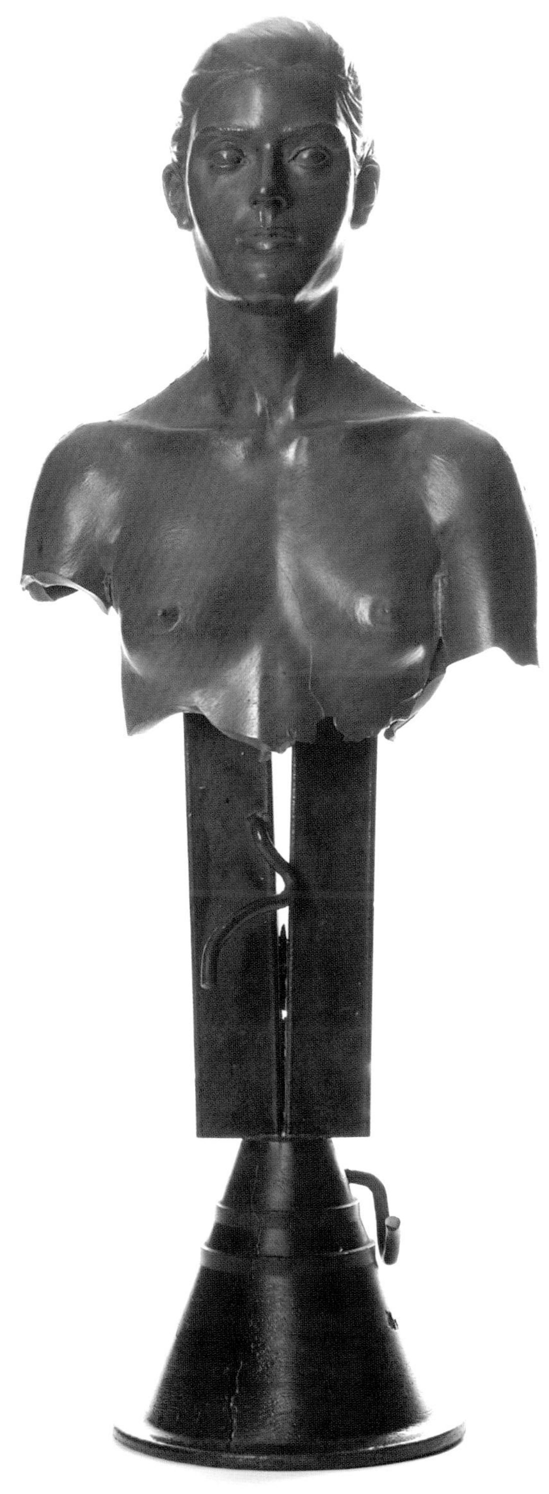

Stephanie Fragment 1981
Bronze, unique casting, 23″ x 6″ x 8 3/4″

Hilary Harkness 1971-

"I see all the male artists, or at least all the dead ones, having so much fun painting the female form," Hilary Harkness once said. "I wanted to claim some of that for myself."[1]

Though her Lilliputian societies, constructed in miniature on a comic strip grid, encourage us not to take them too seriously, it is difficult to dismiss Harkness's work as pure visual entertainment. Instead, one is drawn to the detailed conflation of the commonplace and the bizarre sex, violence, domesticity, and militarism that make up Harkness's paintings, and we are left to wonder what sort of broad statements the artist actively manipulates.[2]

It is not easy to pin down: given a voyeuristic cross section of several interior spaces, we are privy to naked and scantily clad women—French maids with blonde hair and voluptuous bodies sewing, cleaning, bathing, massaging, and pleasuring each other and themselves. In this light, they seem to stand as symbols of sexual fantasy, or as toys engaged in activities that compete for attention by projecting a prevailing imagination. Yet when recast as heirs of a Hieronymos Bosch riot and sin, these women become figures at war with the existing male-dominated order. In either interpretation, Harkness refused to criticize or endorse: her figurines are autonomous and busy, but somewhat devoid of personality and too easily multiplied. They should neither be honored, nor destroyed.

Accordingly, the twisted dollhouse of Harkness's *Air Raid* becomes a world of magical realism that one is neither eager to embrace nor apt to reject. It is seductive because it reveals a glimpse of scenes that fulfill our wildest expectations, but equally off-putting through its melting pot of lesbian utopia, brothel, and a military headquarters.[3]

Still, Harkness seemed to anticipate such a reaction, toning down some of the more overt scenarios with others that are bent more toward their comic origins: one maid vacuums the rooftop amidst incinerating bombs, while another rocks a baby—perhaps the product of an immaculate conception—to sleep. Similarly, Harkness allows her scale and perspective to remain slightly imperfect, creating a safety zone by breaking the presented universe from reality.

Though these measures do tend to undercut the message of Harkness's work, they also create some of the tensions and frictions that make the work so poignant and irresolvable in the first place.

[1] Quoted in Wakefield, "Hilary Harkness," 30.
[2] Amy, "Hilary Harkness at Bill Maynes," 151.
[3] Johnson, "Bill Maynes: Hilary Harkness," 31, c. 4.

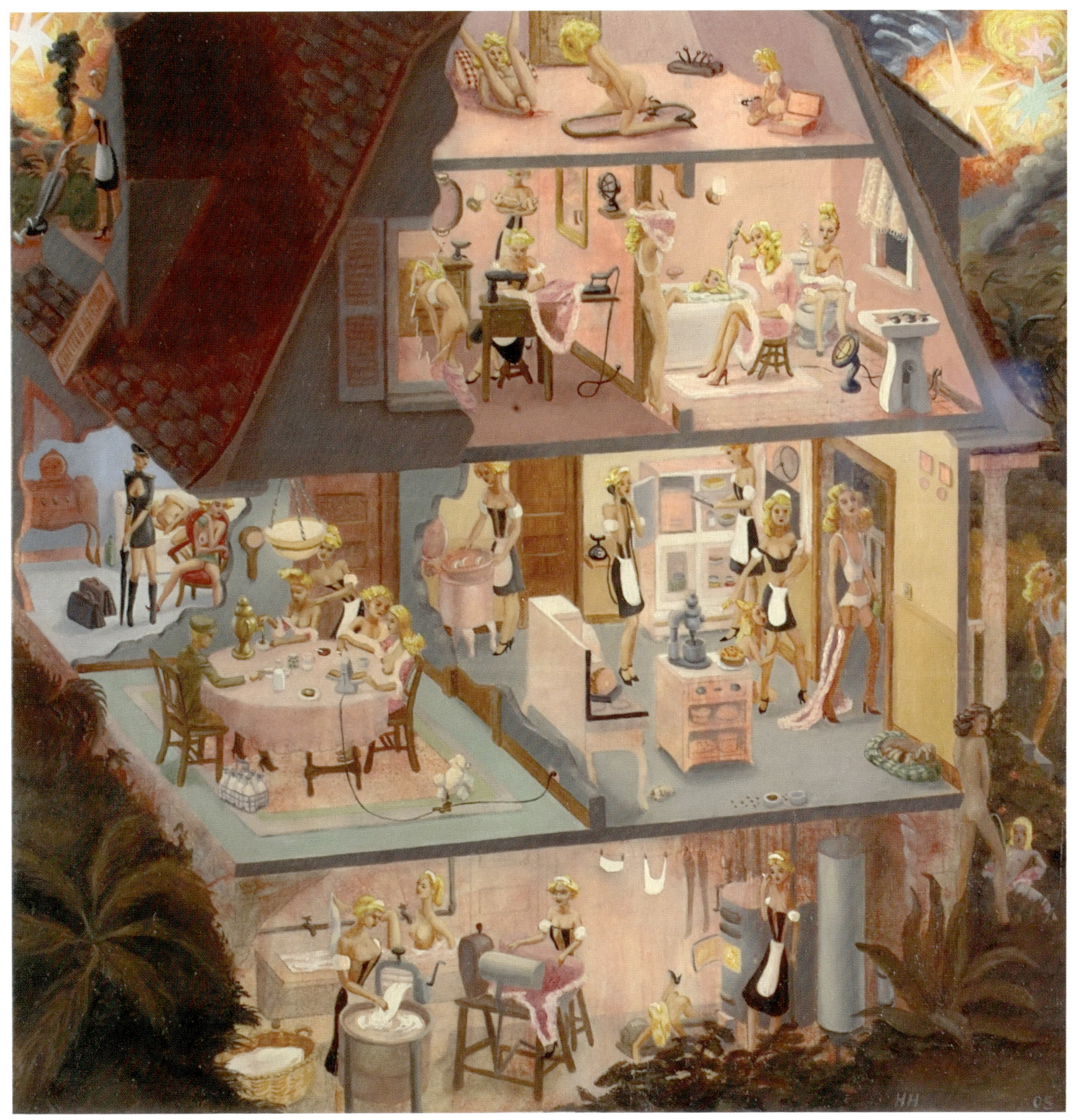

Air Raid 2005
Graphite and watercolor on paper, 10 1/2″ x 10 1/2″

Don Brown 1963-

With their sheen alabaster surfaces, Don Brown's sculptures seem intent to reflect modern Western society's current ideals of youth and beauty, functioning in much the same way as the famed kouroi nudes of ancient Greece.[1] Indeed, most critics, like Ken Johnson of the *New York Times*, have received Brown's figures optimistically as "sexy, finely made, half-size sculpture...[in] underwear and platform shoes."[2] Others, however, are quick to reject Brown's proposed notions of beauty, characterizing the orphan-like, prepubescent qualities of his statues as unsettling, if not pedophilac. As Sarah Valdez described, "The young women, by fiat of the artist, engage in a Lolita-esque game of dress-up, milking the hapless power of their innocent, underaged sexuality. Through variations in hairstyles and visages, all of Brown's subjects have the same coltish physique. Long, bony legs, flat stomachs, tiny breasts, and flat buttocks are of a much-coveted body type that is physically powerless, yet also aristocratic and expensive."[3]

That Brown's work elicits such a reaction seems to validate his effort to dislocate modern beauty criteria from their familiar posts in airbrushed, high-glossy photo spreads: once recast in classical materials, the same adolescent figures begin to issue societal caveats rather than induce mindless envy.

In many pieces from his *Yoko* series, however, which feature the artist's wife as his model, Brown also sought to endow his beacons of beauty with a dignity that challenges the shallow modern ideals they might otherwise propagate. In *Yoko VII*, his model is once again dressed in high heels and provocatively slipping underwear, firmly entrenching Yoko in connotations of fetishism and Lolita formation, despite her relationship to the artist. Indeed her physique is unapologetically culled from Brown's aesthetic mold, but unlike in other works, *Yoko VII* does not appear entirely complicit in her presentation; with downcast eyes and a demurely turned hip, she displays a fragility that belies her presentation as a modern kouros. Sadie Coles HQ frames Brown's *Yoko* similarly in its gallery notes: "The natural way in which Brown allows the body to seek and offer support, from furniture, from another person, from itself, contrasts with the conventions of classical sculpture, where celebration of physical prowess called for the figures to stand strong."[4] In this way, Brown succeeded at calling attention to modern beauty standards for the body without sacrificing the reserved humanity he saw underlying such explicit sexuality.

[1] Valdez, "Don Brown," 45.
[2] Johnson, "West Side: The Armory Show," 33, c. 1.
[3] Valdez, "Don Brown," 45.
[4] Sadie Coles HQ, "Don Brown."

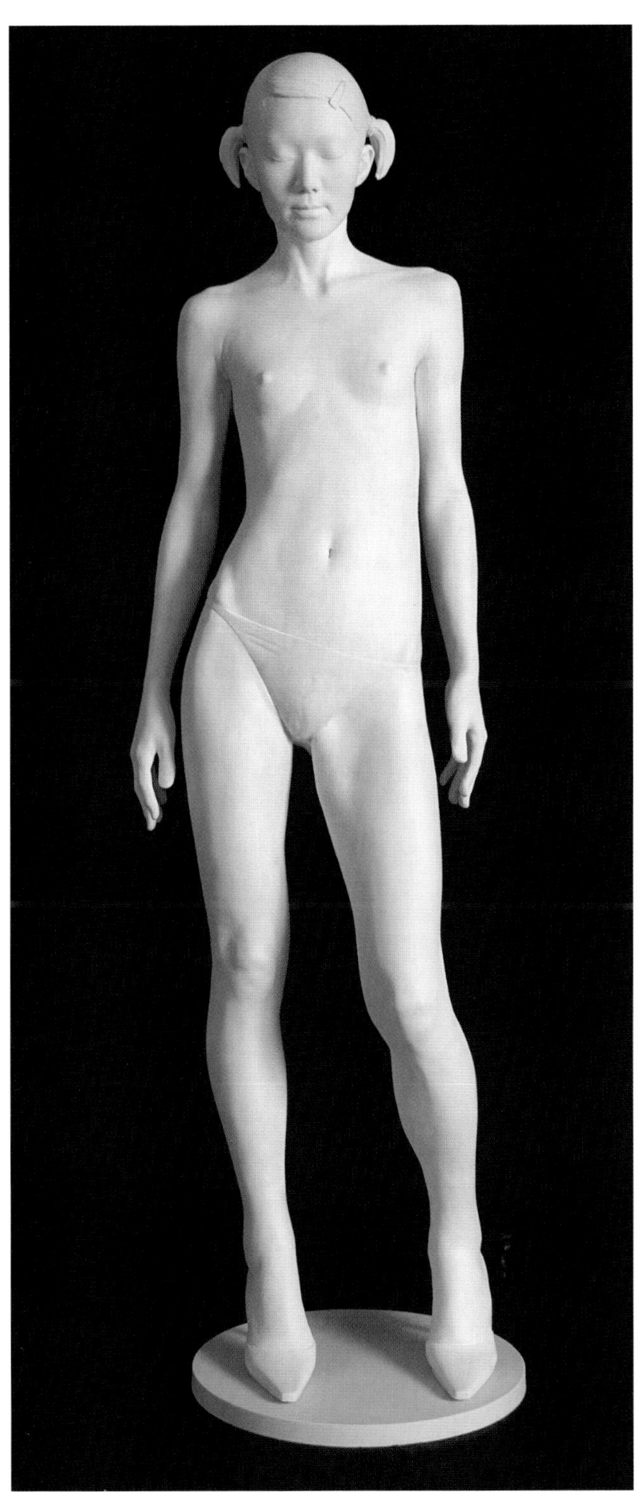

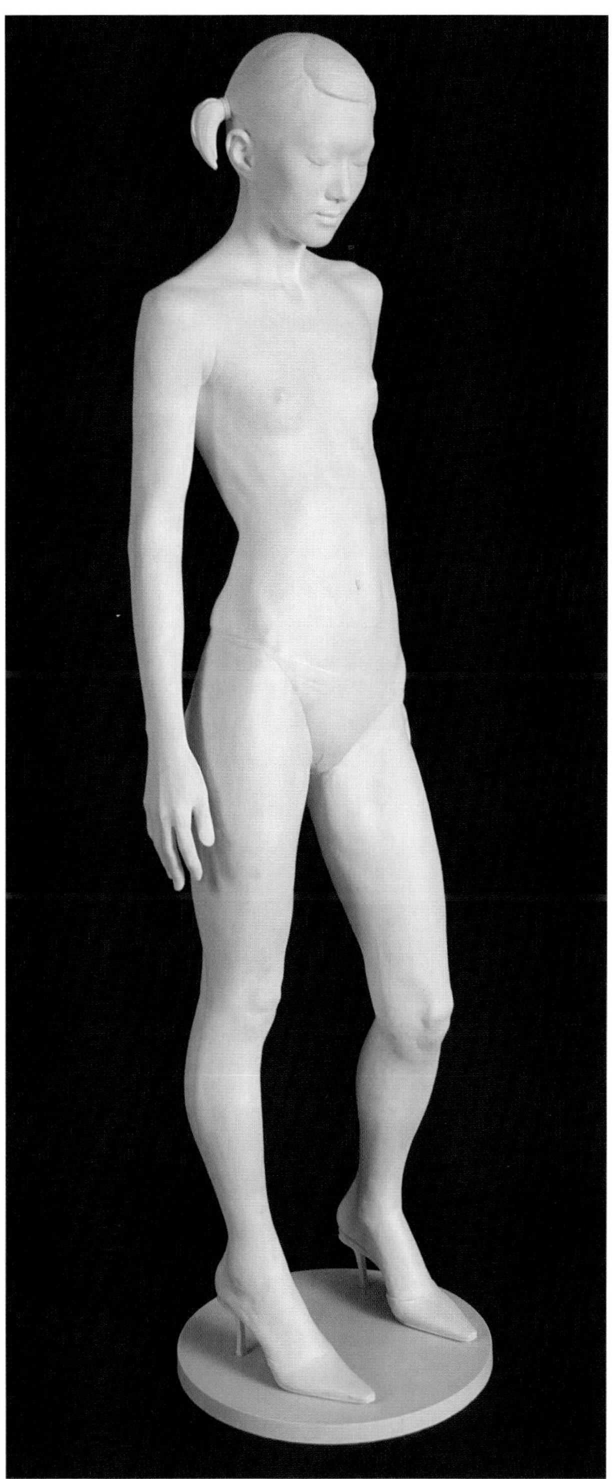

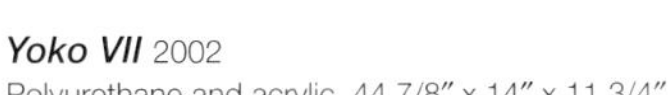

Yoko VII 2002
Polyurethane and acrylic, 44 7/8″ x 14″ x 11 3/4″

Marcus Harvey 1963-

Marcus Harvey first captured international attention for his provocative depiction of the Moors child-murderer, Myra Hindley, which was featured at the 1997 *Sensation* exhibit at the Royal Academy in London. His reproduction of the popular media photograph of the killer, *Myra* (1997) garnered unprecedented protest, owing as much to its content as to its medium of children's handprints. Eager to reproduce his success, Harvey sought out other confrontational subjects only to then obscure their content in pictorially challenging and unusual ways. In his *Readers Wives* series, for example, Harvey applied thick layers of impasto oil paint onto a black canvas mapped with masking tape, which preserved just enough of the original canvas to outline close-ups of pornographic scenes.

In *Soldier and Girl*, Harvey again adapted this formula, merging it with his Door Paintings series (2002) in order to develop a voyeuristic tone for his usual semi-lewd material. As a result, the viewer has no choice but to peer through the rippled glass at a couple in a state of undress, seeming to portray the aftermath of a brief encounter, complete with appropriately vague details. Of course, the rippled glass is nothing more than another of Harvey's painterly veils, applied to the canvas with thousands of small riffs of paint in order to delay the underlying subversive content.

Like so many of Harvey's other works, the central theme of *Soldier and Girl* captures a sense of the elemental—food, sleep, shelter, human contact, and sex—and in this way serves as an allegory for the necessities of life as the painter sees them. Along the way, art itself is subtly entered into his prescription, not only as an additional necessity itself, but as a method for taming and containing its counterparts. The resulting "found" scene presupposes a snapshot aesthetic if only to preserve Harvey's notion that such an encounter is an essential component of life and, as such, could take place in countless variations simultaneously across the world. His aim, as it was in *Myra*, was simply to codify this abstraction into an actual event, to "restore physical recollection" to an image and to provide it with "textural reality."[1] In the process, Harvey continually engages the viewer with a sensuous, pictorial friction that is far more dynamic than its derivative photograph.

[1] Delgado, "Outrage at 'Children's' Portrait," Quoted in Young British Art, 265.

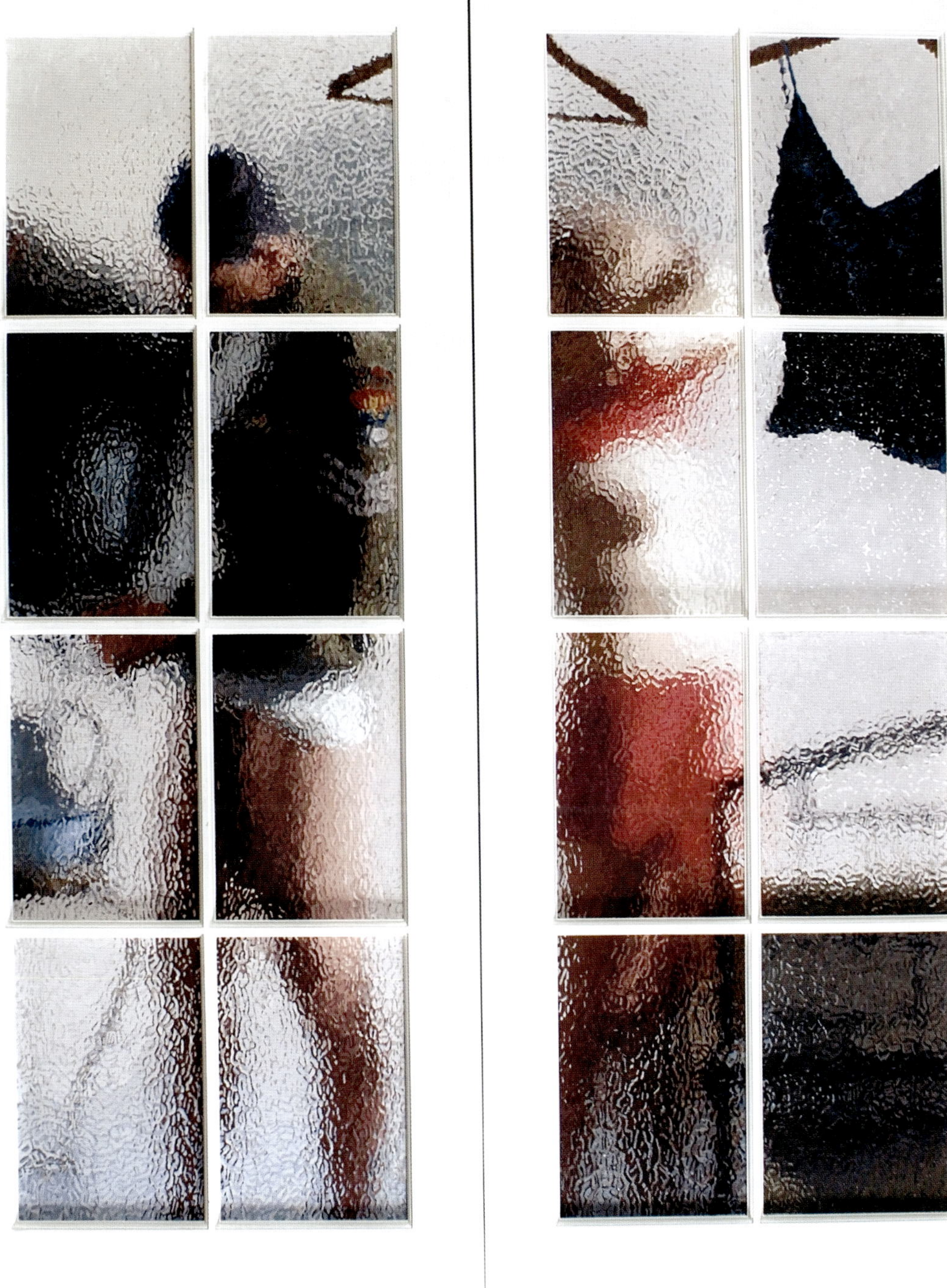

Soldier and Girl 2002
Oil and eggshell on two panels, 96″ x 72″

Neil Jenney 1945-

When Neil Jenney's work was exhibited at the New Museum in 1978, it was included in Marcia Tucker's show entitled *"Bad" Painting*, a figurative reference to his defiance of classical tenets of "good" painting. Jenney, who described his work as "good drawing/bad painting," reveled in the opportunity to publicly separate himself from both the emerging Photorealists and their dependence on the principle of good draftsmanship. The fissure was to be as wide as his brushstroke.

Wet and Drying is a product of these *Bad Years*, 1969–1970. Its pairing of image and title establishes a conditional paradox typical of the series, and its troping of an otherwise hidden cause-and-effect deviates from the litany of predigested images common to Photorealism.[1] The work also serves as a rare insight into the personality of a SoHo recluse like Jenney, by tackling the self-referential realm of painting as its subject. Departing from the human and social values that populate other *Bad Years* works, and, from the fertile political ground of works like *Us and Them*, which depicts two fighter planes in combat bearing U.S. and Russian insignias, *Wet and Drying* instead comments on the parallel that exists between Jenney's lofty themes and the cyclical process through which he enters them.

Jenney's representational painting owes much of its public success to his effortless merger of paint, image, text, frame, and concept, each of which enjoy equal attention in the series.[2] The effect is such that the viewer is caught balancing every element between the aesthetic of its surface and the depth of its content.

A great deal of Jenney's content hinges on his deadpan word games and verbal fragmentation, such as in *Fish and Pole*, where the pole has irreparably broken in half, thereby separating the two ends of the contest and dissolving the usefulness and coherency of the original fishing pole into its parts. Jenney permanently affixes this layer of meaning to his works by constructing his own frames, which are always painted black with bold white stenciled writing, and it has been said that "no one has ever used frames more effectively than Jenney."[3] *In Wet and Drying*, Jenney converted the simple observation on the quality of paint to a reflexive and analogical statement about the always-evolving role of art and its many movements within society.

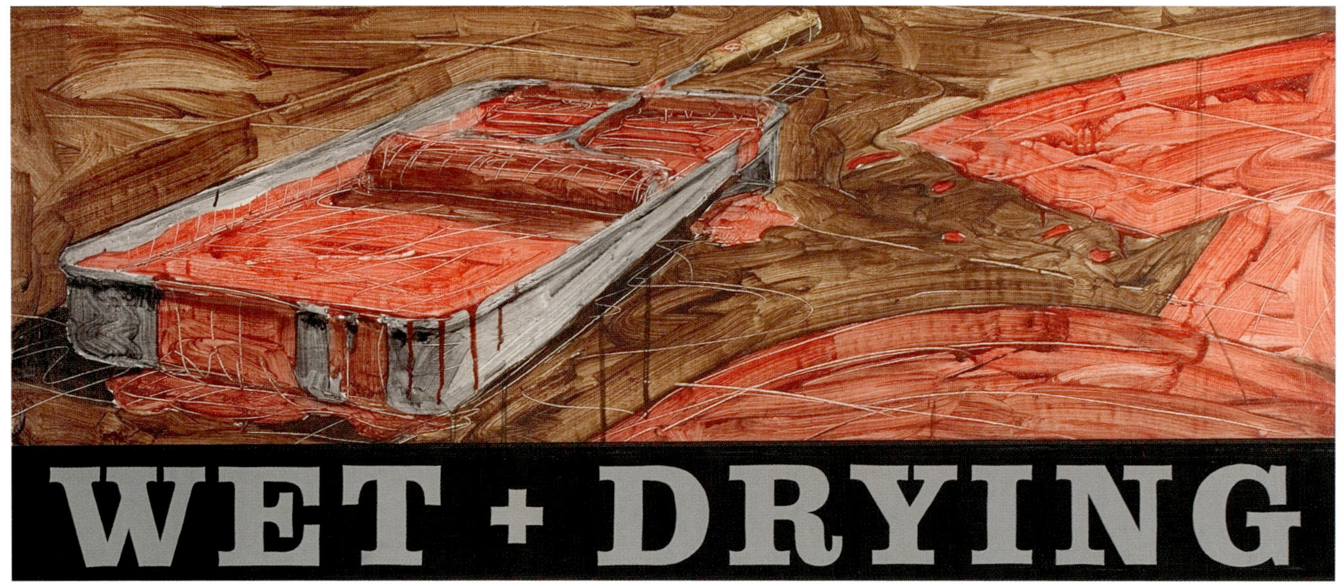

Wet and Drying 1969-70
Acrylic on canvas, 35 1/4" x 74 1/4"

[1] Gardner, *Neil Jenney*, 11.
[2] Smith, "When He Was Bad," 36.
[3] Raynor, "Exhibition of Neil Jenney," C.

Kent Bellows 1949-

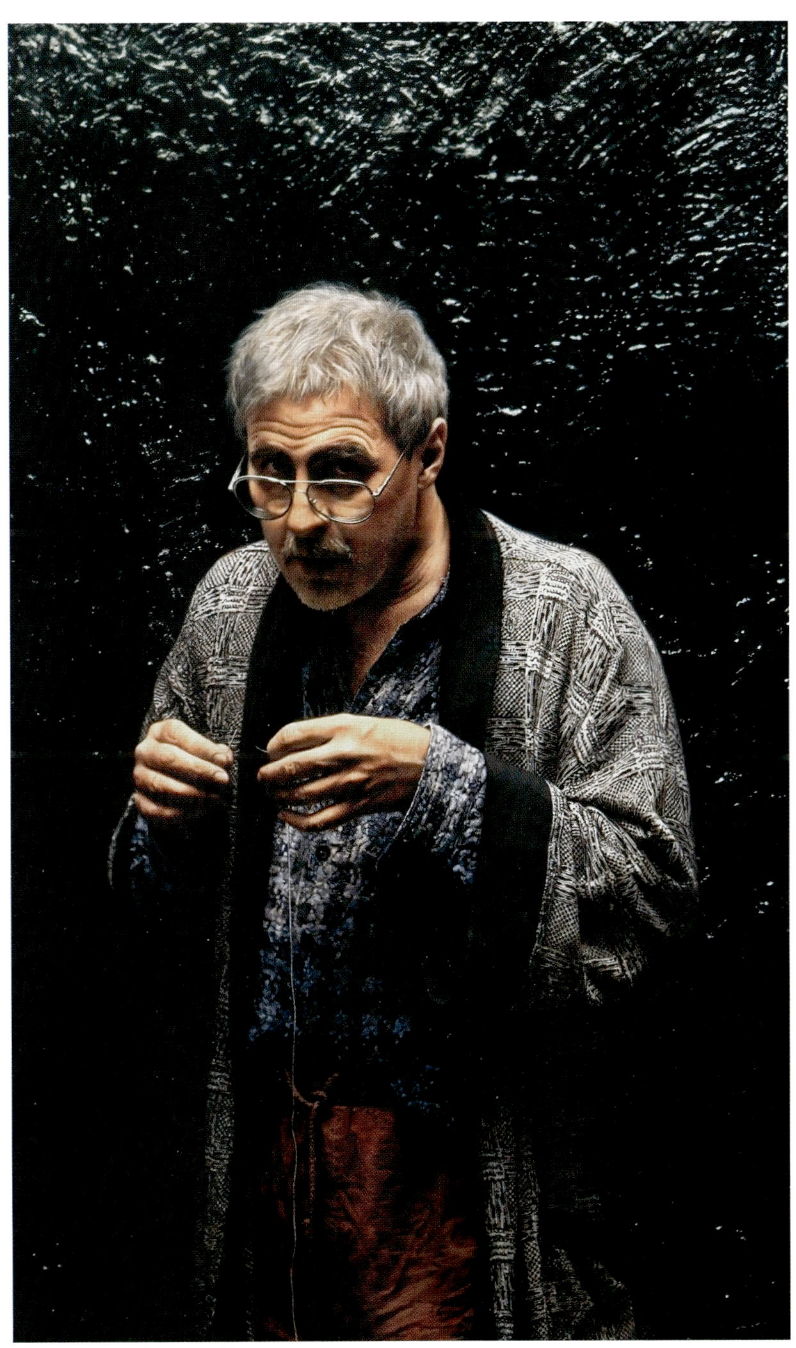

Self-Portrait (Threading a Needle) 1999
Oil on wood panel, 27 1/4″ x 17″

Ron Kleeman 1937-

Ron Kleemann first garnered critical attention as a Photorealist in the 1970s when his close-ups of race cars began to question the vanity implicit in the worship of such objects. As Kleemann once wrote, "We reflect our personalities by the objects we surround ourselves with—a narcissistic reflection of our own importance in accordance with our individual choices...It isn't the reflective quality of chrome as a painting problem that interests me—it's the evidence that people need a certain amount of 'chrome' in their lives, in a figurative sense, in order to see themselves. Perhaps to remind them that they do, in fact, exist."[1]

In 1987, Kleemann applied this approach to yet another macho, "in-your-face, up-front" vehicle: the fire engine.[2] Adopting a composition similar to his race car series, Kleemann positioned the bright-red, municipal monsters to fill the entire canvas, spilling out of the picture frame as if eager for the day's activity and speed. In works such as *(20/20)*², this masculine power motif is pushed to its logical limit, as the truck seems to take on nearly phallic connotations, protruding into the foreground at a rakish, aggressive angle.[3] But as much as a work like *(20/20)*² celebrates the social importance of such a visual icon, it is the subtle challenge offered to its overtly male vanity that seems to resonate. Through the allusion to vision in the title, which poses as an homage to the number twenty emboldened in chrome on all sides of the truck, Kleemann asks his viewer to reconsider the way we look at ourselves and our personalities as contingent to the objects that surround us. As Meisel reminded, "Unlike the other Photorealists, [Kleemann] is very concerned with titles, all of which have cryptic meanings and are very much a part of his work."[4] Truly, *(20/20)*² is no exception, as the double entendre of its title drives much of the social commentary embedded at the heart of the work.

In the wake of September 11, much has been written about the appearance of Kleemann's fire engines as symbols of the "Great American Machine," and, of course, his meticulously rendered portraits of large, polished vehicles can be seen as just such a celebration.[5] However, while it was surely never Kleemann's intention to criticize the values embodied by the affected men and women (in fact, Kleemann even traded two of his serigraphs for a helmet, boots, and coat to become an honorary fireman), such a simplified reading does not take into account the full accord of all of the painting's elements, either as a unified whole or as an artifact of its time of creation.[6] For only when one considers the complex interplay of *(20/20)*²'s style, composition, content, title, and context can the true meaning of the piece ever be realized as it was initially intended.

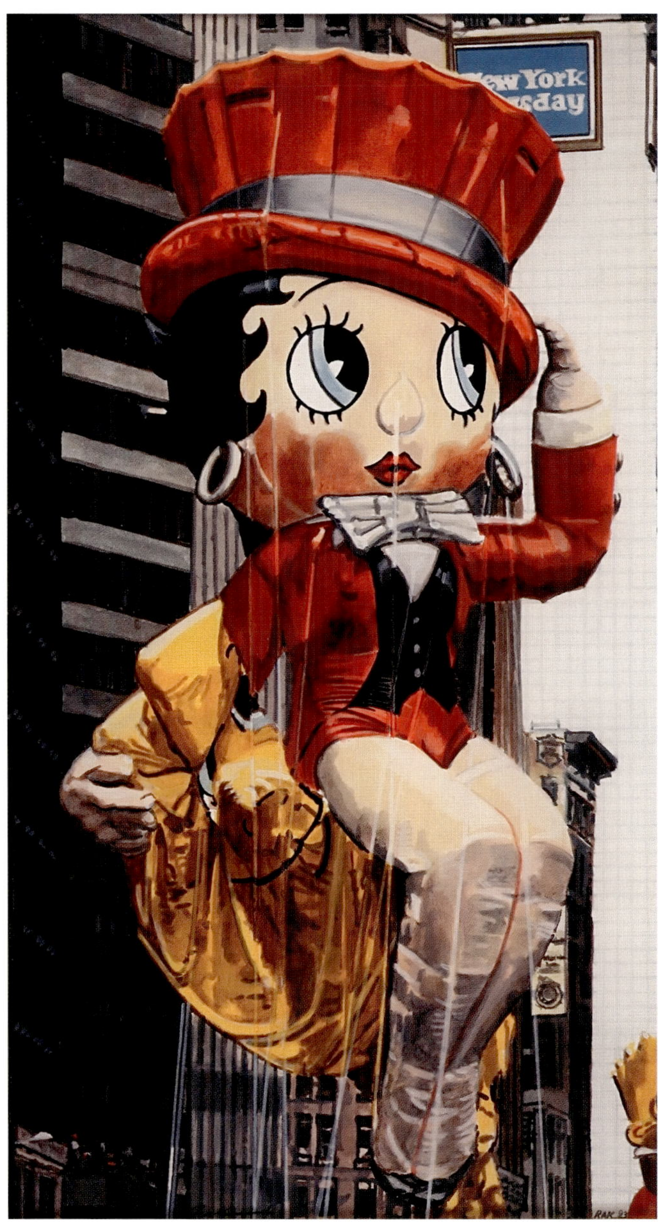

Boopsy 1993
Acrylic on board, 18″ x 10″

[1] Kleeman, "Voice of the Icon," 306.
[2] Meisel, *Photorealism at the Millenium*, 161.
[3] Meisel, *Photorealism*, 303-304.
[4] Ibid, 304-305.
[5] Meisel, *Photorealism Since 1980*, 267.
[6] Meisel, *Photorealism*, 304.

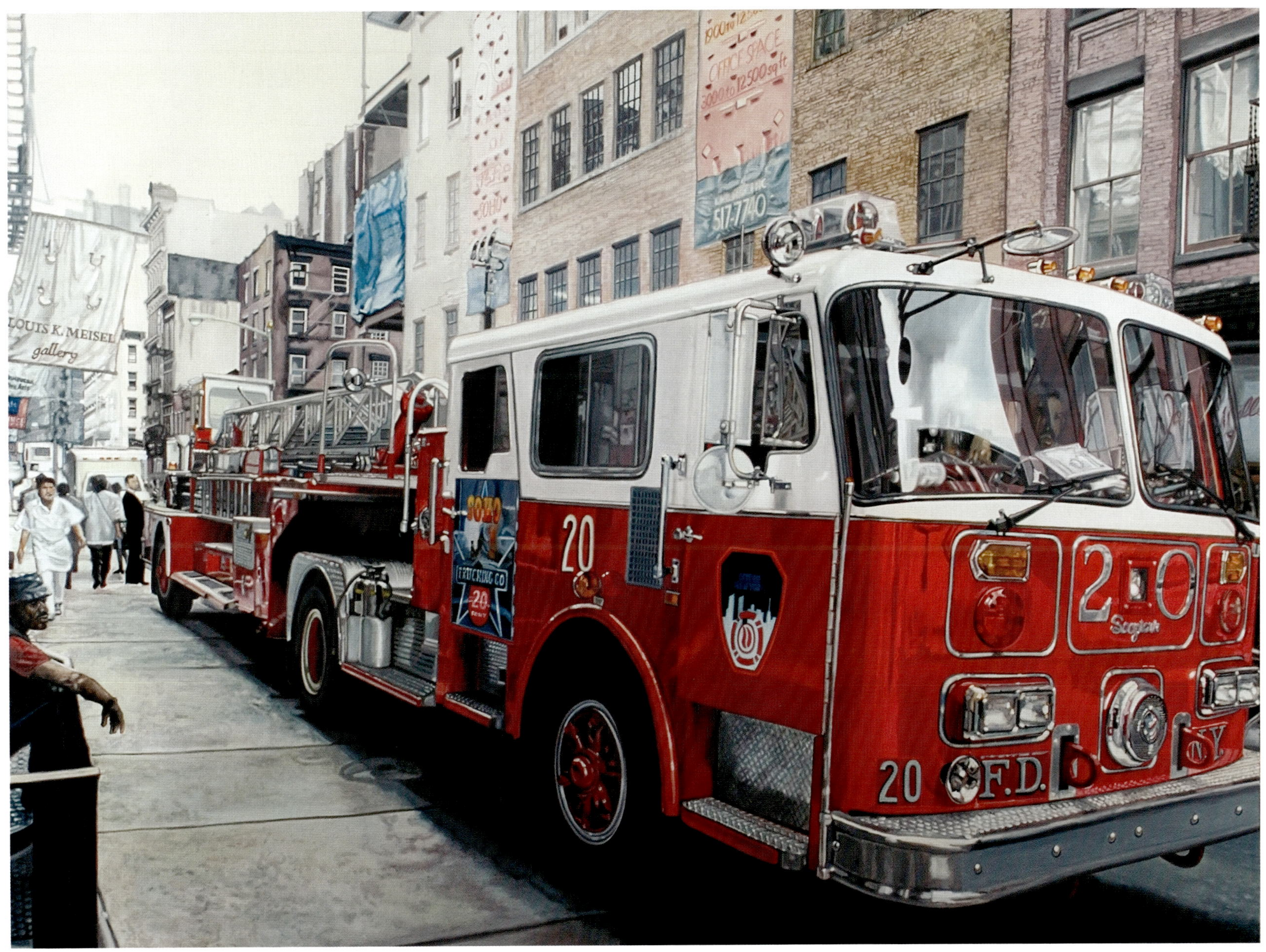

(20/20)^2 1990
Oil on linen, 44″ x 60″

Robert Rauschenberg 1925-

"You are the author,"[1] instructs the exhibition catalog for Robert Rauschenberg's *Short Stories* show at the Waddington Gallery in London in 2002. It is a declaration that represents the artist's persistent drive to find new ways of closing the perceived space between art and the world it seeks to imitate and inform. As he wrote early in his career, "Painting relates to both art and life. Neither can be made. (I try to act in that gap between the two)."[2]

In 1973, for example, Rauschenberg forced his viewers to bring their own lives and narratives into his work, providing nothing more than an artistic tabula rasa. He traveled to France to craft his own paper at the centuries-old Moulin à Papier Richard de Bas, but rather than paint his creations, Rauschenberg left the papers unadorned, molding them into simple shapes such as a flat circle or horseshoe. As Mary Lynn Kotz described, "The rich, uneven texture of the paper and the simple design [led] viewers to create their own images."[3] Rauschenberg gave this work the simple title *Pages*.

Over twenty years later, Rauschenberg revived both the title and mission of *Pages* through works such as *Page 42, Paragraph 1*, though as the name suggests, his *Short Stories* series provides the viewer with slightly more guidance. Employing photographic collages screened onto polylaminate and then painted over with rare vegetable dyes and acrylic paints, Rauschenberg supplied his audience with a series of jumbled, half-erased, and often bizarre images "that appear almost as fragments ripped from some wider text. The viewer is left to fill in the spaces in between, to make the narrative and visual connections between figures that range from power lines to pelicans to potted plants."[4]

As the title suggests, the work serves as an incomplete storyboard to an absent narrative, upon which viewers are invited to "read into it something of their own experience,"[5] or, in other words, to finally become Rauschenberg's esteemed author. Even though *Page 42, Paragraph 1* suggests that the roles of author and painter might be too closely linked for such freedom—Rauschenberg places the truncated word "Stud" above a blank portion of the canvas, inviting simultaneous interpretations such as "study" and "studio"—the incorporation of a foreign language on the storefront sign allows for multiple narratives, each equally foreign to the next.

As Robert Mattison wrote, Rauschenberg's work is often "the sign of an activist who thinks that the world can change for the better and that art can participate in, or even lead, such change."[6] Perhaps nowhere does Rauschenberg believe in this more strongly than when he invites the world to participate directly in his art—to become not only the recipients of his images, but the imprimaturs of their very meanings.

[1] Batchelor, Robert Rauschenberg: Short Stories, 1.
[2] Quoted in Kotz, Rauschenberg/Art and Life, 7.
[3] Kotz, Rauschenberg/Art and Life, 193.
[4] Campbell-Johnston, "Robert Rauschenberg: Short Stories."
[5] Kotz, Rauschenberg/Art and Life, 299.
[6] Mattison, Robert Rauschenberg: breaking boundaries, 260.

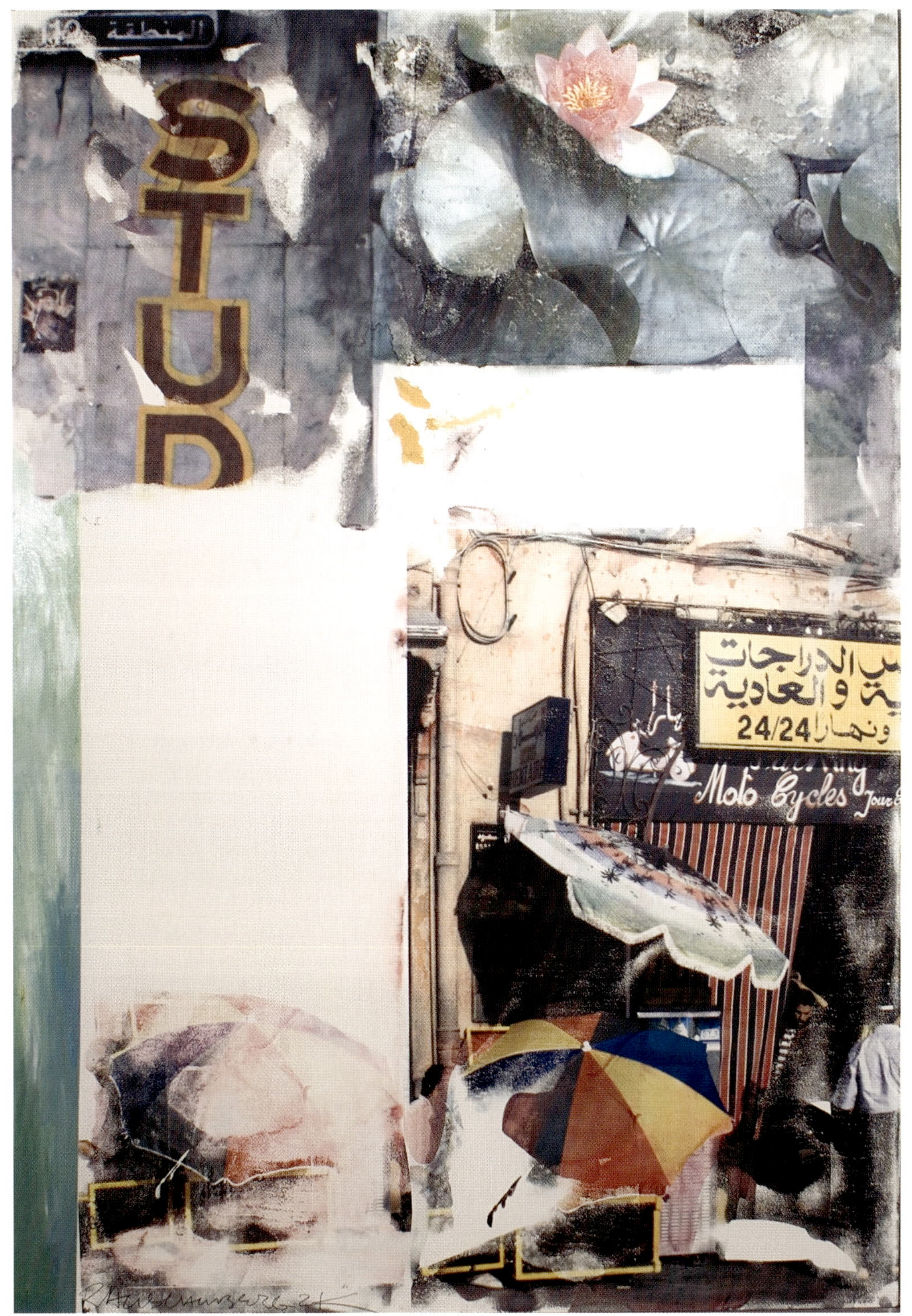

Page 42, Paragraph 1 (Short Stories) 2000
Vegetable dye transfer and acrylic on polylaminate, 85 1/2″ x 60 1/2″

Damian Loeb 1970-

The literary theorist Mikhail Bakhtin famously wrote, "How often the words 'he says,' 'people say,' 'he said' are repeated...In the everyday speech of any living person in society, no less than half (on the average) of all the words uttered by him will be someone else's words."[1] Through his work, Damian Loeb seems to suggest the same can now be said for the operation of memory, for he postures that we have come to interpret the world through an amalgam of collectively shared, previously known images. In his 2002–2003 series titled *Horror/Sci-Fi 1.1.9b2*, Loeb furthered this theory by appropriating screen stills from popular films such as Steven Spielberg's *Close Encounters of the Third Kind* and Stanley Kubrick's *The Shining* in order to challenge the way we instantly recognize certain images through a "dream-like sense of déjà vu, echo[ing] back from the giant storehouse of media mythology in haunting fragments which can never quite be placed."[2] As Carey Lovelace described it in a review for *Art in America*, "These are effective paintings [because their] seemingly unintended subtext is the degree to which 'reality' nowadays is shaped by secondhand images."[3]

I'm Getting To You...(Very Slowly) is typical of the series. It seems to derive from a "hauntingly familiar" scene in the 1980 horror film *Friday the 13th*, though such a desire to place the referent is frowned upon by Loeb, who cautions that his art is only "weakened by a dependence on external signifiers."[4] Instead, he prefers to superimpose additional fragments and details onto the scene to test the limits of recognition and demonstrate how easily our minds fuse diverse stock images in order to digest and come to grips with new experiences.

Still, Loeb's primary interest is simply to reproduce the emotional experience of film in his medium of high art. As the gallery guide for the series states, "Damian Loeb has chosen the often undervalued genres of horror and science-fiction film" because such movies anchor "the unknown and the fantastic in images that are familiar and realistic, lulling us into a false sense of security and then undercutting this with brief and shocking interludes of horror."[5] Like his chosen genre of film, Loeb's work coaxes his viewers into the scene through familiar imagery, only to undercut all expectations with the insertion of new—and often incongruous—supplementary images. Only then can Loeb truly disrupt the dominant mechanism of collective consciousness by forcing the viewer to access his or her own personal memories to mend the disparate familiar images presented. For, as Bakhtin wrote, "within the arena of almost every utterance an intense interaction and struggle between one's own and another's word is being waged."[6] In his paintings, Loeb forces a similar struggle between internal and external lenses of interpretation, challenging our unthinking reliance on shared experience alone.

[1] Bakhtin, "From *Discourse*," 530.
[2] Dannatt, "The Art of Allusion."
[3] Lovelace, "Damian Loeb," 125-126.
[4] Quoted in Dannatt.
[5] "Damian Loeb: Horror/Sci-Fi," 11.
[6] Bakhtin, "From *Discourse*," 539.

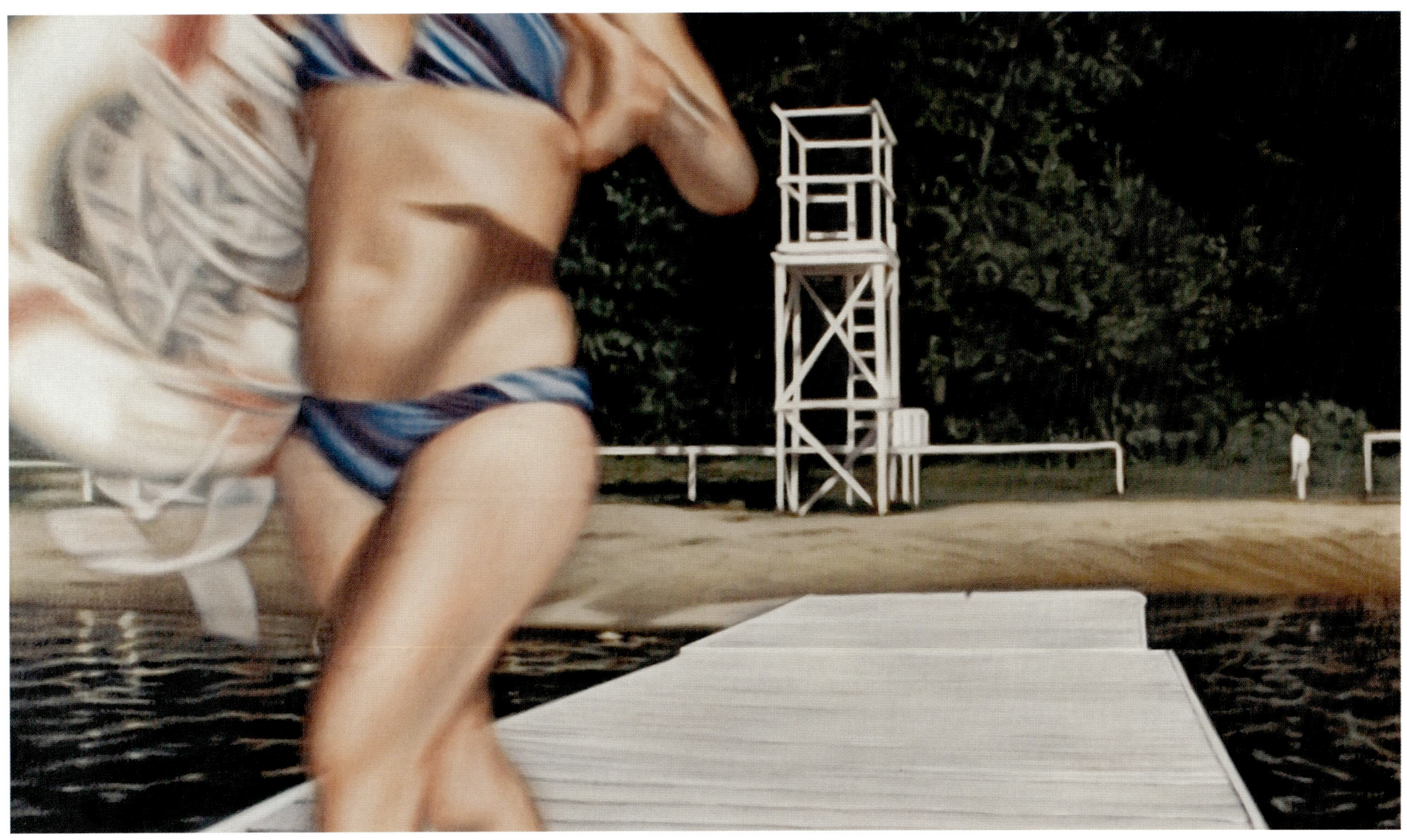

I'm Getting To You... (Very Slowly) 2002
Oil on linen, 42″ x 72″

Alan Magee 1947-

As the critic Richard West once wrote, the beauty of Alan Magee's work is that "while the eye is being *trompe*'d, the mind is being trumped."[1]

Magee's realist work has consistently functioned in this manner, preserving a simple visual truth that bleeds seamlessly into a multifaceted narrative. Always deliberate in his use of fictional threads, Magee likens his compositional strategy to Franz Kafka's literary approach, specifically his delicate propelling of descriptivist realism into more magical realms—a process Kafka termed "going over."[2] Magee explained the parallel in an interview with the writer Barry Lopez: "In working with realist painting...I hope to bring observation to the point where it can go over, where somebody looking at that drawn version of a real thing feels that the drawing has invited them into another realm, and I don't know a better way of doing that than passing thoroughly through the solid ground of real experience."[3]

Magee's approach in *Braid* is no different. Taking his wife, Monika, as his model, Magee transforms her simple profile into a moment of "illusionistic serenity," employing the commonplace braid as a point of entry for a contemplative experience.[4] As with his use of other everyday items—drills, wrenches, and motor parts—Magee's objects involve the viewer with their tangible familiarity, inviting a further exploration of one's own personal associations, be they daily preoccupations, future agitations, or even secret passions.[5] Of course, Magee does not unleash such a personal bombshell on his viewer without any guidance: his selectively colored braid asserts and reveals itself slowly, unhurriedly becoming part of a greater whole and shedding its everyday banality piece by piece. In this way, Magee encourages his viewer to ease into the process of going over. For Magee, such a visual unfolding actually simplifies life, revealing each day to be nothing more than an encounter with successive utilitarian objects as familiar as a braid—objects that we typically recognize for their functionality and not their beauty. But Magee's realistic representation invites a retreat from such an existence, a moment for the mind to wander along the strands of the braid and to appreciate the beauty of its everyday life.

Nevertheless, it also seems as though the braid might just as easily fade as reveal itself, thereby interrupting the aroused digression with a startling sense of impermanence and loss. In this way, Magee concedes that life cannot linger in a dream state forever. Ultimately, like the viewer's eye, it must return to reality, retreating away from the magical haze of the transparent profile and back to the symbolically real beginning of the perfectly rendered braid.

[1] West, "Exact Anatomy," 15.
[2] Quoted in Lopez, Alan Magee, 23.
[3] Ibid.
[4] West, "Exact Anatomy," 15.
[5] Weiner, "Alan Magee," 18.

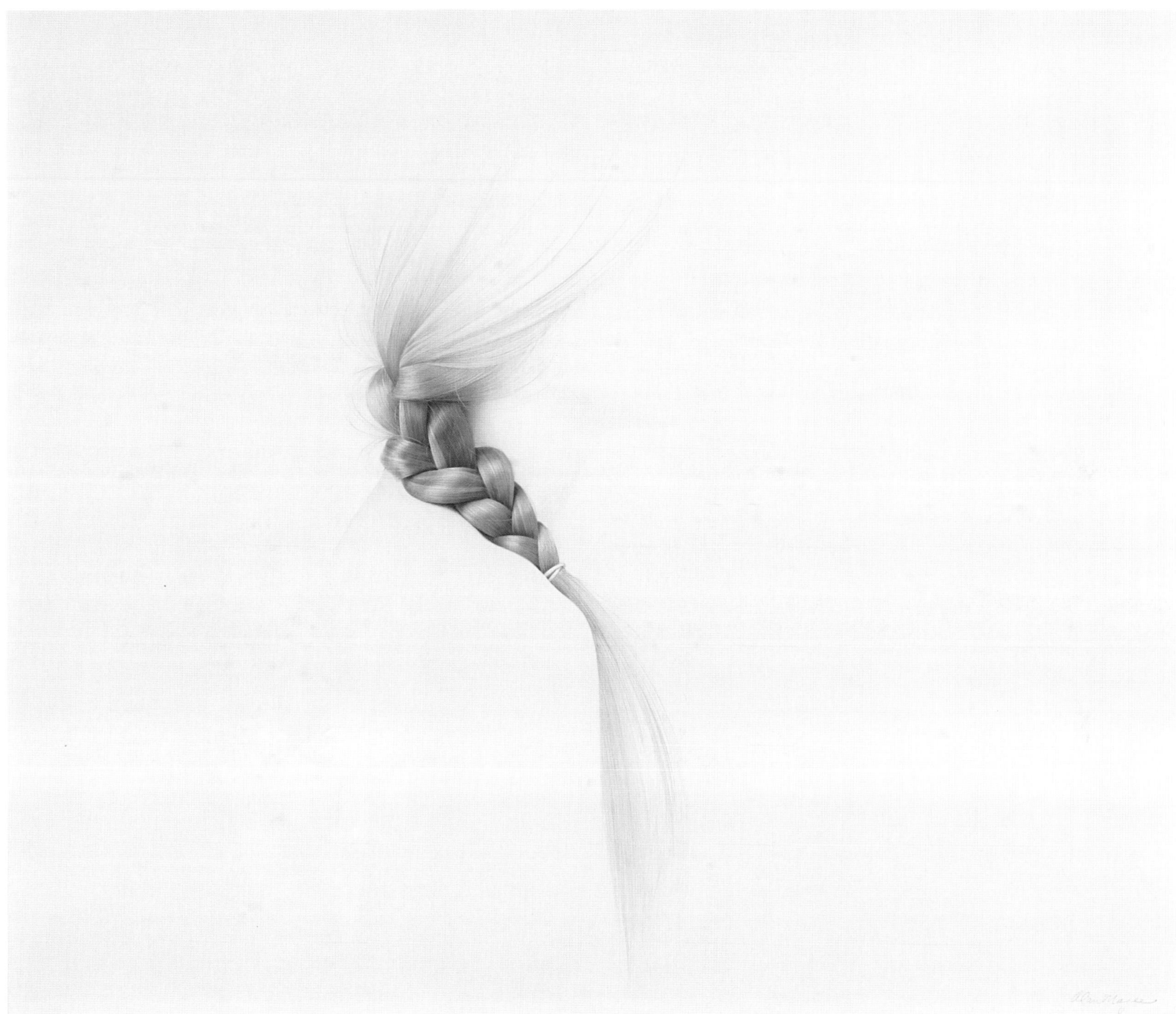

Braid 1980
Colored pencil on paper, 22 3/4″ x 29″

Philip Pearlstein 1924-

While leading a workshop at the Pratt Institute in 1959, a young Philip Pearlstein challenged his students to develop a single source photograph into a series of paintings that would mimic the whole course of art history. Although the experiment was meant to provoke resourcefulness and curiosity in his students, its lesson on the realist tableau presented a surprising hiccup to Pearlstein himself. "I had them make an abstraction that fought the picture plane," he reflected in an interview with Robert Storr, "and then asked them to translate it into a still life, a realist still life. It was a terrific problem."[1] As it turned out, the problem spawned an illustrious career for Pearlstein himself, who substituted live studio models for the photograph before launching his own perspectival assault on the resistant realist picture plane.

Working at a distance of only a few feet, Pearlstein painted from an uncomfortable proximity that resulted in such perceptual distortions as his famously elongated hands and feet. What little room survived the claustrophobia, Pearlstein then filled with household ornaments from his collection of American folk art, as well as their many shadows, created through the artist's use of multiple light sources. Pearlstein seemed to find himself a successful formula for "folding figure and background together so that they form[ed] a single impenetrable surface."[2] In turn, Pearlstein then utilized this visual complexity not only to create aesthetically stimulating geometries but also to shield his work from exploration of its possible symbolism. As Robert Storr wrote, "Pearlstein has made room for all manner of imagery that invites all kinds of speculation, but in the final analysis, these subtexts operate as bait to draw viewers into situations that stubbornly refuse to yield to interpretation but more than generously reward the eye."[3]

In a work such as *Two Nudes with Horse Weathervanes & Punch*, the potential for such metaphorical subtext is undeniable: Two naked females sit opposite one another, nearly touching but without acknowledgment of their immediacy. An equal number of inanimate horses appear mid-stride, far more capable of movement than their real-life counterparts, while a mischievous Punch doll lurks behind the support structure of the smaller horse.[4] It is an eccentric cast, staged so as to intimate some elusive dimension of meaning—symbolic or literal—but Pearlstein's denial of any conceivable narrative proclaims his intent to begin and end at a "highly abstracted still-life arrangement."[5] As Pearlstein said, "The big problem for the realist artist has to do with the choice of subject matter, and its meaning. Once I decided that the models and those objects in my paintings just added up to a kind of big still life, I felt that I had dispensed with the problem."[6] Having freed himself of such an overriding concern, Pearlstein was then able to devote his career to a problem much closer to his true interests—one that has occupied him since he first posed it to his students over forty years ago.

[1] Quoted in Storr, "Exchange with Robert Storr," 27.
[2] Smith, "Taut Paintings of Philip Pearlstein," Weekend Desk, C.
[3] Storr, introduction to *Philip Pearlstein: Since 1983*, 14.
[4] Bourdon, "Up Close and Impersonal," 94.
[5] Kino, "Philip Pearlstein at Robert Miller," 90-91.
[6] Quoted in Storr, "Exchange with Robert Storr," 29.

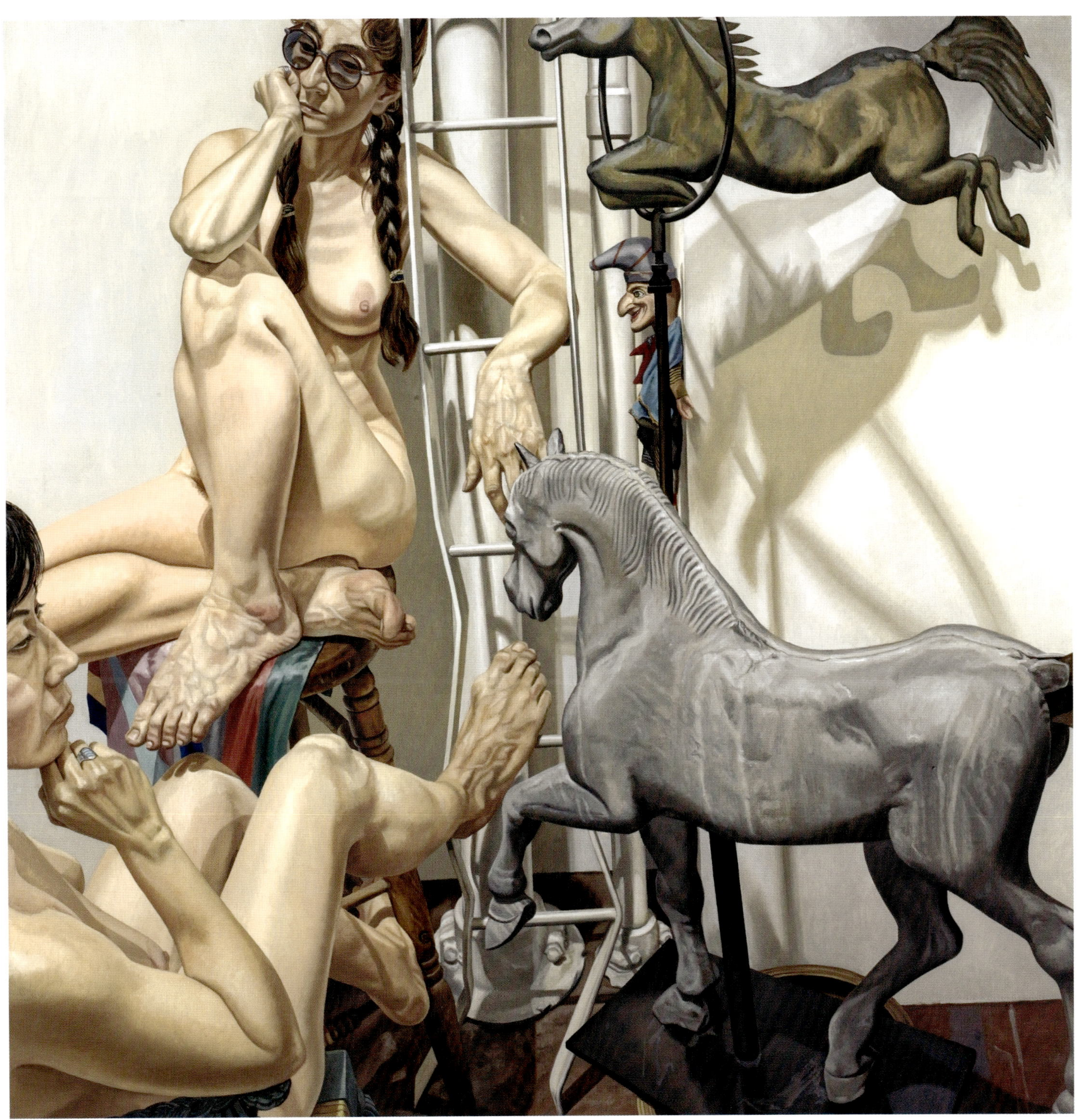

Two Nudes with Horse Weathervanes & Punch 1988
Oil on canvas, 72″ x 72″

Marilyn Minter 1948-

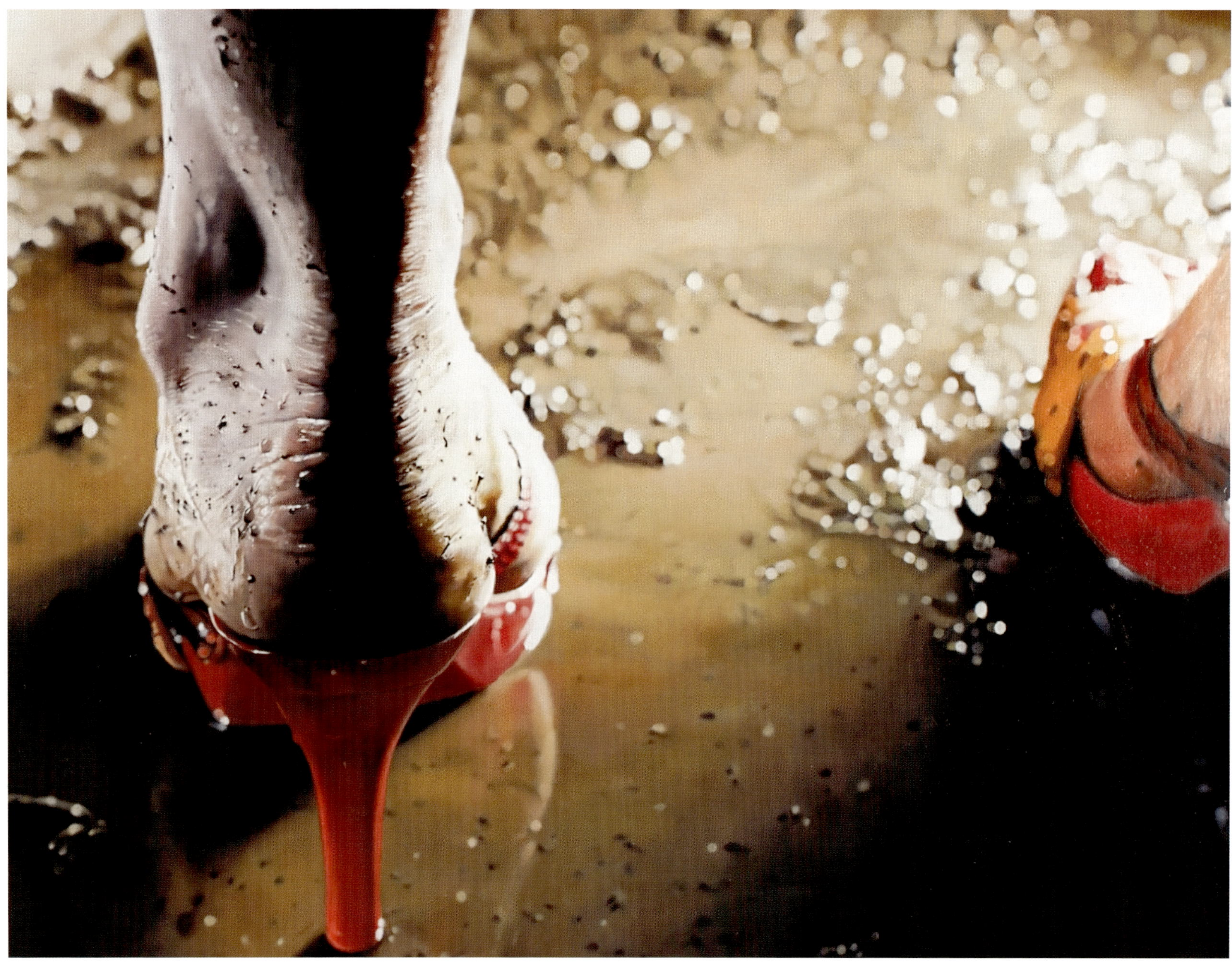

Ruby Slippers 2006
Enamel on metal, 35 7/8″ x 48″

Richard Estes 1936-

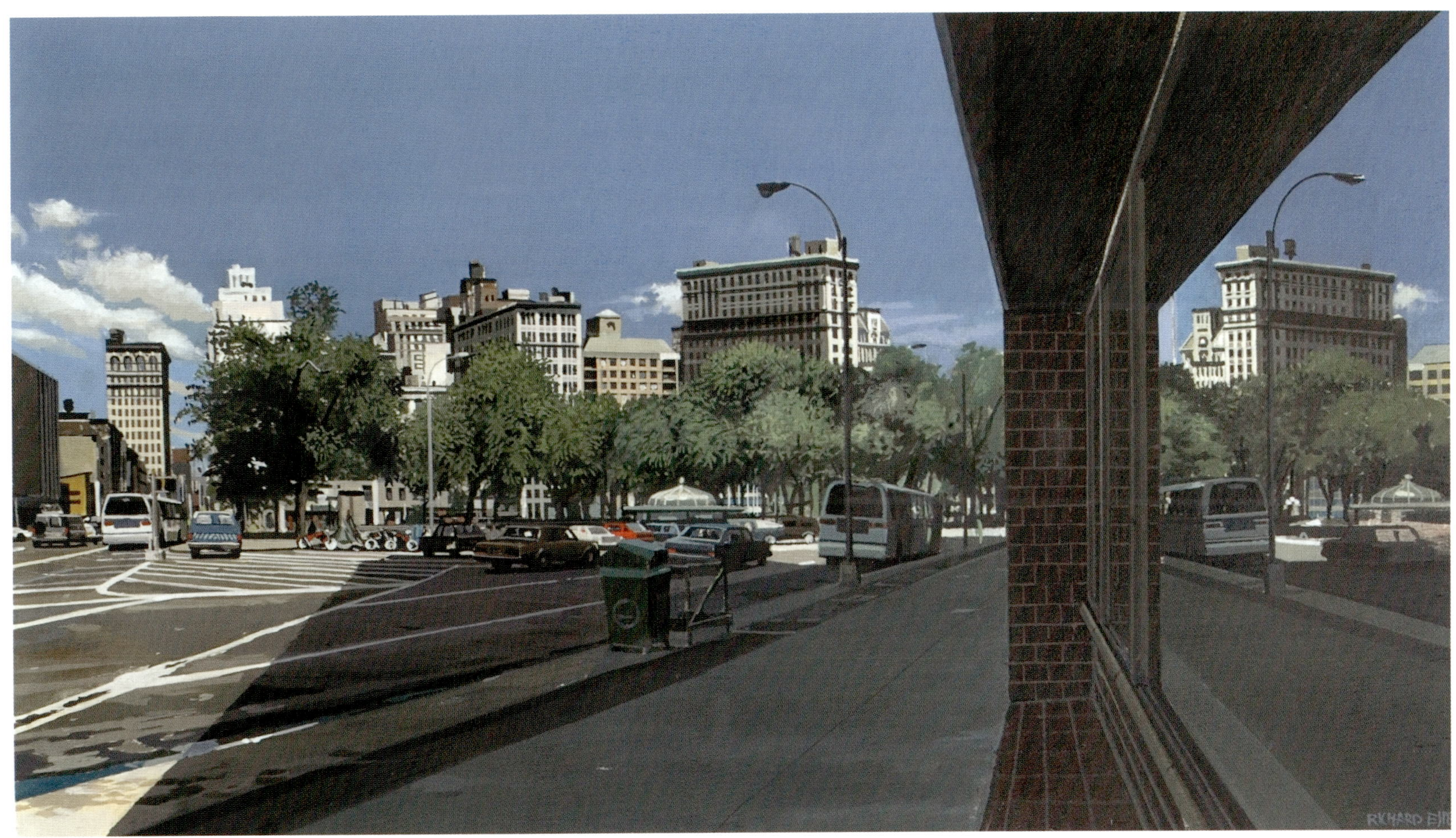

Union Square Looking Northeast 1993
Acrylic on board, 9″ x 16 1/4″

Kara Walker 1969-

> *"Clytie, not inept, anything but inept: perverse, inscrutable and paradox: free, yet incapable of freedom who had never once called herself a slave...Clytie who in the very pigmentation of her flesh represented that debacle [of slavery]...as though presiding aloof upon the new, she deliberately remained to represent to us the threatful portent of the old."*[1]

In 1936, William Faulkner sought to confront the haunting legacy of the Old South in *Absalom, Absalom!,* a novel aimed at the lingering racial stereotypes, difficult inheritance of miscegenation, and deeply ingrained attitudes of the antebellum system in latter-day America.

Nearly sixty years later, Kara Walker presents herself as a modern adaptation of Faulkner's Clytemnestra, once again seeking to represent the enduring psychological and physical threat of the Old South today. While Walker's mythological concoctions of rape, incest, cross-species sexuality, racial violence, and power struggle often seem "perverse, inscrutable and paradox," critics have argued that they are nonetheless "vivid and shocking evocations of an antebellum world, rooted in stereotypes, comment[ing] on the system of slavery and its continuing legacy in the American consciousness."[2]

While the vocabulary may be easy to recognize, the messages of Walker's deceptively simple silhouettes are often far more obscure. In *Shiny Penny*, for example, a poor white soldier is pictured life-sized, presenting both a penny and his erect phallus with equal enthusiasm as he holds his bayonet in abeyance. That such a scene ever took place is improbable and even humorous, yet inconsequential so long as Walker generates a silhouette, which, in her own words, "presents just enough detail and eliminates just enough information for me to create my own stories."[3] The viewer can only imagine the particular story: Is he enticing a slave, a farmer, or a child into performing a sexual act? Is it a trap, with the latent violence of his gun ready to strike? Or is he offering a gift, unable to hide his true intent all the while? We need not know exactly, for it is the spirit of the time—and accordingly the spirit of the likely sin—through which Walker communicates "one of her central messages...that slavery visited degradation equally on all concerned and that its tragic legacy poisons life for all Americans."[4]

Though the poor white soldier of *Shiny Penny* was certainly not a driving force behind slavery, his seemingly eager participation in the violent, sexual mélange of slavery's worldview makes him equally culpable in Walker's eyes, and she is found "wreaking her revenge in visual vignettes based on both history and fantasy" in absurdist scenes such as this.[5] While it is often difficult to construct a clear message from Walker's works, the undeniable blackness of the silhouettes, like Clytie's "pigmentation," reminds us that race is always the issue at hand, the "threatful portent of the old" that Walker revised.

[1] Faulkner, Absolom, Absolom!, 126.
[2] Dixon, "Negress Speaks Out," 12.
[3] Quoted in Hayt, "Simple, Austere," 51, c. 1.
[4] Smith, "Black on White," PT2.
[5] Dixon, "Negress Speaks Out," 19.

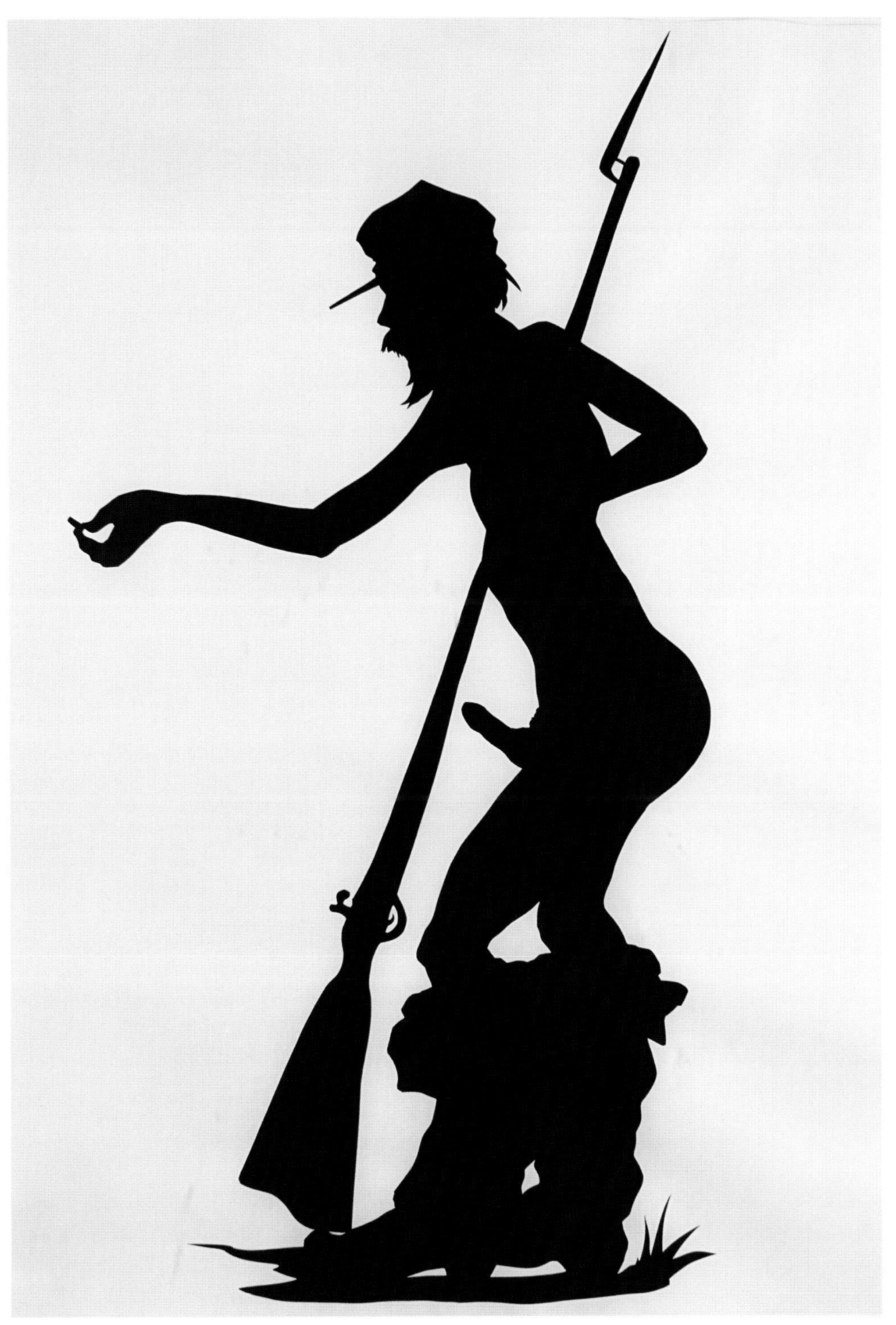

Shiny Penny 1995
Cut out construction paper on paper, 54″ x 41″

Robert Cottingham 1935-

Edward Hopper once described his 1930 painting *Early Sunday Morning* as "almost a literal translation of Seventh Avenue" in New York City.[1] Nearly sixty years later, Robert Cottingham's *Barber Shop* brought Hopper's transcription of Seventh Avenue to its logical extreme, cropping and refocusing his urban landscape through the eager lens of photorealism. In the process, Cottingham not only revived Hopper's iconography but also his painterly aim, as Hopper famously described it, to "project upon canvas my most intimate reaction to the subject as it appears when I like it most."[2]

Cottingham showed a similar reverence for his subject: his work proudly displays the complicated architectural patterns and nuanced advertising graphics of the urban setting, zooming in on the gritty details of the storefront without embarrassment for the slight imperfections that belie its crisp presentation. Yet Cottingham's work, which has been described as a "coda to Pop Art," also goes beyond the confines of photorealism, creating in its wake a sentimental but brooding glimpse at the legacy of early American commercial life.[3]

In *Barber Shop*, Cottingham chose to center on a lone barber pole. Unlike Hopper, for whom the colorful pole stood in contrast to a bleak, unbroken string of closed storefronts, Cottingham's barber pole functions in concord with its homogenously blue-toned environment—a beacon for the stir of activity within. Since the viewer is unable to back far enough away from the close-up to place it within any greater economic message, he is instead compelled simply to bear witness to the pole's modern transformation into a commercial decal for "Stephan's Barber Shop." In the microeconomic world depicted, Cottingham's predisposition for advertising has taken on a narrow, yet poignant force, which is oddly at ease with the composition's aesthetic balance and polish.

Nevertheless, there is a tensile relationship evoked by the presence of the acid-green framed storefront window, which serves as a microcosm of the work itself, a painting within the painting that attempts to accommodate both the stylized logo of the barber pole and the impulsively abstract red brushstroke in close proximity.[4] The claustrophobic juxtaposition of the two elements serves as a pressing reminder that despite his penchant for Photorealism's precision, Cottingham is continuously aware of the many divergent influences pulling on his work. It is this ambivalence that actually allows Cottingham to regard his subject with such painterly reverence, for it becomes a facet of life that can never be easily captured or represented in the advertising aesthetics. His storefronts, then, contain as much nostalgia for the ennui of small-town retail as they do admiration for their enduring vitality in the face of modern commercialism.[5]

[1] Quoted in Hobbs, *Edward Hopper*, 77.
[2] Ibid., 1.
[3] Anderson-Spivy, "Robert Cottingham at the MacDowell Colony," 37–39.
[4] Bonito, *Get Real*, 30.
[5] Auer, "Cottingham's Sign Language," E8.

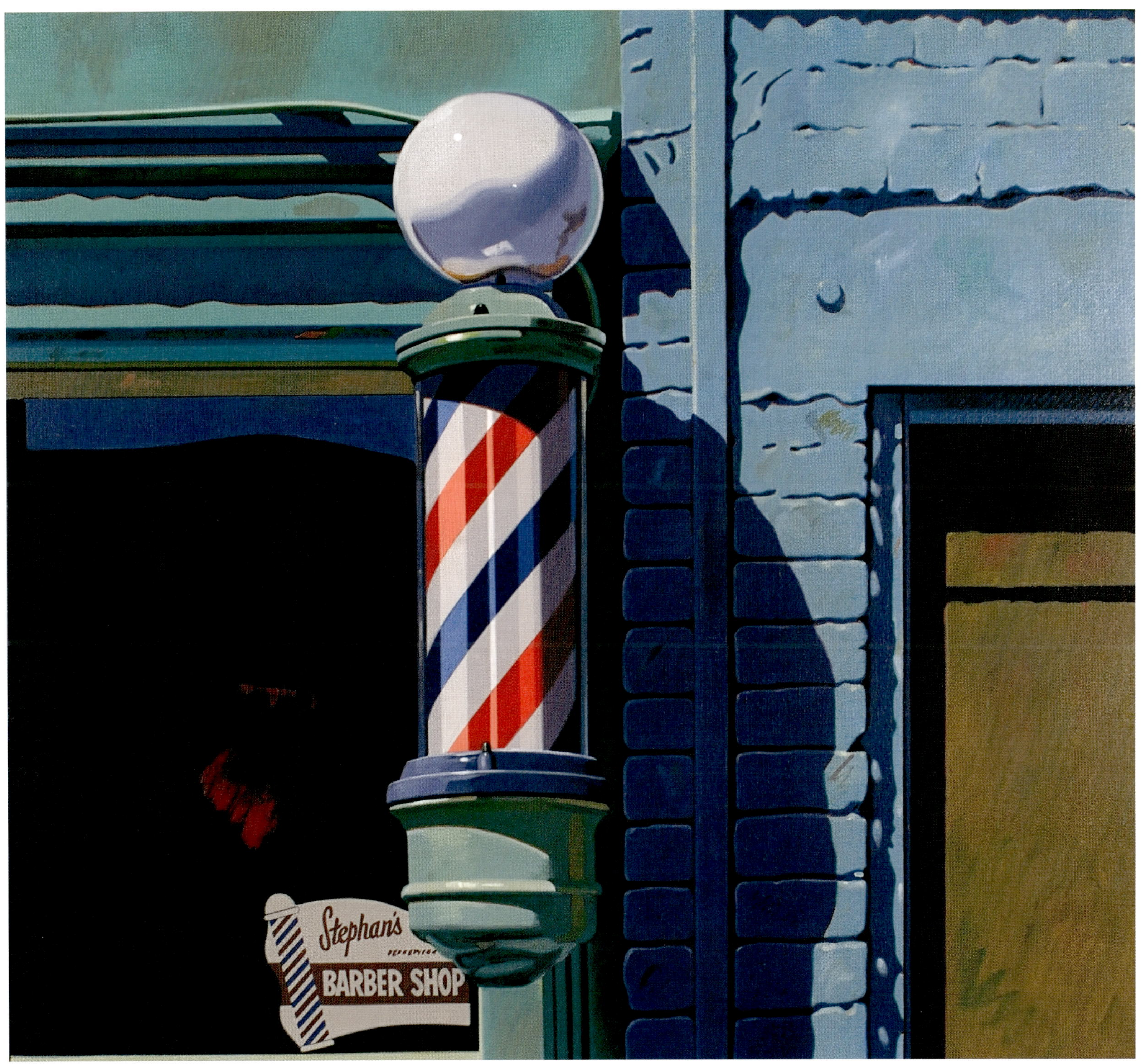

Barber Shop 1988
Oil on canvas, 32″ x 32″

Robert Longo 1953-

Robert Longo's black-and-white drawings appear as simple as they are large: at eight feet by four feet, Longo presents a single figure against a starkly blank background. As Eleanor Heartney wrote for *Art in America*, "Longo has always had a cinematic sense of scale, exploiting size in his drawings and sculptures to evoke a sense of awe."[1] Yet his figures obviously present more than a simple towering effect: Intentionally cropped too closely by their frames, Longo's portraits impart a sense of urgency and frustration that immediately begins to assault the viewer, harassing him or her with the violence of a pent-up movement that refuses to resolve.

In Longo's *Men in the Cities* series in particular, from which this untitled selection derives, works were created from a series of photographs taken by the artist, which he later faithfully translated into ultra-realistic drawings. Despite the accuracy of most pieces in the series compared to their source photographs, the most striking detail of the collection's example—the vertical tie—was actually absent from the original photograph, added later by the artist. Longo is believed to have included the tie to create a high-impact moment in which the man appears to be both hanging and flying, and possibly even impaled, all at the same time. Longo also elongated the legs of the businessman, brought them in tighter, and tilted the upper body farther back to heighten the effect.[2] In this way, his filmic use of the image reminds viewers of familiar slow-motion and stop-action footage, which prolongs the audience's initial reaction. Through such devices, Longo's work adheres to his vision of abstract symbolism and the creation of a violent gesture that perpetually accosts and discomforts his viewer.

Longo created many of the poses in the series by shooting tennis balls at his models and allowing them to dodge or catch the flying objects without instruction while he took photographs. The resulting images tend to separate the human figure from its easily recognizable and expected positioning, thereby creating another layer of action in which the viewer attempts to reconcile the twisted, existing image with preexisting anatomical ideas of the human shape.[3] For Longo, this is just another method of instilling his work with movement—a challenge which always seems to be at the center of Longo's intentions. Whether by tricking the eye into correcting an image to its proper shape, anticipating the figures' subsequent fallout, or simply forcing the viewer to travel the monumental length of the image, Longo perpetually finds new and inventive means for capturing a suspended but nevertheless perceivable motion in an otherwise stagnant genre.

[1] Heartney, "Robert Longo at Metro Pictures," 127.
[2] Longo, "Save the Last Dance," 92.
[3] Ibid., 93.

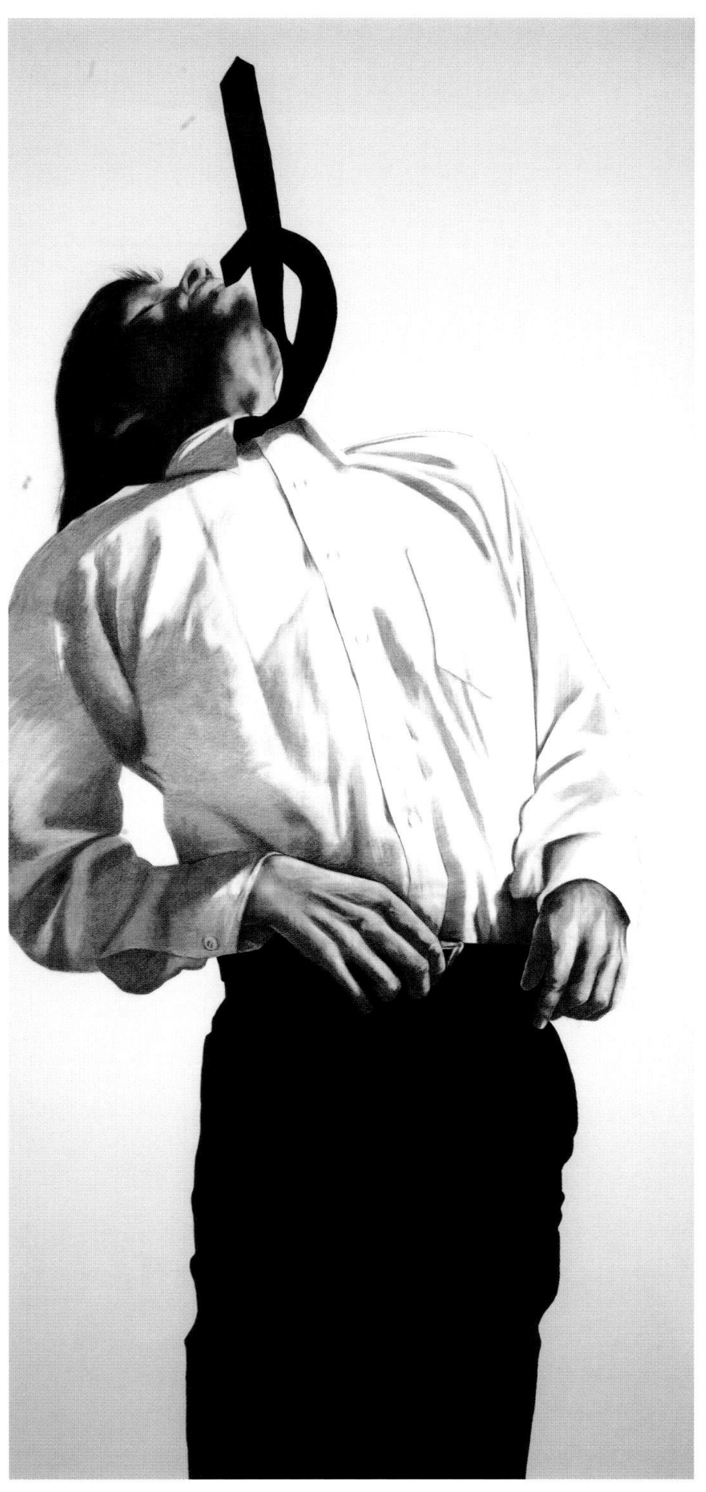

Untitled (from Men in the City series) 1982
Charcoal, graphite and ink on paper, 96″ x 48″

Grayson Perry 1960-

When invited to explain his dark, self-referential pottery, Grayson Perry once remarked, "It's no good asking me. I put forward the question in the work, I don't answer it."[1] For Perry, the role of the authoritative artist runs in opposition to the nature of his vases, which spiral in a directionless, three-dimensional storyboard of images, photographs, and truncated texts. To forcefully put these fragments in order—to explicate a beginning, a middle, and an end to the narrative—would be to undercut the representative psychology of the chaos at hand.[2] Perry's designs are endlessly complicated for a reason: the cyclical repetition and variation of images enables a Freudian deferral of fulfillment and prolongation of a certain image-oriented pleasure for which its anticipation outweighs its completion.[3] The vase is not only a landscape dotted with free association but a preferred illusion as well.

Perry's pottery is replete with scenes of fantasy and fetish for a similar purpose: as pure thought and visual artifact, they can never disappoint, and the illusion can be sustained. Once converted to reality, they are sure to fall short of their idealized depiction.[4] But the realms of fantasy, fetish, and daydreams are not always visually pleasant: a hypodermic needle, a sickly fetus, and a sword-like phallus jar the viewer from thinking of the piece as just another domestic craft or household clutter. His works are as dramatic and obsessive as they are personal and confessionary. In *He Comes Not in Triumph*, the artist appeared to be reflecting upon and grieving for his lifelong journey as a transvestite to live as a man constructing a woman. Those praying toward the assembled figure seem to show the mental and physical hardships of the process, yet they are undeterred in elevating and revering her nonetheless, for all affix their gaze firmly to the young girl. In this way, Perry simultaneously proclaims and mourns for his life, humbly assuming his position at the center of a small universe while acknowledging the materials of demise—the rope and the gallows—that are ever present in the background.

In addition to his mastery over complex, infinite, and often sinister meanings, Perry has been praised for the artistry of his works as well, receiving the famed Turner Prize in 2003. Rather than throwing his pottery, Perry lays down hundreds of coiled snakes of clay one by one, and then gradually smoothes them into the recognizable shape—a process he calls "a war of attrition." His high-gloss glazes and liberal use of gold project the atmosphere of a precious object that is befitting for the amount of labor required by a single vase with his level of detail.[5] Thus, while Perry insists, "There's something humble about a vase—it's not a big, show-offy thing," one quickly begins to believe that his prefacing is yet another ploy in Perry's lifelong obsession to flirt with truth while simultaneously avoiding any measure of disappointment.[6]

[1] Quoted in Jardine, "Grayson Perry," 6.
[2] Jardine, "Grayson Perry," 6.
[3] Ibid., 11.
[4] Ibid., 8.
[5] Ibid., 3-4.
[6] Quoted in Jardin, "Grayson Perry," 3.

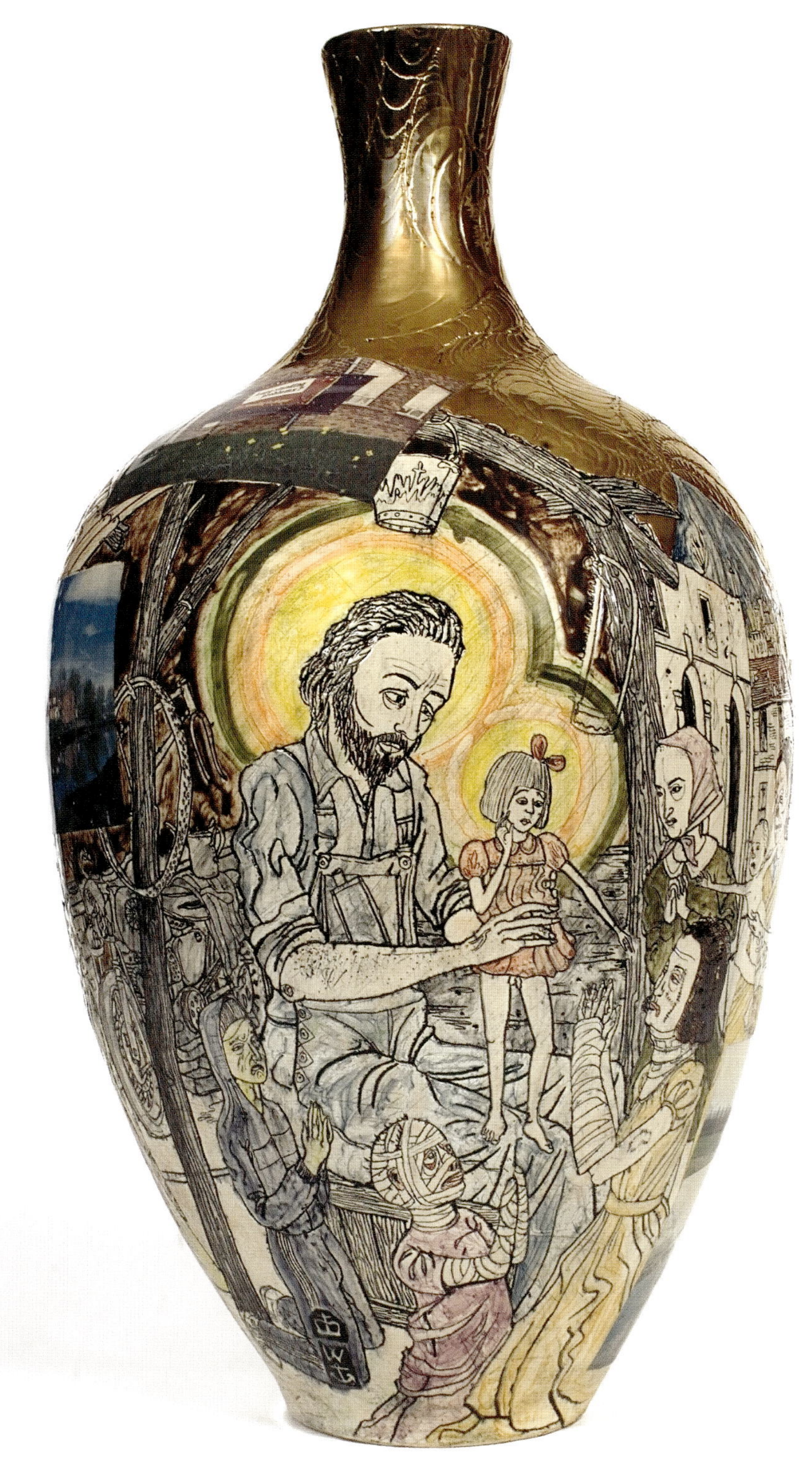

He Comes Not In Triumph 2004
Glazed ceramic, 20 7/8″ x 11 3/4″

Robert Kushner 1949-

After standing at the forefront of the 1970s Pattern and Decoration movement, Robert Kushner's work in the 1980s began to incorporate the most diametrically difficult of shapes—the human figure—into the "ageless currency" of fruit, flowers, and geometric patterns that dominated his formalistic framework.[1] Seeking a way to incorporate his growing interest in the dramatic effect of "gesticulating bodies" in the performance arts, Kushner developed a technique to overlay and bleed opaque Technicolor outlines of the human form onto medium as varied as patterned fabric, cotton, and wallpaper. It was a sharp deviation from the ornamentation that characterized Pattern and Decorations, largely antithetical to the vocabulary of Islamic patterns, Hindu poster art, and Oriental macramé typically brought together in the movement's unified, multi-cultural expression.[2]

In many ways, it was as if the presence of the nude figure, which is so heavily connoted by the Western canon, required an extensive overhaul of Kushner's artistic process. He ceased working from photographs, as was the custom of the avant-garde, preferring for the first time the spontaneity and freedom offered by live models. He then sought to convey the weightiness and volume of the figures in the language of his movement's flat compositions, rendering them in negative space while dismantling their support to allow for a more authoritative, heightened floating effect.[3]

Even the title of *Model and Painting* speaks to these changes, simultaneously recognizing the fluid importance of the live model while insisting that its inclusion has allowed his work to further bridge the gap between the decorative arts and the hallowed history of painting. Indeed, the classicized, thoughtful pose assumed by his model seems to function as one element of this bridging effort. But it is the work's principle of repetition and permutation that truly achieves the painting's cyclical success, as the fully figured female reappears in the facial features of her intertwined counterpart. Through this emphatic reiteration, Kushner was able to coerce the novel, supposedly out-of-place motif of the figure into a traditional, decorative format.

Always fighting against the critical world's inability to see past the dialectic definitions of high and low art, Kushner sought to unite his joyous, loquacious, colorful works with the canon of accepted forms through the integration of the human figure.[4] The resulting interaction of his figures with each other and with a disjunct background, richly steeped in both sensuality and control, carried a new anecdotal element of eroticism that was easier to digest and provided further distance from the typical attack on his work's thematic frivolity.[5] Through this technique, Kushner reached the height of his critical public appeal in the early 1980s, in large part due to innovative works such as *Model and Painting*.

[1] Cotter, "Robert Kushner," 9.
[2] Cotter, "Robert Kushner," 7-10; Anderson-Spivy, *Robert Kushner*, 50.
[3] Anderson-Spivy, *Robert Kushner*, 50.
[4] Ibid., 50-52.
[5] Ibid., 50-54.

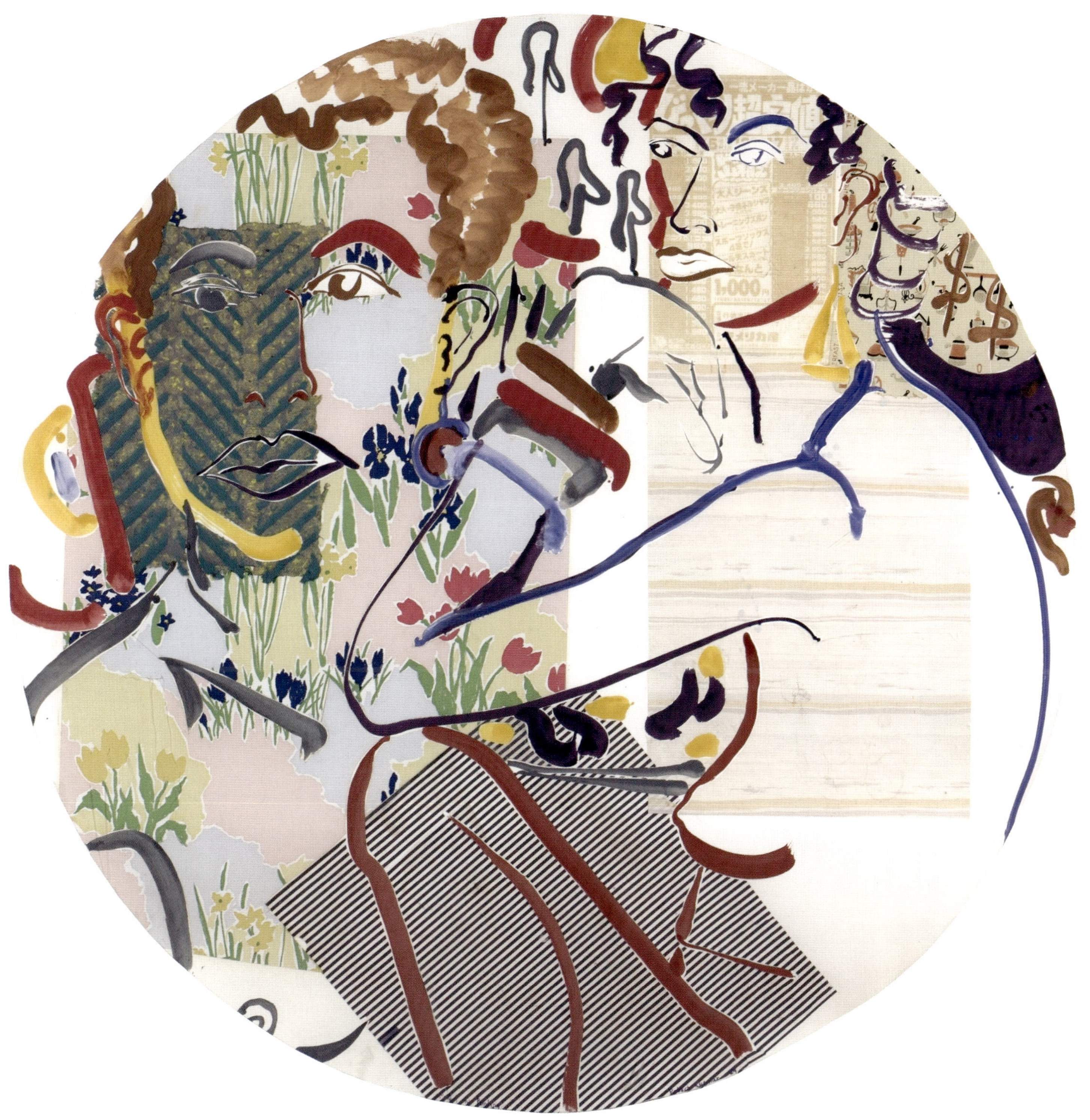

Model and Painting 1984
Acrylic and wallpaper collage on paper, 59″ (diameter)

Malcolm Morley 1931-

Nearly every review of Malcolm Morley's 1990s images of fighter planes and battleships is oriented around the traumatic biographical event that Morley uncovered in psychotherapy in which his beloved boyhood model of the H.M.S. *Nelson* was destroyed during a WWII bombing of London. Conveniently, critics have seized upon this anecdote for its strong metaphorical evocation of violence and lost innocence.

Certainly, Morley has done nothing to discourage this reception: he not only admitted painting from real toy models as sources, but also attached several of the models he built himself directly to his work, allowing them to serve as fourth-dimensional appendages, bridging the realms of fantasy and reality. The toy-like depiction of such massive weapons also serves this end, presenting planes as both agents of destruction and agents of fantasy, fulfilling their dualistic role in the innocent re-creations of war that children invent with small plastic figures.

Before ever receiving such critical reviews, Morley himself claimed, "I think it would be nice to make an adventure painting. It would appeal to a special kind of ecstasy of the eleven year boy."[1] Since Morley hardly anticipates his audience to be composed entirely of adolescent males, such a statement becomes evocative of the type of puerile reaction he sought to generate in the untapped recesses of his viewer. As Ken Johnson wrote, "It is as if the artist were giving his younger self a chance to live out the imaginative life that the war interrupted," and indeed, Morley seems to extend his opportunistic nostalgia to his viewers in every way possible.[2]

But others have rejected this view as overly simplistic. For many, his work is more about "the literal depiction of objects and their limitations on two-dimensional surfaces,"[3] or as Morley termed it, "The pun of putting an aeroplane on the picture plane."[4]

In a recent retrospective, Brooks Adams argued another vantage point entirely, claiming that Morley's work centers on historical images of war and conquest because they represent "Morley's coming to terms with his own 1950s and '60s history as a painter."[5] To make his case, Adams cited the pop and color field target paintings that Morley transformed and marginalized into targets on the wings of his planes to suggest his need for their destruction, despite their significance as badges of past success. In many ways, *Hiding Behind History* seems the paradigmatic support for Adam's theory: through the work's enigmatic title, Morley hints that his recent 1990s works may in fact hide behind his history as a painter, since they revive the naval subject matter of his superrealist works in the 1960s and '70s. At the same time, however, he introduces the possibility that the series is in fact a covert, militaristic mission meant to eliminate his former iconographic legacy entirely. The struggle is complex, as attested to by the canvas's fragmentation into Cezannist blocks, which protects his earlier work—symbolized by the ship—beneath a mask of abstraction. If the conclusion of the complex visual battle is unknown, it is intentionally so, for it sets the stage for yet another of Morley's re-creations in the lifelong struggle to preserve his youthful vision in the immense sea of adult formalism.[6]

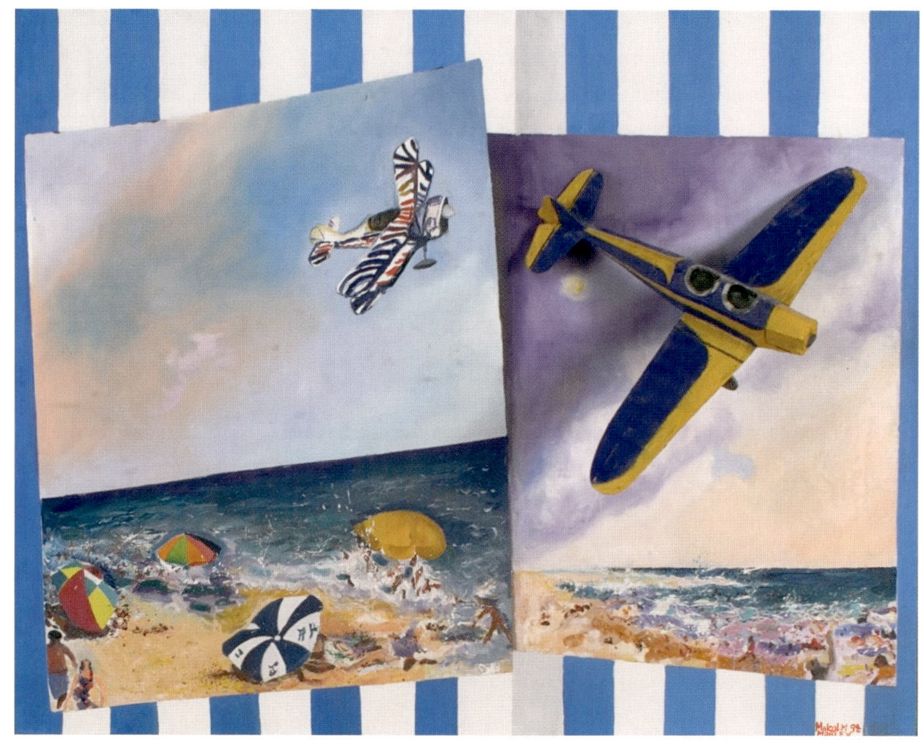

Pictures from the Azores 1994
Oil on canvas with painted model plane, 29" x 35" x 14"

[1] Quoted in Adams, "1900s Morley," 52.
[2] Johnson, "Malcolm Morley, Sperone Westwater," E 42.
[3] Budzynski, "Critical Moments: Malcolm Morley," 32-35.
[4] Quoted in Kent, "Portrait of the Artist," 18-19.
[5] Adams, "1900s Morley," 56.
[6] Johnson, "Malcolm Morley, Sperone Westwater," E 42.

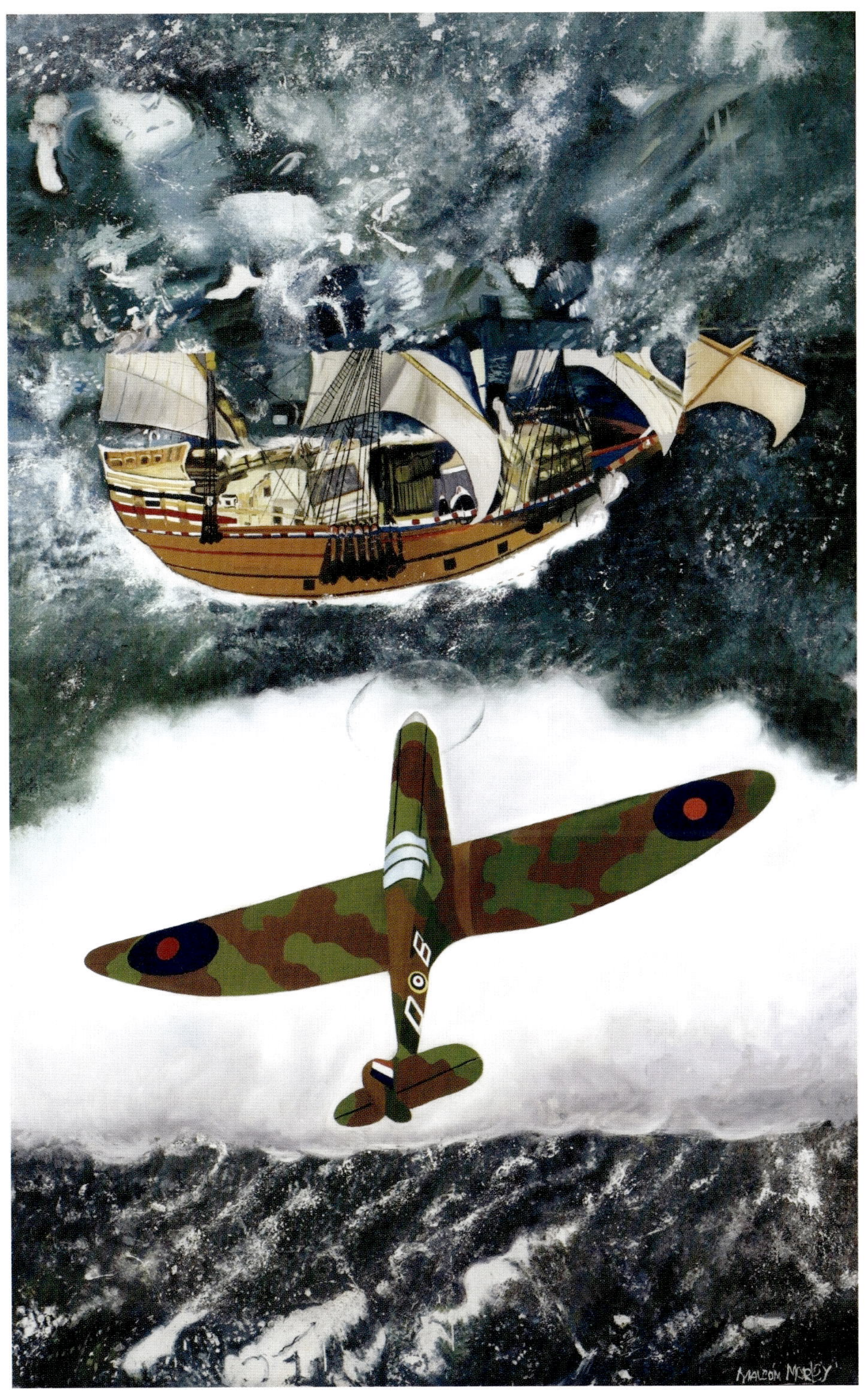

Hiding Behind History 1999
Oil on linen, 88″ x 56″

Alice Neel 1900-1984

Alice Neel's extensive portraiture forms a seldom paralleled oeuvre, both in its volume and its variation. Though her unrelenting loyalty to a single genre lent itself well to a timeline of her career and an outline of the American landscape she was capturing, her course is not without significant digression—brief respites from the social commentary through which she was said to be "collecting souls."[1] Her Portrait of Ben Medary appears as just such a pause, offering an opportunity for personal catharsis and an unapologetic review of the fiancé of her friend and studio mate Rhoda Myers.

At the time, Neel was incapable of accepting Rhoda's impending marriage. She had only recently recovered from the collapse of her own marriage to Carlos Enríquez de Gómez and she knew firsthand the devastating effect such a union could have on an artist's career. To some extent, Neel used the portrait of Ben Medary as a means for displacing her own sadness and anger onto a new subject, and as such, his portrayal was a long-overdue opportunity for introspection. Moreover, Neel genuinely failed to understand Rhoda's attraction. Neel saw Ben Medary not for his potential but for what he was at the time: the directionless son of renowned architect Milton Bennet Medary Jr. In Neel's eyes, Ben Medary represented everything inimical to art; he was a rich Anglo-Saxon, the heir to a fortune he didn't earn, and the proprietor of a bourgeois morality that was inflexible and suppressive.[2]

As a result, her portrait of Ben Medary is rather cutthroat. Combining a new, expressionistically flat style with a lifeless palette, Neel portrayed her subject as fundamentally gray. His suit, his tie, and even his personality are gray, browned and sullied. Neel's lines are no less critical: Rendered with uncluttered simplicity, he appears to lack any depth—the cookie-cutter representative of upper-class banality and a spiritual void left in the wake of wealth.[3] Discovering that she could not "collect" his soul, since she found it missing, Neel simply transcribed his empty shell as faithfully as she could, not stopping to imbue it with any of the detail or character for which she was known. His image is as asymmetrical and misshapen as the ideology he represents.[4]

Neel once told another subject of her work, "You won't like this portrait because I am making you look a little askew, but you are a little askew."[5] Certainly, Ben Medary was also the recipient of such a perspective. Sadly, Neel's warning went unheard. Rhoda Medary had two children with Ben Medary in a marriage marked by constant unhappiness until he took his own life in 1963.

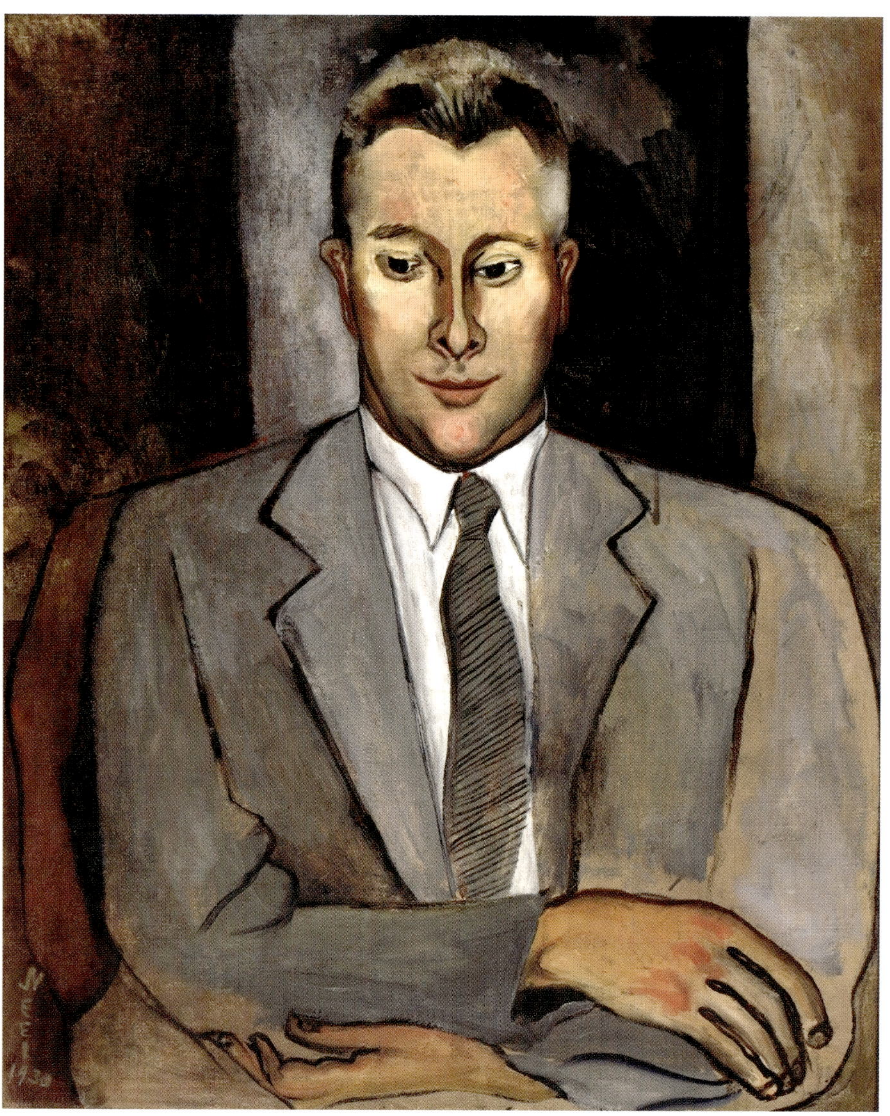

Portrait of Ben Medary 1930
Oil on canvas, 30″ x 25 1/8″

[1] Gruen, "Collector of Souls." 174-179.
[2] Belcher and Belcher, *Collecting Souls, Gathering Dust*, 116.
[3] Ibid., 125.
[4] Ibid.
[5] Quoted in Johnson, "Alice Neel: Fifty Years," 175.

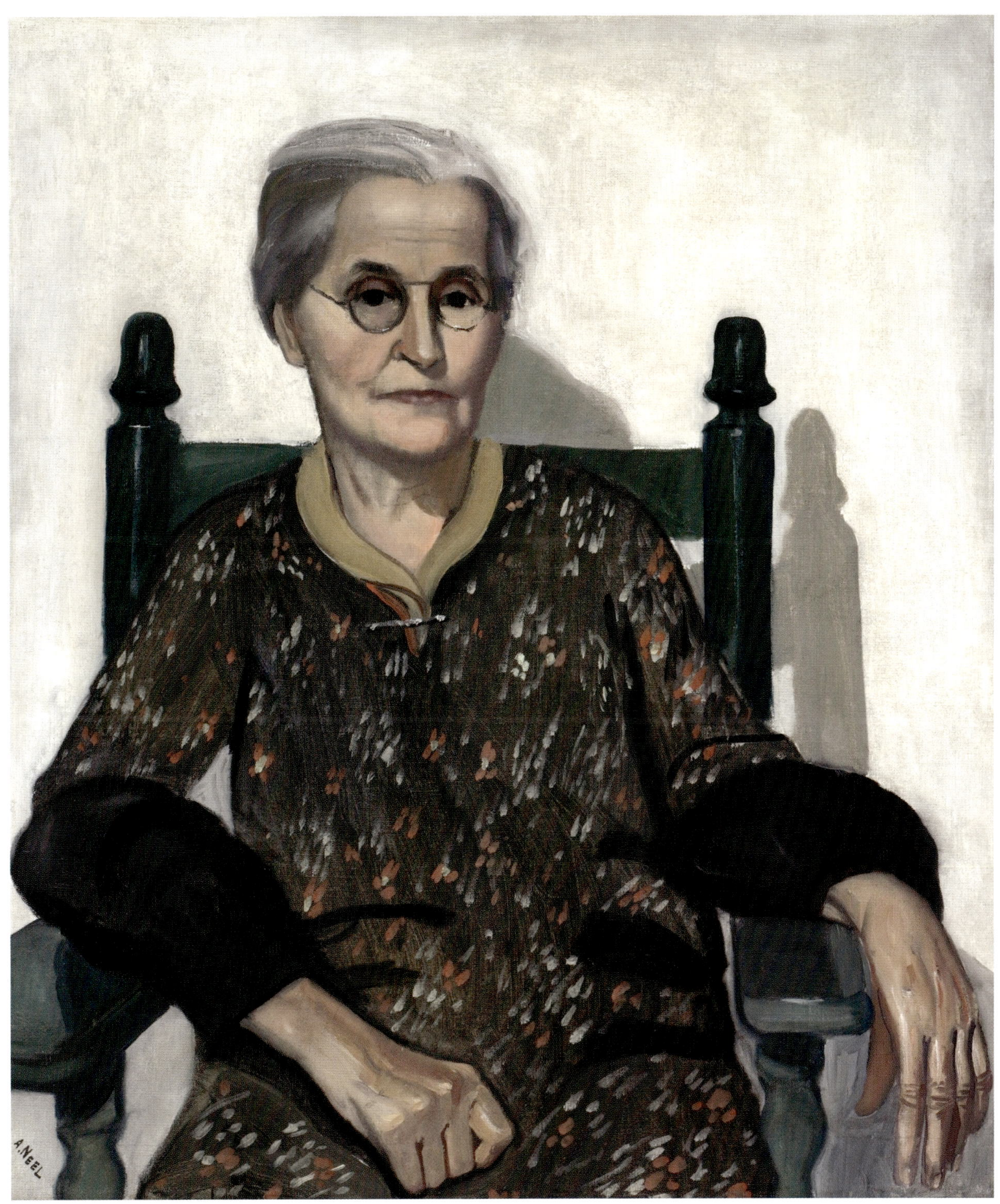

Portrait of the Artist's Mother 1930
Oil on canvas, 30″ x 26″

Richard Phillips 1962-

Best known for an au courant style in which he appropriates images from beauty magazines, fashion photo shoots, and the glamorous side of entertainment, as well as the "B-quality" sources of hard-core pornography and prostitution, Richard Phillips has crafted an oeuvre largely dominated by female power and pulchritude.[1] Along with it, Phillips has revealed a distinctly male projection of such beauty by positioning women with sultry, seductive glances so far above the viewer that they cannot help but look down with disdain and pity, all too aware of their control over the situation. On the surface, *Sissel* portrays a woman who is perfectly in line with such qualities. A blonde, blue-eyed beauty stares down at her onlooker as she now does at her audience, head tilted back to impart an air of seduction.[2]

Extratextually, *Sissel* serves Phillips's greater interest in the autobiographical function of painting as a pragmatic tool for freezing and preserving one's memory.[3] The work documents the occasion on which Phillips proposed marriage to Sissel Kardel, a fellow New York City artist, only to receive her prompt rejection. Of course, such narrative is undoubtedly in keeping with his leitmotif of female empowerment and control, but it is the psychological depth of the context, as well as the introduction of known pain rather than emotional distance, that seems to truly govern the painting.[4] For once, it is not the collective cultural memory bank of fashion and entertainment images that Phillips draws upon but rather his own personal memory.[5]

Not surprisingly, however, the two modes of painting share many thematic elements, as both aim to memorialize the unattainable, be it the impossible standards of beauty presented in the pages of magazines or, more plainly, the love of Sissel Kardel.[6] Though Phillips seems to clutch onto *Sissel* for just a moment longer, cropping her tightly as if trying to hold on, *Sissel*'s icy beauty snubs his physical encroachment as it did his proposal and, to a larger extent, halts the persistent masculine attempt to advance on female autonomy with one strikingly apathetic gaze.

[1] Rebentisch, "Richard Phillip's Psycho-Realism," 86; Molon, "Richard Phillips," 248.
[2] Jones, "Gleams of Past Existence," 56.
[3] Ibid.
[4] Bürgi, "Innocence," 50.
[5] Rebentisch, "Richard Phillip's Psycho-Realism," 84.
[6] Molon, "Richard Phillips," 248.

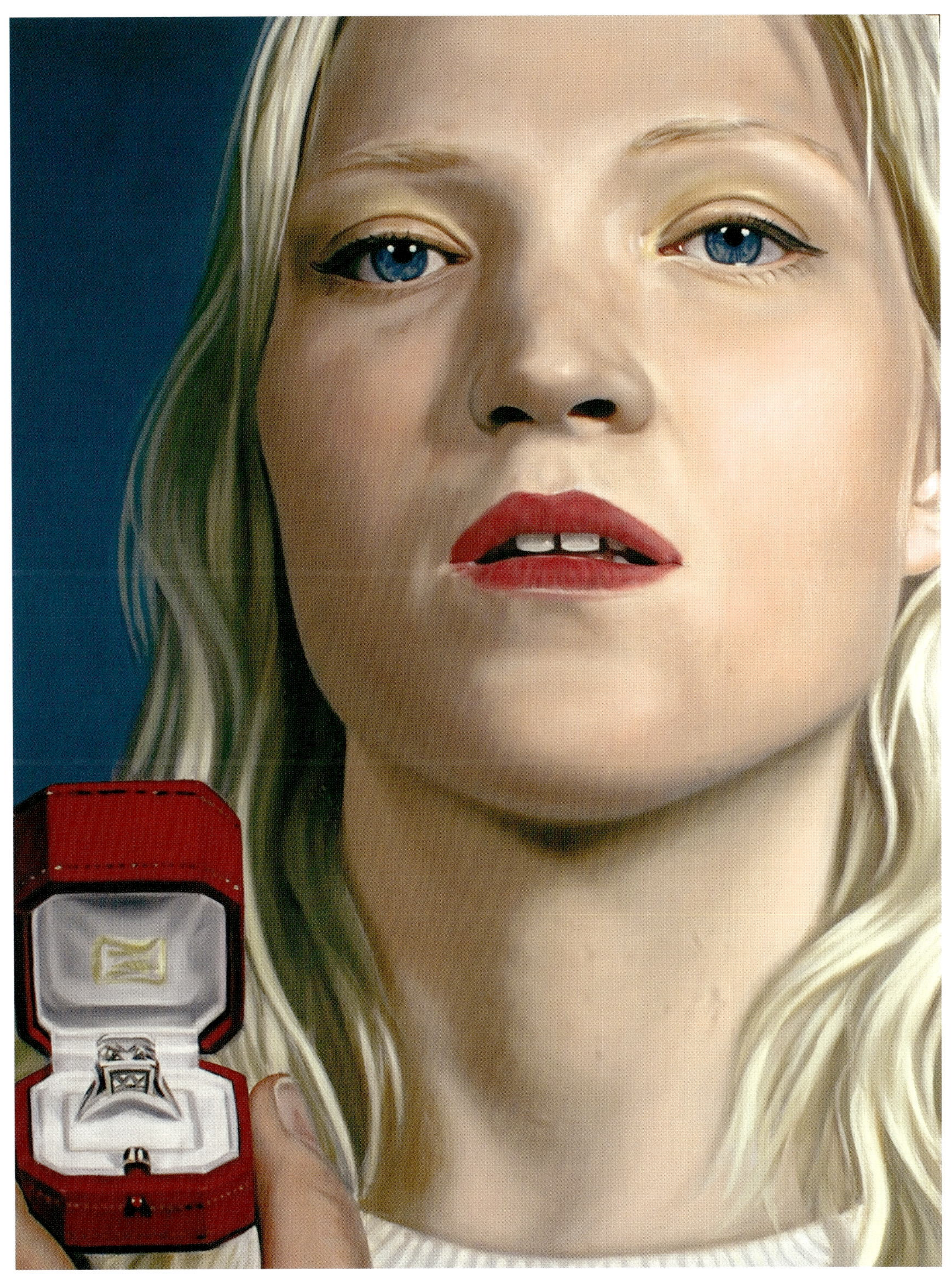

Sissel 2002
Oil on linen, 36″ x 27 1/4″

Martin Eder 1968-

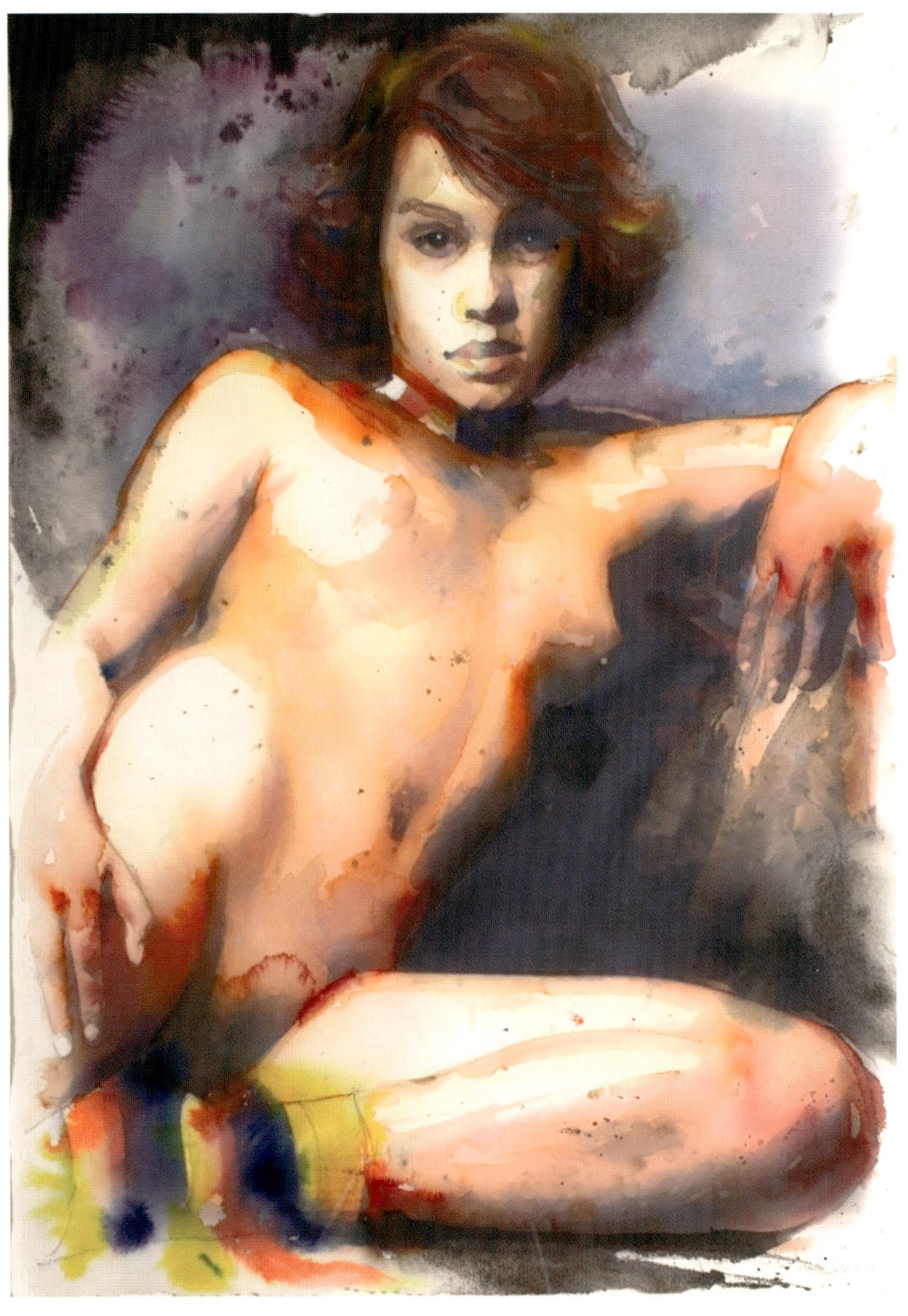

Untitled 2002
Pencil and watercolor, 29 1/8″ x 21 1/4″

Machiko Edmondson 1965-

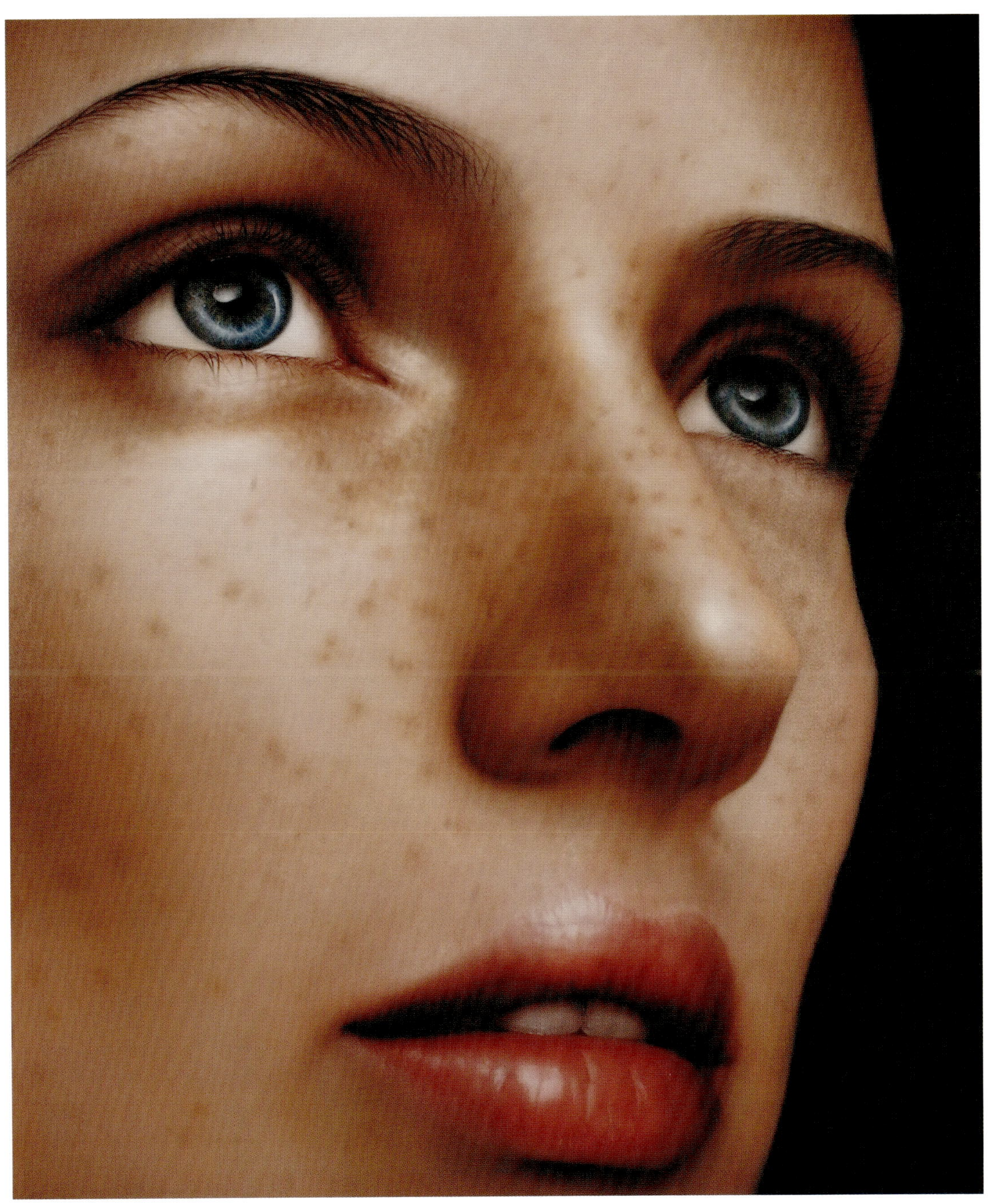

Serendipity (Sugar Cane After Sonic Youth) 2003
Oil on canvas, 72″ x 60″

Robert Overby 1935-1993

As Michael Duncan wrote for *Art in America* in 1996, "Perpetually out of sorts with the art world, Overby showed only rarely in his lifetime. Yet since his death three years ago from Hodgkin's disease, two solo exhibitions in L.A. have established him as a classic California experimenter whose works reveal a buoyantly independent spirit in the vein of [Bruce] Nauman, [Jonathan] Borofsky or 1990s dynamo Tim Hawkinson."[1]

Overby acquired his posthumous reputation through his wild experimentation with latex rubber castings of indoor spaces, architectural structures, and open-air suburban environments—including stairwells, building façades, and sidewalks, respectively—yet he also attempted such varied genres as renaissance portraiture, classical oil landscape, and irregularly shaped abstraction. When dismayed by his reception in any of these artistic fields or simply exhausted by his own frenetic rate of production, Overby would refocus on his career in graphic design, where he produced MoMA catalogs, magazine spreads for the Kiwanis charity, and even the most recent Toyota logo.[2] As a result of his schizophrenic approach, Overby's artistic output often combined elements of computer-aided design, avant-garde or synthetic materials, and traditional techniques as he mixed and matched influences and resources in purposefully asynchronous combinations, prompting David Rimanelli to comment, "[With Overby], it's not a question of two competing styles, but maybe ten, twenty styles, all of which the artist worked in at more or less the same time."[3]

Yet no matter his chosen style or subject, Overby consistently returned to a relatively limited set of overarching concerns, namely the effects of abstraction and texture, the limits of mimesis, and the artist's ability to manipulate illusionistic space.[4] In a work like *If Only (01.07.89)*, Overby seemed to confront all these concerns at once, jumbling the hard edges of ink with a softer layer of watercolor. Subverting expectations, Overby allowed the easily controlled pen to dart frenziedly around the picture frame, while the traditionally unpredictable watercolor appears tamed and purposeful. At the same time, he proved his capacity for realism, crafting the subject's face with precision and care, only to destroy the viewer's perception of authenticity by inserting details of an abstractionist, incongruous hand growing out of a truncated nude and by obscuring patches of the face with repetitious blocks of color. The result of this strange amalgamation proves a rather fitting microcosm of Overby's career, as it represents a variety of styles and techniques all centered on the human figure and the boundaries of its deterioration before rendering it unrecognizable.

Though Charles LaBelle termed Overby's constant churning of ideas and styles a "dismissal of continuity and adoption of a self-reflexive circularity," it is just as easy to argue, as Michael Duncan had, that Overby viewed "art-making as a progression and as a learning process."[5] In this light, *If Only (01.07.89)* stands as a poetically transitional testimony to Overby's process, momentarily defining the artist's place on his journey while informing his next move into untried ideas and mediums.

[1] Duncan, "Ruins and Replicas," 76.
[2] Rimanelli, "Robert Overby," 83.
[3] Ibid.
[4] Duncan, "Ruins and Replicas," 76.
[5] LaBelle, "Robert Overby: UCLA," 108; Duncan, 76.

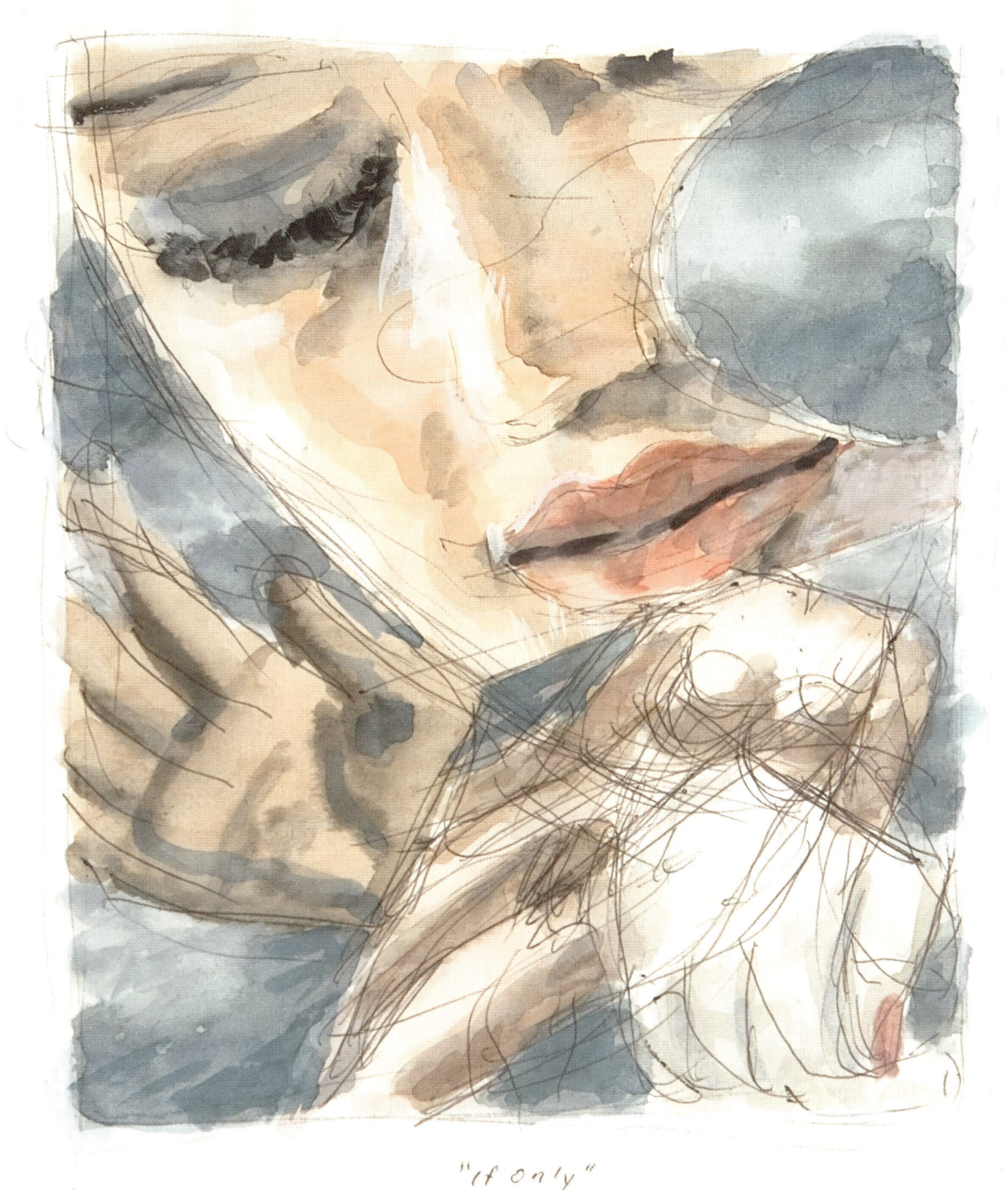

If Only (01.07.89) 1989
Watercolor and ballpoint pen ink on paper, 6 3/8″ x 5 1/2″

Niki de Saint Phalle 1930-2002

After attaining fame for her *Rifle Shot* series, in which male-figure assemblage sculptures were displayed and shot from close range, consequently exploding paint containers across their surface, Saint Phalle turned her eccentric brand of feminism to a new subject matter: sculptures she dubbed simply the *Nanas*. These imaginative Ruben-esque figures occupied Saint Phalle for great lengths of her career and through many permutations, including a massively scaled environment sculpture titled *Hon*, Swedish for "she." Erected at the Moderna Museet in Stockholm, *Hon* had its visitors enter through the vagina, where they were confronted by a carnival atmosphere: an aquarium, a planetarium, a twelve-seat cinema devoted solely to Greta Garbo films, and, most notably, a milk bar in the breasts.

Though constructed on a much smaller scale, Saint Phalle's other *Nanas* were no less imaginative and always displayed a similar affection for the joy inherent in the body, in life, and in the celebration of its many experiences. Like all her *Nanas, Three Graces* exudes this "pure and free fantasy;" Its figures recognize the possibility of human weakness and in turn provide an elegantly simple and cheerful solution: they turn their backs on it and dance.[1]

Saint Phalle herself viewed each of her Nanas as joyful, liberated women ready to become heralds of a new matriarchal age by taking control of a world gone awry.[2] She located her sculptures in a long line of such female mythical archetypes and pointed to works like the Venus of Willendorf as proof of their validity, ubiquity, and timelessness. To Saint Phalle, all such figures represent "the independent, benign, giving, contented, mother," and as such, reflect their necessity as an ideal in society.[3]

Always concerned with the approachability of her art, Saint Phalle's *Nanas* shrank progressively smaller and smaller, ultimately taking form as miniature compositions like *Three Graces*. They invite viewers into their universe, rather than repelling them through aura. Created with familiar red hearts, childlike flowers, a playfully mosaic coloration reminiscent of Gaudi, and a sense of lightness that belies their voluptuous shapes, Saint Phalle's *Nanas* greet their audience as mother-goddesses of a female cosmos that has yet to abandon its post in the imagination but which is ready to reclaim its proper place in reality.[4]

[1] Schulz-Hoffman, "All-Devouring Mothers," 14.
[2] Ibid.
[3] Ibid.
[4] Restany, preface to *Niki de Saint Phalle*, 6.

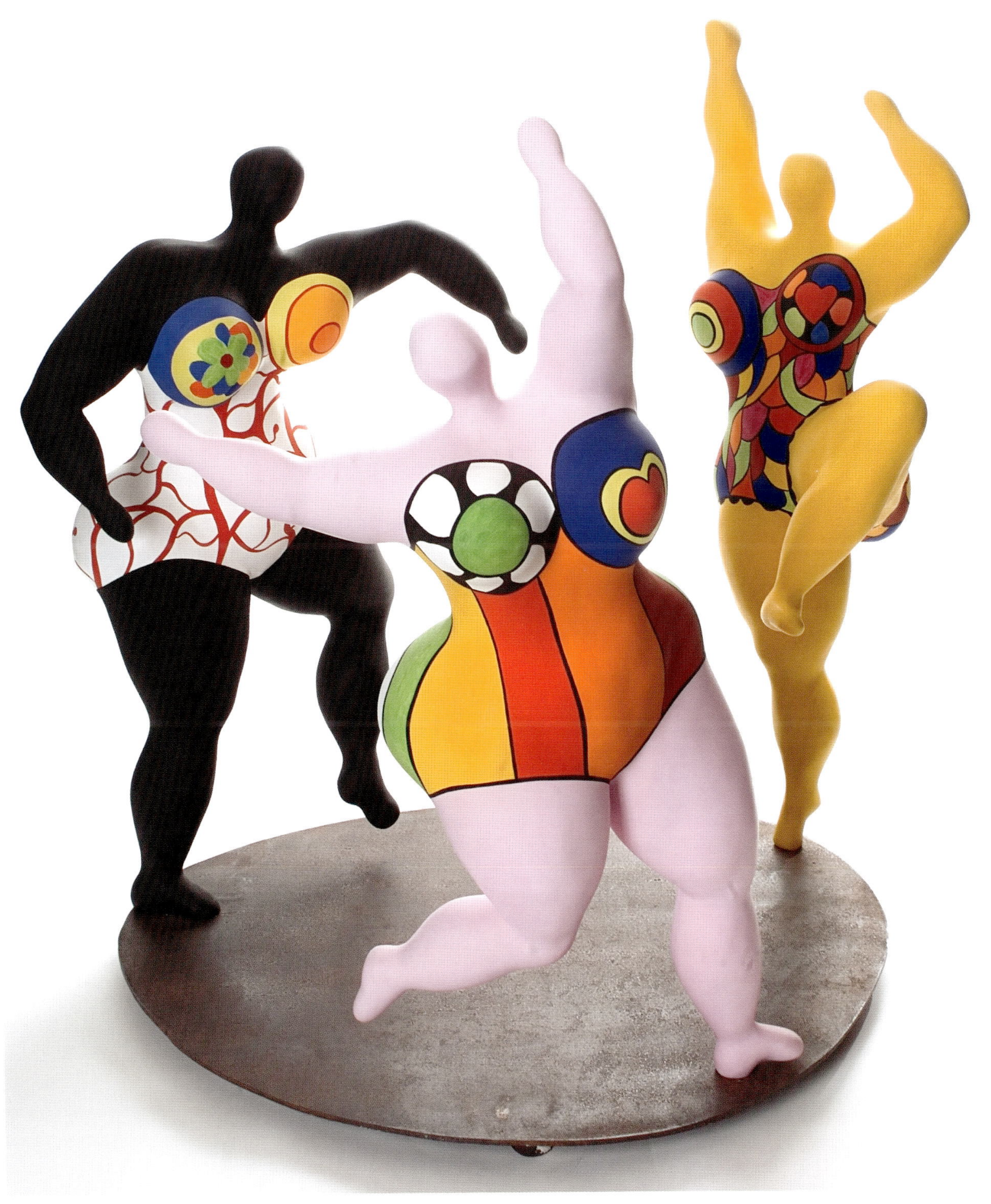

Three Graces 1994
Painted polyester on steel base, 25″ x 23″x 18 3/4″

Lisa Yuskavage 1963-

Though less audacious and provocative than her earlier works, which were branded with such titles as *Asspicking, Foodeating, Headshrinking, Socialclimbing, and Motherfucking Bad Habits* (1996), Lisa Yuskavage's recent paintings continue to marry the classical female nude with authentically déclassé, contemporary sexuality.[1] After abandoning wholly fictional characters in favor of a real-life model, Yuskavage again changed her source material to found pop-culture images, painting most often from 1970s *Penthouse* photo spreads. As part of this new approach, *Pajamas* appears as an idealized-but-real figure, simultaneously evocative of the clichéd props, passive demeanor, and open bits of clothing associated with soft-core pornography but firmly rooted in a seductively beautiful style that restricts the viewer from an exaggerated erotic reaction.

Like many others, Yuskavage faced the difficulty of depicting the female nude while remaining a contemporary artist. In earlier work, Yuskavage found the solution in the mannerist distortions of "bloated bellies, elongated necks," and hyperbolic buttocks that symbolized the burden of sexual attributes and their use in modern culture.[2] The appropriation of conventionally attractive women from the pages of *Penthouse*, however, drew her work further away from the grotesque, staging a more seductive relationship with the viewer that is, ironically, less confrontational.[3]

Pajamas also develops its modernity by serving as a contemporary reworking of Degas' pastels of women in intimate settings. Employing a similar use of a single color, the work abandons Degas' monotype gray in favor of a soft red that unites the figure and foreground. Yuskavage also adopts Degas' alchemical backlighting of the figure, using the technique to imply a narcissistic admiration that nearly succeeds in containing the light from escaping behind her reach.[4] In order to save the nude from any such stereotype, though, Yuskavage portrays her with downcast eyes that suggest she has accepted her role as a sex symbol but that she still yearns for something more real.[5]

Through its elegant and meditative silence, Yuskavage continues to obliquely remind her viewer of the absence of such qualities in their sexual realities, all the while harkening the "enduring possibility of their renascence."[6] The result is a *Penthouse* image painted with a tenderness that combats and ultimately overwhelms its role as an idiomatic commodity.[7]

[1] Seigel, "Local Color," 15-16.
[2] Ibid., 15, 17.
[3] Ibid., 19.
[4] Seigel, "Local Color," 20; Hall, "Painterly Paradoxes," 26-27.
[5] Hall, "Painterly Paradoxes," 28.
[6] Ibid.
[7] Ibid., 27.

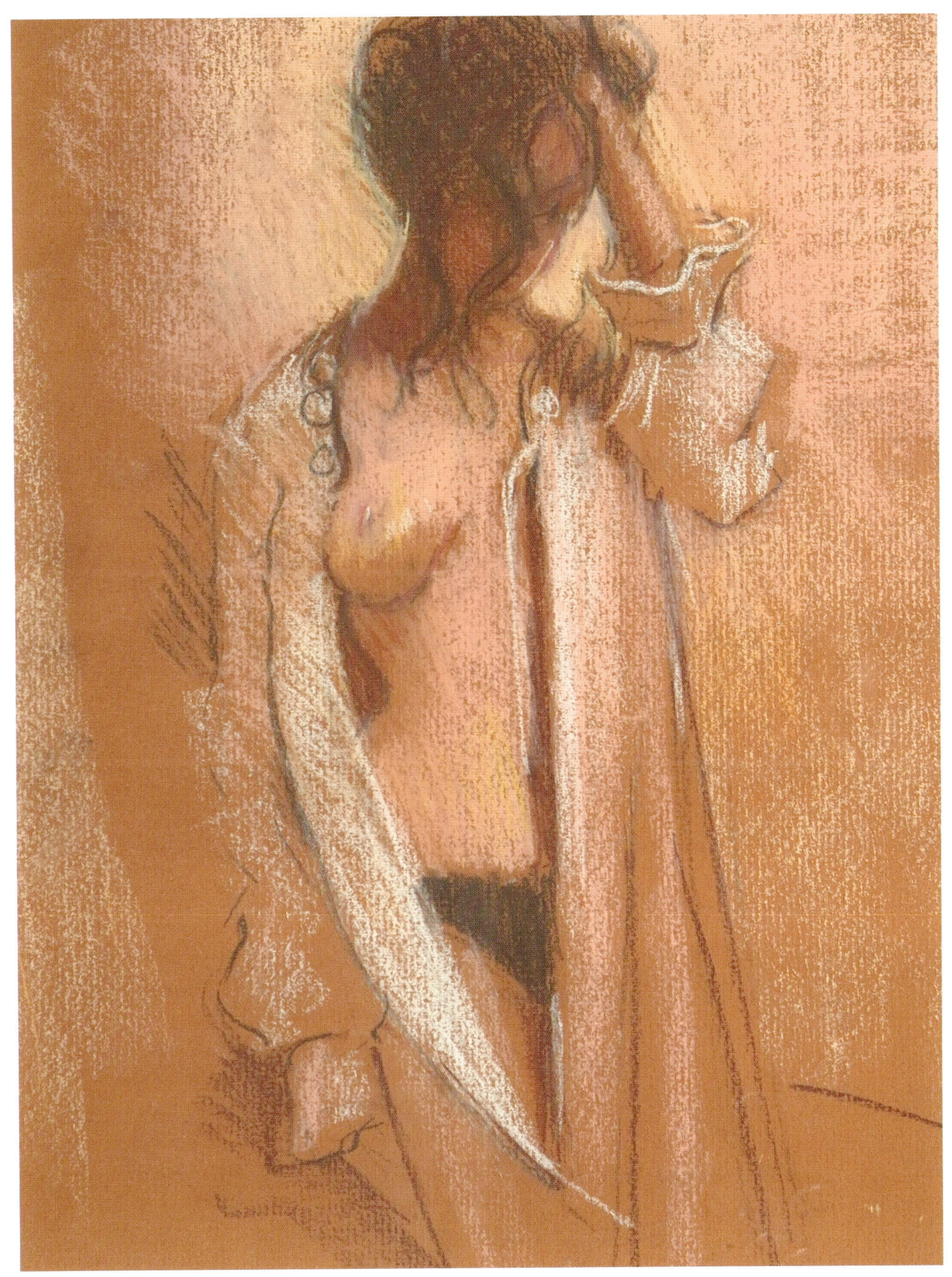

Pajamas 2002
Pastel on paper, 12 1/2″ x 9 1/2″

Evan Penny 1953-

A rubber impression serves as the mold for thin sheets of silicone and rayon into which Evan Penny paints his arsenal of wrinkles, blemishes, freckles, and eye bags onto eight layers of artificial human skin. After several treatments, a coat of liquid resin and fiberglass permanently sets the chosen facial features in place before glazed eyes and individual strands of human hair are added to complete the illusion.[1] At first glance, the deceptively simplistic virtuosity of the resulting figure warrants nothing more than space in a wax museum or a Hollywood soundstage, which, in fact, is where Penny first learned the craft. But set against the backdrop of its contemporaries, Penny's eerily lifelike creations begin to fill a significant artistic void, attacking the perceived "truth" of photography in three dimensions as Photorealism has in two.

To this end, Penny himself has said, "My intent is to situate the sculptures perceptually between the way we might see each other in real time and space, and the way we imagine our equivalent in a photographic representation."[2] Through a work like *L. Faux: CMYK*, for example, Penny began to achieve his aim with a perfectly accurate, albeit out-of-focus, bust in order to carry the planar distortions typical of trick photography into sculptural form. "We try to imagine a technology that created these effects; a technology that doesn't exist," David Clark wrote, and in the process of our searching, we realize Penny has convincingly shown "the project of realism...entangled with the trajectory of photography."[3]

In the Collection's *Aerial*, Penny is once again at work conflating the planar realm with the sculptural. As David Moos described in the exhibition catalog chronicling *Aerial's* debut, "Penny's work takes over the effects of photography and translates them into sculpture. A work such as *Aerial* accentuates this ambition by rendering a nude male figure simultaneously in two and three dimensions. The aluminum base of Aerial is flush with the wall, and the feet of the man are nearly flat. As our gaze ascends this drastically foreshortened figure that we see from above, the sculpture acquires dimensional volume. Penny signals this transition, from image to sculpture, by having the man reach back with one hand to touch the wall, to stabilize the illusion of this palpable perception."[4]

William Ganis commented on the effects of this transition, claiming that Aerial befits "our digital zeitgeist" because it reveals that "the difficult-to-realize anamorphoses and planar distortions...are now push-button available and have entered the common visual lexicon."[5] The accessibility to unreality in everyday life that Penny augments, however, is not without its own set of concerns, as he commented in a recent interview: "Any shift in the representation of the body produces a deep anxiety...Today, the question of what is real and what is not is in such a constant state of flux. You can't look at the representation of a body without feeling its implications in your own sense of self."[6] Although Penny does provide some relief from the existential crisis he has created—through elements like the extended hand in Aerial—it is nevertheless impossible to deny that Penny "has taken his work outside the canonizing traditions of figurative sculpture and thrown in his lot with a radical rethinking of visual culture."[7]

[1] Shattuck, "What it Takes," 24.
[2] Penny, "Artist Statement."
[3] Clark, "Evan Penny's Uncertainty Principle."
[4] Moos, "Evan Penny."
[5] Ganis, "Evan Penny: Sperone Westwater," 75.
[6] Quoted in Milroy, "Skin Deep," R1.
[7] Clark, "Evan Penny's Uncertainty Principle."

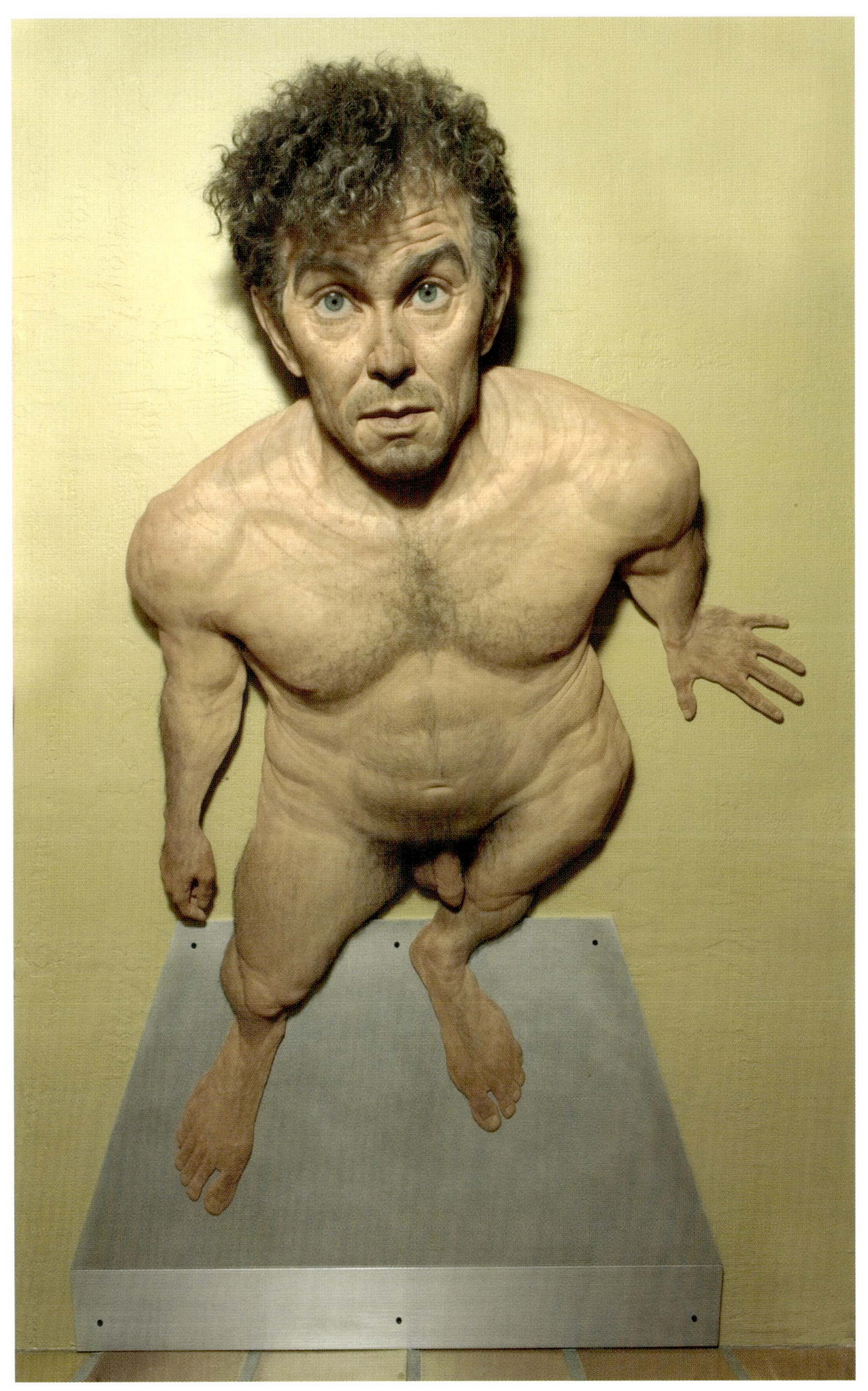

Aeriel 2005
Silicon pigment, hair, fabric, aluminum, 106″ x 60″ x 13″

John Salt 1937-

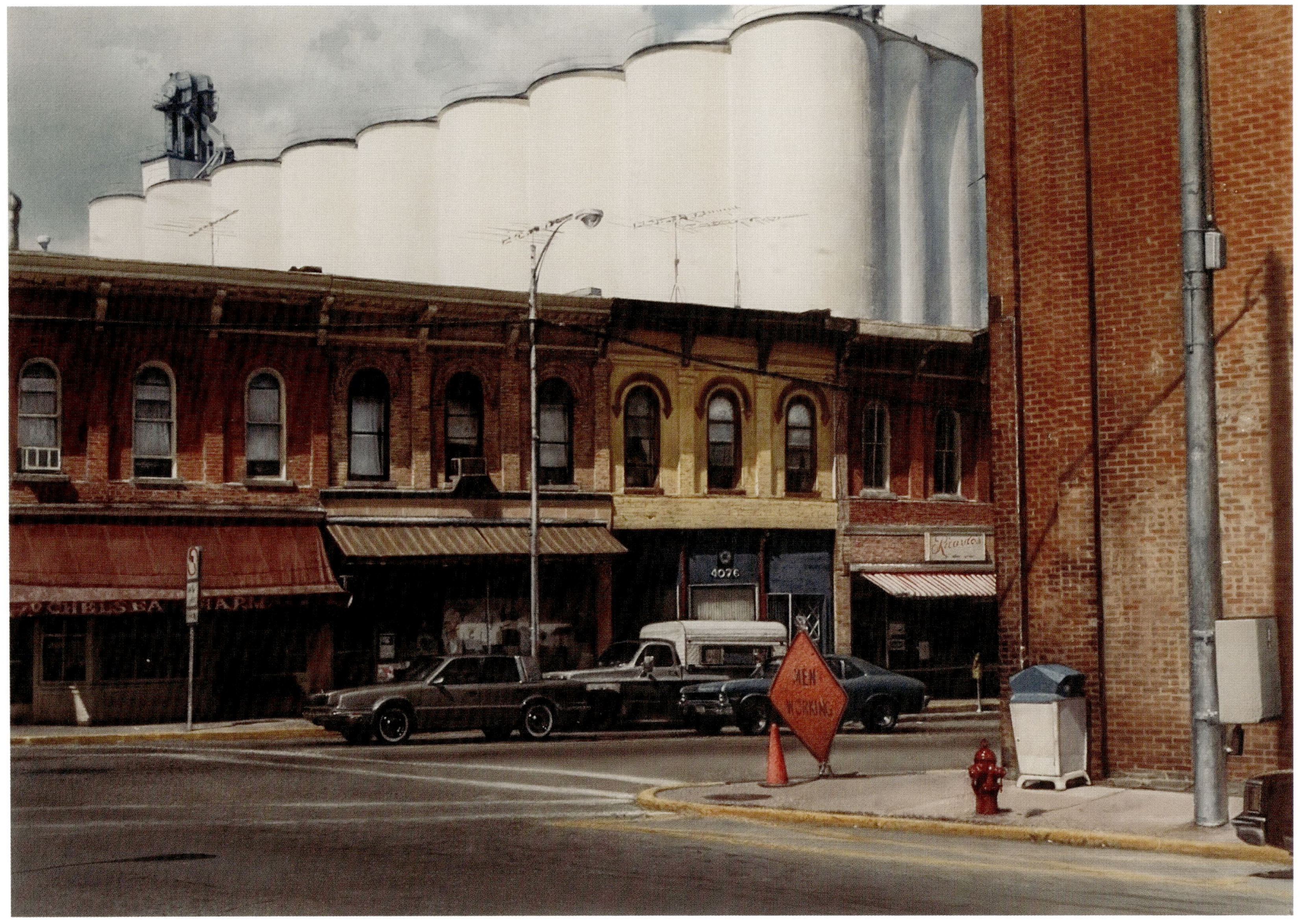

Street Profile with Grain Elevators 1990
Watercolor on paper, 24″ x 36″

Barry Flanagan 1941-

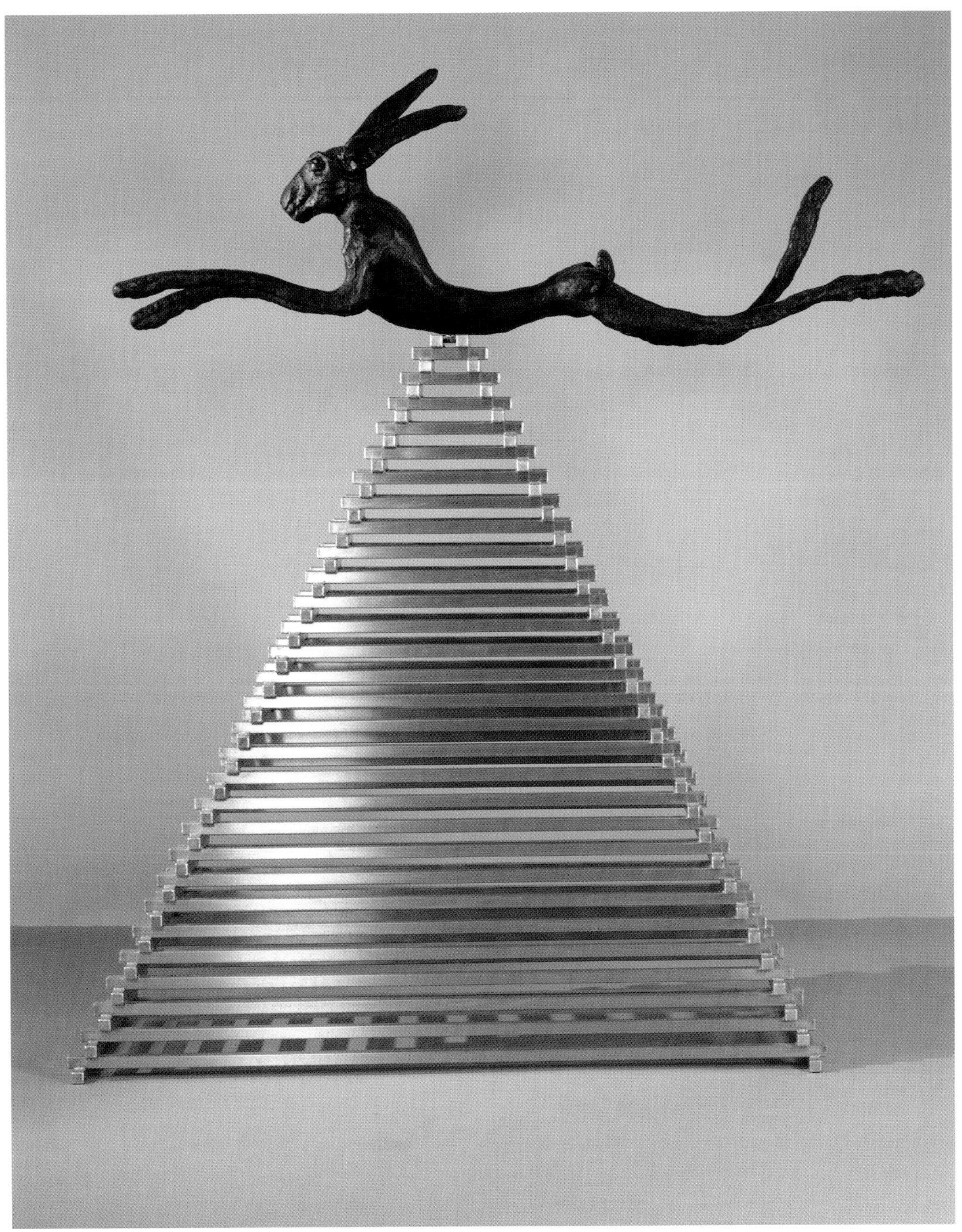

Hells Bells 2005
Bronze on Steel Base, 95 1/4″ x 86 5/8″ x 26 3/8″

Marc Quinn 1964-

In a series of marble portraits, Marc Quinn explored the curious visual similarity between sculptures of living amputees and sculptures from antiquity that have fragmented over time. To achieve this effect, Quinn employed the poses and materials of Greek and Roman art, entrenching his sculptures firmly within a classical realm. In stressing this similarity, however, he also revealed the paradox that, as viewers, we are taught to read deformed, classical figures as though whole—and still fully capable of communicating the beauty of their age—but we see amputees as though ruined, stripped of their role as ambassadors to our culture.[1] Quinn instead chose to take such classical works literally, exploring how a modern audience might react if the statue were to instantly materialize as flesh.

The model for *Selma Mustajbasic* lost her leg while at a bar in her native country of Bosnia, when a bombing raid destroyed her hometown. She was an appropriate subject for Quinn, whose series *Group Portrait* also includes victims of car accidents, a thalidomide baby, and a woman once afflicted by meningococcal septicaemia, all of whom lost limbs to their respective tragedies. Quinn portrayed only those who had adequate time to reflect on their loss, believing they better understood that their new external reality undermined neither the world they represented nor their own inner beauty.[2]

Quinn also allowed the model to choose his or her own pose, which he saw as an inquiry into body image self-perception.[3] *Selma Mustajbasic*, who has one of the more tame abnormalities in the series, is posed discreetly; from the front and back, her deformity is all but erased. Yet from the side, her bent, intact leg frames the negative space created by her accident, highlighting her injury.

Of course, Quinn does not see her injury as a loss at all, but rather as an opportunity to dispel the physical limitations of our exteriors and to focus on the infinite possibilities of our interiors.[4] As such, his work transforms what might be considered a physical violation of the laws of nature into its polar opposite: a spiritually beautiful phenomenon that renders our worship of the ideal body image rather irrelevant.[5]

[1] Celant and Quinn, "About *Peter Hull*," 60.
[2] Celant and Quinn, "About *Peter Hull*," 59-61.
[3] Ibid.
[4] Celant, "On the Path to Eden," 12.
[5] Ibid.

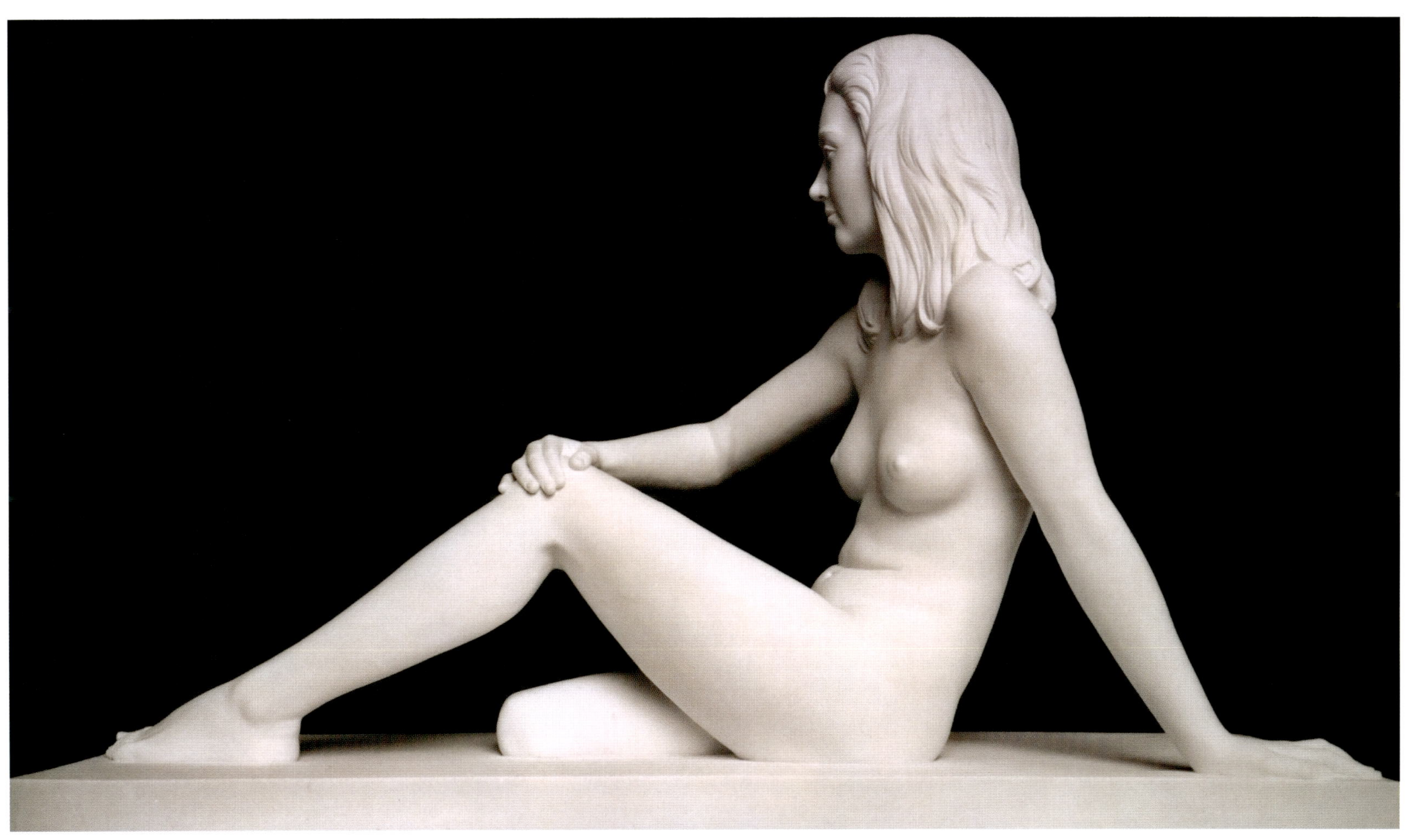

Selma Mustajbasic 2000
White marble, 35″ x 22″ x 57″

George Segal 1934-2000

After breaking the taboo against direct-cast plaster sculptures, from which he creates starkly white figures of convincing corporeality, George Segal turned to bas-relief as a means for synthesizing sculpture and painting.[1] The fusion allowed Segal to return to the wall and to his painterly instincts without sacrificing his already established identity as a contemporary sculptor. By the late 1980s, however, this pursuit evolved again, merging with an earlier interest in female nudes.[2]

To simplify the many new facets of his evolving form, Segal revived the spartan environments of his 1970 nudes, which were able to define a setting without detracting from the featured figure. *Woman Against Black Window* serves as a telling example of this marriage of interests: the thinly clothed plaster bust is portrayed with a single piece of fragmented furniture and the architectural element of a window—just enough for the rough-hewn background color to provide the necessary accompaniment of emotion and narrative.

Like so many of Segal's previous experiments, the bas-reliefs form a ghostly tableau that is affected as much by a sense of spiritual isolation as by the artist's sincere attempt to convey his compassion for humanity. In part, Segal derives his need to depict this fragile inner life from the direct contact he has with his sitters during the casting process, a procedure that Segal claims forces sitters to be "just as stoic and brave, or screaming and hysterical as they really are...They can't pretend with me."[3] In contrast to the wit and distanced irony associated with Pop Art of the time, Segal's approach seems sated with the dignity and individuality of his sitters.[4]

In *Woman Against Black Window*, Segal blended classical elements with his new style, introducing the Old Master technique of chiaroscuro into his cast to convey an acutely somber mood. As Segal explained, the resulting shades of black and white not only define the emotional environment, but also "indicate some of those strange lights and darks that are purely imaginative."[5] Against this ageless tactic, Segal merged Duchamp's contemporary use of the ready-made, placing a found chair and window around the featured cast figure, suggesting that beyond its environs, the body itself is the most natural point of departure for expressing the human experience.[6]

[1] Livingstone, *Retrospective George Segal*, 23, 15.
[2] Ibid., 92.
[3] Segal, "Sense of 'Why Not?'," 149.
[4] Théberge, Preface to *Retrospective George Segal*, 8.
[5] Quoted in Livingstone, *Retrospective George Segal*, 136.
[6] Livingstone, *Retrospective George Segal*, 57.

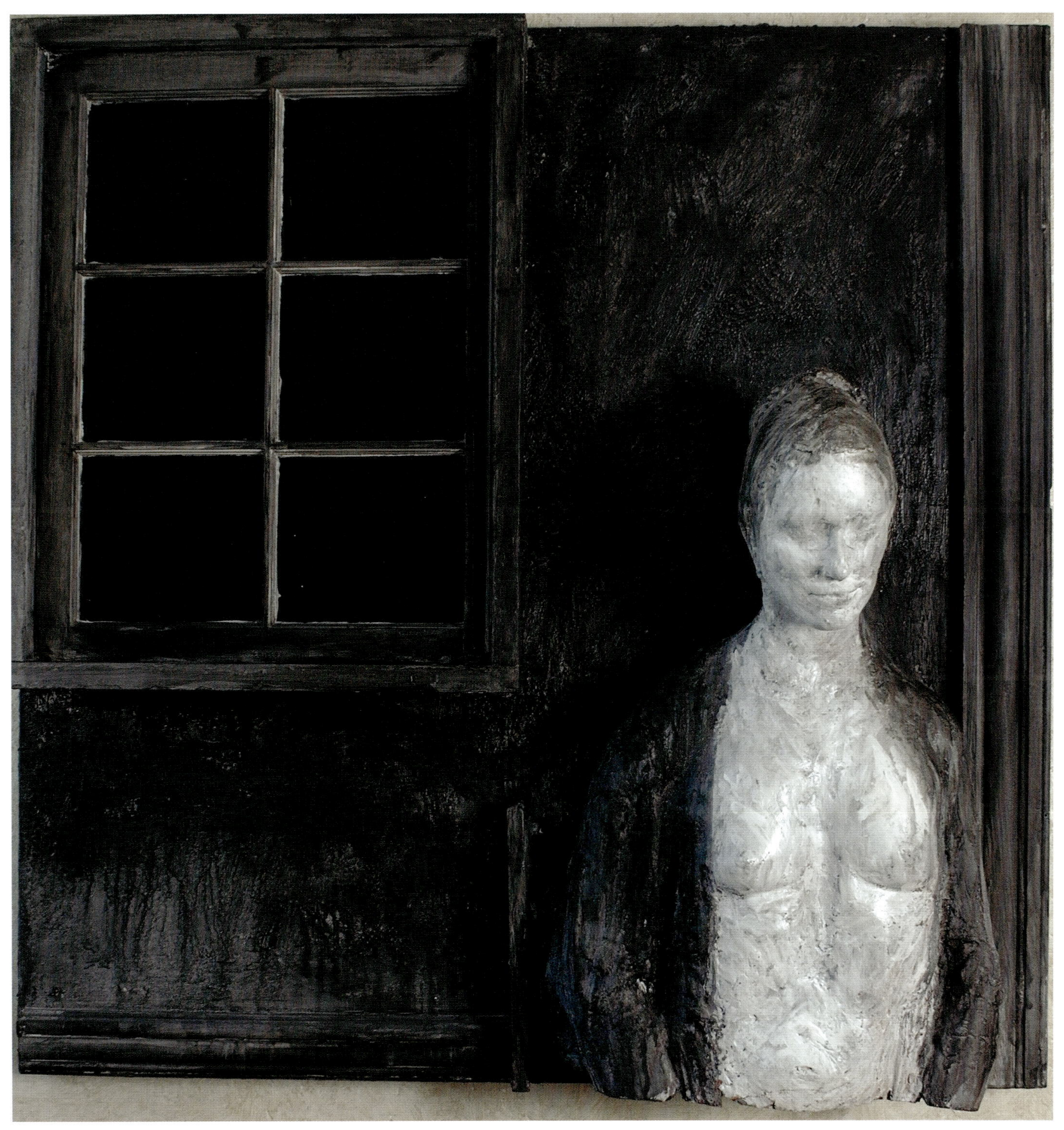

Woman Against Black Window 1989-90
Plaster, acrylic paint, wood, and glass, 48″ x 48″x 14″

Al Hansen 1927-1995

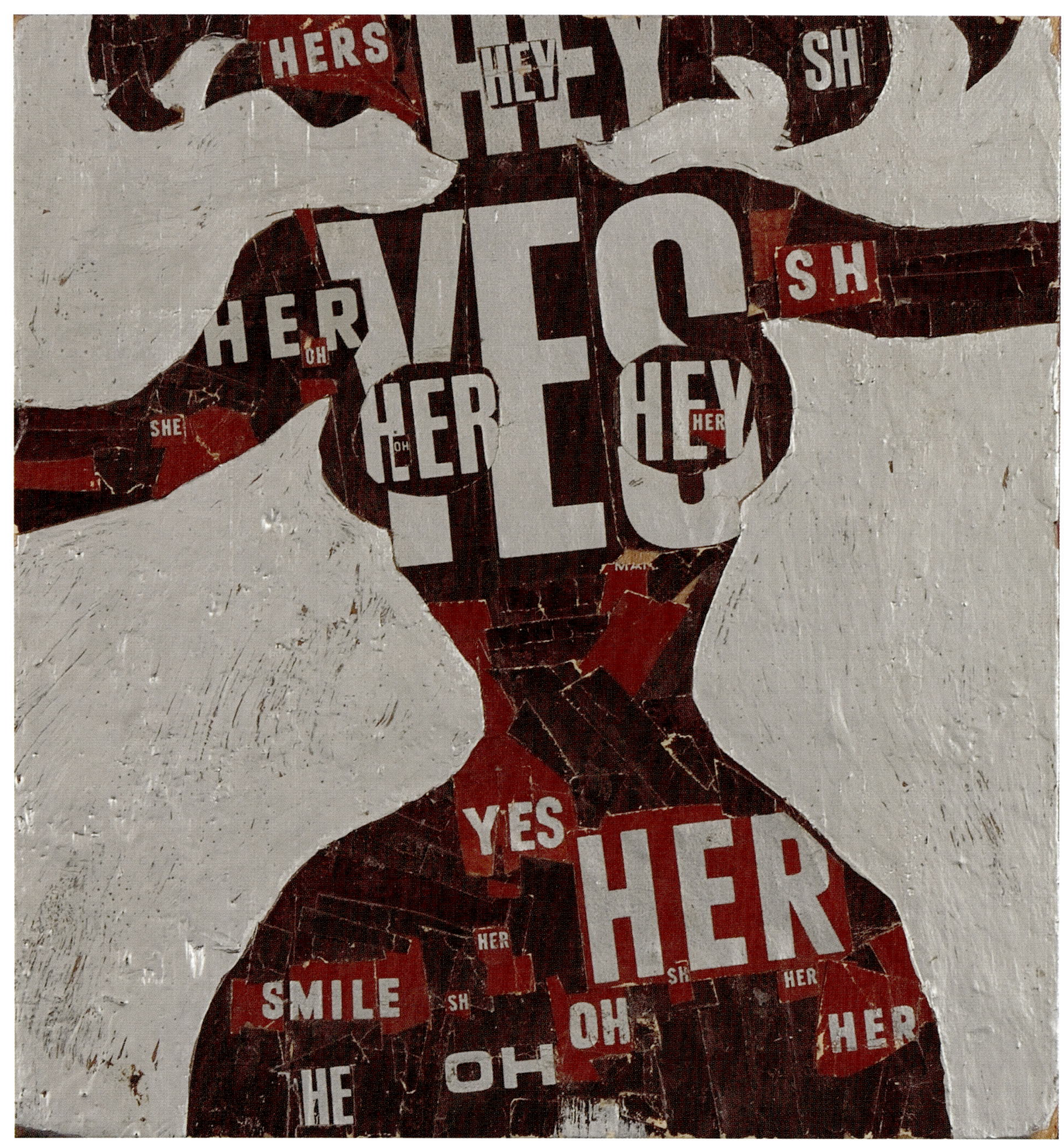

Happy Birthday Joan with Love (or whatever that is) 1972
Hershey wrappers on wood, 6″ x 5 1/2″

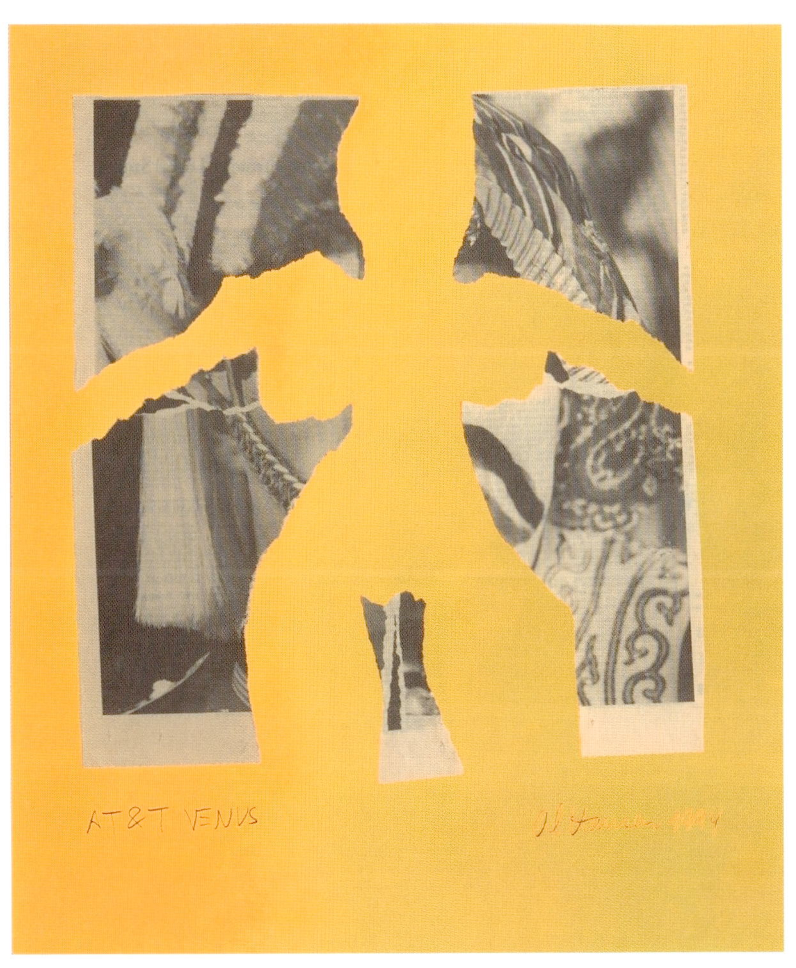

AT&T Venus (Orange) 1994
Newspaper collage, 16 3/4″ x 13 3/4″

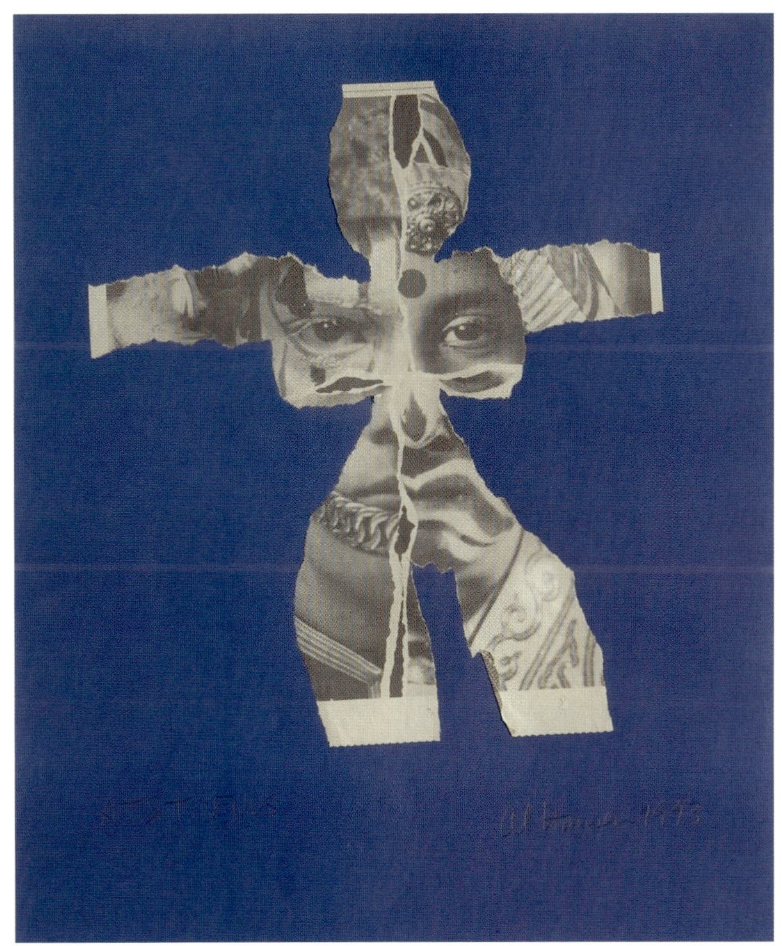

AT&T Venus (Blue) 1994
Newspaper collage, 16 3/4″ x 13 3/4″

Larry Rivers 1923-2002

Following his dark reworking of Leutze's *Washington Crossing the Delaware* (1953), Larry Rivers again found himself with a macabre but patriotic scene in a *LIFE* magazine photograph. Bearing the caption, "End of the Gallant Rebs," the image showed the coffin of the last Civil War veteran, Walter Williams, draped in a Confederate flag and attended by a marine—the perfect blend of American folk history and national iconography for a Rivers work.[1]

As with *Washington Crossing the Delaware*, Rivers sought to capitalize on a familiar headline narrative by subverting the expected visual content and deconstructing the imagery into distinct, fragmentary planes. The violent rupturing of the scene, in turn, alludes to other dialectic splits particular to the given narrative—its concurrent presence of life and death, the remnants of a confederate South in a reunited nation, and the simultaneity of a past-lived history and its inherited present reincarnation.[2] Through the use of such appropriation, cropping, and fragmenting of images pulled from the collective memory bank, Rivers aimed to parallel the way we receive and ultimately come to understand significant historical moments.[3]

Nevertheless, Rivers's work is not aimed entirely at dispelling public misconstructions of history; his collage style and repetition of subject matter also reveal many of his own personal uncertainties, such as his search for an acceptable national identity. In life as in his paintings, Rivers seems to settle upon an accretive approach, combining traces of his Jewish heritage with fragments of the American identity, all the while mocking elements of both.[4]

In a time when abstraction still dominated the artist's New York school, Rivers's historical paintings remained faithful to a figurative, anecdotal method, melding clichéd images of mass circulation with mechanisms of high art until they became both comprehensible and—like the mass media stories he sought to trace—more fleeting than of historical import. Only later in works such as *The Last Civil War Veteran* did Rivers succumb to the type of severe visual distortion and abstraction of tonality that carried a far darker message, intended to transcend the initial moment of interpretation that Rivers coveted in *Study for Last Civil War Veteran*.

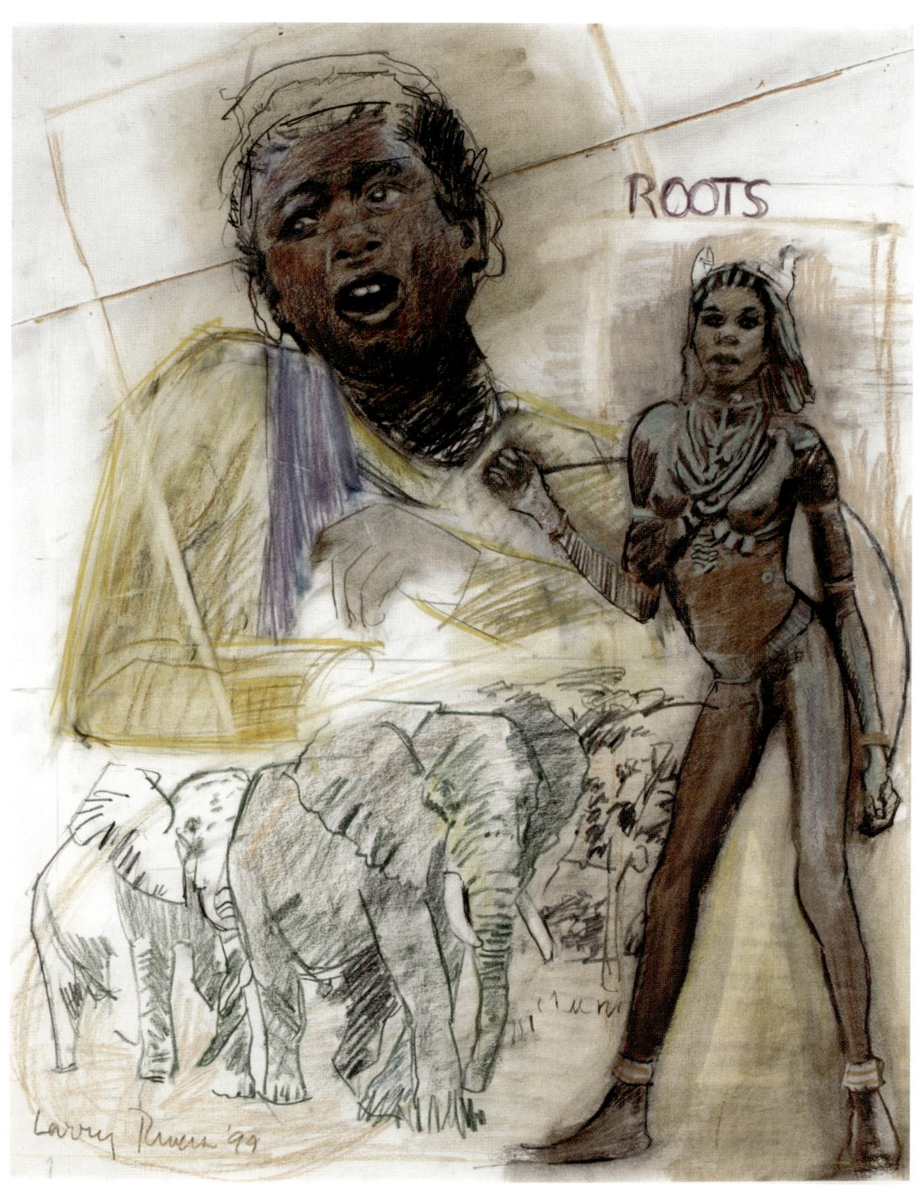

Roots, The Auction and Other Visions of Slavery 1994
Pencil and colored pencil on paper, 27 5/8" x 23 1/2"

[1] Hunter, introduction to *Larry Rivers*, 28-29.
[2] Hunter, "Larry Rivers, Public and Private," 47.
[3] Bonito, *Get Real*, 118.
[4] Hunter, introduction to *Larry Rivers*, 11.

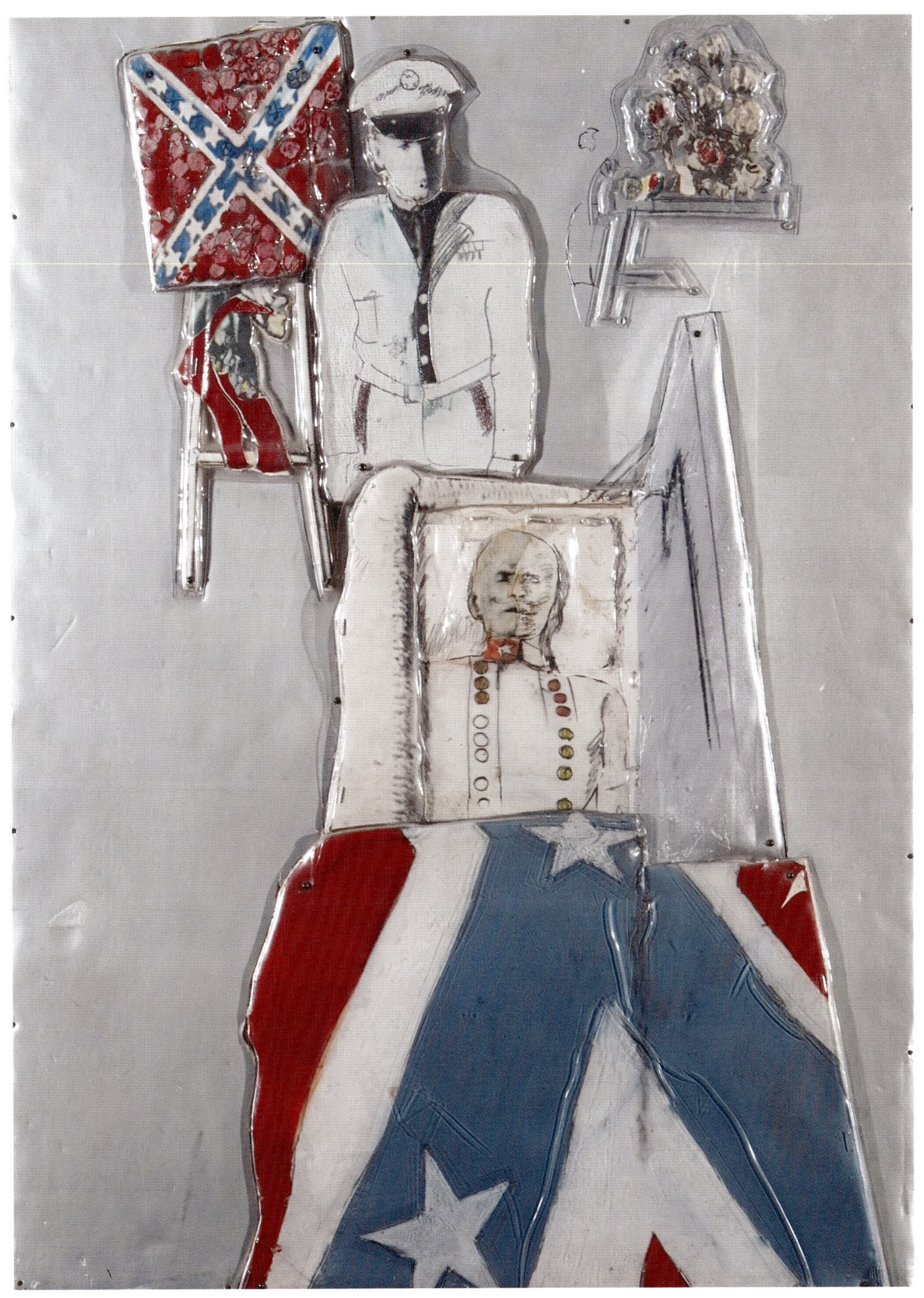

Study for Last Civil War Veteran 1970
Mixed media, 31″ x 23″ x 1 1/2″

Su-en Wong 1973-

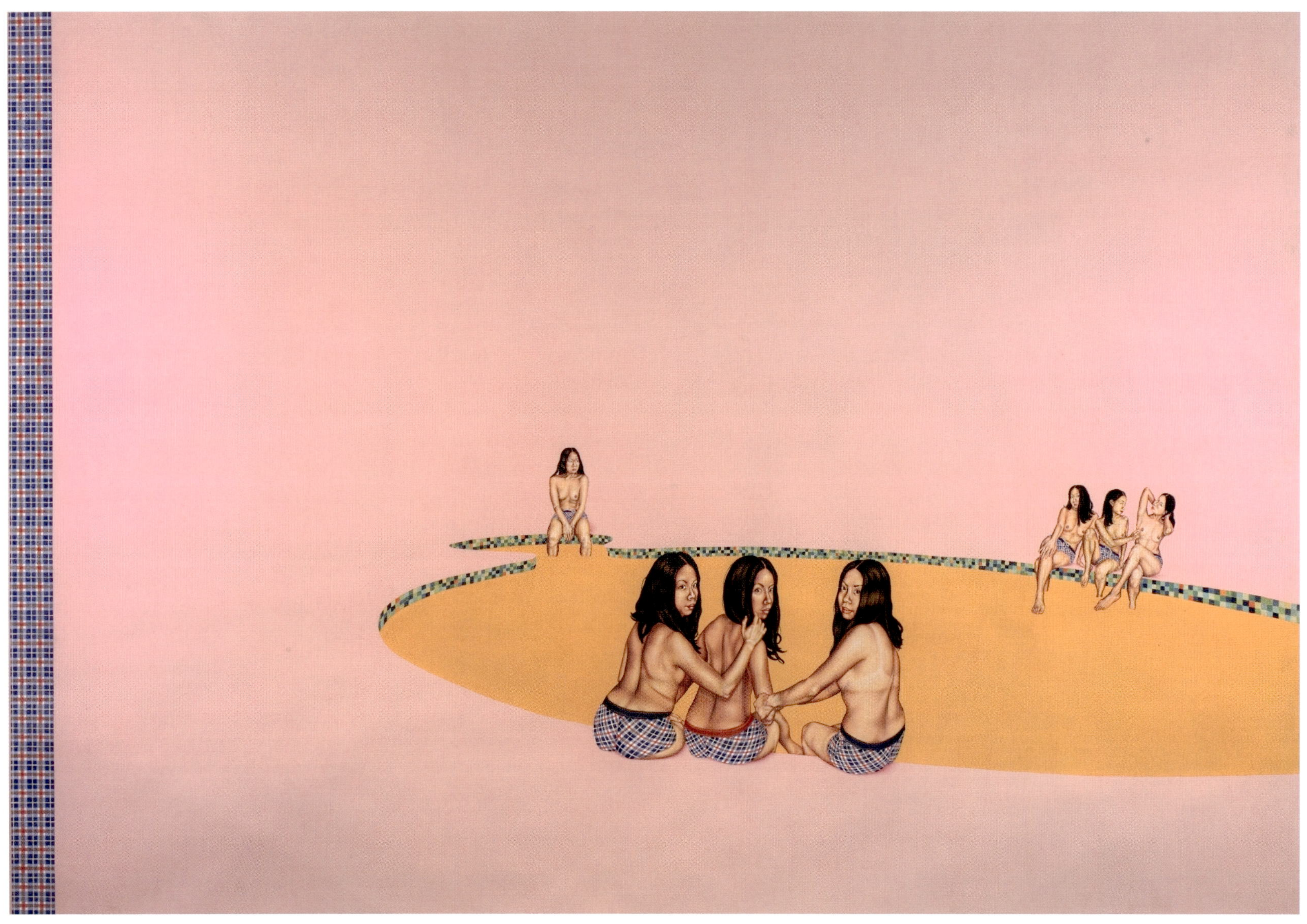

Full Bloom 2002
Colored pencil on paper, 80″ x 118″

Jenny Saville 1970-

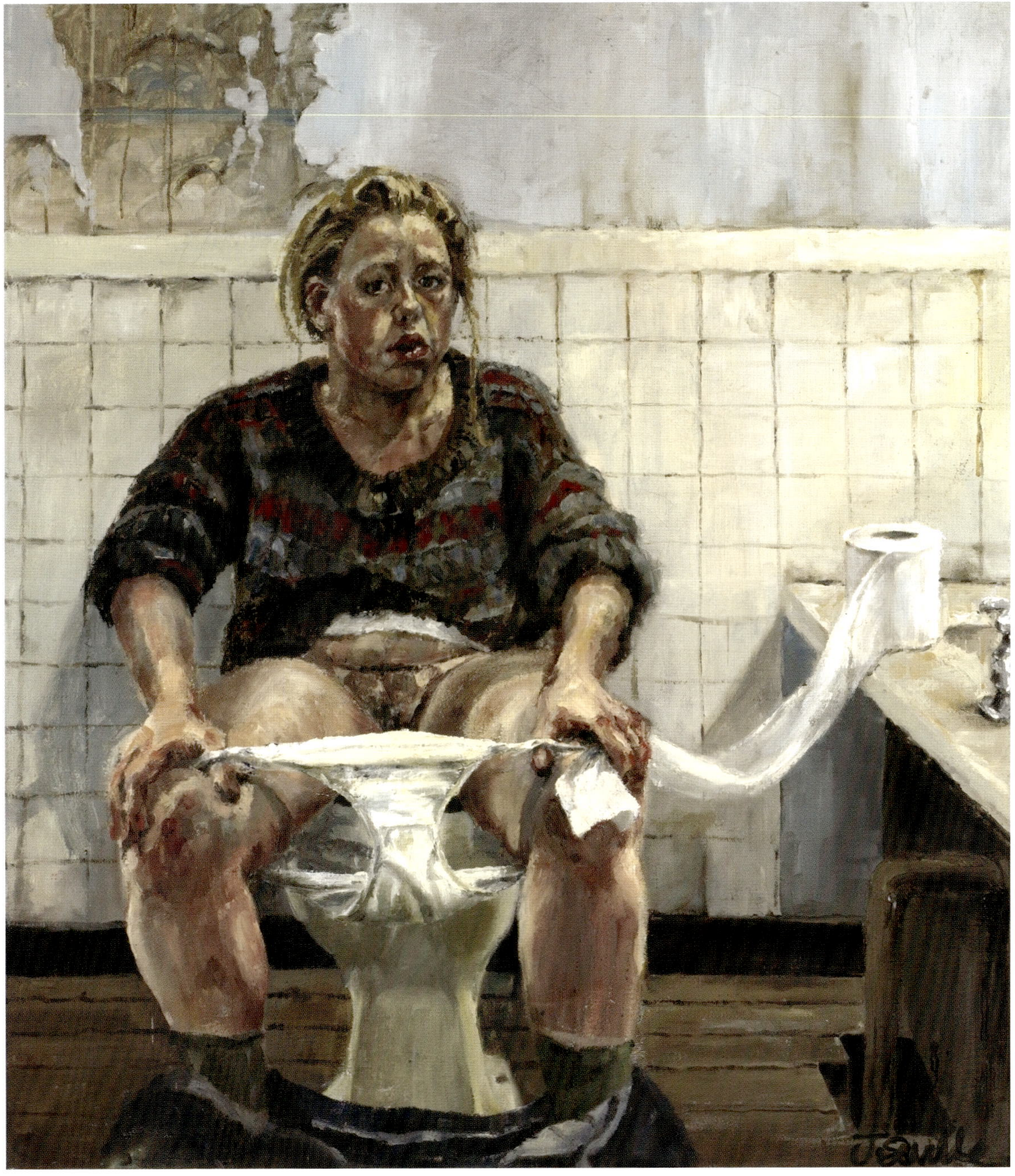

Self Portrait 1991
Oil on canvas, 53 7/8″ x 48″

Richard Diebenkorn 1922-1993

At the height of his success in the abstract style, Richard Diebenkorn abruptly turned to figure drawing. Though he experimented with the genre and its propensity for narrative sensuality through a variety of different media, he almost always adopted the same subject matter: the female form and its relationship to new surroundings.

In *Untitled (RD 850)*, one of his more elaborate charcoal works, Diebenkorn developed an interior landscape replete with architectural and geometric motifs that blur the line between simple, domestic furnishings and free-floating patterns evocative of his earlier abstractions. His female model, who serves as the visual and emotive centerpiece of the work, struggles to free herself from the potency of these geometric abstractions. Her outer elbow and knee form playfully akimbo diagonals that force the viewer's eye into the patterned background, while Diebenkorn's loose stroke spares his nude nothing, treating her with the same irregular and overlapping line.

Despite the lingering echoes of his earlier work, Diebenkorn was eager to consider the psychological potential of figural drawings, and he sought to stage an appropriate and worthy scene, making no attempt to conceal his model's calculated pose behind a candid snapshot aesthetic. Instead, Diebenkorn spent great energy posing his nude to maximize the subtle effects engendered by her relationship with strange surroundings, focusing on the juxtaposition of textures, the blending of color, and the properties of light and shadow—all of which he viewed as integral to the scene's honesty and intimacy. Ironically, many critics have argued that Diebenkorn betrayed this vision of intimacy through the distortion of his model's facial expression, which is reduced to an impression rather than a particular likeness.[1] Nevertheless, his work stands as both a compelling portrait of the emotion derived from posture and as a landscape of a dark interior that is nothing if not idiosyncratically Diebenkorn.

[1]Norland, *Richard Diebenkorn*, 93.

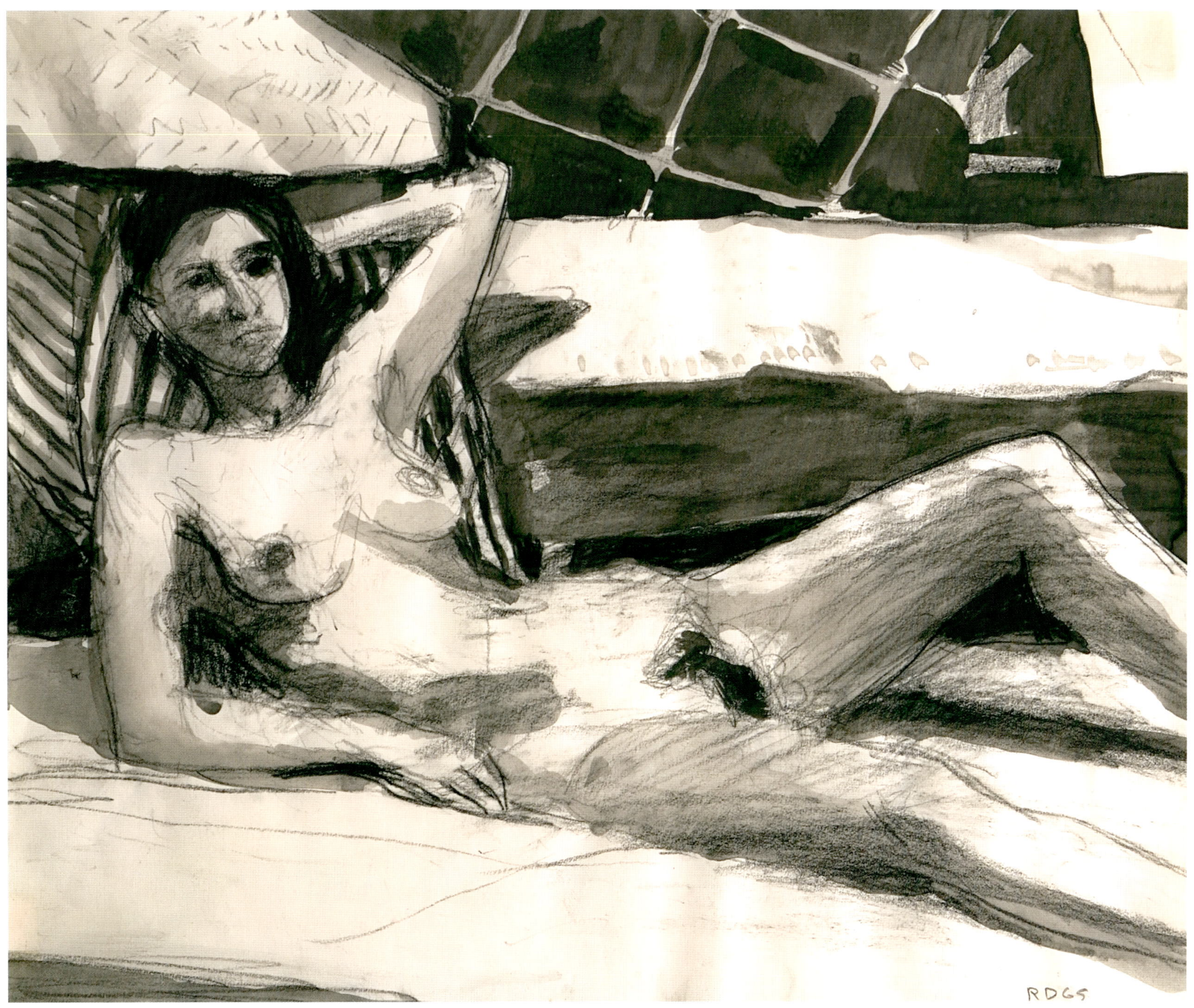

Untitled (RD 850) 1965
Charcoal and ink wash on paper, 14″ x 17″

James Rosenquist 1933-

In 1906, Claude Debussy wrote a short piano piece for his two-year-old daughter titled *Serenade for the Doll*. Its simple staccato rhythm mimicked a mechanical wind-up doll with accelerating and decelerating ostinatos, rendering the listener unsure of the piece's ultimate optimism or pessimism. Debussy complicated the question by dedicating the work, "To my little daughter Chouchou, with her father's tender apologies for that which follows."[1]

James Rosenquist's series *The Serenade for the Doll After Claude Debussy* functions not only as an artistic sequel to the musical piece, but also as an attempt for the sake of his own daughter to reinterpret Debussy's ambivalence toward the unknowable future of one's child. As such, *Gift Wrapped Doll #37*, the last installment in the series, takes a retrospective, adult view of another childhood plaything: the unwrapped, untouched doll.

Yet clearly, Rosenquist did not intend the doll to stand simply as a blissful symbol of childhood pleasure; instead, the doll is foregrounded with such force that the background is destroyed entirely, rendering the large canvas overtly claustrophobic.[2] His technique also spoils the intimacy associated with the subject, as the paint presses forward beyond the picture plane, intruding on the otherwise safe domain of the viewer.[3] Such aggression may suggest the artist's desire to create a world in which his dire warning is necessary, but at the same time, Rosenquist was conscious not to let his creation of an off-putting world slip too aggressively into the realm of fantasy. He needed it to remain perfectly real, so he rendered the doll with the crispness and exactitude typical of the Photorealist genre, so that she serves as an eerie, believable symbol of his daughter.

In the end, as much as the *Gift Wrapped Doll* series creates yet another lens for Rosenquist's social commentary on the commodification of humanity, it is the personal message to his daughter that endures. Like Debussy, Rosenquist was not yet ready to let his daughter into the world, choosing instead to wrap her in cellophane, thereby preserving her innocence forever.[4] But, also like Debussy, Rosenquist conceded that such a vision could never be a reality, no matter how realistically it was rendered. As a result, Rosenquist followed in his inspiration's footsteps yet again, offering two antithetical versions of his daughter's future as it rushes to penetrate the thinly protective cellophane—both an optimistic hope symbolized by the glinting, reflected light and, conversely, a pessimistic apology symbolized by the possibility of endless darkness.

[1] Claude Debussy, *Coin des Enfants; Petite Suite pour Piano Seul.* Paris: A. Durand, 1908.
[2] Hopps, "Connoisseur of the Inexplicable," 8.
[3] Ibid, 6.
[4] Rosenquist, "Painting, Working, Talking," 107.

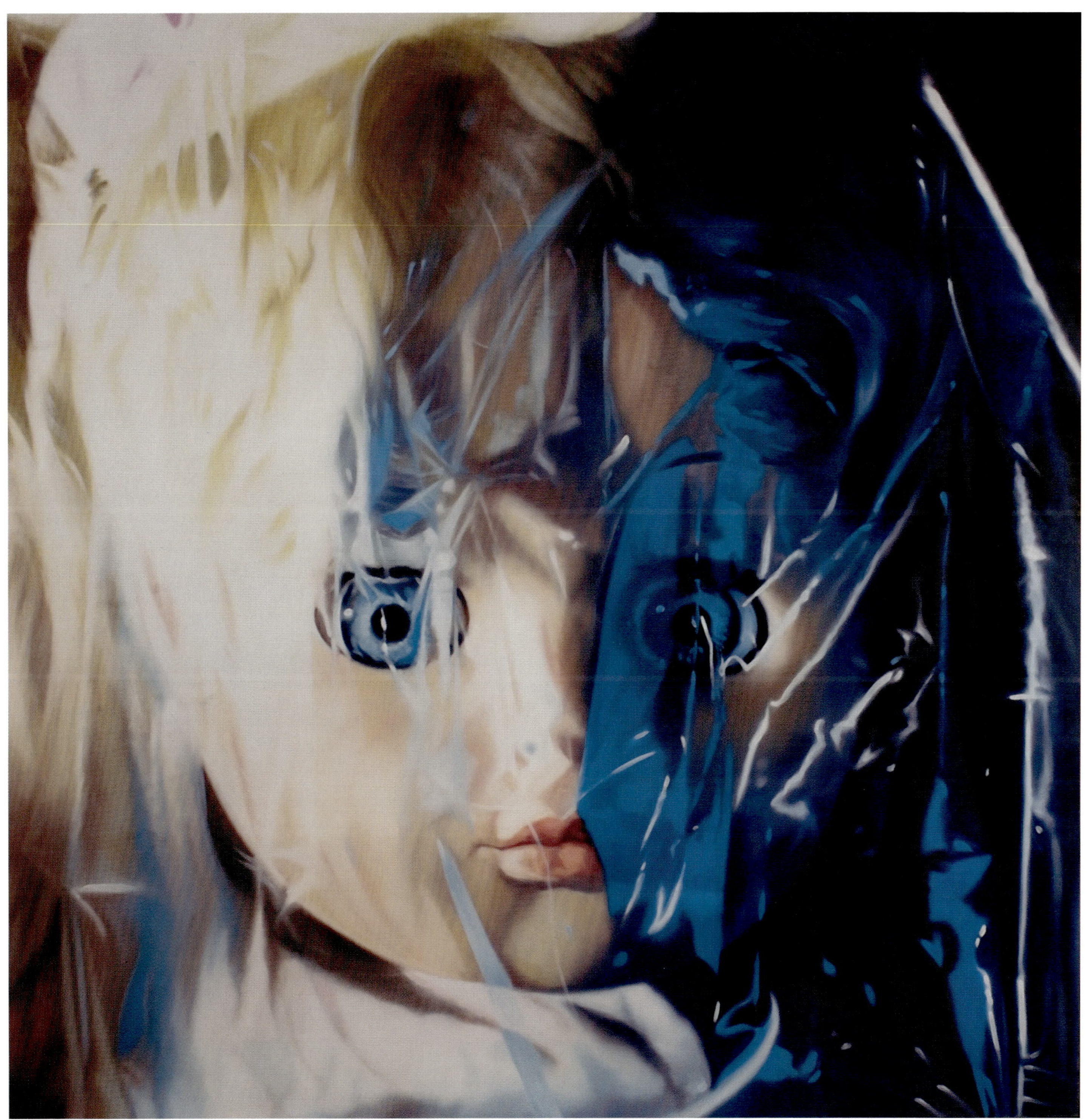

Gift Wrapped Doll #37 1997
Oil on canvas, 60″ x 60″

Raphael Soyer 1899-1987

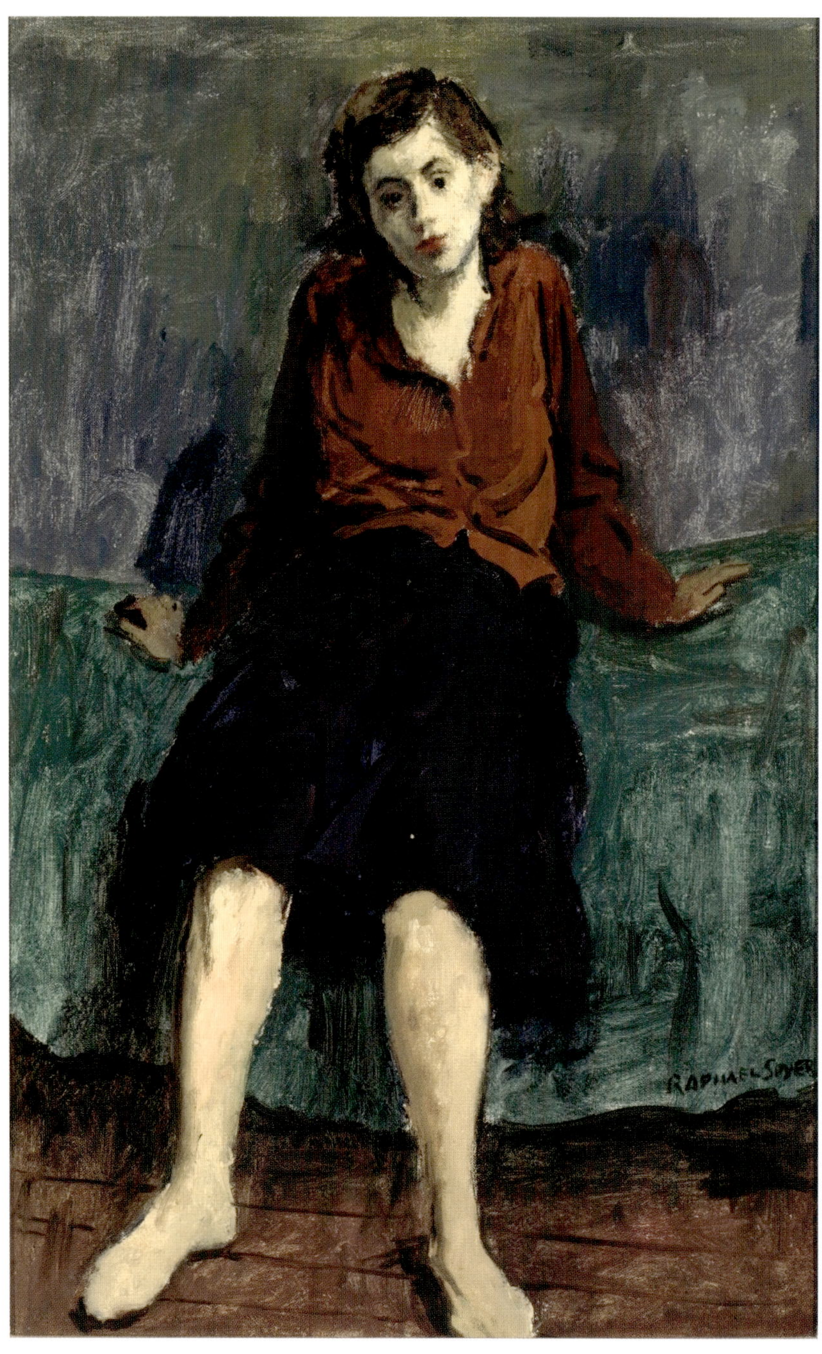

Untitled Seated Woman circa 1935
Oil on canvas, 26 1/4″ x 15 1/2″

Raphaella Spence 1978-

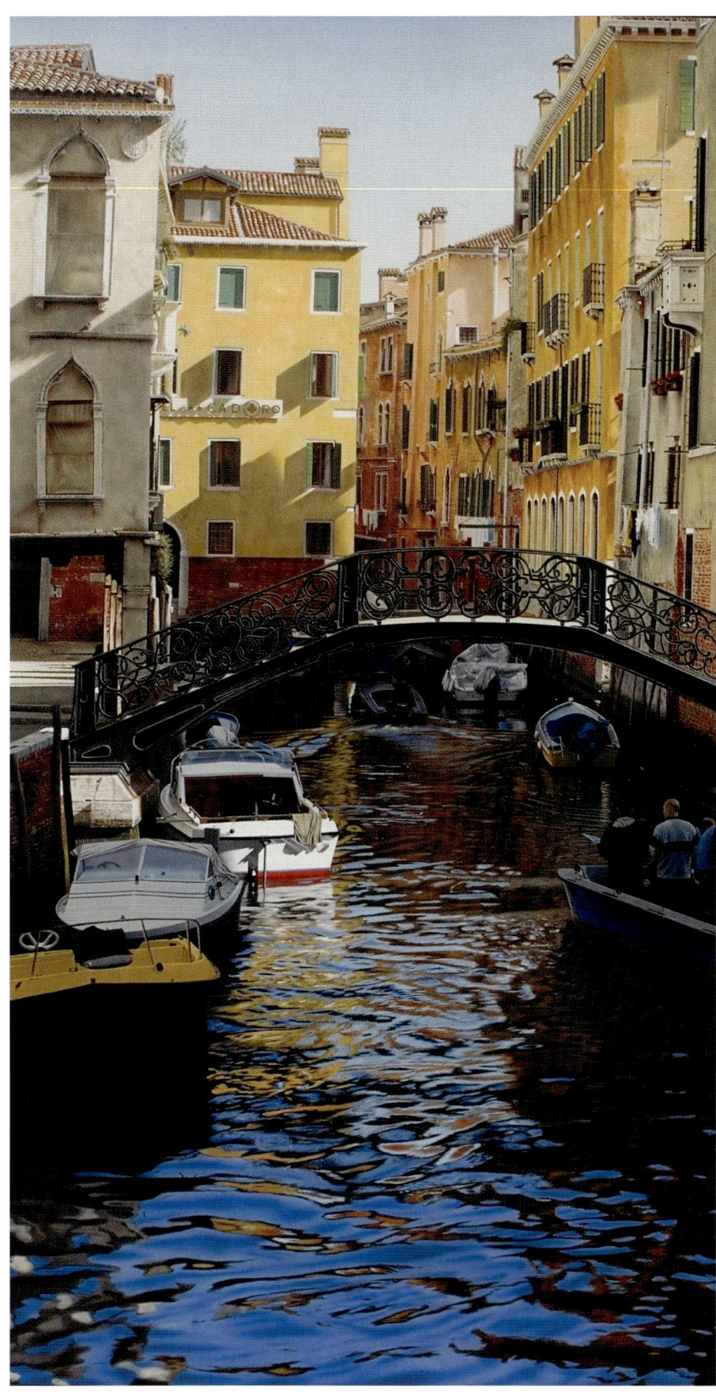

Bridge of Colors 2004
Oil on Canvas, 59″ x 31 1/2″

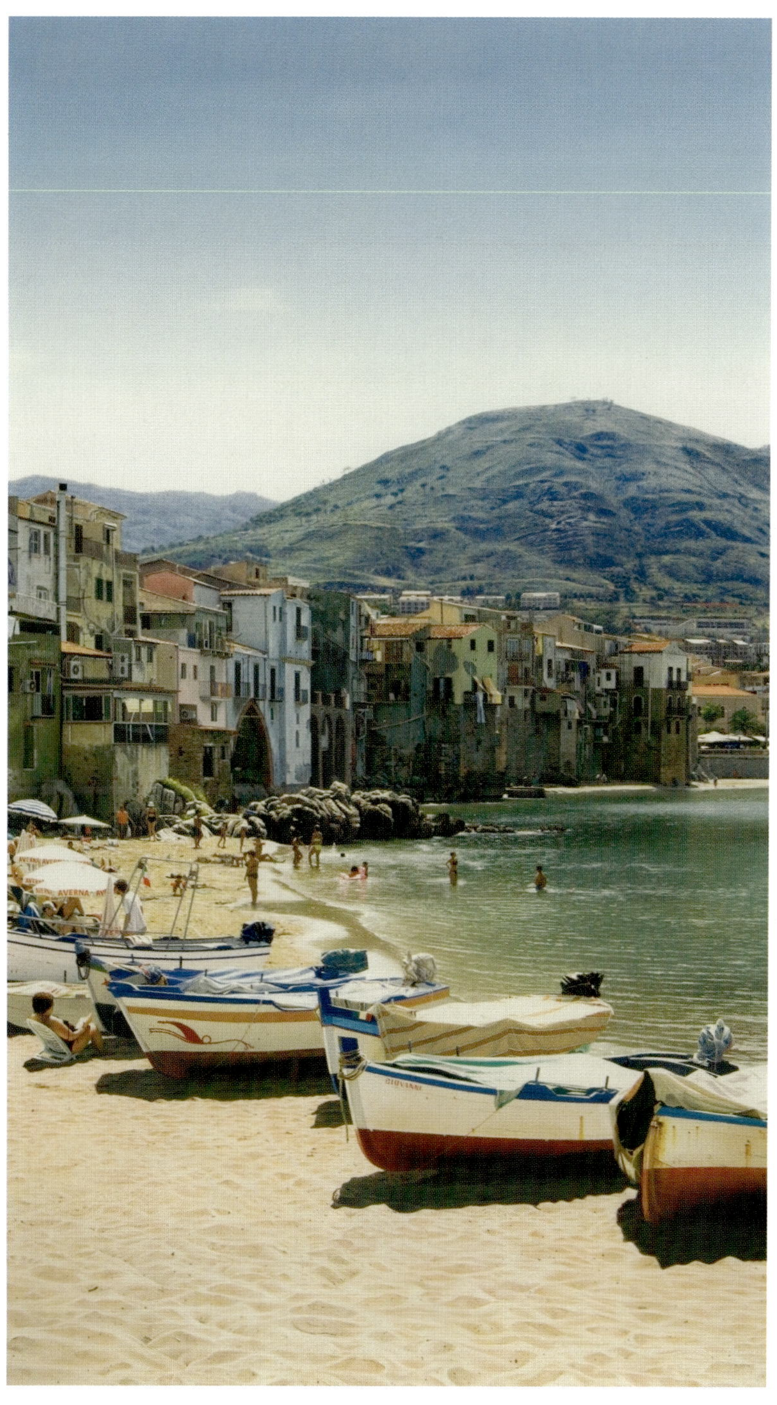

Cefalu 1978
Oil on canvas, 59″ x 34″

Cynthia Westwood 1969-

Much of the historical bias against Photorealism has been focused on artists' common use of photography for source material, as many have maintained that transposing an image from photograph to canvas generally requires less artistic consideration than capturing the image of a model or still life. Cynthia Westwood, however, who paints from photographs, models, and imagination, rejects the claim. "A painting is a series of choices...Photographs often have an out-of-focus background—the camera has made that decision. With a painting, the artist makes all the decisions," she said. "A painter decides what goes in and what doesn't. It is a painter's own vision, which can be determined by the artist's state of mind. The end result is very particular."[1]

For Westwood, the end result has most often involved intimate scenes of women bathing—a construct typically too personal and private to tolerate the interjection of a camera and its operator. Though Westwood tepidly admits that imposing on such a scene involves a degree of discomfort, as her models often seem to be in a suspended state of anxiety before their inevitable calm, Westwood's presence remains largely unacknowledged. As Eric Fischl wrote, "Westwood's almost invisible manner of applying paint suggests an unself-conscious celebration of female physicality with all the transparency of a freshly cleaned window."[2]

Though Fischl has claimed that Westwood's paintings are simply "some of the best 'flesh' paintings to be found today," he has also championed Westwood's art for its infusion of detail and memory.[3] Her work often conjures intense psychological energy that is both sexual and confident, establishing a temporary equilibrium removed from the pressures of an outside world. It is this energy, this heightened state of being to which Fischl credits Westwood's success: "We want to feel that the object is, for the moment, more alive than we are...[We] want the object to still the moment. Our being frozen gives us the chance, the fighting chance, to peer into and perhaps grasp the substance of meaning. Art is, after all, about revelation, and you can't have a revelation unless you are, for an instant, pulled out of the dark flow of your life."[4]

In its stillness, *White Bath* offers us this rare opportunity, a moment to remove ourselves from the world, like its bather, and begin the personal and private search for revelation.

[1] Quoted in Neild, "Painting Makes a Comeback."
[2] Fischl, "Eleven Artists from Everywhere," 23.
[3] Ibid.
[4] Ibid., 22-23.

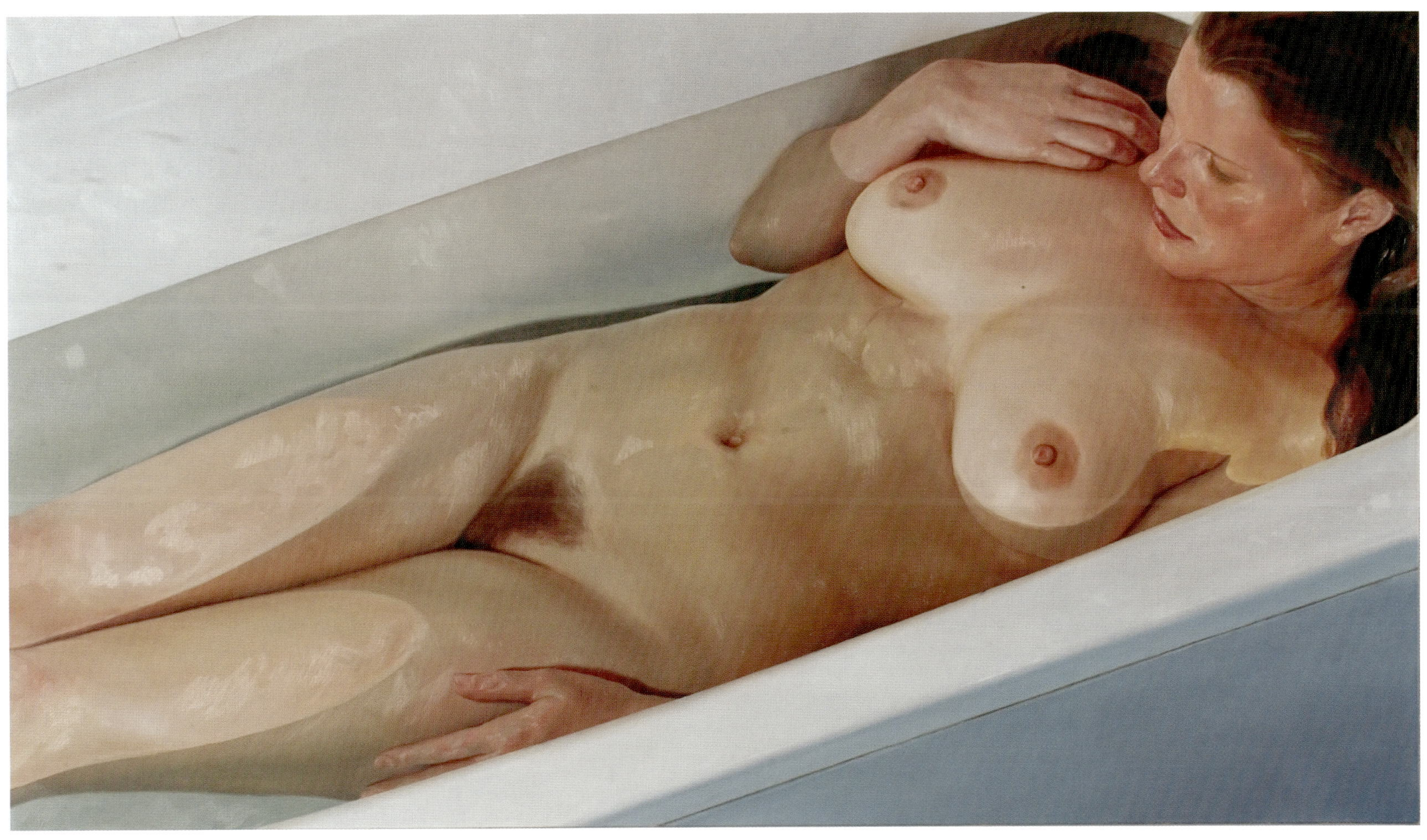

White Bath 2004
Oil on linen, 36″ x 64″

Bernardo Torrens 1957-

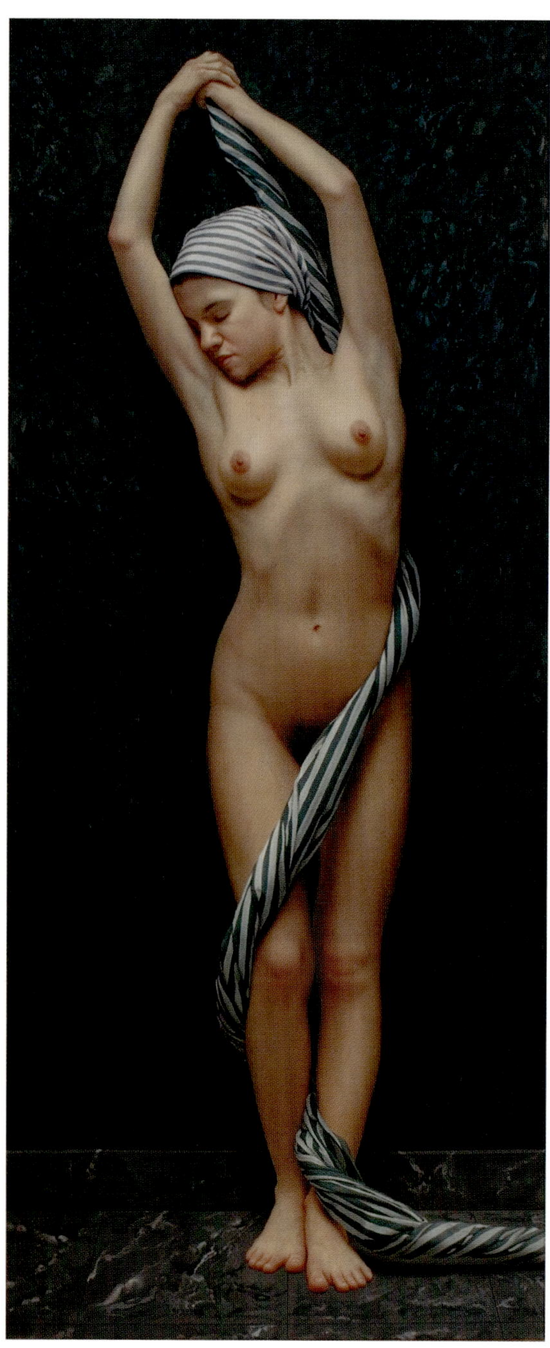

Lakme 1995
Acrylic on panel, 68″ x 29″

Jack Mendenhall 1937-

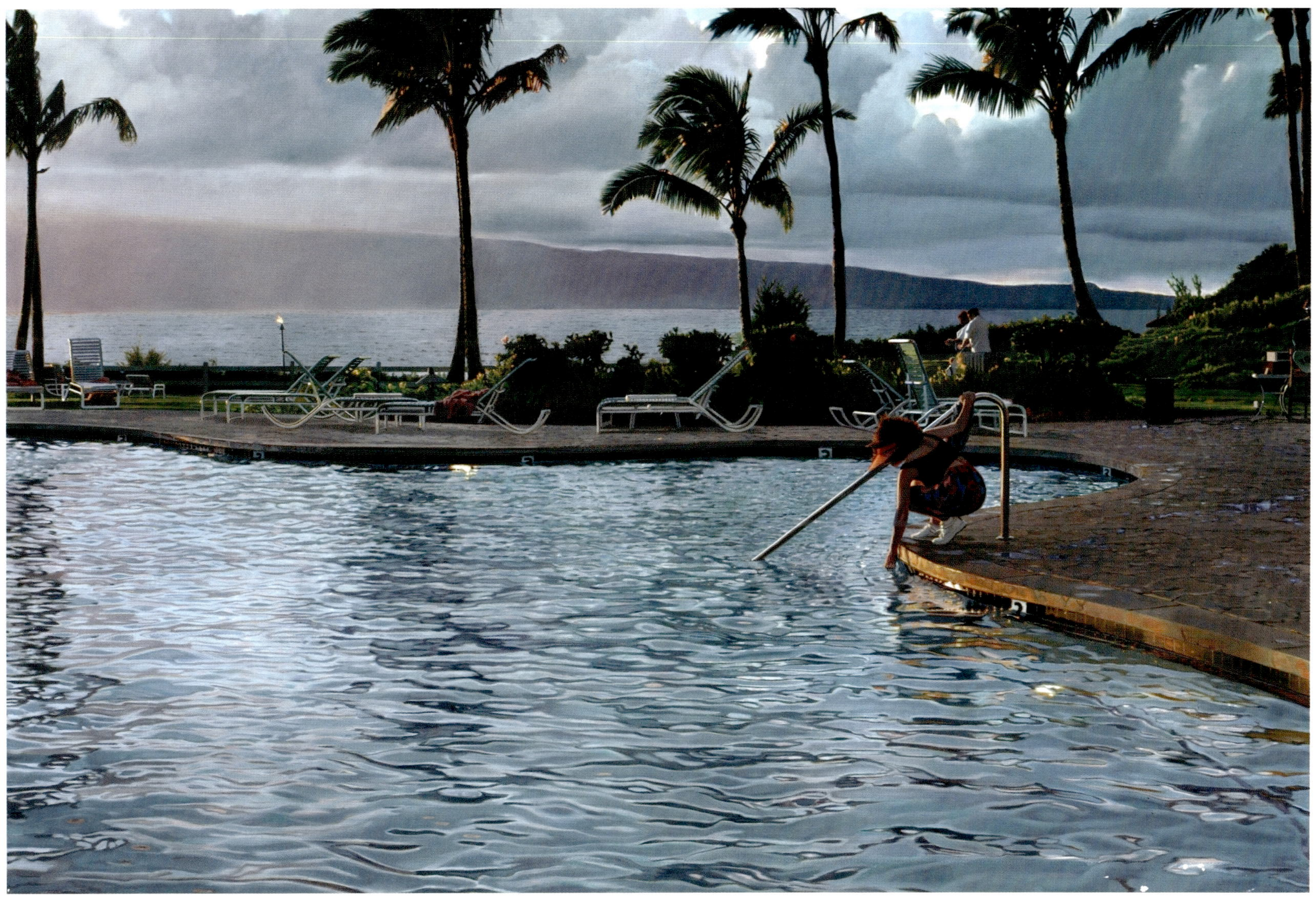

Kapalua 1995
Oil on canvas, 48 1/4″ x 72″

Kiki Smith 1954-

Kiki Smith famously explained in 1990, "I think I chose the body as a subject not consciously, but because it is the one form that we all share; it's something that everybody has their own authentic experience with."[1] Through laboratory vials of human fluids, sketches on flesh-like paper, and, most commonly, various approaches to figurative sculpture, Smith utilizes the undeniable relationship between her viewers and their bodies to present a provocative issue, such as the AIDS crisis or the subordination of women, and subsequently deny any possibility of extrication from it.

But beyond merely engaging viewers in broad representational experiences, Smith focuses on the body as an individual's only connection to the surrounding world, and consequently, as the battleground upon which facets of the surrounding world inevitably stake their claims on the inhabitant's identity. As Helaine Posner wrote in a retrospective chronicling the midpoint in Smith's career, "She [has] always been concerned with the diverse social, political, and economic forces fighting for control of the body, and attentive to the destructive effect these competing agendas have on an individual's ability to establish a coherent sense of self."[2]

In the Collection's *Now*, it is evident that concern over such internal schisms is still at play in Smith's recent work. Although it is unclear whether a single woman is presented in duplicate or if in fact there are two different women, their similarities in facial structure, dress, and body position suggest that the two figures represent emotional counterparts of the same individual. One is comfortable at center stage, staring directly at the viewer, while the other is relegated to her peripheral position and turns her glance aside. Despite this split, however, Smith left open the possibility of their eventual merge, providing a visual link at the nexus of their hands and situating the center figure's weight to carry her naturally into the other's position, should the latter's thigh ever become an unstable source of balance. This hope for reunification is one that Smith herself has admitted to striving for in her art: "Our bodies have been broken apart bit by bit and need a lot of healing; our whole society is very fragmented...Everything is split, and presented as dichotomies—male/female, body/mind—and those splits need mending."[3]

In Now, Smith acknowledged the fracture of the individual as she has throughout her career, but not without providing a possible path toward healing and eventual redemption.

[1] Smith, "Interview with Kiki Smith," 132.
[2] Posner, "Approaching Grace," 26.
[3] Quoted in Jennifer Wells, Projects 24.

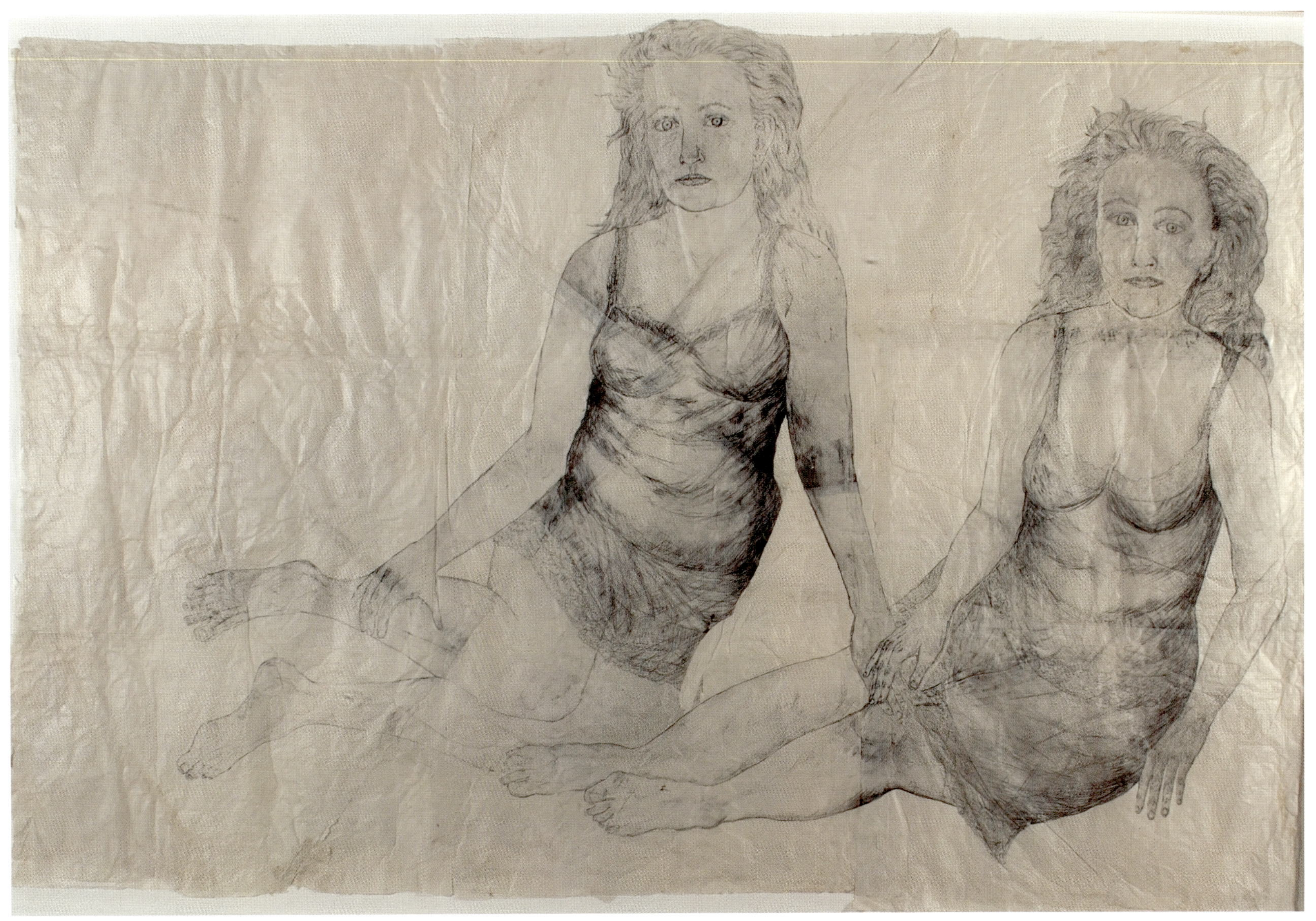

Now 2005
Collage, ink on nepal paper, 56 1/2" x 87"

Xavier Veihan 1963-

Xavier Veilhan's art often seems motivated by the mischievous pleasure of eliciting surprise from his audience. His work's apparent simplicity begs the viewer to examine it more closely, to see and feel it at a distance of mere inches. In Veilhan's *David*, for example, the artistic ploy goes beyond the mere allusion of the statue's celebrated namesake to mimick Michelangelo's material so as to appear crafted out of traditional marble or stone. One touch to its surface, however, achieves the desired effect, startling the viewer and revealing the truth behind Veilhan's ruse: the lightweight polyurethane foam is not at all the expected solid and is already threatening to give way to the audience's mistakenly firm advance.

Throughout his career, Veilhan has mastered similar tactics, toeing the complex and ever-changing line between art and technology and placing his viewers in perpetual limbo while they judge whether Veilhan has finally gone too far. One would not be surprised to find Veilhan's photographs rendered to the point of incomprehension, or to discover varying distances impossibly focused at the same time. As a result, Veilhan's technical skill as an artist is often blurred with his skill as a graphic designer or as a mastermind of the digital world. Veilhan's *David* adapts this strategy to the medium of sculpture: his figure appears hand-carved from solid marble, but in reality is the result of a specialized computer laser that shapes the figure from a solid block of foam. By exploring such new avenues of illusion, Veilhan demonstrates that there is more than one way to accurately represent reality.

At the same time, Veilhan refuses to assure his audience that the aspects of reality he has chosen to represent are either his favorite or even important.[1] *David* stands as yet another everyman—hands in pocket, caught in a moment of distraction or perhaps at an impasse between irresolvable decisions. The indeterminacy of the piece is generalized to the point that we begin to invent a narrative for the details we are lacking. But the narrative can only go so far without suggestive details; isolating his figures and stripping them of such background, Veilhan suggests a rudimentary, semiotic approach to figuration along the lines of "A is for Apple, D is for David."[2] Through this paradoxically simple package, Veilhan's sculptures suggest that only certain fundamental features are necessary to induce an audience's acknowledgement of his figures as sufficient representatives of reality. As such, it seems Veilhan is content to play several games with his viewer, asking not only when he has gone too far but also when he has gone far enough.[3]

[1] Gillick, "'Eastworld,'" 27.
[3] Ibid., 40.
[3] Cameron, "Keeping Up Appearances," 9.

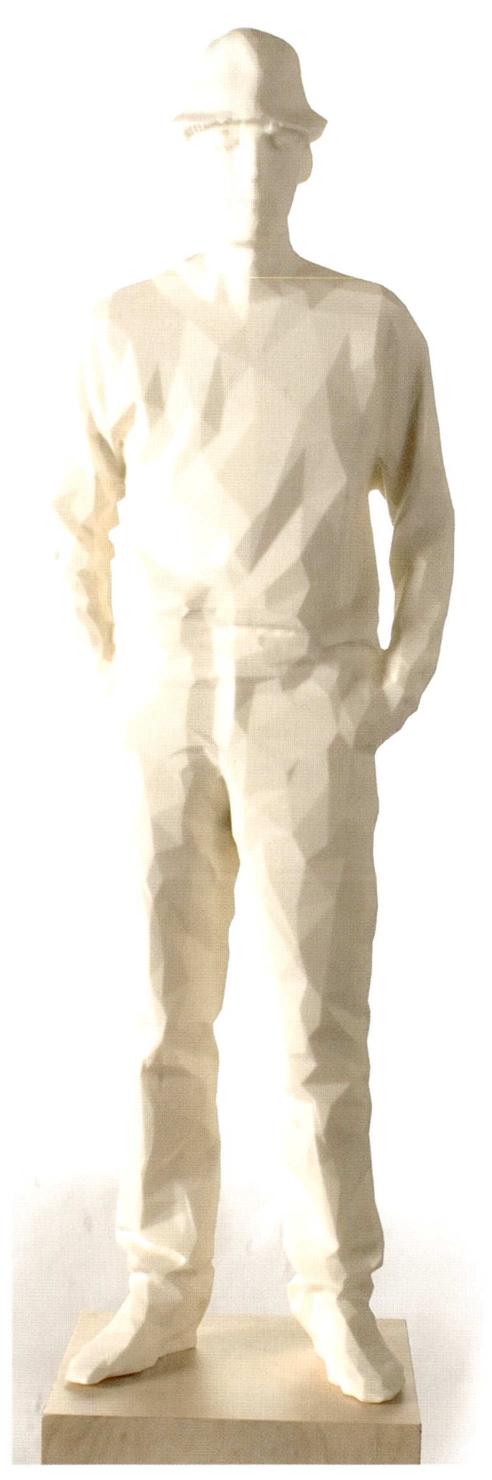

David 2005
Polyurethane foam, 35 3/8″ x 11 3/4″ x 6 3/4″

Idelle Weber 1932-

In an interview with the *New York Times Book Review*, Vladimir Nabokov once said, "I prefer to accept only one type of power: the power of art over trash, the triumph of magic over the brute."[1]

In her series of trash paintings, Idelle Weber seems to have literalized this conviction, capturing with haunting realism what appears to be the subject matter least fit for high art: piles of garbage. Composed primarily between 1974 and 1979, Weber's trash paintings depict the littered debris that accumulates on city streets, from empty and shattered Heineken beer bottles at the foot of the curb (*Heineken*, 1976) to a crumpled Land O'Lakes butter carton discarded in a gutter (*Land O' Lakes*, 1979). Throughout the series, Weber painted the residue of our society's material culture, suggesting not only the gross waste entailed but also a sense of the ease with which we shift between various labels and products in the never-ending chase after a transient, faddish identity in our throwaway culture.

In *Cooper Union Trash*, an early sample from the series, Weber raised her trash up off the sidewalk and piles it atop an overflowing garbage can outside Cooper Union College for the Advancement of Science and Art. Well-known in New York City for its avant-garde art and architecture programs, the college makes a fitting locus for the power of art to supply magic to anything, even a functionless, bursting trash can. Unlike later works in the series, *Cooper Union Trash* is strikingly devoid of labels, focusing its viewer's attention instead on the classic still-life composition of the painting and the play of shadow and light across the overlapping, highly textured bottles, glasses, cans, and bags. Similarly, the piece highlights its own use of contrasting surfaces, such as the juxtaposition of the pebbled can and crinkly plastic bag with the smooth, glossy areas of glass and aluminum.

The accidental amalgamation that has produced this still-life scene is depicted as a magically pure and unified whole: none of the pedestrians who contributed to the temporary sculpture remain in the scene, nor is there a single strewn piece of trash left on the sidewalk or road. Instead, the intricate parts have come together as a fragile but complete composition, ready to be painted in the most meticulously detailed and visually clear method possible, for they, it seems, have nothing to hide.

Like contemporary "second-generation realists" John Baeder and Hilo Chen, Weber largely adhered to one specific subject matter at a time, following in the tradition of Ralph Goings and Richard Estes.[2] Although she relentlessly captured different trash scenes during the late 1970s, other works in the series rarely approached the variation of color, complicated shifts in texture, or fragile beauty of the isolated and sculpturesque composition *Cooper Union Trash*. Accordingly, the work seems to stand as one of her greatest statements on the power of art—especially photorealistic art—to "triumph" in the most unfavorable conditions, even when pinned down by the most challenging elements of reality.

[1] Quoted in Shenker, "Old Magician at Home."
[2] Meisel, *Photo-Realism*, 434.

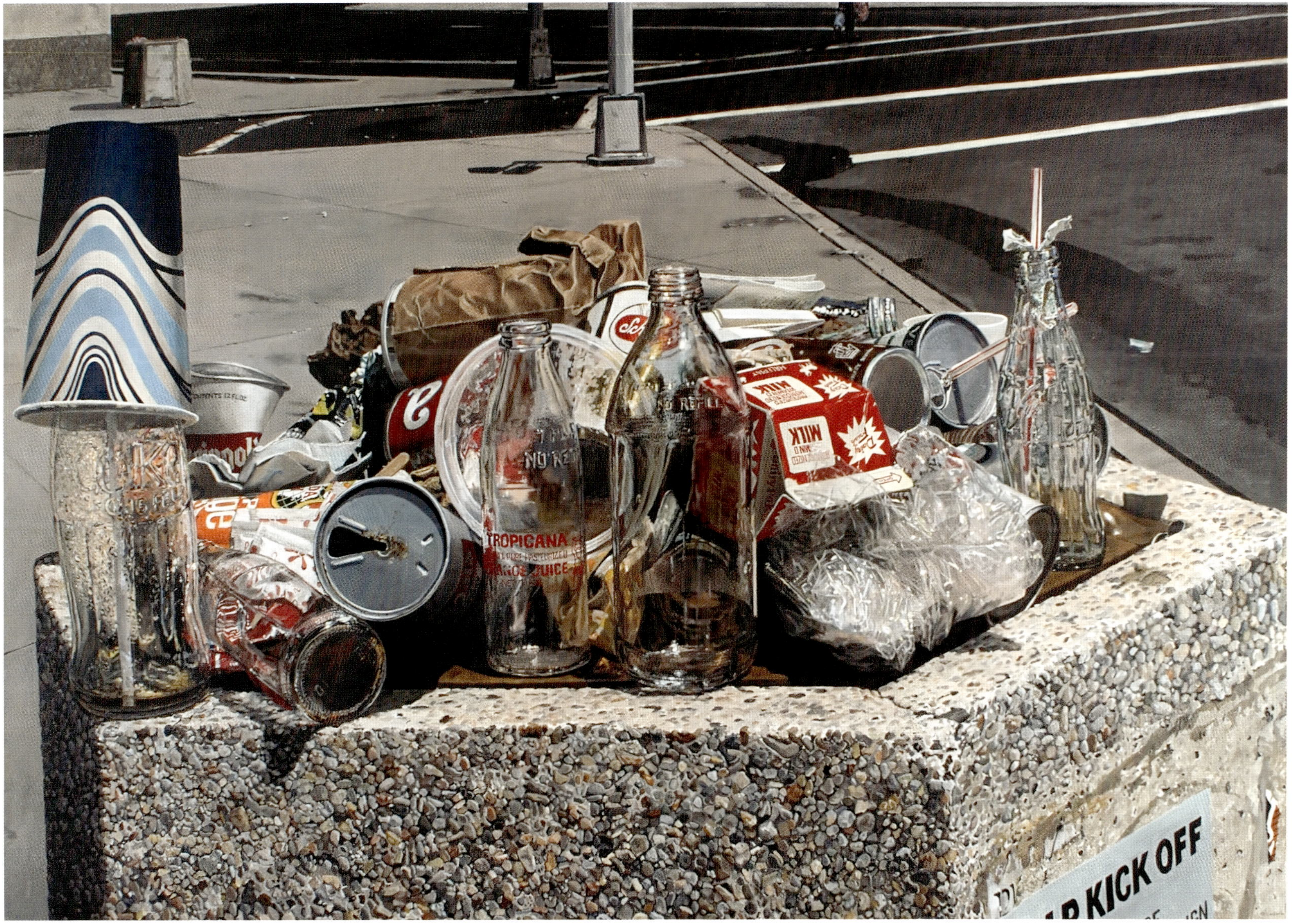

Cooper Union Trash 1974
Oil on canvas, 45″ x 64 1/4″

David Salle 1952-

The French critic, essayist, and novelist André Gide once beseeched his audience, "Please do not understand me too quickly." A viewer of David Salle's work is faced with a similar responsibility, as multi-paneled canvases challenge the eye to identify and even reconcile seemingly unrelated figurative moments. Nudes, props, masks, furniture, ghostly outlines, and still-life fruits and flowers all contend for attention in a prepositional struggle for being, as they seem able to exist only in the context of other corporeal objects—above, below, and next to them but never simply alone.[1] To complicate and prolong the challenge of understanding, Salle employs a private vocabulary of unfamiliar and bizarre objects, from bears on bicycles to truncated anime heroines, amounting to what Mimmo Paladino calls "an inexhaustible reservoir of non-symbolic images" that defy instant or universal comprehension.[2]

Salle's *Sideways Moon* encapsulates the artist's unique ability to derive endlessly layered meaning from the simple juxtaposition of such images. The three-paneled canvas portrays many events as they simultaneously unfold, indirectly clashing with one another despite the clearly defined boundaries. The visual organization also dictates moments of direct encounter—a knifelike boat attempts to further fragment the anime figure, a woman's progress is checked by nature's presence, and, most strikingly, the foundational image of an artist literally and symbolically vies for spatial dominance with the superimposed outline he seems to be painting. What results is a totality that suggests an inability to settle on any one object, space, or identity—a split consciousness that, for Salle, is the only faithful account of self we can attain: "the self revealed in the juxtaposition of images."[3] Section by section, his paintings form new meanings and alter existing relationships through Bakhtinian dialogues, rhymes, and puns that pose an internal threat to the autonomy of the work and the agency of the artist's voice in order to force a new understanding of self as an aggregate of external influences.[4]

Owing to his interests in film and performance art, Salle has time and again privileged those styles and techniques that defy the static quality of painting, those "pictorial constructs of montage and split-screen...[in which] powerful images unite and there's no need for explaining."[5] It is here that his panels cinematographically collide, subsequently hatching the disorientation between work and audience that is Salle's hallmark.

[1] Koestenbaum, "The Empty Cup," 29.
[2] Paladino, "David Salle, Screen Paintings," 122.
[3] Quoted in Tuten, "At the Edges," 78.
[4] Tuten, "At the Edges," 78.
[5] Liebmann, *David Salle*, 17-18.

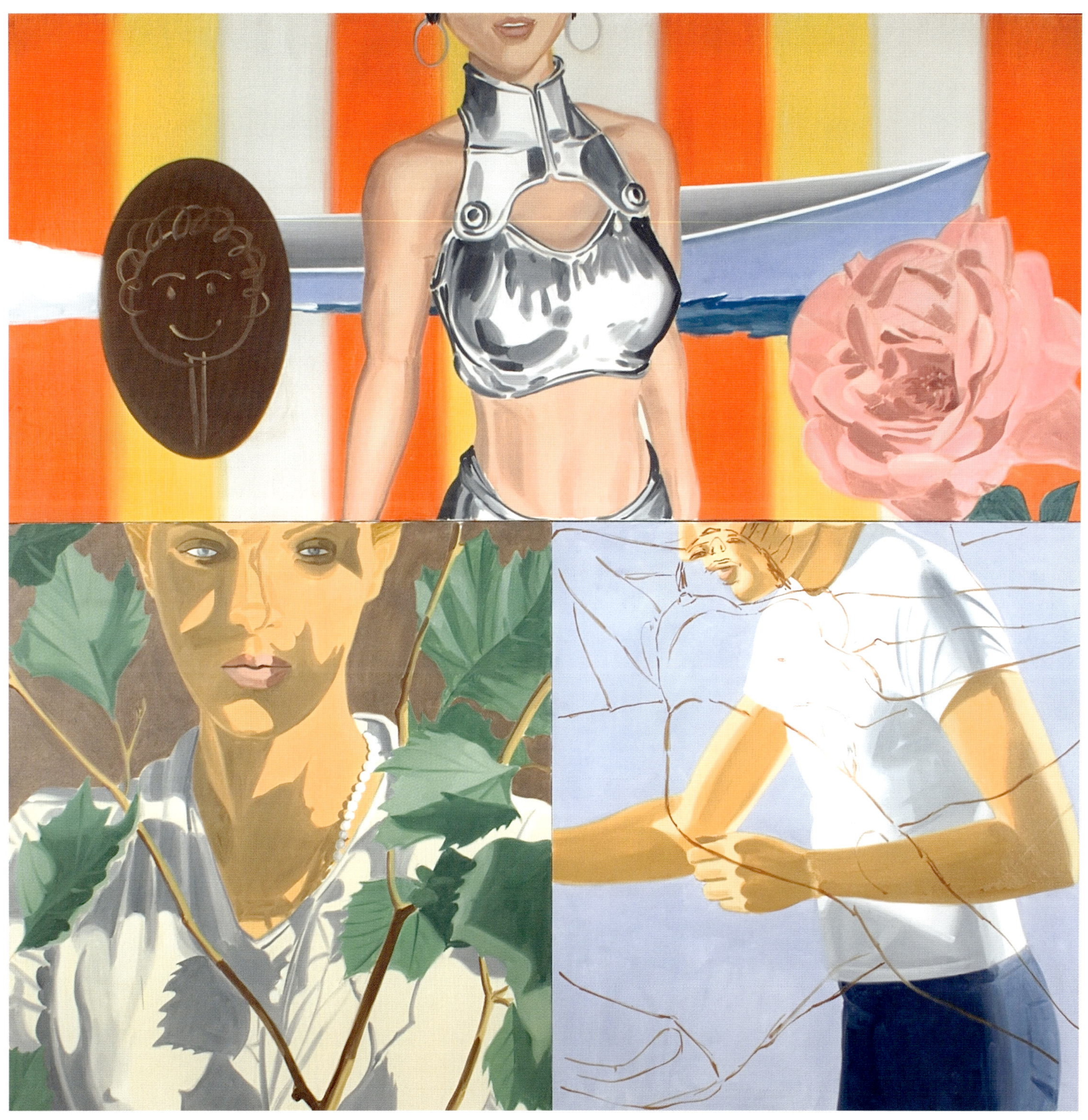

Sideways Moon 2002
Oil on linen 89″ x 90″

Mel Ramos 1935-

In 1993, Barnaby Conrad, a friend of Mel Ramos, was compiling a book on the history of the martini. Conrad asked the artist if he had ever painted a martini, to which Ramos responded blithely, "No, but I'll do one for the book."[1] Soon thereafter, Ramos found himself revisiting the very themes that had made him a figurehead for West Coast Pop Art during its explosion in the 1960s. Draping a perfectly tanned nude inside an oversized martini glass, Ramos was again at work pairing larger-than-life consumer products with the equally amplified sex that sells them. He found renewed satisfaction in the endeavor and decided to continue his earlier exploration of media-saturated female nudes in his series *The Lost Paintings of 1965*, based on old studies and drawings never before brought to fruition.

Almond Joy carries Ramos's levity and joy for his subject candidly in its title, situating his work to affirm and observe the link between market culture and the female body rather than critique or condemn it. Ramos's hyperreal stylization of startlingly familiar figures introduces an element of reality into his fictional world, producing a realm in which the dualities of art and life merge: the artificial becomes precise, the natural turns synthetic, and depth seems smoothed into flatness.[2] Still, Ramos's subjects are never objects imported from reality, but "objets trouvés" imported from the parallel world of mass media, giving a tertiary distance to his work that appears incongruous with its superreal style.[3]

Ramos plants artifacts from contemporary reality inside a universe that simply cannot be real—too skewed in its scale and simplistic content—to prove that the self-declared absurdity makes it feel no less truthful. In fact, all of his work's elements are instantly recognizable and easily digested, pulled from some segment of our reality that we otherwise choose not to acknowledge. His nude materializes from an Almond Joy wrapper as if emerging from an enormous birthday cake, and the viewer is able to assimilate its imagery into his or her ever-swelling vocabulary of pop culture.

Ramos's "archetypal playmates" stand starkly in front of their bold backgrounds, unaware of any illogicality and certainly unashamed of their circumstances. They relinquish the "ennobling excuse" for nakedness of historical distance, choosing instead to engage with the present, posing as a pinup might alongside massive cigars, bottles of wine, and cans of motor oil.[4] Ramos's nudes seem to be centerfolds freed from their concealment in the center of taboo magazines, released instead to serve as placebos for the collective erotic fantasies of mass media.[5] His temptresses self-assuredly play with their products rather than submit to the passive role of plaything.[6] In this way, they serve as a celebration of strength and sexuality in a post-pop mold so often carved out for parodistic criticism of market culture.

[1] Quoted in Gardner, *Mel Ramos: Heroines*, 225.
[2] Gardner, *Mel Ramos: Heroines*, 8.
[3] Ibid., 11.
[4] Ibid., 24, 17.
[5] Ibid., 18.
[6] Ibid., 19.

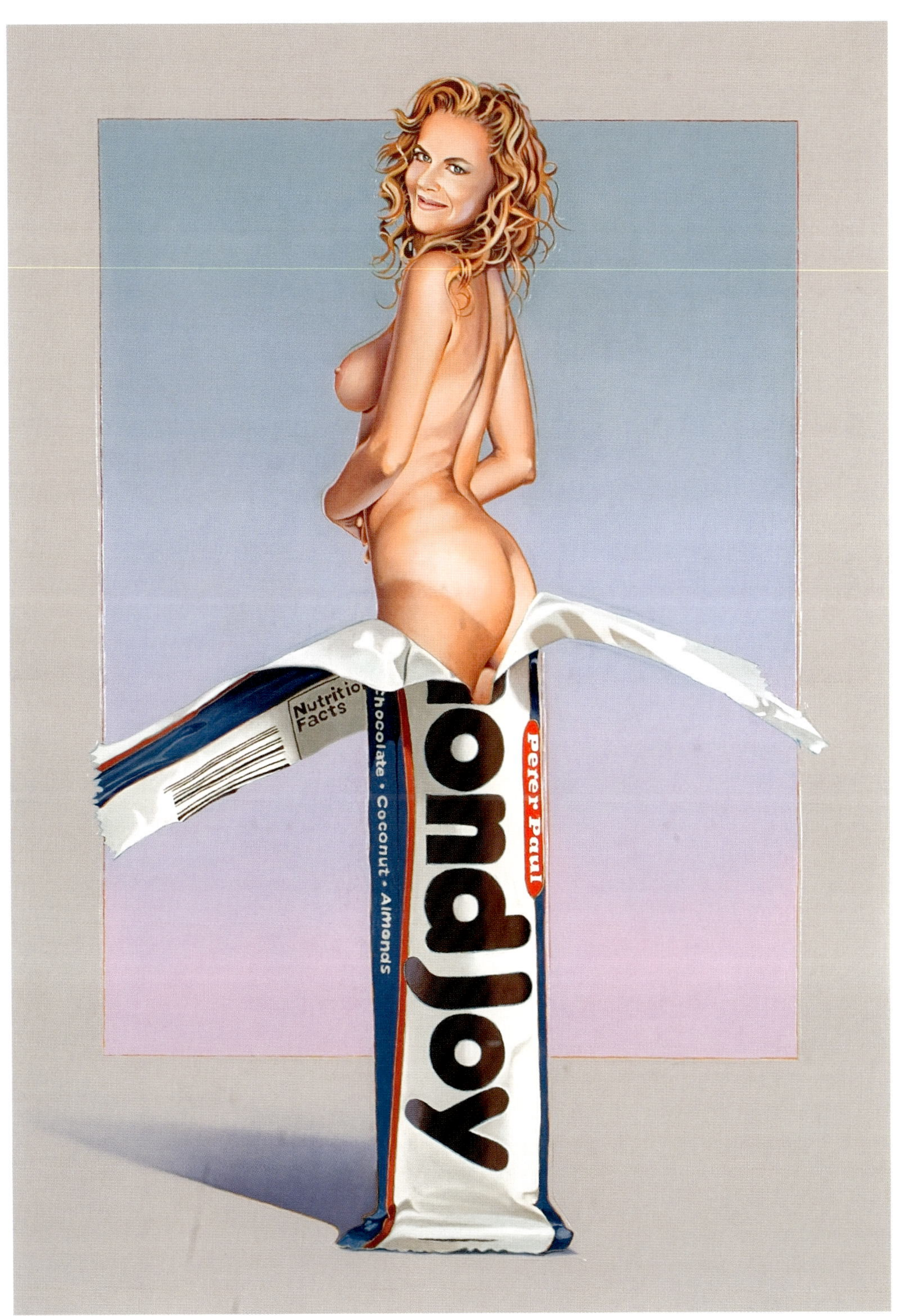

Almond Joy: The Lost Painting of 1965, #29 2002
Oil on canvas, 36 1/4″ x 25 1/2″

Tom Wesselmann 1931-

Upon seeing her image in Tom Wesselmann's *Great American Nude #12* (1961), the model depicted famously exclaimed that she felt the urge to return the kiss offered by the painting.[1] Innocently and succinctly, this chance remark seemed to define Wesselmann's primary goal in his figurative works of the 1960s, in both his *Great American Nudes* and his *Bedroom Paintings*. Wesselmann's assertive canvases aimed to directly confront and engage the viewer with the circumstance of the painting in order to incite a more personal and intimate response.

Of course, the erotic subject matter of his figures imparts this sense of intimacy as deeply as the formal elements of the painting, for there is no mistaking the litany of pleasurable objects presented, from the smoking cigarette and the ripe orange to, most noticeably, the brilliant red lips and erect nipple, each of which seems ready to slide off the canvas and onto the viewer due to the "drop-out" edgeless table at the forefront.[2] As a result, Wesselmann's work places his viewer as the literal recipient of the intended pleasure and the metaphoric participant in the action of the painting, both as the sexual partner and as the voyeuristic gazer. His *Study for Bedroom Painting #2*, as well as its derivative final work, adopts the new open sexuality of the 1960s and embraces its fulfillment of bodily desires in every sense of the word, from the oral satisfaction derived from the depicted objects to the visceral satisfaction derived from the work itself.

Like every other work in the Bedroom Paintings series, *Bedroom Painting #2* was formed out of a multitude of earlier studies; each study is a finished oil canvas, only on a smaller scale.[3] In *Study for Bedroom Painting #2*, Wesselmann explored the notion of sexual anonymity through a featureless face (except for the charged lips), and he later adopted and transformed this notion by pushing the rest of the face beyond the boundary of the painting. In this study, Wesselmann also developed the dividing element of the cigarette smoke, which he retained almost exactly in the finished work. Through this vertical figure, Wesselmann fragmented and fetishized the balanced sexual features of the lips and the nipple.[4] By fragmenting these features in this way and through an outlining technique evocative of his earlier collages, Wesselmann's nude becomes even less representative of a person and more representative of an abiding abstract sexuality. As Marco Livingstone put it, Wesselmann's focused fragmentation celebrates "the idea, rather than the reality, of sex."[5]

In the end, Wesselmann established this fragmentation and then tried everything in his power—through the softened orange, the hazy transparency of the smoke, and the edgeless table—to mend the rift. For it is exactly this sort of tension that is at the heart of a successful Wesselmann work in the first place: he provides "a momentary glimpse of a possible situation" that could have been otherwise and could have involved further details, but that is already so perfectly satisfying in its current stripped-down form.[6]

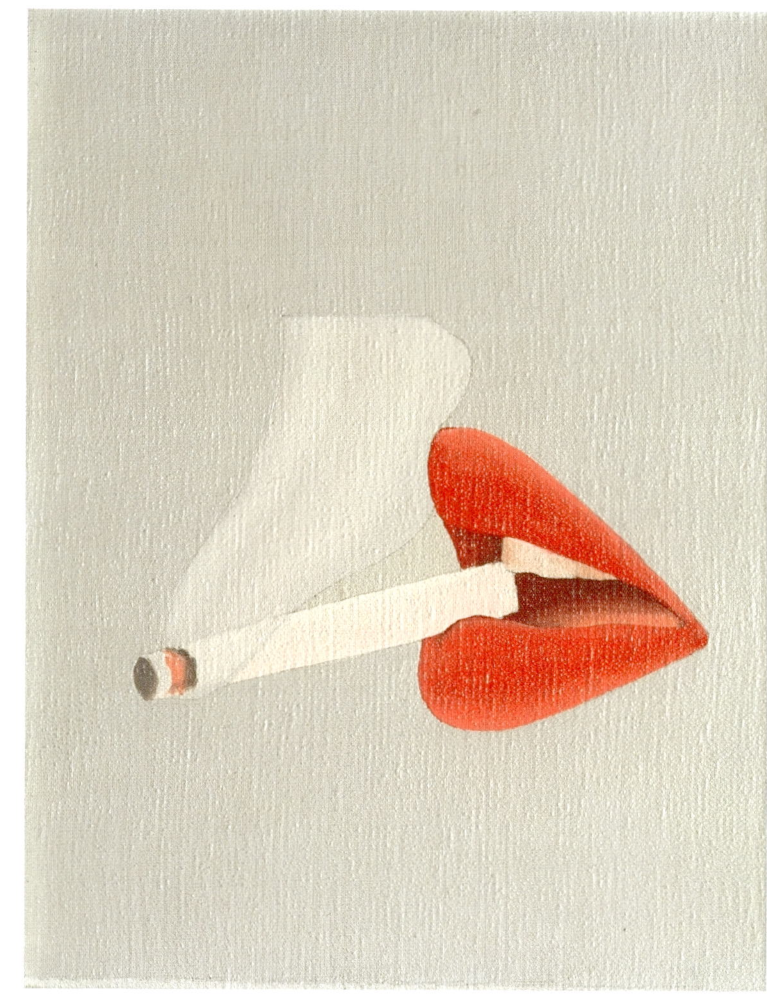

Smoker Study #9 1967
Oil on canvas, 10″ x 8″

[1] Livingstone, "Telling it," 11.
[2] Stealingworth, *Tom Wesselmann*, 56.
[3] Davidson, M., III and Maxwell Davidson IV, *Tom Wesselmann*.
[4] Livingstone, "Telling it," 20.
[5] Ibid., 11.
[6] Stealingworth, *Tom Wesselmann*, 56.

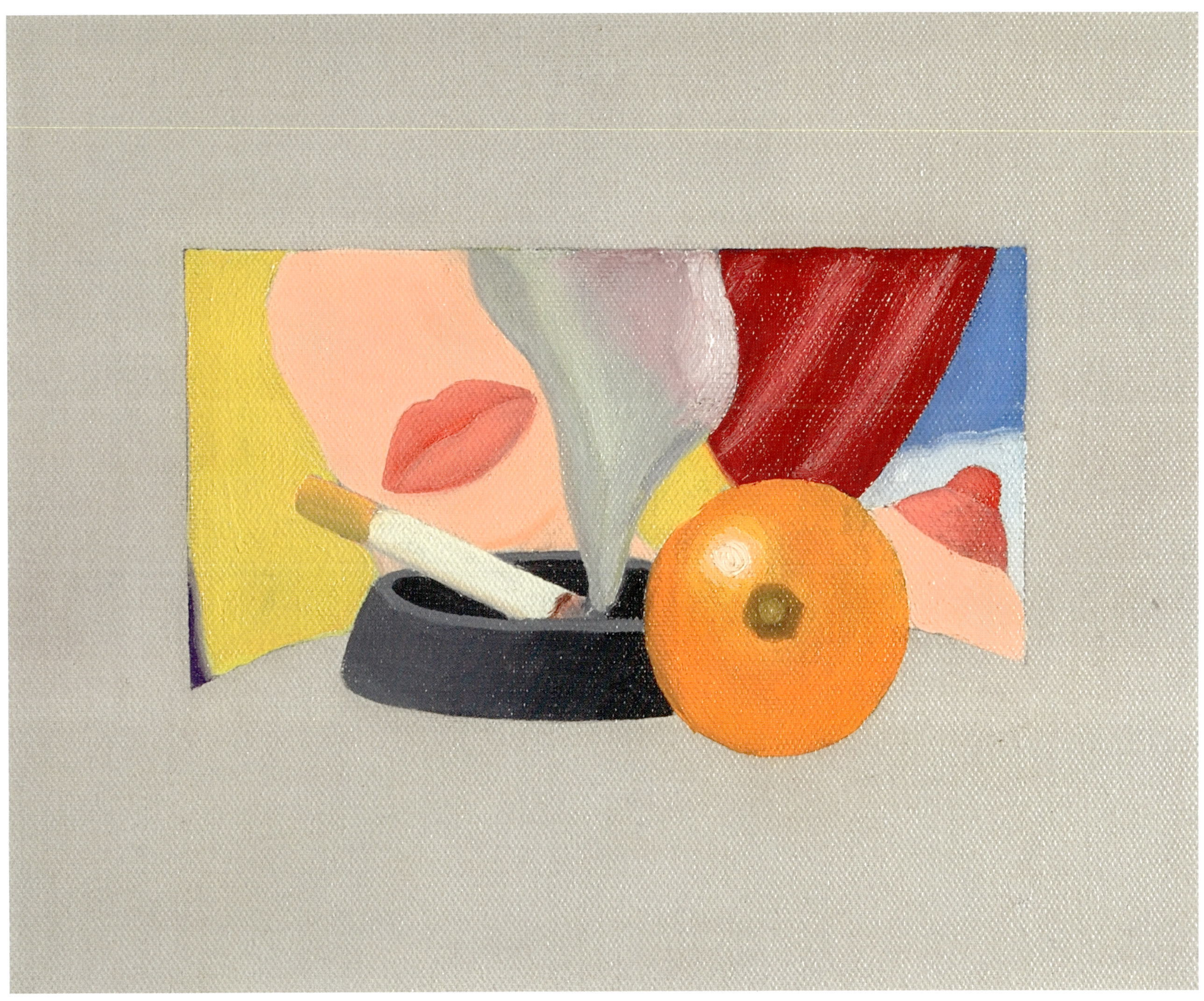

Study for Bedroom Painting #2 1967
Oil on canvas, 8″ x 10″

Richard Prince 1949-

In a series based on pulp-fiction paperback covers from the 1950s and 1960s, Richard Prince's nurse paintings provide yet another specialized lens for exploring the insidious symbols and biases of American culture. Taking dime romance novels such as *Park Avenue Nurse* and *Nympho Nurse*, Prince appropriated their covers, silk-screening all contents onto a solidly colored background as if digesting the full meaning of such a book in one swift, complete act. From there, Prince set about mashing, veiling, and silencing his image, covering the canvas in blocks of color reminiscent of Mark Rothko and drips of paint evocative of the furious gestures of de Kooning.[1] His work preys on the appeal of the fetishized nurse, embellishing the masculine fantasy and its ideals of a playboy lifestyle for which a nurse is the perfect, attentive servant. Yet through the juxtaposition of dramatic, end-scale colors—as seen in *Mission Nurse's* clashing moss green and pale blue—Prince's work is also intended to upend the masculine fantasy. To this end, the work is purposely unsettling: many paintings in the series are blood-colored, a mechanism that violently extracts the nurse from her stereotyped role in soap operas and Halloween costumes and places her firmly back in the grim, visceral side of the profession.

While Prince based his work in the requisite imagery necessary to conjure such associations, he was also quick to attack it, silencing the communicative value of the sexualized nurse in as many ways as possible. Accordingly, the nurse's mouth is hidden behind a surgical mask, not only blocking one of her most attractive features but literally inhibiting her ability to communicate verbally.[2] He also covered her with a fully buttoned uniform on one planar level and color blocks of smeared paint on another. In essence, while the connotations are not destroyed, the nurse no longer exists simply to arouse and satisfy a fetish, and as a result, her presence is intensified. She becomes an ambiguous force, scarcely accessible and distinctly forbidden, a subtle attack on the myth of American male power.

At the same time, however, Prince remains a man painting fetishized servants and it seems inevitable that some measure of Freud's pleasure principle sneaks into his work; certainly, his series succumbs to its treatise of repetition compulsion so that, on some level, Prince's work seems subject to the very same development of seduction that he aimed to criticize.

[1] Collings, "Richard Prince: Nurse Paintings," 4-6.
[2] Ibid., 7.

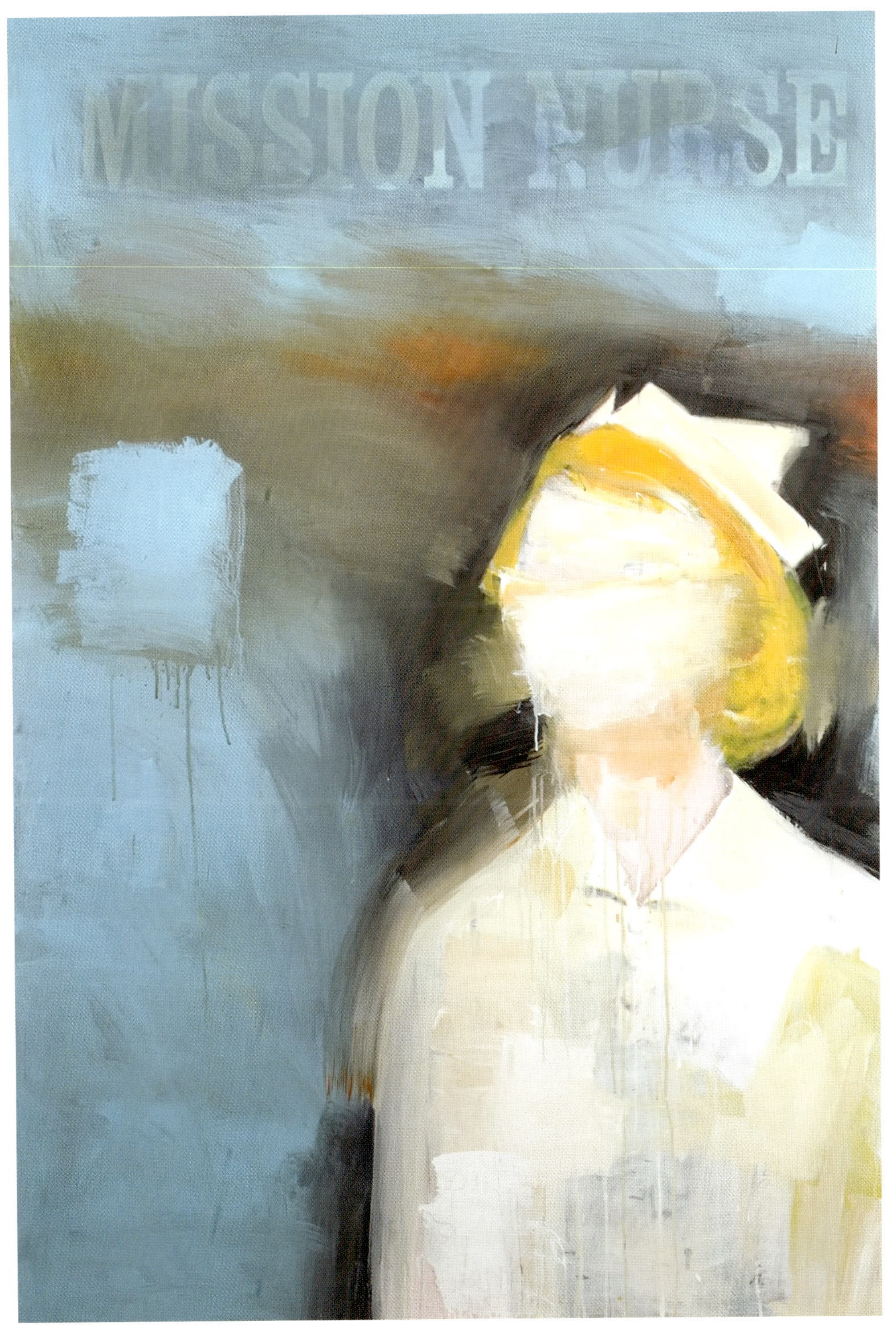

Mission Nurse 2002
Ink jet print and acrylic on canvas, 70″ x 48″

Joseph Stella 1877-1946

At a time when Joseph Stella was largely preoccupied by the machinery and motion of industrial metropolitan life, *The Red Hat* marked a sharp departure from the crisply defined forms of his futurist and precisionist works. Though its chronology suggests a simple, curative role for the painting as an interlude between movements, there appears to be much more at stake for the artist's identity, especially given the striking similarity between the featured figure and Stella's hatted profile image in his self-portraits of the time.

For an Italian-born painter working in America, the pastoral scene seems to reflect Stella's growing "nostalgia for Italy," not only for the "shining visions of his youth" but for "the great artistic traditions of the Renaissance" so absent from the American artistic vanguard of the 1920s.[1] In both its style and in its content, *The Red Hat* stands as a momentary reprieve from contemporary life and the modern demands of painting. Stella was quick to adopt an expanded and more vibrant palette of tropical tones through which he engaged an otherwise taboo sentimentality. Its brightest horizontal—to mention nothing of the title—centers the focus of such sentimentality on the figure's red hat before dispatching the eye into "the light filled space of Stella's imagination."[2] Its abstract patterning of sky and surrounding terrain similarly depicts a surreal landscape that is as much indebted to the imagery of magical realism as it is to the fantastic "joy and pictorial innocence of early masters."[3] Accordingly, *The Red Hat*'s sweet and lyrical colors depict an overall utopian calm, even as it contends with the looming, oversimplified bull, which stands as the only indication that such a reprieve might be too idyllic to last.

It is difficult to reconcile *The Red Hat's* radical reduction of forms and heavy geometric masses with the sharply defined, floating figures of Stella's precisionism, the soft, hazy atmosphere of the bucolic scene with the clear, busy backdrops typical of his futuristic works.[4] Yet, the artist, like his substitutive figure in the painting, seemed content to linger on this temporary excursion into the sentimental symbolism of the Italian countryside and to "immerse himself in the art of antiquity and [of] the Renaissance."[5] In fact, he personally retained the escapist piece until the day of his death.

[1] Baur, *Joseph Stella*, 45.
[2] Ibid., 48.
[3] Ibid., 46.
[4] Ibid., 51.
[5] Ibid., 47.

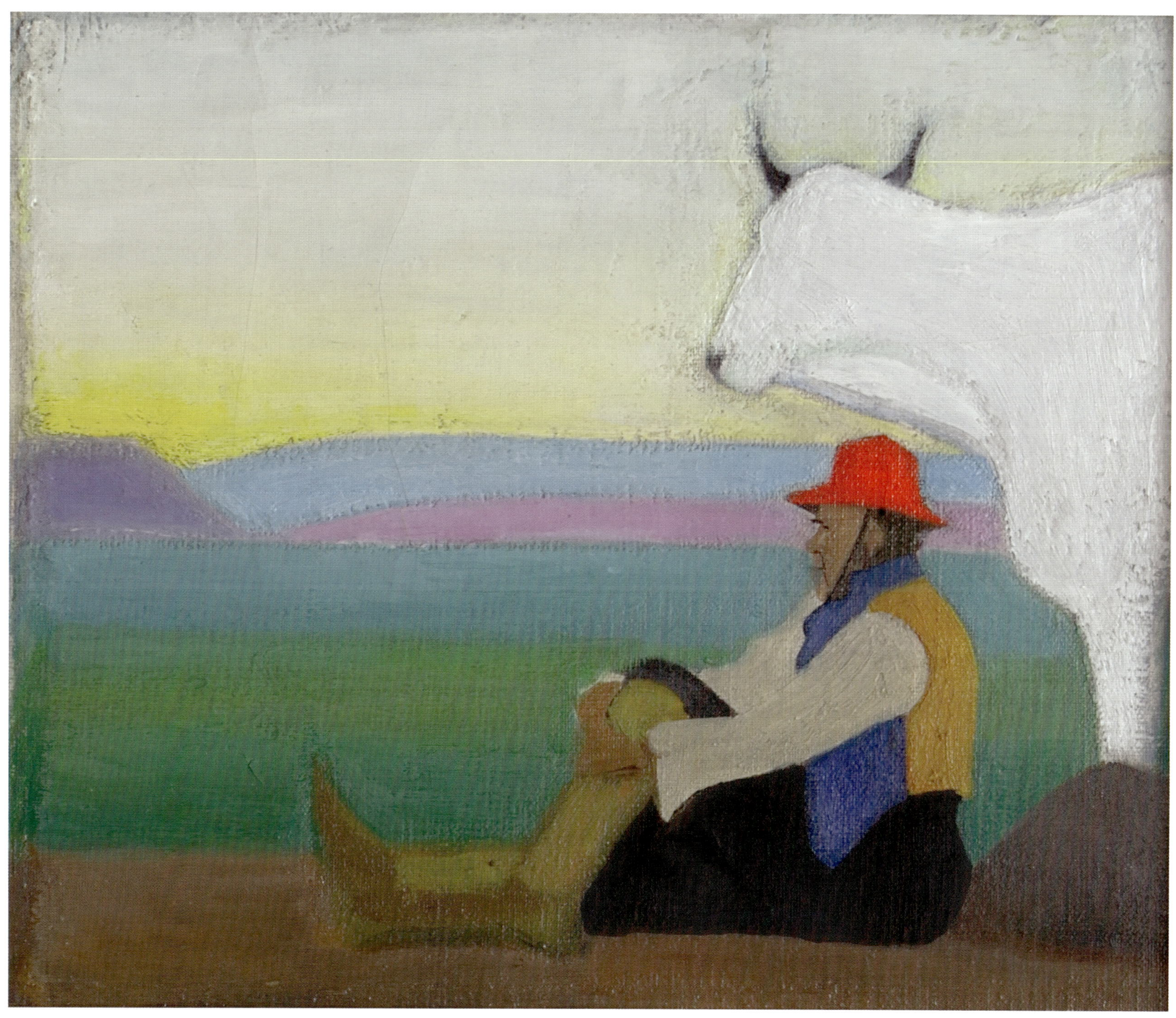

The Red Hat 1924
Oil on canvas, 9 3/4″ x 12″

Bibliography

Adams, Brooks. "*1900s Morley: The Return of the Prodigal Son." In Malcolm Morley, 1965–1995: exposición*, edited by Asunción Cabrera and Casilda Mora, 53–72. Madrid: Fundación "la Caixa," 1995. An exhibition catalog.

Adrian, Dennis. *The Real and Ideal in Figurative Sculpture: John De Andrea, Duane Hanson*. Chicago: Museum of Contemporary Art, 1974. An exhibition catalog.

Alloway, Lawrence. Quoted in Vivien Raynor, "Art: Marisol Sculpture from Leonardo Painting." *New York Times*, June 1, 1984.

Amy, Michael. "Hilary Harkness at Bill Maynes." *Art in America*, November 2001.

Anderson-Spivy, Alexandra. "Robert Cottingham at the MacDowell Colony." *Drawing*, Winter 1998–99.

———. *Robert Kushner: Gardens of Earthly Delight*. Edited by Paul Anbinder. New York: Hudson Hills, 1997.

Arteaga, Agustín. "Robert Graham, Sculptor." In *Robert Graham*, edited by Noriko Fujinami, translated by Mónica Mayer, 15–29. Mexico City: Instituto Nacional de Bellas Artes, 1997. An exhibition catalog.

Auer, James. "Cottingham's Sign Language Speaks Loudly in Oshkosh Show." *Milwaukee Journal Sentinel*, September 9, 1990.

Baeder, John. Diners, *Revised and Updated*. Edited by Robert Morton. New York: Harry N. Abrams, 1995.

Bakhtin, Mikhail. "*From Discourse in the Novel*." In *The Critical Tradition: Classic Texts and Contemporary Trends*, edited by David H. Richter, 530–39. New York: Bedford Books, 1998.

Batchelor, David. *Robert Rauschenberg: Short Stories*, London: Waddington Gallery, 2002. An exhibition catalog.

Baur, John I. H., and Irma B. Jaffe. *Joseph Stella*. New York: Preager, 1971.

Bearden, Romare. *Collages: Profile/Part II: The Thirties*. Edited by Albert Murray. New York: Cordier & Ekstrom, 1981. An exhibition catalog.

Belcher, Gerald and Margaret Belcher. *Collecting Souls*, *Gathering Dust: The Struggles of Two American Artists, Alice Neel and Rhoda Medary*. New York: Paragon House, 1991.

Bell, Clare, Germano Celant, and Jim Dine, "Walking Memory: A Conversation with Jim Dine, Clare Bell, and Germano Celant." In *Jim Dine: Walking Memory, 1959–1969*, edited by Germano Celant and Clare Bell, 47-208. New York: Guggenheim Museum, in association with Harry N. Abrams, 1999.

Belz, Carl. "Gregory's Vision." In *A Unique American Vision: Paintings by Gregory Gillespie*, by Gregory Gillespie, Donald D. Keyes, Rani M. Carr, and Carl Belz, edited by Thomas S. Holman, 23–47. Athens, GA: Georgia Museum of Art, 1999.

———. *William Beckman*. Seattle: Frye Art Museum, 2002.

Blackwell, Tom. *Tom Blackwell: New Paintings*. Edited by Linda Chase. Manchester, NH: Currier Gallery of Art, 1985. An exhibition catalog.

Bonito, Virginia Anne. *Get Real: Contemporary American Realism from the Seavest Collection*. Durham, NC: Duke University Museum of Art, 1998.

Bourdon, David. "Up Close and Impersonal." *Art in America*, May 1997.

Bovier, Lionel, and Yves Aupetitallot, eds. *Xavier Veilhan*. Paris: Magasin—Centre National d'Art Contemporain, 2000.

Briganti, Giuliano, and John Hollander. *William Bailey*. Translated by Peter Glendening and Maria Fitzgerald. New York: Rizzoli International Publications, 1991.

Budzynski, Scott. “Critical Moments: Malcolm Morley.” *Art Criticism* 14, no. 1 (1999): 32–35.

Bürgi, Bernhard. “Innocence.” In München, *Richard Phillips*, 50–54.

Cameron, Dan. “Keeping Up Appearance.” In Bovier and Aupetitallot, *Xavier Veilhan*, 9–11.

Campbell-Johnston, Rachel. “Art-Exhibition-London; Robert Rauschenberg: at Waddington Galleries, W1 Until Jul 6.” Times (London), June 8, 2002.

Celant, Germano. “Marc Quinn: On the Path to Eden.” In Quinn, Celant, Leader, and Prada, *Marc Quinn*, 9–13.

Celant, Germano and Marc Quinn. “About Peter Hull, *Selma Mustajbasic, Jamie Gillespie, Alexandra Westmoquette, Tom Yendell, Catherine Long, Stuart Penn, Helen Smith: Group Portrait*.” In Quinn, Celant, Leader, and Prada, Marc Quinn, 58–171.

Chase, Linda. Hollywood on Main Street: *The Movie House Paintings of Davis Cone*. New York: Overlook, 1988.

Casteras, Susan. “Breaking the Mold: Audrey Flack’s Sculptures.” *In Breaking the Rules: Audrey Flack: A Retrospective 1950-1990*, edited by Thalia Gouma-Peterson, 103-129. New York: Harry N. Abrams, Inc., 1992.

Clark, David. “Evan Penny’s Uncertainty Principle.” In *Absolutely Unreal*, edited by Nancy Tousley and David Clark. London, ON: Museum London, 2003. An exhibition catalog. http://www.evenpenny.com/essay_clark_l.php.

Clark, Garth. “Cracks in the Sidewalk: A Chronological Study of the Art and World of Viola Frey.” In *Viola Frey Retrospective Catalogue*. Sacramento: Crocker Art Museum, 1981. An exhibition catalog.

———. “Viola Frey [Obituary].” *Crafts* (London), no. 192 (January/February 2005): 75.

Collings, Matthew. *Richard Prince: Nurse Paintings*. New York: Barbara Gladstone Gallery, New York, 2004. An exhibition catalog.

Cotter, Holland. “Brooklyn-ness, a State of Mind and Artistic Identity in the Un-Chelsea.” *New York Times*, April 16, 2004.

———. “Robert Kushner.” In Anderson-Spivy, *Robert Kushner: Gardens of Earthly Delight*, Edited by Paul Anbinder. 7–10.

Dannatt, Adrian. “The Art of Allusion: Damian Loeb’s Work Relies on the Viewer’s Recognition of the Visual Sources that He Quotes Liberally.” *Art Newspaper*, June 2003.

Davidson, Maxwell, III, and Maxwell Davidson IV. *Tom Wesselmann: The Great American 60’s*. New York: Maxwell Davidson Gallery, 2003. An exhibition catalog.

Delgado, Martin. “Outrage at ‘Children’s’ Portrait of Hindley.” Quoted in *Young British Art: The Saatchi Decade*, edited by Robert Timms, Alexandra Bradley, and Vicky Hayward, 265. New York: Harry N. Abrams, 1999.

Desmarais, Charles. *Stephan Balkenhol*. Cincinnati: Contemporary Arts Center, 2000. An exhibition catalog.

Dixon, Annette. “Introduction: A Negress Speaks Out: The Art of Kara Walker.” In *Kara Walker: Pictures from Another Time*, edited by Karen Goldbaum, 11–25. Ann Arbor, MI: University of Michigan Museum of Art, 2002.

Duncan, Michael. “Ruins and Replicas (sculptor and painter Robert Overby).” *Art in America*, July 1996.

———. “The Self and Its Symbols.” *Art in America*, May 2000.

Faulkner, William. *Absolom, Absolom!* New York: Vintage International, 1990.

Fernandez-Cid, Miguel. "A Matter of Weight." In Stephan *Balkenhol: Centro Galego de Arte Contemporanea*, edited by Maria do Céu Bapista, translated by Helena Cornide, Elena Expósito, Interlingua Traducións, Nadia Poloni, Catherine Schelbert, and Josephine Watson, 143–47. Galacia: Xunta de Galicia, 2001. An exhibition catalog.

Fine, Ruth. "Romare Bearden: The Spaces Between." In *The Art of Romare Bearden*, 2-137. Edited by Judy Metro. Washington, DC: National Gallery of Art, in association with Harry N. Abrams, 2003.

Fischl, Eric. "A Dialogue with Eric Fischl: New York, May–June 2003." By Frederic Tuten. In *Eric Fischl: Paintings and Drawings, 1979–2001*, edited by Annelie Lütgens, 97–101. Ostfildern-Ruit, Germany: Hatje Cantz, 2003.

———. "Eleven Artists from Everywhere: Twenty-Two Frozen Moments, Believably Represented." *Believer*, December 2005/January 2006.

———. "Fischl on Fischl: Selected and Arranged by Robert Enright." By Robert Enright. In *Eric Fischl: 1970–2000*, edited by Arthur C. Danto, Robert Enright, and Steve Martin. New York: Monacelli, 2000.

Flack, Audrey. *Art and Soul: Notes on Creating*. New York: E. P. Dutton, 1986.

French, Sarah, ed. *David Salle: Immediate Experience*. Milan: Alberico Cetti Serbelloni Editore, 2002.

Frey, Viola. *Unpublished Statement for the Ceramics Symposium 1979*. Los Angeles: Institute for Ceramic History, 1979.

Ganis, William. "Evan Penny: Sperone Westwater." *Sculpture*, March 2006.

Gardner, Belinda Grace. "Wonder Women—Heroines, Goddesses, Beauty Queens: Mel Ramos' Erotic Pop Power Princesses." In *Mel Ramos, Heroines, Goddesses, Beauty Queens*, edited by Thomas Levy, 7–35. Bielefeld, Germany: Kerber Verlag, 2002.

Gardner, Paul. *Neil Jenney: The Bad Years 1960-1970*. New York: Gagosian Gallery, 2001. An exhibition catalog.

Gillespie, Gregory. "Interview with Gregory Gillespie." By Donald D. Keyes. In Gillespie, Keyes, Carr, and Belz, *A Unique American Vision*, 49–56.

Gillespie, Gregory, Donald D. Keyes, Rani M. Carr, and Carl Belz. *A Unique American Vision: Paintings by Gregory Gillespie*. Edited by Thomas S. Holman. Athens, GA: Georgia Museum of Art, 1999.

Gillick, Liam. "'Eastworld'. Xavier Veilhan's mirrored context." In Bovier and Aupetitallot, *Xavier Veilhan*, 26–29.

Giovannini, Joseph. "The Acts of Devotion Begin with the Doors," *New York Times*, December 1, 2002, Arts and Leisure.

Gluek, Grace. "Art People; A French Invasion." *New York Times*, January 22, 1982, Weekend section.

Goldwater, Marge. "Jennifer Bartlett: On Land and Sea." In *Jennifer Bartlett*, edited by Marge Goldwater, Roberta Smith, and Calvin Tomkins, 39–75. New York: Abbeville, 1985. An exhibition catalog.

Gould, Claudia, ed. *Lisa Yuskavage*. Philadelphia: Institute of Contemporary Art, University of Pennsylvania, 2000. An exhibition catalog.

Gruen, John. "Collector of Souls." *Herald Tribune*, January 9, 1966.

Hall, Marcia B. "Lisa Yuskavage's Painterly Paradoxes." In Gould, *Lisa Yuskaage*, 23–28.

Hammond, Anna. "Alexis Rockman at Gorney + Lee." *Art in America*, April 2001.

Harrison, Helen. "Rodin and His Descendants, of a Sort." *New York Times*, December 5, 1999.

Harvard University Art Museums. "Pictorial Strategies Are Focus of John Wesley's Painting in the Sert Gallery Exhibition." Press release, 2001. http://www.artmuseums.harvard.edu/press/released2001/wesley.html.

Hawkins, Margaret. "Modern Spins on Classical Beauty." *Chicago Sun-Times*, August 7, 1998.

Hayt, Elizabeth. "Nature Painting that Looks Unnatural." *New York Times*, October 15, 2000.

———. "Simple, Austere, An Old Genre Is Daringly New." *New York Times*, November 16, 1997.

Heartney, Eleanor. "Marisol: A Sculptor of Modern Life." In *Marisol*, edited by Lucinda H. Gedeon, 9–23. Purchase, NY: Neuberger Museum of Art, 2001. An exhibition catalog.

———. "Robert Longo at Metro Pictures." *Art in America*, September 2004.

Hindry, Ann. "Will Cotton's Giant Confections." In *Will Cotton: Paintings 1999-2004*, translated by Charles Penwarden, 6-13. Paris: Galerie Daniel Templon, 2005. An exhibition catalog.

Hobbs, Robert. *Edward Hopper*. New York: Harry N. Abrams, 1987.

Hopps, Walter. "Connoisseur of the Inexplicable." In *James Rosenquist: A Retrospective*, 2-15. New York: Solomon R. Guggenheim Museum, 2003.

Hunter, Sam. Introduction to *Larry Rivers*. New York: Rizzoli, 1989.

Jana, Reena. "Viola Frey: Survey of Work, 1969–1981." *Ceramics, Art and Perception* (Sydney, Australia), no. 41 (2000): 83–87.

Jardine, Lisa. "Grayson Perry—Very Much His Own Man." In *Grayson Perry*. London: Victoria Miro Gallery, 2004. An exhibition catalog.

Johnson, Ellen H. "Alice Neel: Fifty Years of Portrait Painting." *Studio International* 193 (March 1977): 174–79.

Johnson, Ken. "Bill Maynes: Hilary Harkness—Mary Carlson," Art in Review, *New York Times*, April 27, 2001.

———. "From Modernism Backward: Jim Dine's Multiple Styles," Art in Review, *New York Times*, April 9, 2004.

———. "Jack Shainman Till Freiwald," Art in Review, *New York Times*, September 24, 1999.

———. "Malcolm Morley, Sperone Westwater." Art in Review, *New York Times*, March, 12, 1999.

———. "Mary Boone: Eric Fischl," Art in Review, *New York Times*, May 28, 1999.

———. "West Side: The Armory Show on the Piers Just Keeps Growing," *New York Times*, February 23, 2001.

Jones, Ronald. "Gleams of Past Existence." In München, *Richard Phillips*, 55–68.

Katz, Alex. "On Art and Artists: Alex Katz." By Kate Horsfield and Lyn Blumenthal. *Profile 2*, no. 1 (January 1982): 1–11.

———. "Plunk 'Em Down and Pain 'Em: Alex Katz Interviewed by Vincent Katz." By Vincent Katz. *Ritz Newspaper*, no. 92 (1984): 59. Quoted in Sandler, *Alex Katz*.

Katz, Vincent. *Janet Fish Paintings*. New York: Harry N. Abrams, 2002.

———. "Symbols for the Self." *Art in America*, December 1999.

Kennel, Sarah. "Bearden's Musee Imaginaire." In *The Art of Romare Bearden*, 138-155. Edited by Judy Metro. Washington: National Gallery of Art, in association with Harry N. Abrams, Inc., 2003.

Kent, Sarah. "The Company of Strangers." In *Stephan Balkenhol: Sculptures 1988-1996 in the Saatchi Collection*, edited by Jenny Blyth, 1-8. London: Saatchi Galley, 1996. An exhibition catalog.

Kent, Sarah. "Portrait of the Artist." *Time Out London*, June 2001.

Kilimnik, Karen. Karen *Kilimnik Paintings*. Patrick Frey Edition. Zurich: Scalo, 2002.

Kino, Carol. "Philip Pearlstein at Robert Miller." *Art in America*, January 2002.

Kleeman, Ron. "Voice of the Icon, 1978." In Meisel, *Photo-realism*, 305–6.

Koepplin, Dieter. "Stephan Balkenhol." In *Stephan Balkenhol: Centro Galego de Arte Contemporanea*, edited by Maria do Céu Bapista, translated by Helena Cornide, Elena Expósito, Interlingua Traduccións, Nadia Poloni, Catherine Schelbert and Josephine Watson, 149-150. Galacia: Xunta de Galicia, 2001. An exhibition catalog.

Koestenbaum, Wayne. "The Empty Cup of Not Loving Myself." In French, *David Salle: Immediate Experience*, 27–33.

Kotz, Mary Lynn. *Rauschenberg, Art and Life*. New York: Harry N. Abrams, 2004.

Kramer, Hilton. "The Art of Conservation." *New York Times*, February 9, 1969.

Krulik, Barbara. "Sean Henry: The Scale of the Commonplace." In *Sean Henry: Sculpture and Drawings*, 3–7. London: Berkeley Square Gallery, 2001. An exhibition catalog.

Kuspit, Donald B. "Spiritual Realism: Don Eddy's Paintings." In *Don Eddy: The Art of Paradox*, edited by Paul Anbinder, 7–89. New York: Hudson Hills, 2002.

LaBelle, Charles. "Robert Overby: UCLA Hammer Museum, Los Angeles." *Frieze*, November 2000.

Leffingwell, Edward. "Will Cotton at Mary Boone." *Art in America*, May 2000.

Liebmann, Lisa. *David Salle*. Edited by David Whitney. New York: Rizzoli, 1994.

Lindey, Christine. *Superrealist Painting and Sculpture*. New York: William Morrow, 1980.

Livingstone, Marco. *Retrospective George Segal: Sculptures, Paintings, and Drawings*. Montreal: Montreal Museum of Fine Arts, 1998. An exhibition catalog.

———. "Telling It Like It Is." In *Tom Wesselmann*, edited by Thomas Buchsteiner and Otto Letze. 9-16. Ostfildern, Germany: Cantz Verlag, 1996.

Lombardi, D. Dominick. "A Master of Contemporary Art." *New York Times*, August 12, 2001.

Longo, Robert. "Save the Last Dance for Me." Interview by Richard Price. In *Men in the Cities*, 87-103. New York: Harry N. Abrams, Inc., 1986.

Lovelace, Carey. "Damian Loeb at Mary Boone." *Art in America*, February 2002.

Lucie-Smith, Edward. "Ralph Goings: America's Vermeer." In *Ralph Goings: Four Decades of Realism*, 3. Youngstown, OH: Butler Institute of American Art, 2004. An exhibition catalog.

Magee, Alan, Alan Magee: *Paintings, Sculpture, Graphics*. New York: Forum Gallery, 2003. An exhibition catalog.

———. "Conversation with Barry Lopez." By Barry Lopez. In Magee, *Alan Magee: Paintings*, Sculpture, Graphics, 23–34.

Mark Moore Gallery. *Till Freiwald: January 10-February 14, 2004.* Press Release, 2004. www.markmooregallery.com/indexphp?mode=past&objectid=69&view=pressrelease

Mary Boone Gallery. "Damian Loeb: Horror/Sci-Fi 1.1.9b2 at Mary Boone Gallery, Chelsea." Press release, 2003. http://www.damienloeb.com/history/horrorscifi.html.

———. "Description of Will Cotton's *Ice Cream Cavern*." Press release, 2003.

Mattison, Robert. *Robert Rauschenberg: Breaking Boundaries*. New Haven: Yale University Press, 2003.

McManus, Irene. Dreamscapes: *The Art of Juan González*. New York: Hudson Hills, 1994.

McQuaid, Cate. "Adding a Stroke of Originality to a Staged Scene." *Boston Globe*, October 31, 2003.

Meisel, Louis K. *Photo-Realism*. New York: Harry N. Abrams, 1980.

———. *Photorealism at the Millennium*. New York: Harry N. Abrams, 2002.

———. Photorealism Since 1980. New York: Harry N. Abrams, 1993.

Milroy, Sarah. "Skin Deep." *Globe and Mail* (Toronto), March 1, 2004.

Molon, Dominic. "Richard Phillips." In *Schwabsky*, Vitamin P, 248.

———. "Tim Gardner." In *Schwabsky*, Vitamin P, 120.

Moncrieff, Elspeth. (*Here and Now*). London: Berkeley Square Gallery, 2004. An exhibition catalog.

Moos, David. "Evan Penny—How We See Ourselves Now." In *Evan Penny: No One—In Particular*. New York: Sperone Westwater, 2005. An exhibition catalog.

München, Mosel, ed. *Richard Phillips*. Translated by Catherine Schelbert. Munich: Schirmer/Mosel, 2000. An exhibition catalog.

Neild, Barry. "Painting Makes a Comeback: But Can Contemporary Artists Brush Up Their Skills?" CNN.com, Entertainment, March 17, 2006. http://www.cnn.com/2006/SHOWBIZ/03/14/modernmasters.painters/index.html.

Norland, Gerald, ed. *Richard Diebenkorn: Paintings and Drawings, 1943–1976*. Buffalo, NY: Albright-Knox Art Gallery, 1976. An exhibition catalog.

Paladino, Mimmo. "David Salle, Screen Paintings." In French, *David Salle: Immediate Experience*, 122.

Pearlstein, Phillip. "An Exchange with Robert Storr." By Robert Storr. In *Philip Pearlstein: Since 1983*, edited by Elisa Urbanelli, 17–33. New York: Harry N. Abrams, in association with Robert Miller Gallery, 2002.

Penny, Evan. "Artist Statement: *L. Faux and No One—In Particular*." 2003. http://www.evanpenny.com/essay_statement_1.php.

Posner, Helaine. "Approaching Grace." In *Kiki Smith*, 7–35. New York: Monacelli, 2005.

Quinn, Marc, Germano Celant, Darian Leader, and Miuccia Prada, eds. *Marc Quinn*. Milan: Fondazione Prada, 2000. An exhibition catalog.

Raynor, Vivien. "Art: Exhibition of Neil Jenney Work," *New York Times*, November 23, 1984. Weekend edition.

———. "Art: Marisol Sculpture from Leonardo Painting," *New York Times*, June 1, 1984.

Rebentisch, Juliane. "Richard Phillip's Psycho-Realism." In *Richard Phillips: Kunstverein in Hamburg*, edited by Yilmaz Dziewior, translated by Christopher Jenkin-Jones, 86–92. Ostfildern, Germany: Hatje Cantz Publishers, 2003. An exhibition catalog.

Reed, Arden. "Nicolas Africano at Allene Lapides." *Art in America*, December 1999.

Resource Library Magazine. "Painting on the Edge: The Art of William Beckman." Traditional Fine Arts Organization and Frye Art Museum. http://www.tfaoi.com/aa/3aa/3aa340.htm.

Restany, Pierre. Preface to *Niki de Saint Phalle: My Art, My Dreams*, edited by Carla Schulz-Hoffman, 6. New York: Prestel, 2003.

Richard, Frances. "Nicolas Africano." In *Curve: The Female Nude Now*, edited by Isabel Venero Tricia Levi, 19. New York: Universe Publishing, 2003.

Rimanelli, David. "Robert Overby." *Artforum*, April 1997.

Rosenquist, James. "Painting, Working, Talking." Interview by Michael Amy. *Art in America*, February 2004.

Sadie Coles HQ. "Don Brown." http://www.sadiecoles.com/brown3.html.

de Saint Phalle, Niki. *Retrospektive*. Duisburg, Germany: Wilhelm-Lehmbruck-Museum der Stadt Duisburg, 1980. An exhibition catalog.

Salle, David. "David Salle: At the Edges." By Frederic Tuten. *Art in America*, September 1997.

Sánchez, Alberto Ruy. "Robert Graham, the Nude Seen from Within or Four Letters for a Vocabulary of the Body." In *Robert Graham*, edited by Noriko Fujinami, translated by Margarita Nieto, 31–37. Mexico City: Instituto Nacional de Bellas Artes, 1997. An exhibition catalog.

Sandler, Irving. *Alex Katz: A Retrospective*. New York: Harry N. Abrams, 1998.

Schulz-Hoffman, Carla. "All-Devouring Mothers—On Niki de Saint Phalle's Artistic Programme." In *Niki de Saint Phalle: My Art, My Dreams*, edited by Carla Schulz-Hoffman, 7–17. New York: Prestel, 2003.

Schwabsky, Barry. "Karen Kilimnik." In Schwabsky, *Vitamin P*, 174.

———, ed. *Vitamin P*. New York: Phaidon, 2002.

Schwendener, Martha. "Doug Wada: Dee/Glasoe." *Time Out New York*, May 17–24, 2001.

Scully, Vincent. Preface to Baeder, *Diners, Revised and Updated*, 6.

Segal, George. "The Sense of 'Why Not?': George Segal on His Art." Lecture, Albright-Knox Art Gallery, Buffalo, NY February 28, 1967. Quoted in *Studio International* 174, no. 893 (October 1967): 146–49.

Seigel, Katy. "Local Color." In Gould, *Lisa Yuskavage*, 15–21.

Shattuck, Kathryn. "What it Takes to Get Ahead." *New York Times*, October 23, 2005.

Shenker, Israel. "The Old Magician at Home." *New York Times*, January 9, 1972.

Sholis, Brian. "Traces of Beauty among the Ruins," *Void*. Rotterdam, Netherlands: Artimo-Gijs Stork, 2004.

Smith, Kiki. "An Interview with Kiki Smith." By Robin Winters. In *Kiki Smith*, edited by Paolo Colombo, Elizabeth Janus, Eduardo Lipschutz-Villa, and Kiki Smith, 132. Amsterdam: Institute of Contemporary Art; The Hague: Sdu Publishers, 1990.

Smith, Roberta. "And When He Was Bad, He Certainly Was Busy." Art in Review, *New York Times*, March 30, 2001.

———. "Black on White: Contrasts in Silhouette." Art in Review, *New York Times*, March 24, 2006.

———. "Flooding the Mind's Eye: Jennifer Bartlett's Comissions." In Jennifer Bartlett, edited by Marge Goldwater, Roberta Smith, and Calvin Tomkins, 79-137. New York: Abbeville Press Publishers, 1985. An exhibition catalog.

———. "Realism with a Vengeance." *New York Times*, June 13, 1997.

———. "The Taut Paintings of Philip Pearlstein." Art in Review, *New York Times*, March 4, 1988.

Spike, John T. *Fairfield Porter: An American Classic*. New York: Harry N. Abrams, 1992.

Stealingworth, Slim. *Tom Wesselmann*. Edited by Mark Greenberg. New York: Abbeville, 1980.

Storr, Robert. "An Exchange with Robert Storr." In *Philip Pearlstein: Since 1983*, edited by Elisa Urbanelli, 17–33. New York: Harry N. Abrams, in association with Robert Miller Gallery, 2002.

———. Introduction to *Philip Pearlstein: Since 1983*, edited by Elisa Urbanelli, 7–14. New York: Harry N. Abrams, in association with Robert Miller Gallery, 2002.

Taplin, Robert. "Robert Graham at Gagosian." *Art in America*, September 1994.

Théberge, Pierre. Preface to *Retrospective George Segal: Sculptures, Paint ings, and Drawings, 8-9*. Montreal: Montreal Museum of Fine Arts, 1998. An exhibition catalog.

Valdez, Sarah. "Don Brown." In *Curve: The Female Nude Now*, edited by Isabel Venero Tricia Levi, 45. New York: Universe Publishing, 2003.
Valdez, Sarah. "Don Brown." In Curve: *The Female Nude Now*, edited by Isabel Venero Tricia Levi, 45. New York: Universe Publishing, 2003.

———. "William Beckman at Forum." *Art in America*, February 2004.

van Zeil, Wieteke. "The Promise of Beauty," *Void*. Rotterdam, the Netherlands: Artimo-Gijs Stork, 2004.

Wakefield, Neville. "Hilary Harkness: And the Battle Goes On." *Interview*, June 2004.

Weiner, Jonathan. "Alan Magee: An Appreciation." In *Alan Magee: Paintings, Sculpture, Graphics*, by Alan Magee, 17-20. New York: Forum Gallery, 2003. An exhibition catalog.

Wells, Jennifer. Projects 24: *Kiki Smith*. New York: Museum of Modern Art, 1990.

West, Richard. "An Exact Anatomy of Alan Magee." In Magee's, *Alan Magee: Paintings, Sculpture, Graphics*, 15.

Yablonsky, Linda. "New York's Watery Grave." *New York Times*, April 11, 2004.

Yoskowitz, Robert. "Hilo Chen." *Arts Magazine*, December 1980.

———. "Hilo Chen," *Arts Magazine*, December 1981.

Music Scores

Claude Debussy, *Coin des Enfants; Petite Suite pour Piano Seul*. Paris: A. Durand, 1908.

Credits

Nicolas Africano, *Untitled (Reclining Nude)*, 1998. Courtesy Nancy Hoffman Gallery

William Bailey, *Arezzo Still Life, 1979* © William Bailey. Courtesy Robert Miller Gallery, New York

Romare Bearden, *Johnny Hudgins Comes On, from Profile/Part II: The Thirties Series, 1981* © Romare Bearden Foundation/Licensed by VAGA, New York, NY

Don Brown, *Yoko VII, 2002* © Don Brown/Courtesy Sadie Coles HQ, London

Colette Calascione, *Illumination, 2004*. Courtesy Nancy Hoffman Gallery

Davis Cone, *County, 1999* © Davis Cone/courtesy of Forum Gallery, New York, NY

Will Cotton, *Ice Cream Cavern, 2003*. Courtesy: Mary Boone Gallery, New York

Don Eddy, *Silver Shoes, 1972*. Courtesy Nancy Hoffman Gallery

Don Eddy, *Aqueous Lumina, 1993*. Reproduction courtesy Artists Legacy Foundation, which represents the estate. Courtesy Nancy Hoffman Gallery

Eric Fischl, *Lapping Sounds Along the Shore, 1996-97*. Courtesy: Mary Boone Gallery, New York

Eric Fischl, *Untitled, 2005*. Courtesy: Mary Boone Gallery, New York

Eric Fischl, *Untitled (Arching Woman), 2005*. Courtesy: Mary Boone Gallery, New York

Janet Fish, *Dog Days, 1993* © Janet Fish/Licensed by VAGA, New York, NY

Barry Flanagan, *Hells Bells, 2005* © Barry Flanagan/Courtesy Waddington Galleries

Viola Frey, *Man and Vase, 1996*. Reproduction courtesy Artists Legacy Foundation, which represents the estate. Courtesy Nancy Hoffman Gallery

Viola Frey, *Conversation Urn: Viola's Theory, 2000*. Courtesy Nancy Hoffman Gallery

Juan Gonzalez, *Rembrandt's Hands, Vermeer's Frame and the Passing of the Moth, 1990*. Courtesy Nancy Hoffman Gallery

Juan Gonzalez, *Memory Piece, 1990*. Courtesy Nancy Hoffman Gallery

Hilary Harkness, *Air Raid, 2005*. Courtesy: Mary Boone Gallery, New York

Marcus Harvey, *Soldier and Girl, 2002* © Marcus Harvey/courtesy Jay Jopling/White Cube, London

Sean Henry, *T.P.O.L.R. (The Path of Least Resistance), 2002* © Sean Henry, courtesy of Forum Gallery, New York

Alex Katz, *Amanda, 1973* © Alex Katz/Licensed by VAGA, New York, NY
Damian Loeb, *I'm Getting To You... (Very Slowly), 2002*. Courtesy: Mary Boone Gallery, New York

Alan Magee, *Braid, 1980* © Alan Magee, courtesy of Forum Gallery, New York

Marisol (Escobar), Magritte VI (Pushed Out Face), 1998. Art © Marisol/Licensed by VAGA, New York, NY

Alice Neel, *Portrait of Ben Medary, 1930* © Estate of Alice Neel. Courtesy Robert Miller Gallery, New York

Fairfield Porter, *Still Life, 1975*. On behalf of the estate of Fairfield Porter

Marc Quinn, *Selma Mustajbasic, 2000* Courtesy: Mary Boone Gallery, New York

Mel Ramos, *Almond Joyce: The Lost Painting of 1965, #24, 2002* © Mel Ramos/Licensed by VAGA, New York, NY

Robert Rauschenberg, *Page 42, Paragraph 1 (Short Stories), 2000* © Robert Rauschenberg/Licensed by VAGA, New York, NY

Larry Rivers, *Study for Last Civil War Veteran, 1970* © Estate of Larry Rivers/Licensed by VAGA, New York, NY

James Rosenquist, *Gift Wrapped Doll #37, 1997* © James Rosenquist/Licensed by VAGA, New York, NY

David Salle, *Sideways Moon, 2002* © David Salle/Licensed by VAGA, New York, NY

George Segal, *Woman Against Black Window, 1989-90 Art* © The George and Helen Segal Foundation/Licensed by VAGA, New York, NY

Kiki Smith, *Now, 2005*. Courtesy of the artist and John Berggruen Gallery, San Francisco

Kara Walker, *Shiny Penny, 1995*. Courtesy Sikkema Kenkins & Co.

Tom Wesselman, *Study for Bedroom Painting #2, 1967* © Tom Wesselmann/Licensed by VAGA, New York, NY

Index

In the artist section of this index, the numbers in bold indicate the pages dedicated to individual artists. Non-bolded numbers indicate where artists are mentioned in text throughout the book.

In the art section of this index, the numbers in bold indicate the page(s) where the named piece appears in the book. Non-bolded numbers indicate where individual named pieces are mentioned in text throughout the book.

The Artists

Art

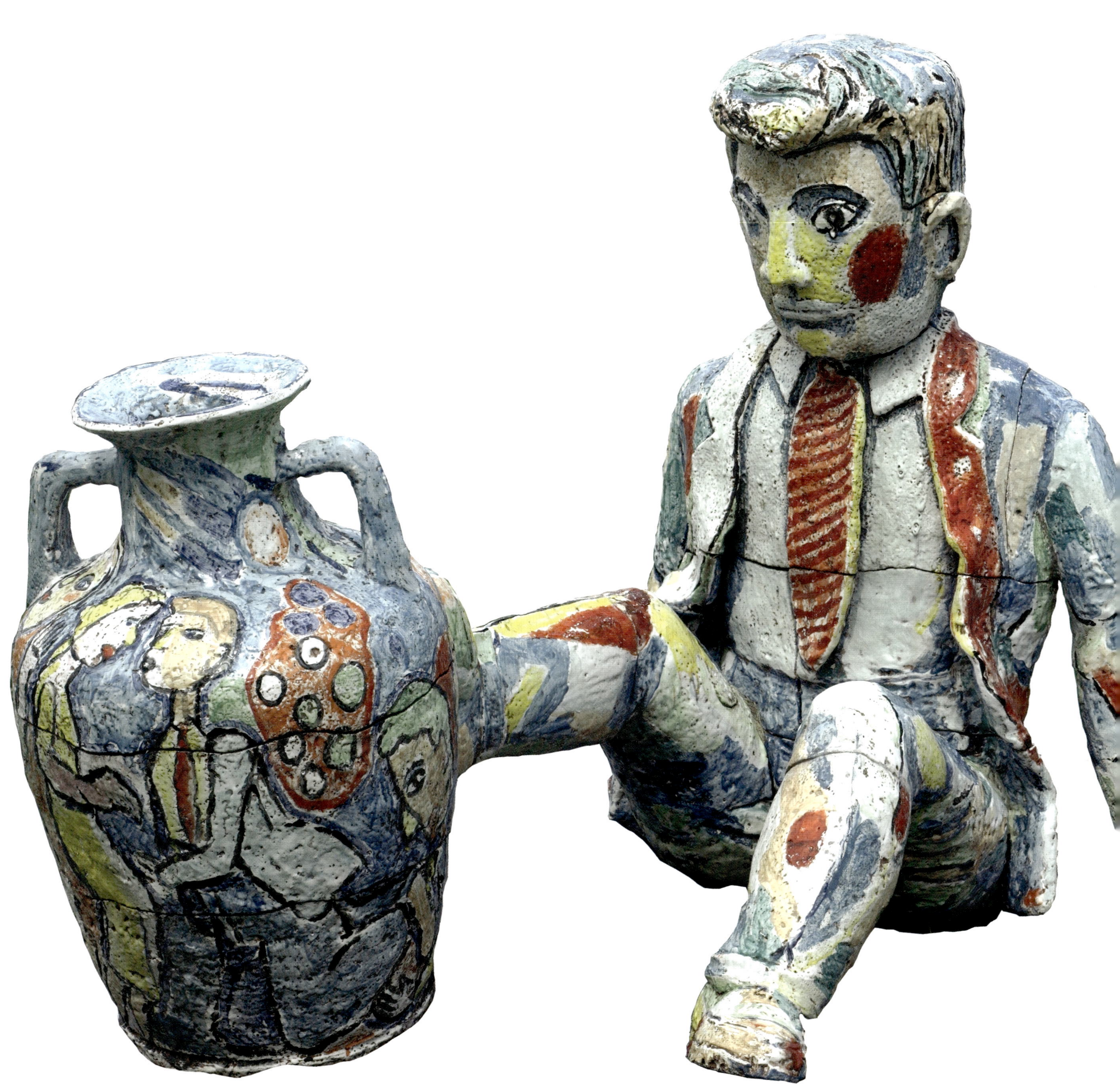

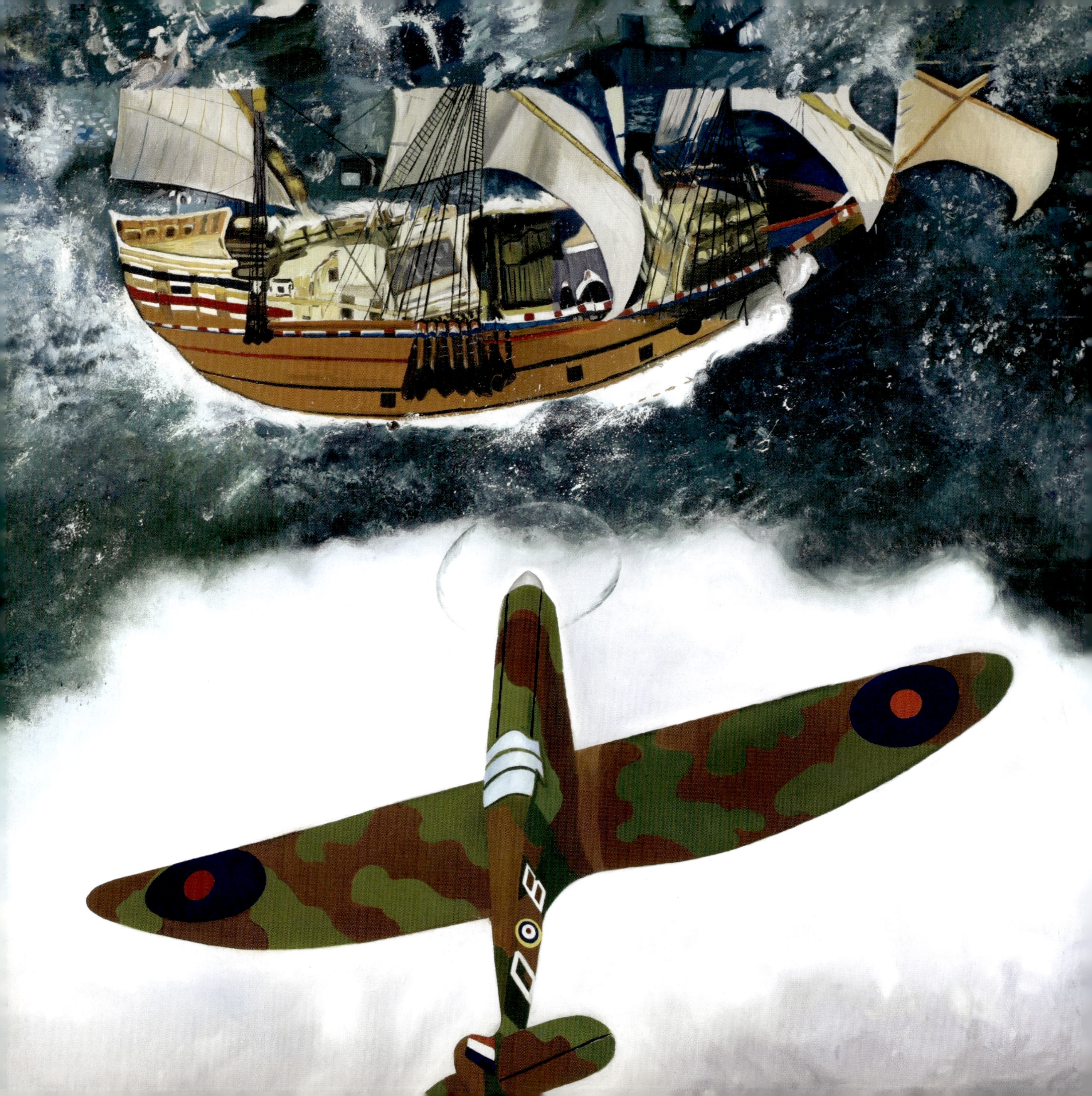

Acknowledgements

First and foremost, we would like to thank Jared Pruzan for his extraordinary efforts in writing the essays which accompany the illustrations in the book. His insights and observations immeasurably enhance the understanding and appreciation of the works. Secondly, we would like to thank Dede Young, Curator of Contemporary Art at The Neuberger Museum, for writing the introductory essay to the book. Dede is a quiet but persistent and persuasive voice for the power and pleasure that is embodied in the art. We would also like to thank Louis Meisel for his invaluable assistance with the launching of this book, Nancy Hoffman, Mary Boone, Frank Bernaducci, and the myriad gallery owners and directors who have helped us over the years. We thank Joan Caron Miloscia for her patient assistance in tending to the innumerable administrative details of cataloging, photographing, and compiling the many works in this book and in the collection. We would like to thank Jessica McIntyre for her aid in securing the necessary authorizations for the reproductions, and Uly Mayer for her meticulous proofreading. We would like to thank Richard Perry, Lindsay Brown, and Jerry Soga of Collectors Press for their creativity in framing the vision and design of the book. Finally, we thank all of the artists in the book, in the collection, and in the world.

-Rick & Monica Segal

I would like to thank Rick and Monica for their extraordinary trust and unending generosity; Noelle for her thankless support and loving patience; and Paula & Kent for their selfless grace in all that they do for their son.

-Jared Pruzan

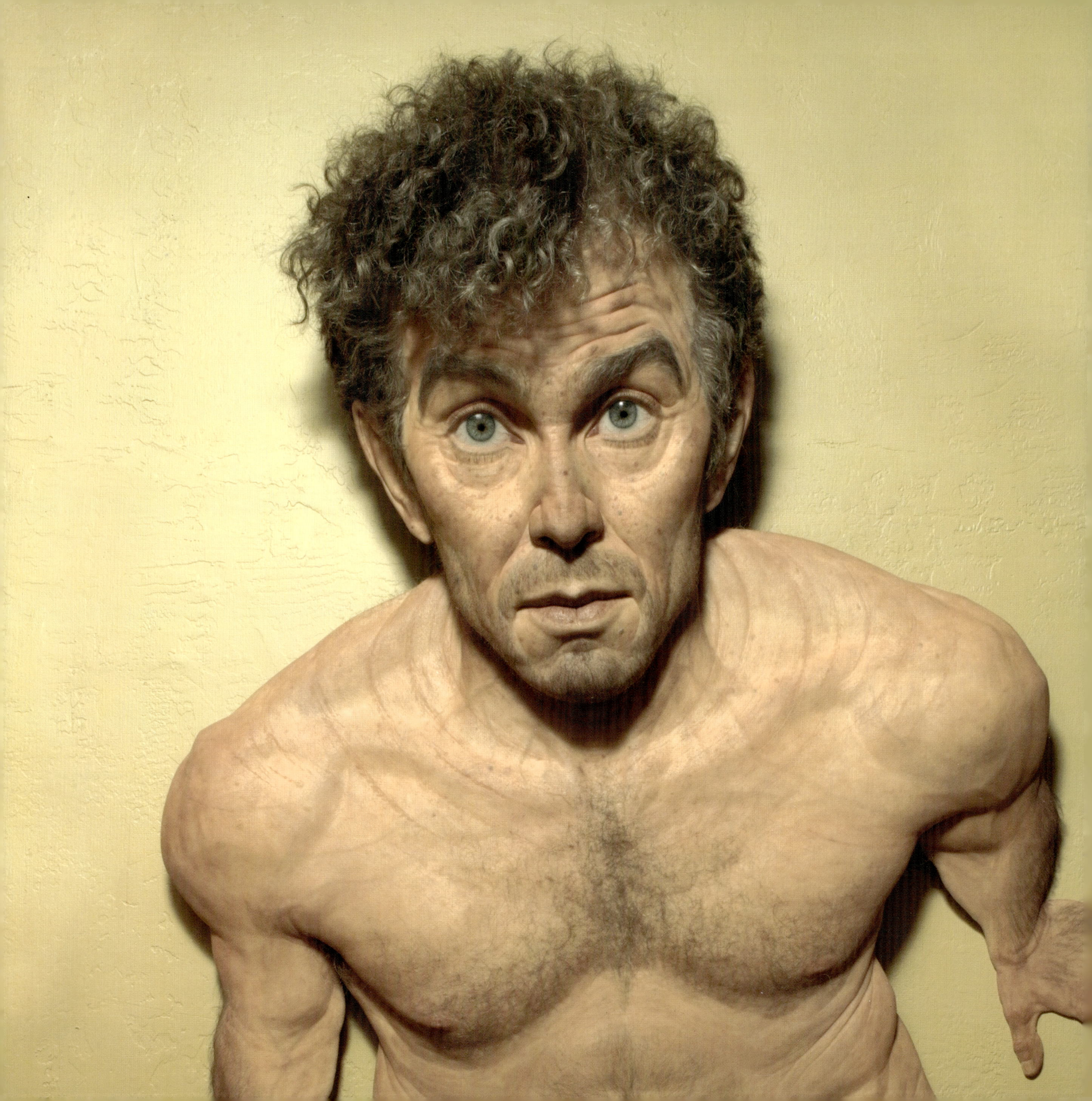